P9-DNU-682

Saying What the Law Is

Saying What the Law Is

THE CONSTITUTION
IN THE SUPREME COURT

CHARLES FRIED

HARVARD UNIVERSITY PRESS

Cambridge, Massachusetts, and London, England   2004

Publication of this book has been supported through the generous provisions of the
Maurice and Lula Bradley Smith Memorial Fund.

Library of Congress Cataloging-in-Publication Data

Fried, Charles, 1935–
    Saying what the law is : the constitution in the supreme court / Charles Fried.
        p.   cm.
    Includes bibliographical references and index.
    ISBN 0-674-01302-6 (alk. paper)
        1. Constitutional law—United States.   2. United States. Supreme Court.
3. Judicial process—United States.   4. Judicial review—United States.   I. Title.

KF4550.F728   2004
342.73—dc22   2003062495

For Anne, again

Contents

Preface

This book is neither a treatise nor a reference work. Rather it offers an understanding of the main topics of constitutional law. The Constitution sets up the government of the United States more or less from the ground up, with amendments adopted over a period of some two hundred years. One cannot sensibly expect the law of the Constitution to offer some single unifying theme, but there is a coherence to the law of each of the main topics, considered here, which are of the most general interest and which give our national life its distinct and admirable texture. It is this coherence (or these coherences) that makes constitutional law a subject that can not only be learned but understood. As in anatomy there is something beyond learning the names of nerves, bones, and muscles; there are the great systems of the living body: the nervous, the circulatory, digestive, and musculo-skeletal systems. So in constitutional law there are the principal themes and systems and their articulation one with another that make this a subject that may properly be presented in more general terms. It is these coherences that make it possible to offer an account of constitutional law that can be illuminating to the educated layman and non-specialist lawyer without condescension or the slighting of crucial nuance. And it is the search for these coherences that may make a work like this illuminating even to the specialist in constitutional law, to the mature lawyer, or to the student entering on a study of the subject. At the same time the search for coherence can be pressed too far. Constitutional law is a human and a political creation; tensions and contradictions, gaps and questions on the way to answers are inevitable. These ragged edges and outright failures must be noted as faithfully as are noted the instances in which constitutional law seems, in Lon Fuller's phrase, to be working itself pure. Above all, a book like this must be aware of its own prejudices and predilections and must guard against mistaking them for some underlying best explanation of what is really there.

My first encounter with the subject was in 1958 as a student of Herbert Wechsler, the greatest law teacher I have known in forty-five years in legal education. His high and astringent intellect sought, and where it did not find, imposed, the rule of reason on law. When I entered teaching he was my model. My first practical encounter with constitutional law had been as a law clerk to Justice John Marshall Harlan. He too believed that reason ruled in the house of the law. This devotion to reason was perhaps more remarkable in his case because he had spent his professional life before going on the bench as a highly successful New York practitioner. He treated his two law clerks as collaborators in a great work. When we could not persuade him and he could not move us before he gave his vote in conference, he would say sadly as he left the room, "Well, I guess I'm the Justice." In that Term he wrote a number of dissenting opinions—in *Monroe v. Pape, Mapp v. Ohio, Poe v. Ullman*—the wisdom of which now seems prescient. After that year I did not return to constitutional law until 1985 when I was first Deputy Solicitor General and then Solicitor General. For four years the Supreme Court was my principal scene of activity. Among the cases discussed in this book which I and my office presented to the Court were *Morrison v. Olson, Bowsher v. Synar* (Chapter 3—Separation of Powers), *Nollan v. California Coastal Commission* (Chapter 6—Liberty and Property), *Cleburne v. Cleburne Living Center*, and *City of Richmond v. J. A. Croson Co.* (Chapter 7—Equality).

When I returned to teaching I made constitutional law my subject. I also had the opportunity to participate as an advocate in some of the cases discussed in this book, particularly *United States v. Morrison* (Chapter 2), *Zelman v. Simmons-Harris* (Chapter 5—Religion), and the commercial speech cases discussed in Chapter 4. I had written one book on my experiences as Solicitor General, *Order and Law: Arguing the Reagan Revolution* (1991). (Here Chapter 3, on the separation of powers, draws on Chapter 5 of that work; I am grateful to Simon & Schuster for permission to repeat some of its passages.) I then decided to do a book on constitutional law itself, and published two articles that announced my project and are adapted here as its first chapter ("Constitutional Doctrine," 107 *Harv. L. Rev.* 1140 (1994) and "Types," 14 *Constitutional Commentary* 55 (1997)).

My writing on constitutional law since then has all been done with this project in mind and I draw on that writing in several places. In Chapter 1 and the Afterword, I make use of some of the ideas in "Five to Four: Reflections on the School Voucher Case," 116 *Harv. L. Rev.* 163 (2002). In Chapter 3, I draw on "Perfect Freedom, Perfect Justice," 78 *B.U. L. Rev.* 717 (1998) and "Perfect Freedom or Perfect Control?" 114 *Harv. L. Rev.* 606 (2000). Material from "Revolutions?" 109 *Harv. L. Rev.* 12 (1995) appears in Chapters 1, 2, and the Afterword.

My project was delayed by my four years' service as an associate justice of the Supreme Judicial Court of Massachusetts. Deciding, as well as teaching and arguing, constitutional cases has greatly influenced the perspective in this book. All of this experience has strengthened my faith that to a remarkable extent here reason rules.

Many colleagues at Harvard and elsewhere have commented on drafts of one or more chapters. David Shapiro read an earlier draft of the whole book and his encouragement was particularly valuable. The chapter on speech benefited from the expertise and careful suggestions of Elena Kagan (who also commented on other chapters), Robert Post, Frederick Schauer, Laurence Tribe, and Eugene Volokh. Lon Berk, Scott Brewer, Stephen Breyer, Richard Fallon, Heather Gerken, Mary Ann Glendon, Ryan Goodman, John Manning, Frank Michelman, Martha Minow, Robert Nozick, Joseph Singer, and William Stuntz commented on one or more chapters. In every instance their help was an act of friendship as well as of scholarly assistance, and the encouragement that their criticisms gave me sustained me through this effort. I am very grateful to them. I did not follow all their advice, so they must stand absolved of any responsibility for errors in the book. And it is obvious to those who know these distinguished critics that their views on many of the subjects touched on here are often not mine. That is why their comments were particularly useful. I presented early drafts of individual chapters at faculty workshops at Berkeley, Cardozo, Harvard, New York University, and University of Pennsylvania law schools. I learned from the colleagues who took part in those discussions. Tara Kole of the Harvard Law School class of 2003 worked through the whole text with me more than once. Her help was invaluable. Jaime Dodge Byrnes, Justin Dillon, and Michael Dimino also provided research assistance while students at Harvard Law School. Matthew Seccombe provided valuable editorial assistance. I am grateful to the Harvard Law School and Dean Robert Clark for providing me with material support and occasional relief from other duties as I was working on this book. Finally, I owe a great debt to the students who studied constitutional law with me over many years.

August 2003

Saying What the Law Is

CHAPTER ONE

Doctrine

The Constitution was written in 1787 and came into effect in 1789; its most important amendments were adopted in 1791 (Amendments I–X) and 1865–1870 (Amendments XIII–XV). The text of the Constitution and its amendments comes to just over seventy-five hundred words. If the purpose of this book were to understand that text, it would be a work of history. But this is a book about understanding constitutional law, and that law principally comes out of the decisions of the Supreme Court of the United States, which as of this writing consist of more than five hundred and thirty volumes (although probably less than half of those decisions touch on constitutional issues). It is for this reason that this book quotes—often at length—from important Supreme Court opinions: they state the law, and sometimes with a signal eloquence and pungency. They are not only the words but the music of our constitutional law. To a lesser extent constitutional law also comes out of decisions of lower federal courts and state courts dealing with federal constitutional issues, the practices and pronouncements of Congress and the executive branch, and to a small degree the teaching of constitutional scholars. The rules and principles that emerge from all of these sources are what is compendiously called constitutional doctrine.[1] The constitutional doctrines in the domains of federalism, the separation of powers, speech, religion, liberty, and equality are the subjects of the chapters that follow. But before presenting these topics, this chapter offers a discussion on the nature of constitutional doctrine in general.

The first issue about doctrine is whether it exists at all. The decisions of the Supreme Court of the United States certainly resolve disputes—a striking recent example is *Bush v. Gore*.[2] But do they make law? In a trivial sense they must make law—they are what lawyers call the law of the case, because they are the definitive resolution of particular disputes that have invoked the legal system. But the ambition of law goes further: each legal decision should be referable to a rule or principle; it should be justifiable not just by the good that it does but as part of the fabric of the law. This is what Felix Frankfurter meant when he said, "we do not sit like a kadi under a tree dispensing justice according to considerations of individual expediency."[3] It is what is necessary if constitutional law is to be *law,* rather than just a set of political decisions made by politicians. We want courts—and the Supreme Court is above all a court—to be bound by rules and principles. Some of these principles are fundamental; they go deeper than political expediency. And in the larger number of cases not governed by some fundamental principle of political morality, individual liberty is only secure if government is limited by rules.[4] Courts are the natural agency of government to assure both adherence to fundamental principles and regularity in the application of rules. These normative judgments about the nature of a well-functioning legal system are sometimes collected under the rubric of the rule of law,[5] to which I devote some attention in Chapter 3 on the separation of powers.

A challenge to this conception of the rule of law doubts that generalities are capable of constraining particular judgments, and so for better or worse the Supreme Court does not and cannot adhere to rules and principles. If courts cannot adhere to rules and principles as they decide particular cases, then doctrine is not possible, because doctrine is the web that courts spin as they decide cases in a lawful way. That courts cannot adhere to rules and principles is a radical challenge, rooted in deep philosophical disputes, that I shall not address.[6] Rather I shall assume that doctrine is possible, because creating and following rules are pervasive human activities. Whether the Court is in fact constrained by doctrine or whether it is just fooling around as it goes about painstakingly formulating and referring to it is something that readers can judge for themselves as I describe in subsequent chapters the course of decisions in particular difficult areas. In the balance of this chapter, I turn to the nature and sources of constitutional doctrine in general, to the role of precedent in the formulation of that doctrine, and to the question of what it means for a court to adhere to doctrine.

Precedent

American constitutional doctrine has two principal sources: the text of the Constitution itself and prior court decisions, especially the decisions of the Supreme Court of the United States. That the Constitution's text is a source of constitutional law (constitutional doctrine) is not surprising, and needs explaining only in a work of legal philosophy—which often takes as its task explaining the obvious. It is enough to say that that text *is* the Constitution, and it is that text that judges and other officials swear to support as the "supreme law of the land."[7] It is more problematic that court decisions should be as important a source as they are—so important, indeed, that in many constitutional disputes the text receives only a passing, as it were polite nod, as courts go about their business of parsing not the text but the prior decisions of the Supreme Court, which are treated as controlling the outcome. It is a source of frustration to many that constitutional doctrine—and that means those hundreds of volumes of cases—stand between us and the Constitution itself.[8] Like the Protestant cry, "Only Scripture," there is a longing to refer all decisions directly to the constitutional text.[9] There must be judges, and citizens must accept their rulings in their particular cases, but the citizen should be able to plead his case person to person in terms just of the Constitution, unmediated by the distorting filter of doctrine. This is a fantasy, but it is worth pausing to see why.

The believer struggling with his God is fighting about ultimate truth and the salvation of his soul. The citizen coming to court procures a judgment between himself and his adversaries, a judgment that may ultimately have to be enforced by the power of the state, a judgment to which other citizens will look to infer something about what they too might expect if they come into controversy with their neighbors or officials. Unmediated, fresh reference in contemporary disputes to the spare and distant text of the Constitution cannot possibly offer the regularity and rationality which is the indispensable characteristic of a government of law. The Constitution's text must be mediated by doctrine before it can yield decision. But that does not mean that precedent—prior court decisions—must be a source of that mediating doctrine. It is said that Continental judges are supposed to decide cases under the governing codes by direct reference to the authoritative texts, without regard to prior decisions, although in practice that reference too is mediated by doctrine: the rules and principles developed by scholars and text writers, who in turn draw on what is called the "jurisprudence," that is, the course of decisions on a particular matter.[10]

American courts both before and after the Revolution followed the English courts' practice of accompanying their decisions by opinions which explained those decisions by reference to prior decisions and opinions—that is precedent. From the very start the Supreme Court was thought of as a court like the other courts with which the founding generation was familiar, albeit with a special jurisdiction. It too decided cases—and only cases, not abstract and general disputes—after hearing opposing counsel, and the Court's decisions were accompanied by the opinions of the judges disposing of the arguments made to them by the parties.[11] So it was quite natural for the Supreme Court more or less from the beginning to treat precedent as an essential element in reasoning about constitutional law. This does not mean that past decisions had an unbreakable grip on the future. Anglo-American courts have always been adept at the casuistry that allows prior decisions to be acknowledged but distinguished from the case at hand. And American courts interpreting the Constitution could not be rescued from a precedential dead end by an omnipotent legislature, as could the English courts developing the common law, so that the Supreme Court, in addition to sometimes unconvincing distinctions, also has had to resort to occasional outright overruling. But distinguishing and overruling aside, because the Supreme Court in deciding constitutional cases has acted like a common law court developing the law according to its precedents, those five-hundred-odd volumes of Supreme Court Reports are the principal source of constitutional law, of constitutional doctrine.

Although any decision that explains itself implies some generalization, and to that extent a commitment to that generalization, some may object that this commitment cannot be taken to justify deference to prior decisions as elements or building blocks of doctrine, because the commitment need not extend beyond that occasion. It is conceivable that judges and other officials might disregard prior court decisions and decide each case by a fresh consideration of how the text and the principles standing behind the text bear upon it, although of course the unencumbered judge might look to past decisions as a source of wisdom—as he might to the arguments of counsel or to law review articles. (I put aside whether the authentic meaning is arrived at by reconstructing the intentions of those who wrote, debated, and ratified the text, or by discerning the meaning of the text, or by recurring directly to whatever fundamental truths of morality and justice the Constitution is believed to embody.) This "fresh start" conception is quite different from the notion that a decision need imply no commitment or generalization at all. Imagine that a court strikes down, as violating the First Amendment, a state statute that punishes speech disrespectful of the legislature. If the court then declined to invalidate a statute punishing speech disrespectful of the governor, it would either have to explain why such a statute is different (thus honoring the prior decision) or acknowledge, while disregarding, the similarity. When deciding for the governor, the court may acknowledge that its decision against the legislature was incompatible with its new decision and therefore wrong. Convinced of its prior error, why should the court not shift ground completely? In each case a responsible court would offer—or at least have in mind—a justification for its decision, a justification that should point to how this decision fits with, or criticizes, other decisions that have been or might be made. There would be doctrine in the first case, maybe even quite an elaborate doctrine, and contrary doctrine in the second—doctrine at every turn. Not only doctrine, but even commitment. It is not just a commitment that survives reevaluation in light of the acknowledged ultimate criterion of correctness. This way there is not a deficiency, but a surplus of doctrine—as much as one doctrine for each decision. Of course such a from-the-ground-up, fresh-each-time mode of reasoning is quite unrealistic. No merely human judge would have the time or the intellect to think every case out afresh. Doctrine not only mediates between first principles and particular results along the timeless dimension of inference, but it in fact—if not in logical necessity—provides continuity between a particular decision and those that have gone before. It is respect for precedent that makes for continuity in doctrine. Such continuity gives Supreme Court decisions the regularity and predictability they must have to make the Court's exercise of power both be and seem to be lawlike and acceptable.

Continuity and Character

Although precedent—regard for what came before—in some form or other is necessary to the continuity of law and persistence in doctrine, it has a particular salience in the decisions of the Supreme Court and the constitutional doctrine that that court generates. Supreme Court justices have hardly cultivated the colorless impersonal style of their European counterparts. The supreme bench has been populated by strong personalities. Their selection has sometimes been attended by fierce political battles. And once on the bench they have tended to stay for a very long time—life tenure being guaranteed by the Constitution. In its two-hundred-and-fourteen-year history, during most of which the Court had nine members, there have been only one hundred and eight justices. From the Marshall Court onward the Court's judgments have almost always been announced as having been written by a single named justice, in which the other justices joined or to which they responded in concurring or dissenting opinions. Thus the institutional voice of the Court has always been suffused with a strong personal element. This personal element invites a greater, not a lesser emphasis on precedent. An unelected justice, wielding great power, is naturally moved to demonstrate that his judgment is supported, if not compelled, not just by the force of logic but by the authority of what others before him have concluded, conclusions that have won acceptance and proved themselves, if not wise, at least workable. More personally, a judge writing under his own name cannot help but wish to appear consistent, first of all with what he himself has written in earlier cases and more remotely with opinions others have written and which he is recorded as having joined. More remotely still, a judge when she must write or vote in a case similar to one decided before her accession to the Court, while not moved by the same tug of consistency as moves her more senior colleagues, will feel some strong part of that pull herself: lest each new appointment signal the possible undoing of a line of precedent developing until that time, the new judge may wish the promise of some persistence in the doctrine in whose development she will participate. And so precedent is like a rope woven of fibers, none of which stretch through its whole length. None of this is logically compelled, as the fantasy example of the hypothetical judge who considers each case anew shows. Nor is it just a practical necessity, although it is that. Respect for precedent is what gives both a judge and a court character. And character inspires confidence in those who must submit to a court's power and imposes discipline on the exercise of that power.

We require continuity in legal doctrine. Yet we also require each new decision to be more or less right on its merits. The only way we can have both is for the new decision to be right, in part at least because it accords with established doctrine. We encounter here an instance of what may seem a general paradox of rationality: a rational person is always in principle open to reason, yet any human pursuit—certainly the pursuit of reason—would be thwarted if those committed to it kept returning to first principles to make sure that the beginning was right. I call this a paradox because we try to have it both ways: to shut down argument after some reasonable point and yet to be unwilling to put any proposition permanently and in principle beyond question. (We want to avoid being like the man who cannot get to work in the morning because he must keep returning home to make quite sure that he has turned off the gas.) The paradox appears in its most intimate form in the design of our own life plans—and it manifests itself in the law, even though the judge's plan is not her personal life plan, but a plan for the law.[12]

The solution to the paradox at every level begins by noticing that we are time-extended, not punctuated, beings. The ends we pursue, the thoughts we entertain, the sentiments that grip us are all time extended, not punctuated. Our affections, commitments, and projects are also time extended. Just as we could not whistle a tune if at every moment we started afresh, so we could be neither friend nor enemy, we could not keep promises, do acts of kindness, nor take revenge, if every momentary and discrete movement were the occasion of a fresh choice. Steadiness and commitment are not just virtues that keep us unswervingly on course to some goal or end point: they make our lives more or less coherent; they allow us to understand and describe what it is that moves us at all. They give character. They give character to a judge as she pursues a course of decision, but this same steadiness and commitment give character to the Court. Without such steadiness the Court's work would not only be unpredictable and the law unreliable, it would be threatened with incoherence. Unless doctrine persists, unless doctrine itself is prolonged, it cannot sufficiently order social action. The Constitution promises that kind of persistence, and it can only deliver if its commands are instantiated in doctrines that persist. If what the Constitution meant were open to reinterpretation from the ground up (from the text, or original intention, or fundamental values up), if a new story could be started, a new argument made at each instance of its application—not just by the Supreme Court, but by lower courts, state courts, and officials at all levels—then, whatever might be said about the "correctness" of some of these interpretations, the ensemble of purportedly constitutional activities would exhibit an incoherence that must be much further from the reason for having a Constitution than the departure worked by any particular doctrine, no matter how far afield it might have wandered.[13]

The public expects steadiness and commitment in the courts; the Supreme Court as an institution should have a collective character, as men and women have character.[14] The Court should be like a careful, sober, and reliable trustee of someone else's assets. Imagine how such a person goes about some project. She is unlikely to conceive every detail and ramification at the first moment of action. Our important undertakings have a life cycle. And so, too, there are the rhythms and sequences by which doctrine, like the doctrine about takings or the establishment of religion, is brought into being, elaborated, modified, and perhaps eventually abandoned. In fact, the great organizing doctrines of constitutional law have come into being in a variety of ways. Some, like judicial review or the decisions stating the relation between state and federal courts, did indeed seem to issue from early and sweeping decisions—*Marbury v. Madison*,[15] *Martin v. Hunter's Lessee*[16]—with the whole course of later jurisprudence working out the implications of their large generalizations. But others, like the First Amendment jurisprudence protecting expression presented in Chapter 4, had a late and halting beginning, and only later, through an accumulation of distinctions and expansions, did anything like a comprehensive principle emerge.

The case for reason displayed over time must take account not only of how commitments come into being, but also of changed plans and understandings. Neither a person nor a social institution like the Supreme Court can lead a punctuated existence, in which reason turns afresh at every moment to determine what is the best thing to do NOW. Large stretches of life and attention are taken up with moving according to a plan already set, playing according to a score already written, adhering to commitments already made. But just as a punctuated existence is inhuman, so a life lived strictly according to plan is mad—

and dangerous. Whole projects may be cast aside as mistaken, and what follows can be liberating, thrilling, or full of promise. Those who don't get trapped have a kind of peripheral vision that allows them to notice the chance of a new departure even while they keep their eye on the ball. This is a manifestation of the paradox of rationality to which I referred earlier. A judicial decision too is both an intellectual and a moral act, and the commitment to the argument behind it correspondingly is made both to oneself and to others. Of course, like the rest of us a judge must recognize at some point that he—carried along by doctrine—has been moving down a blind alley, and then he may have to retrace his steps, perhaps all the way to the start of his journey. But still, if we did not proceed with some considerable measure of confidence in our prior steps, we could not progress at all.[17] Reasoning about the Constitution certainly requires at least that kind of commitment to our own thought, and in this sense implies respect for precedent.

Finally, doctrine spreads not only across time and over judges but conceptually as well. It is not a mere collection of rules. Just as coherence in doctrine over time and over the judges who develop it entails a rational, not a punctuated, structure, so also doctrine is not limited—or not generally limited—to small, discrete topics. For instance, as we shall see in Chapter 4, there is doctrine about commercial speech and doctrine about child pornography, but these doctrines are connected in a principled way to the more general theme of freedom of expression. Developments in one aspect of that theme will come to have a bearing on other aspects. And the same is true, though to a lesser extent, even across topics. Doctrinal developments in freedom of expression have a bearing on analogous aspects of doctrine about religious freedom. And more generally still, modes of reasoning, terms of analysis, developed in one area, will crop up in other quite different areas.[18] Thus some constitutional prohibitions and limitations (for instance, on laws impairing the obligation of contracts and on what counts as a regulation of interstate commerce) are said to constrain only weakly, while others (like the prohibition on laws impinging on political expression or on classifying by race) impose very stringent constraints. Although these are very different topics, the terms in which doctrine describes the degree of stringency in each will be limited in number, and in mature doctrines will be expressed in similar ways.

This coherence across topics and themes is not surprising. Not only is the development of doctrine an exercise of reason, but it is the work—largely—of the same small body of judges, a body whose membership changes quite slowly. The justices may hear a federalism case at the start of a day and a free speech case right afterward. There may be rational connections over themes and topics because the issues and values at stake may be similar, but even without looking for such convergences, a similarity of analytical modes is a feature of the coherence of doctrine. The human mind can only comprehend a limited number of terms. Coherence comes from recognizing, even imposing, similarities and analogies. The vocabulary and rational structures of doctrine are limited, so that the same terms and argument types show up in quite diverse topical settings. Just as coherence and character require that doctrine persist over time, so they require that the treatment of disparate topics be consistent, that differences in treatment be explained and rationalized into what might be called doctrines about doctrine. Just as a doctrine that lasted only for a moment—however richly elaborated—would not count as doctrine and would not give coherence to the law, so also if each case had its own doctrine, then too the law would lack coherence. Law requires persistence of doctrine over time and extension over cases and topics. Coherence requires consistency both diachronically and synchronically. The chapters on particular topics will show just how much of this synchronic coherence constitutional doctrine displays.

Dissenting Opinions: Doctrine in a Minor Key

In considering the meaning and trajectory of constitutional doctrine my discussion will often take up not only the opinions of the Court but also dissenting opinions. When the Court speaks, it almost always speaks in the voice of a named justice.[19] My discussion of precedent has emphasized the continuity of doctrine, the commitment of the Court today to its judgments of a year or even a generation past. But the Court is not only a continuing but also a collegial body. A majority opinion is designated the opinion of the Court. I was taught that it is bad form for an advocate to refer to such an opinion by the name of its author or even to refer to its authorship. The writing justice speaks for the Court and it belies reported experience—and my own personal experience as a justice of a state supreme court—to imagine that the justice assigned to write for the Court just says only and exactly what she believes is right, and then if four others want to sign on, that makes a court. Though signed by a named justice, the opinion takes its place in the rope of continuity not as that justice's personal product, in spite of the fact that the best opinions may be written in a vivid, personal, not at all bureaucratic style. In joining an opinion the four or more justices in a majority make a commitment to each other analogous to that made to prior courts and expected from future courts.

It is striking that the opinion of the Court, which speaks for and to the law, should also be a personal product. It is even more striking, however, that the official publication of the Court's conclusion should include one or more opinions of dissenting justices. So it has been from the beginning of the Court's work. What is the point of writing and publishing dissenting opinions? Given the difficulty of many cases that come to the Court, it is no surprise that there should be disagreements among the justices, and little of importance could be decided if the Court's opinion had to incorporate the views of all of the justices. The publication of dissent is first of all an act of candor. Generally, the majority seeks to answer the dissent's objections, and thus the report of the case hopes to show to the public ruled by the decision that the decision is the product of a process of argument and reason. In this way too the dissent imposes discipline on the majority. After all, the Court's opinion is an argument, a demonstration, and the majority ideally is restrained to make only those arguments that the dissent cannot demolish. But of course many decisions cannot be demolished. They survive the dissent as one of several possible solutions on which reasonable persons may differ. Or the majority and dissent may start from such widely different premises that what the disagreement displays is this fundamental divergence.

What does dissent say about the Court's vaunted collegiality and continuity? If precedent counts, then what is the dissenting justice to do in the very next case which builds on the decision from which he had dissented? Just as a justice coming to the Court does not feel free to ignore all the prior cases on which he did not sit, once established should he not feel equally pressed to go along with a decision even though he had previously dissented from it? Why should his dissent absolve him from his commitment to precedent? These questions bring out a second, crucial function of dissenting opinions, and one that explains why a book like this should pay attention to them: precedent is only a presumption. If constitutional doctrine is not to become rigid, driven by the path-dependence of common law adjudication, there must be room for distinguishing, narrowing, and abandoning precedent altogether. The dissent contains the germ of such changes of direction. Its argument that a particular decision was a wrong turn may be used to justify an about-face, especially if the wrong turn can be shown to be taking the law further and further down a blind alley. These are the prophetic dissents, like Justice Oliver Wendell Holmes's famous dissent in *Lochner v. United States*,[20] protesting against what he believed was the Court's disposition to disenable legislatures from responding to emerging social and economic problems. That dissent did not come into its own for another thirty-two years, but thereafter it has been quoted as if it proclaimed doctrine and the majority's decision in *Lochner* was a precedent only in the sense that it stood as an example of what the law should not be.

Not all dissents are such successes. Indeed most are not, for otherwise doctrine would be quite unstable. Sometimes a dissenting justice is content to point out the unfortunate implications of what the majority is doing, and then accepts the case as precedent, having perhaps restrained the Court from pushing its position to the limit of its logic.[21] And at other times a dissenter after a year or so will simply accept the precedent and reason from it.[22] The second Justice Harlan, a great institutionalist, once wrote, "The passage of time has not made the *Miranda* case any more palatable to me. . . . Yet, despite my strong inclination to join in the dissent . . . I can find no acceptable avenues of escape from *Miranda*. . . . Therefore and purely out of respect for stare decisis, I reluctantly feel compelled to acquiesce in today's decision. . . ."[23]

It is not possible to say in advance which dissents hold prophetic seeds and which at best serve to discipline and restrain a contrary majority. It is not possible to say, because doctrine and precedent constrain more or less loosely. The best I can do is display the continuity that surely does exist and hope to allow the reader in the substantive chapters that follow to develop some instinct of her own for what will wither away, what will be transformed, and what will last.

CHAPTER TWO

Federalism

From the beginning of our history as a nation—even before the framing of the Constitution—no question was more controversial than that of the proper role of the states in the new nation. Alexander Hamilton would have relegated the states to the status of provinces of the national government,[1] while many others would have strictly limited the national government to a small number of defined tasks.[2] The energy in this controversy came as much from strategic concerns about preserving entrenched interests and advantages—high among which was the concern of the southern states to put the continued existence of slavery beyond the reach of the new national government— as from sentimental attachment to familiar places and institutions or a disinterested concern for the arrangement that would best guarantee the liberty, security, and prosperity of the whole. Fueled by these sources of energy, that controversy continued through the Civil War and only began to wane with the definitive advance of the nation's industrialization and economic integration. Two world wars, with universal conscription, and the nationalization of mass culture made increasingly implausible the notion—if it ever was widely felt—that the citizens of the United States consider themselves first of all New Yorkers or Georgians and only secondarily Americans. Yet the notion of "states' rights" has continued to be a theme in political rhetoric and in the last decades of the twentieth century reemerged as a potent and controversial issue in constitutional doctrine. Only in this last period did the Court once again undertake to put constitutional limits, in the name of federalistic concerns, both on the authority of the Congress to impose rules throughout the nation and on Congress's authority to impose rules on state governments themselves.

The most fundamental question for constitutional doctrine in respect to federalism asks whether maintaining the constitutional balance between national and state power is a job for the courts at all. A theological analogy comes to mind: is the Constitution in this regard like the divine watchmaker of eighteenth-century deism, who creates the machinery and then allows it to run on its own, or is the conception rather a theistic one, according to which a higher power intervenes regularly to assure the divine plan? The most famous statement of the deistic view was Herbert Wechsler's "The Political Safeguards of Federalism."[3] Wechsler emphasized the structural features of the Constitution, such as the representation by states in the Congress and the role of the Electoral College in choosing the President, as assuring the states the political power to protect their interests and prerogatives, with no need for judicial interference. Whether this was ever so, it is very doubtful that it is so today. In addition to the social and economic forces already mentioned, there have been structural changes undermining the political safeguards of federalism: among them the early development of national political parties, the direct election of Senators required by the Seventeenth Amendment in 1913, the national funding of congressional candidates by groups interested in national rather than local issues, and the nationalization of the media.[4] The alternative conception, which has the Court continually policing the boundaries between the two levels of government, was very much in the ascendant in the latter part of the nineteenth century and through the beginning of the New Deal until 1937, as the Court sought to preserve some distinct role for the states in the face of the ever-growing reach of the national power. The more recently developed doctrines protecting state power from national encroachment—dating to 1976[5]—have been highly controversial and strongly criticized by many constitutional scholars. (Even the greatest doubters regarding an active constitutional role for the Court have readily agreed that the Court must police the other side of the national-state boundary to prevent state interference with national power.)[6]

There are several possible themes explaining this revival, in the name of federalism, of constitutional doctrine limiting Congress's power: the conviction that smaller, more local units of government are more responsive to the concerns of individual citizens;[7] that state governments if once again accorded sufficient respect and authority would govern more effectively and less extravagantly than the national government; that breaking the monopoly of the federal government in certain areas and devolving its tasks to the states will encourage competition among them and with that competition will come innovation and efficiency;[8] that smaller units of government will simply be inclined to govern less and so individuals will be less subject to government regulation altogether.

But above all, the Court may have come to the conclusion that by limiting the reach of the national government and protecting the distinct authority of the states it was just doing the job that the Constitution assigned to it to enforce the distribution of powers ordained by the Constitution. By enforcing respect for that distribution, the Court was enforcing respect for the rule of law, refusing to accede to a grab for power that—no matter how expedient—was not authorized by the basic law. Larry Kramer has argued that the framers never intended such an interventionist role for the Court as it had once and has now once again assumed.[9] Statements by Chief Justice John Marshall suggest the contrary. This is a book about doctrine, and rather than adjudicating this historical controversy, I consider a question more apt for the constitutional lawyer: is policing the boundaries of federal and state power a job that the Court can do with the doctrinal tools it possesses or can fashion? Are there doctrines sufficiently definite to provide guidance, regularity, and confidence that the Court is doing lawyers' work for lawyers' use? Even if the doctrines meet this test, are they sufficiently realistic and flexible to be serviceable in changing circumstances? And finally, even if they meet these tests, do such doctrines have a sufficient warrant in the Constitution's text and our constitutional traditions, that they cannot be dismissed as arbitrary inventions of an unelected elite? Nineteenth-century doctrine may have passed the first test of definiteness, but failed the second. I shall argue that the Court's recent doctrinal interventions, with one exception, offer some prospect for doctrinal success.

Foundations

The Constitution of 1789 was a new beginning, a *novus ordo seclorum*.[10] The framers of the Constitution not only knowingly exceeded the instructions that called them to their task of revising the

Articles of Confederation, but they also called for the adoption of their draft by procedures that disregarded the explicit limits of that prior constitution. Thus our Constitution represented a juridical— though not a social—revolution: its terms did not proceed in an unbroken line of authorization from a previous charter of national government.[11] The Constitution, though representing such a new beginning, does not claim that it distributes the totality of governing power among the institutions of the national government it establishes. Rather it states at the beginning of Article I: that it assigns to Congress "all legislative Powers *herein granted*." The powers then granted are not expressed as the plenum of governmental power, but rather as a specific enumeration—a structure that is carried forward in the several amendments granting additional powers to the Congress. Nor can we look to the office of the President to make up the balance of what the Constitution might but does not bestow on the Congress, because the principal power of the President, as we shall see, is to "take Care that the Laws be faithfully executed."

The powers of Congress are set out principally in Article I, section 8. Clauses 1, 2, 5, and 6 grant broad power to manage the fiscal affairs of the nation: to raise money by taxation and borrowing, and to establish and protect a national currency. Clauses 10 through 16 deal with Congress's power in military and foreign affairs. Clauses 3 (commerce), 4 (naturalization and bankruptcy), 7 (post offices and roads), and 8 (copyrights and patents) assign power over particular areas in which Congress might think it useful or necessary to establish a uniform national rule. Other powers are scattered throughout the Constitution. For instance, the power to establish the various offices and departments of the executive branch (a topic discussed in Chapter 3) is granted Congress in Article II, establishing the executive branch. Of particular importance are Congress's powers "by appropriate legislation" to enforce the Civil War amendments, comprising the Thirteenth, Fourteenth, and Fifteenth amendments, and the Nineteenth and Twenty-Sixth amendments, guaranteeing the right to vote to women and to eighteen-year-olds.[12]

After we add up all the powers granted, if we find that they are less than all the powers that a government might enjoy, the question arises: who has the rest? The question is answered twice, and it comes to the same answer: the states. The answer comes first in the Tenth Amendment, which addresses the question directly: "The powers not delegated to the United States by the Constitution, nor prohibited by it to the States, are reserved to the States respectively, or to the people." The answer also comes by a different route. Upon independence, the governments of the several states succeeded to the plenary powers of the King-in-Parliament over their territories. Whatever was left of that plenum of governmental power and had not been assumed by the national government, remained in the states. There was from the start and continues to be debate—often conducted at the level of high theory and dense historical argumentation—about whether the Constitution was the creation of the states, which transferred some part of their sovereignty to the new national government, or was an original creation of the sovereign people of the nation as a whole.[13] That debate was rehearsed in the 1819 case of *McCulloch v. Maryland*,[14] in which counsel for Maryland argued for a narrow interpretation of the Constitution's grant of power to the national government, in part on the ground that the national government was after all the creation of the states. He supported that position by pointing out that the Constitution itself called for its ratification by conventions[15] in the states. Chief Justice Marshall rejected this argument—not that any judicial opinion can settle a point of history.

> No political dreamer was ever wild enough to think of breaking down the lines which separate the States, and of compounding the American people into one common mass. Of consequence, when they act, they act in their States. But the measures they adopt do not, on that account, cease to be the measures of the people themselves, or become the measures of the State governments.[16]

There can be no dispute, however, as Jack Rakove puts it, that

> [t]he states clearly preceded the Union in point of time. . . . While the Continental Congress had to be created de novo, the states were natural successors to the thirteen colonies whose legal origins could be traced to particular grants of rights of government by the Crown. Although the collapse of royal authority during the interregnum of 1774–76 suspended lawful government nearly everywhere, antecedent colonial laws remained in force, and the idea that Americans had to emerge from the state of nature into which a vengeful Crown had thrust them required only the restoration of legal government, not the formation of a new social compact. Just as revolution did not alter rights of property or the duties of family, so a map of America drawn in 1776 would show the same boundaries as one drawn in 1773.[17]

And so, although one may debate whether the reservation of powers to the states in the Tenth Amendment represents the assignment to them of their powers of government by the new national constitution or a recognition of the authority they had and continued to enjoy, it is quite clear that as a practical matter the Constitution presupposed the prior and continued existence of the states as loci of governing power. Indeed it is striking that in contrast to the provisions of Articles I, II, and III establishing the new institutions of the Congress, presidency, and federal judiciary there is no corresponding provision in the Constitution establishing the states and authorizing their continued existence and exercise of governmental power.[18] This structural fact about the Constitution offers at least the beginning of a textual and historical warrant for the Court's earlier and recently renewed project to establish in doctrines a correlate for the assumed distinct constitutional status of the states. These doctrines are of two sorts: first, those that would set a limit to the powers granted to the national government beyond which the national power simply runs out, so that not just state governments but individuals are beyond its reach; and second, those that acknowledge the general authority of Congress to regulate a particular subject, but erect a specific barrier to that power's impinging on the states, or impinging on them in particular ways.

A recent controversial example of the first type of disciplining decision, where Congress's power is said to run out, was *United States v. Lopez.*[19] The Court held that Congress's power to regulate commerce did not extend so far as to allow it to make it a crime to carry a firearm in or around a local school. Recent decisions of the second type, erecting a barrier in the name of state sovereignty to what is otherwise conceded to be an exercise of the power of Congress, have put forward the notion that the states' legislatures and officials cannot be enlisted ("commandeered") to administer federal programs lest the states become mere administrative units of the national government. In *New York v. United States*[20] the Court held that although Congress might use its commerce power to regulate the disposal of radioactive waste, including establishing storage sites throughout the nation, it could not require a state government to acquire and deal with the waste generated within its borders. State sovereignty exerted a counterpressure that stopped the otherwise acknowledged national power over the subject. Another doctrine of this second sort holds that although Congress in the exercise of its commerce power may regulate many aspects of the states' employment practices, it may not because of an implication of the Eleventh Amendment grant aggrieved employees the right to sue the state for damages; if the national government wants the enforcement of this right of state employees it must enforce it itself.[21]

These are all decisions of the theistic, court-interventionist sort. It is an open question, which this chapter will consider in detail, whether such decisions are able to generate a body of doctrine sufficiently coherent and workable to sustain them.

Power and When It Runs Out

As has been noted, the grant of power in Article I speaks of "all legislative Powers herein granted," and later in the article lists what those granted powers are. The inference from this wording—that the framers intended a national government of enumerated powers—is not suppositious. They said so over and over, on all sides of the ratification debate.[22] John Marshall, the most nationalistic of the early justices, repeated the point.[23] But does this enumeration mean any more than that any particular exercise of national power must be referable to one of the enumerated grants, although the sum of those grants may nonetheless occupy the whole field of governmental power?

Necessary and Proper

The enumeration was intended to cover those topics that experience and foresight indicated to the founders were necessary to the vitality of a national government.[24] But if the assignment was to assure the effectiveness of that government, it was important to spell out the interpretive principle on which the assignment was made and expected to be carried out. The Articles of Confederation had provided that each state "retains" those powers not "expressly delegated" to the national government.[25] The Constitution by contrast added a final clause, sometimes called the Sweeping Clause, to its enumeration of the powers of Congress: "To make all Laws which shall be necessary and proper for carrying into Execution the foregoing Powers, and all other Powers vested by this Constitution in the Government of the United States, or in any Department or Officer thereof."

This clause received its first exegesis in 1819 in *McCulloch v. Maryland,* and Chief Justice Marshall's treatment was so masterly that it has stood as a definitive cornerstone of doctrine ever since: Maryland challenged the power of Congress to establish the Bank of the United States because such a power was not explicitly enumerated in the Constitution. Marshall interpreted the word "necessary" in this context to mean not necessary as in the sense of a condition *sine qua non*—as counsel for Maryland had contended—but any means "appropriate" or "plainly adapted" to the end of carrying out one of the enumerated powers or ends of national legislation. Obviously, a bank was not indispensable to carrying out the various powers that Marshall said the bank helped to implement: to lay and collect taxes, borrow money, regulate commerce, or raise and support armies and navies. Money is collected and disbursed throughout the nation; a national bank is a means of facilitating this. He offered this example: the Constitution gives Congress the power to establish post offices and post roads. But their establishment does not *necessarily* entail carrying the mail along those roads from one office to another or the punishment of those who steal from the mails. The first function could be fulfilled by private contract carriers and the second by the states against whose laws theft generally was already an offense. But nonetheless such measures were appropriate to the implementation of the enumerated powers, and that was enough.[26]

As for policing the boundaries of this wider terrain, Marshall pulled in two different directions. The tension between his two lines of thought is reflected in the whole subsequent course of doctrine. On the one hand: "The government which has a right to do an act . . . must, according to reason, be allowed to select the means. . . . Let the end be legitimate . . . all means which are appropriate, which are plainly adopted to that end are constitutional." On the other: "Should Congress, in the execution of its powers, pass laws for the accomplishment of objects not entrusted to [it]; it would become the painful duty of this tribunal . . . to say that such an act was not the law of the land." This has ever been the dilemma. Constitutional doctrine has oscillated between the "painful duty" of enforcing limits on the powers of the national government lest they swamp the distinct authority of the states, and declining to spell out such limits because, as Marshall said, "the provision is made in a constitution made to endure for ages to come, and, consequently, to be adapted to the various crises in human affairs." The challenge to doctrine to resolve this dilemma has been particularly acute with respect to two of the enumerated powers: the power to regulate interstate commerce and the power to enforce "by appropriate legislation" the guarantees of the Fourteenth Amendment that no state "shall deprive any person of life, liberty, or property, without due process of law; nor deny to any person . . . the equal protection of the laws."

The Commerce Power

That the Sweeping Clause is an admonition to interpret the enumerated powers generously is a conclusion particularly apt when we consider the power "to regulate Commerce with foreign Nations, and among the several States, and with the Indian Tribes. . . ." This is a power not to attain a defined end—to establish post offices, to coin money—but to exercise power over (to regulate) a determinate subject matter. And that grant of power is limited only by its subject matter. The debate today about the commerce power is fundamental: has that power become in effect a general power of government, the all-encompassing residual power of sovereignty that the Tenth Amendment had assumed remains in the states, except insofar as specific instances of it are "delegated to the United States by the Constitution [or] prohibited [to them]" by it?

From early days our constitutional jurisprudence has recognized the broad sweep of the commerce power, while warning that it is not equivalent to the general power of government. The foundational statement is once more John Marshall's. In 1824 in *Gibbons v. Ogden*[27] he rejected limiting the commerce power to "traffic [as in the modern usage "trafficking in . . ."], to buying and selling, or the interchange of commodities." Such a limitation would not "comprehend[] navigation"—which was the subject of *Gibbons:* competing licenses, one state, one federal, to operate steamers in New York waters. "Commerce, undoubtedly, is traffic, but it is something more—it is intercourse. It describes the commercial intercourse between nations and parts of nations, in all its branches." Marshall also disposed of the attempt to impose a narrow meaning on the other terms of the Commerce Clause. Commerce "among the several states" means that commerce which is "intermingled with them"; it is that commerce which "extend[s] to or affect[s] other states." It is that "commerce which concerns more states than one." Thus the commerce which is the subject of the clause does not "stop at the external boundary line of each state, but may be introduced into the interior." And the "power to regulate" means the power to "prescribe the rule by which commerce is governed." So long as nothing else in the Constitution precludes it, that "power, like all others vested in the congress is complete in itself, may be exercised to its utmost extent, and acknowledges no limitations other than are prescribed in the constitution."

Such a broad definition must have provoked anxiety then, as it does now. Marshall stated its limits:

> The enumeration presupposes something not enumerated; and that something, if we regard the language or the subject of the sentence, must be the exclusively internal commerce of a state. . . . The genius and character of the whole government seem to be, that its action is to be applied to all the external concerns of the nation, and to those internal concerns which affect the States generally; but not to those which are completely within a particular State, which do not affect other States, and with which it is not necessary to interfere, for the purpose of executing some of the general powers of the government.

This reassurance at the same time recalls both themes of *McCulloch*: that the grant of power to the national government also includes the power to do that which is "necessary" for the purpose of "executing" one of the enumerated powers, but with the caveat: "[S]hould congress, under the pretext of executing its powers, pass laws for the accomplishment of objects not entrusted to the government[,] it would become the painful duty of this tribunal . . . to say that such an act was not the law of the land."

The dilemma for constitutional doctrine whether and how it would define the extent of national power was particularly acute in respect to so broad a subject as commerce. At the time of *Gibbons* and for a century after, this dilemma was bound up in another, related concern: in authorizing some particular federal regulation of commerce, say to keep a particular interstate waterway free from obstruction, constitutional doctrine may announce a broad rule of federal competence which extends to subjects that Congress has not yet regulated, and is unlikely to try to regulate. Does acknowledging that the national government might if it chose regulate a particular subject carry the implication that the states may not regulate that same subject even while that national power remains unexercised? It is in part this concern that lay behind the argument—so strange to our ears—that manufacturing, agriculture, and mining are matters of exclusively state concern.[28] If a subject matter must be exclusively in either the state or the federal realm of concern, then assigning it to the national government, even potentially, would preclude state regulation altogether. This in turn would mean that either wide swaths of subject matter would remain free of any government's attention or the ordinary and inevitable laws addressing these subjects would have to issue from Congress—thus forcing on the Congress a far larger role in setting the rules for local activities than it wished to assume. This is the problem (or doctrine) that goes rather unilluminatingly by the name of dual sovereignty. But the problem only arises because of the premise that acknowledging a power, even though unexercised, in the federal government to regulate a subject precludes state regulation. It conceives of the grants of power to the national government as necessarily withdrawing that power from the states. Once again the wording of the Tenth Amendment might plausibly be taken to support such an analysis. It suggests that only "[t]he powers not delegated to the United States by the Constitution . . . are reserved to the States," and because the power to regulate interstate commerce is so delegated, it is therefore not reserved to the states.

Marshall in *Gibbons* offered a practical way out of the dilemma: the same matter might after all be the subject of state or of federal regulation; only the federal government could regulate that matter insofar as it was an aspect of interstate commerce; and if it did regulate it, then the federal regulation might choose, as an incident "necessary and proper" to the exercise of its commerce power, to oust whatever state regulation of the same matter as interfered with it.[29] But Congress might only wish to establish a minimum not a uniform level of regulation, and then states would be free to regulate as they had before that minimum was established. The inconvenience of this analysis is that it requires Congress to preempt—explicitly or by implication—any otherwise valid state regulation that may conflict with what it tries to accomplish, and that has problems of its own. State regulation may conflict with federal regulation in many, often quite unforeseeable ways. Such impediments may be as general and pervasive as the reservation of the use of the highways in each state only to vehicles or drivers licensed by that state, or having qualifications and characteristics peculiar to and perhaps incompatible with those specified in other states.[30] But they may be as discrete and episodic as a town ordinance relating to the passage of heavy trucks through its streets at night. Congress simply could not by explicit preemption remove all such impediments.

It was in part at least in response to this practical need that the Court developed the notion of dual sovereignty, by which not only are certain topics assigned to the Congress, but others are assigned by the Constitution to the states, and neither states nor Congress may stray from their prescribed areas. The doctrine allowed state governments to deal with problems the national government could not conveniently address. The structure that this body of doctrine created worked well enough when the appetite, capacity, and above all the need for national regulation of the economy was slight, but with the accelerating industrialization and integration of the national economy—especially after the Civil War—the constraints of the doctrine were felt to be increasingly unbearable. The Court strained against and sometimes burst free of its logic in that earlier period: the Court ruled that Congress might forbid moving lottery tickets,[31] rotten eggs,[32] or prostitutes[33] across state lines, but only by emphasizing that it was the physical interstate transportation that was forbidden, although the obvious evils against which these measures were directed were exactly the sort that local laws had traditionally addressed (or failed to address). Following Marshall, the doctrine held that regulation included complete prohibition, and an action within Congress's power to regulate interstate movement was valid whatever its ultimate purpose and certainly in spite of the fact that the effect of the regulation would be felt within the state's borders—after all, as Marshall also had said, every effect must be felt in some particular location. But there was a limit to this device for escaping the doctrinal constraints of dual sovereignty. The antitrust laws could not be used to prevent a nascent monopolist from buying up the shares of competing sugar refineries, because sugar refining was—like all manufacturing—a local matter.[34] On the other hand, the Court did allow the application of the antitrust laws to railroads, which were "instrumentalities of interstate commerce,"[35] and to meat dealers because they controlled the "stream of commerce" from producers to stockyards to slaughterhouses, packers, distributors, and retailers.[36] The same logic was used to justify the regulation of stockyards, which while certainly fixed in one locality, were "but a throat" through which this "current of commerce" flowed.[37]

It is the way of doctrine to develop by analogy, moving out from a core of concrete instances by progressive, metaphorical extensions until a new and more abstract statement is achieved. Commerce Clause doctrine prior to 1937 strained toward such abstractions. The metaphorical path ran through a willingness to acknowledge regulation of activities that consisted in the actual interstate movement, to activities (as in the meat cases) that might be conceptualized as a physical part of that movement. The next step would be to extend the reach of the commerce power to activities whose impact on that movement was not physical but economic. And this is where the outward expansion of doctrine ran into intellectual and political trouble. Early in the twentieth century the Court had recognized the authority of the Interstate Commerce Commission to regulate railroad freight rates between locations wholly in Texas, when those rates undercut rates set by the commission between Shreveport, Louisiana, near the Texas border and those same locations deep within Texas.[38] The Court reasoned that there must be this power in the national government because it was a "measure[] necessary and appropriate" to make effective its undoubted power to regulate interstate freight rates. It would be no stretch to apply federal safety standards to wholly intrastate trains running on the same or parallel tracks as interstate traffic: the former might physically endanger the latter.[39] But here the mechanism of harm was purely economic. Once that is admitted, the way is open to forbidding the interstate shipment (or even the production for interstate shipment) of goods produced under substandard factory conditions or by the use of child labor. The cross-border harm would come about not by the carrying of diseased cattle on interstate rail lines, but by the purely economic route of competitive pressure from lower-wage production. And this, until the "turn" in 1937, the Court—over fierce dissents and against much criticism—would not countenance,[40] because it opened the way for unlimited national regulation of the national economy. The Court's intransigence was motivated to some extent by the traditional concern for maintenance of distinct spheres for state governments, which such an extension threatened to swamp, so that the pre-1937 justices imagined themselves fulfilling their "painful duty." But it would be willful blindness to miss a source of energy that was equally strong: several justices despised the substance of these regulatory measures—especially as they intervened in labor markets to protect workers—and struck down analogous measures enacted at the state level, but on the ground that they deprived individuals of liberty or property without due process of law.[41] It was not until after President Franklin D. Roosevelt and his party won a crushing victory in the election of 1936 that the logic of some of the earlier cases was allowed to expand to encompass regulation of activities whose interstate impact was purely economic.

In *NLRB v. Jones & Laughlin Steel Corp.*[42] the Court decisively turned away from its disposition to invalidate national economic regulation as not within Congress's commerce power. In that case the National Labor Relations Board asserted jurisdiction over labor relations in Jones & Laughlin's manufacturing plants in Pittsburgh and Aliquippa, Pennsylvania.[43] In companion cases the Court turned aside challenges to the board's jurisdiction over employees in a tractor trailer manufacturing plant,[44] a clothing manufacturing plant,[45] and an editorial employee in the Associated Press's New York office.[46] In each of these cases the Court emphasized the extent to which the local activities were part of a productive process that drew on inputs from many locations outside of the state and the outputs of which were similarly widely distributed. Chief Justice Charles Evans Hughes, in the *Jones & Laughlin* case, quoted the Labor Board's characterization of the Pennsylvania plants as "the heart of a self-contained highly integrated body. They draw in the raw materials from Michigan, Minnesota, West Virginia, Pennsylvania in part through arteries and by means controlled by [Jones & Laughlin]; they transform the materials and then pump them out to all parts of the nation. . . ." In the tractor trailer and clothing plant cases the Court also emphasized the percentage of raw materials obtained from out of state, transformed at the plants and then shipped all over the nation. In the *Associated Press* case, the news dispatches edited in New York were received from all over the world and the edited product was then transmitted to subscribers all over the world. Disruptions in labor relations in the particular localities, therefore, would affect commerce with and in many places. The act, the Court concluded, "purports to reach only what may be deemed to burden or obstruct [interstate] commerce. . . . It is a familiar principle that acts which directly burden or obstruct interstate or foreign commerce, or its free flow, are within the reach of the congressional power. . . . [It] is the effect upon commerce, not the source of the injury, which is the criterion."[47] In short, in a modern national economy all commerce is interstate, and any regulation of commerce is regulation of interstate commerce.

*   *   *

Thereafter for the next fifty-eight years, almost without dissent,[48] the rationale of the *Labor Board* cases served to ratify a wide array of federal programs. Perhaps the most significant of these came five years later in *Wickard v. Filburn*,[49] which upheld a penalty on a dairy farmer whose wheat crop exceeded his government-allotted quota of wheat "available for market." Some of Filburn's small wheat output on which the penalty was assessed was grown for sale, but most was for home consumption: as seed crop, livestock feed, and flour. Justice Robert Jackson brushed aside the concern that here was a "regulation of production and consumption, rather than of marketing. . . . The Court's recognition of the relevance of the economic effects in the application of the Commerce Clause [has] made the mechanical application of legal formulas no longer feasible. . . . [E]ven if [Filburn's] activity be local and though it may not be regarded as commerce, it may still, whatever its nature, be reached by Congress if it exerts a substantial economic effect on interstate commerce. . . ." As important as was Jackson's emphasis on the *economic* mechanism of the effect on interstate commerce, his method for measuring if the requirement was met, if that effect was substantial, was even more important. "That [Filburn's] own contribution to the demand for wheat may be trivial by itself is not enough to remove him from the scope of federal regulation where, as here, his contribution, taken together with many others similarly situated, is far from trivial. [Homegrown] wheat overhangs the market and . . . in this sense competes with wheat in commerce." It was as if Filburn had been a forger arguing that a few counterfeit bills could not possibly have an effect—let alone a substantial effect—on the national money supply. This rationale was pushed to its farthest extreme in *Daniel v. Paul*.[50] The Court held that Congress's authority under the Commerce Clause extended to prohibiting racial discrimination in the whole of an amusement park, because its snack bar obtained some of its supplies from out-of-state sources.

And so matters stood until the Court's 1995 and 2000 decisions in *United States v. Lopez*[51] and *United States v. Morrison*,[52] striking down two congressional enactments as beyond the commerce power invoked to justify them. At the outset of this *démarche* the Court invoked the "first principle [that] the Constitution creates a Federal Government of enumerated powers. As James Madison wrote, 'the powers delegated by the proposed Constitution to the federal government are few and defined. Those which are to remain in the State governments are numerous and indefinite.'" The statute in *Lopez,* the Gun-Free School Zones Act (GFZA) of 1990,[53] made it a federal crime to possess a firearm at or near a school. The legislation had no requirement that the firearm had moved in interstate commerce. At the time of the prosecution in Texas, forty states had similar laws,[54] and there was no finding that the states had difficulty enforcing these laws because of some interstate aspect of the offense, or for any other reason. In *Morrison* the Court held that it was beyond the power of Congress under the Commerce Clause to give women victims of "gen-der-motivated" violence a federal damage action against their assailants. This provision of the Violence Against Women Act (VAWA) of 1994 for that reason was unconstitutional. Such assaults were already actionable torts by the law of every state.[55] Both statutes had been passed by Congress by large majorities.

The Court's decisions were met with outrage in both political and academic circles.[56] Some of the passion may have come from surprise at the reassertion—after three generations—of a constitutional doctrine, the triumph over which had become an icon of the New Deal welfare-administrative state. One can almost imagine a Renaissance St. George whose spear, firmly planted in the dragon Reaction, bears the banner *NLRB v. Jones & Laughlin Steel Corp.* But there was this difference. There was no doubt in either *Lopez* or *Morrison*—as there had been in some of the pre–New Deal economic cases—that the substantive regulation was well within the constitutional power of state law, no suggestion of judicial hostility either to keeping guns away from schools or to vindicating the rights of battered women. Fidelity to a conception of what the Constitution requires is what lies behind (and is stated on the face of) these decisions.

The cases were critical. Although the Court had not since 1936 found a case in which it concluded that Congress's power had run out in the long march from *NLRB v. Jones & Laughlin Steel Corp.,* the Court had never ceased to recall Marshall's caveat about its "painful duty." In *Jones & Laughlin* itself Chief Justice Hughes had said that "the scope of [the commerce] power must be considered in the light of our dual system of government and may not be extended so as to embrace effects upon interstate commerce so indirect and remote that to embrace them, in view of our complex society, would effectively obliterate the distinction between what is national and what is local and create a completely centralized government." The clearest, more recent statement was Justice John Harlan's in *Maryland v. Wirtz,* approving the extension of federal wages and hours laws to employees of state government but warning that "the power to regulate commerce, though broad indeed, has limits [that] the Court has ample power [to enforce.]"[57] But if the power to regulate commerce might extend to punishing carrying a gun in a local school or even more remotely to a husband brutally dominating his wife, then it might reasonably be concluded that the commerce power could cover anything at all, standing as the basis for a grant of the general power of government to the Congress. Could a formula be found that avoided that conclusion and marked some limit to the commerce power that did not at the same time cut a swath through more than half a century of modern precedents, a swath so broad as seriously to unsettle the working of the nation's government?[58] A decision that repeated the caveats from Marshall to Hughes to Harlan, while finding by some process of reasoning yet again that here too Congress had not passed the limits of the commerce power, would in effect dismiss those caveats once and for all as empty pieties, while lacking the virtue of candor.

The Chief Justice's opinion threaded its way past every major precedent allowing the extension of the commerce power, from *Gibbons* right through the post-1937 decisions of the New Deal era—even including *Wickard,* which the opinion characterized as "perhaps the most far reaching example of Commerce Clause authority over intrastate activity." Although it overruled no single prior decision, the opinion discerned a common theme in even the most expansive of them that had hardly been explicit in those decisions themselves. The case law, stretching well past the "turn" of 1937, had recognized a plenary power under the Commerce Clause to regulate both the channels and the instrumentalities of interstate commerce, for instance, railroads—even when the particular cars do not cross state borders—or a hotel catering to interstate travelers.[59] These cases presented no issue here, because there was no plausible claim that GFZA or VAWA regulated a channel or instrumentality of commerce. Similarly the Court had long granted a plenary power to Congress to regulate commerce by regulating persons or things "in interstate commerce" as they crossed or after they crossed state lines, "even though the threat may come only from intrastate activity."

The Court identified a third category of cases: "those activities having a substantial relation to interstate commerce." It was this category—of which the Chief Justice makes *Jones & Laughlin* the leading example—that had the potential of making of the commerce power a general power of government. The cases were right to recognize that commerce naturally means commercial activity and that commercial activity is measured by the metric and concepts of economics. The exclusion of manufacturing or other modes of production from the domain of commerce is arbitrary from an economic perspective, and the causal mechanisms by which an effect is understood to be produced beyond the boundaries of a single state are mechanisms measured and conceptualized in economic terms. Economic activities carried out locally and in small degree, if generalized and aggregated, produce national repercussions. No single transaction need have any but an infinitesimal effect on market conditions, but those conditions are nonetheless determined by a myriad of such economic events. In its way, this is an insight into how the world works as basic and transformative as the infinitesimal calculus, to which it is conceptually related. The Court's opinion recognized this truth without any squeamishness, reaffirming *Wickard v. Filburn.*

In *Lopez* and then again in *Morrison* the Court tried for a categorical center for the doctrine by which it would mark the limit of the commerce power and thus retain—or reclaim—it as a subject for constitutional doctrine and Supreme Court adjudication. To leave those limits simply as a matter of degree would entail frequent Supreme Court intervention to adjudicate them, and this might have suggested that if the constitutional limits on congressional power are taken as purely a matter of degree, then those limits may not be appropriate for judicial supervision at all. The first two kinds of cases listed by the Court—regulation of the channels of interstate commerce and regulation of persons or things moving in interstate commerce—are marked by categorical distinctions, not distinctions of degree. This third and most important kind—regulation of what bears a substantial relationship to that commerce—the Court also proposed to cabin by a categorical, and therefore judicially manageable, doctrinal limit: the activity Congress seeks to regulate must itself be an economic activity. "The possession of a gun in a local school zone is in no sense an economic activity that might, through repetition elsewhere, substantially affect any sort of interstate commerce." The Chief Justice repeats this point five years later in the *Morrison* case: "Gender-motivated crimes of violence are not, in any sense of the phrase, economic activity. While we need not adopt a categorical rule against aggregating the effects of any noneconomic activity in order to decide these cases, thus far in our Nation's history our cases have upheld Commerce Clause regulation of intrastate activity only where that activity is economic in nature." From the premise that in an integrated economy all commerce is interstate commerce, it does not follow that all conduct is commercial.

Although the post-1937 cases had stated no such limit, it is also true that the Court's formulation does manage to account at least for their results. Recall that Marshall's early canonical formula in *Gibbons* said that the Constitution's term "describes the *commercial* intercourse between nations and part of nations." And looking back at the pivotal labor board cases of 1937, the economic nature of the activities covered certainly does loom large in the account the Court then gave of its decisions. Justice Stephen Breyer in dissent in *Morrison* objected that the Court's new test was importantly narrower than the post-1937 decisions, which emphasized economic *effect* as a sufficient predicate for the regulation of an activity under the commerce power. The activities regulated by GFZA and more obviously by VAWA may not be characterizable as economic, but an economic impact may be shown: school violence detracts importantly from the quality of education, which in turn has an impact on the quality of the workforce and the relative desirability of communities as places for businesses to establish and workers to settle. Women who are the victims of violence lose days at work or are discouraged from entering or remaining in the workforce; and their victimization imposes many direct and indirect costs on them, their dependents, and the communities that would care for them.[60] Justice Breyer wondered, "why should we give critical constitutional importance to the economic, or noneconomic, nature of an interstate-commerce-affecting cause? If chemical emanations through indirect environmental change cause identical, severe commercial harm outside a State, why should it matter whether local factories or home fireplaces release them?" In short, even if the line could be drawn at the regulation of economic activities, Justice Breyer asks why it makes sense to draw the line there. It is, after all, effects about which we should be concerned.

In his dissent in *Lopez,* Justice Breyer had appeared to concede that there must be some point at which the commerce power runs out, where Congress has gone too far. This concession left him open to the Court's rebuttal that although he appears to acknowledge such a limit "he is unable to identify any activity that the states may regulate, but Congress may not." It was in response to this challenge that five years later in *Morrison* Justice Breyer offered a more fundamental objection to the Court's nascent Commerce Clause jurisprudence. He denied the imperative to fix such a limit marking the limit of the commerce power: "This consideration [the inability to fix a limit], however, while serious, does not reflect a jurisprudential defect, so much as it reflects a practical reality. We live in a Nation knit together by two centuries of scientific, technological, commercial, and environmental change. Those changes, taken together, mean that virtually every kind of activity, no matter how local, genuinely can affect commerce, or its conditions, outside the State—at least when considered in the aggregate." It may be that at the time of the founding the enumerated powers would not sustain such a total assertion of authority, but that is only because the way the world was then offered no occasion for such a plenary assertion under the rubric of commerce. The world is different now, and "judges cannot change the world."

The disagreement between the two positions comes down to the structural inference to be drawn from the Constitution's scheme to grant to Congress "all legislative powers herein granted." The dissent asks only whether the particular assertion is fairly within one of those enumerated powers, and if the world has evolved in such a way that one or more of those powers can be a premise for addressing virtually any subject at all, there is nothing in the Constitution to prevent that conclusion. The Court, by contrast, discerns a structure behind the text, an imperative, not just a description of the state of the world as it stood at the time. The Court took it as the task of doctrine to draw lines and limits that articulate that structure.

State Power as a Counterforce to National Power

This structural articulation may also be expressed in doctrines that assign certain powers and subjects to state government, and that discipline assertions of national power impinging on those domains. There is a hint of this in the Court's opinion in *Lopez*: "Under the Government's 'national productivity' reasoning, Congress could regulate any activity that it found was related to the economic productivity of individual citizens: family law (including marriage, divorce, and child custody), for example." Although the Chief Justice's opinion mentioned that schools and security around them are matters of traditional state concern, he did not insist on the point, and certainly did not treat it as if it were determinative. That was left to Justice Anthony Kennedy's concurrence. Suggesting an implicit structural sense of the federal-state balance that is not simply the sum of the several explicit provisions in the Constitution, the concurrence argued that: "In a sense any conduct in this interdependent world of ours has an ultimate commercial origin or consequence, but we have not yet said the commerce power may reach so far. If Congress attempts that extension, then at the least we must inquire whether the exercise of national power seeks to intrude upon an area of traditional state concern." The basic law of crimes—murder, assault, theft—the law of wills, and title to property are other examples of the traditional realm of state law.

But this is a precarious doctrinal basis for limiting the reach of federal authority, as is shown by the abandonment of the doctrine of dual sovereignty that once put mining, manufacturing, and agriculture in the domain of exclusive state concern. And in fact aspects of family law—interstate enforcement of child custody and support decrees—have long and uncontroversially been the subject of federal legislation, albeit by reference to a national power other than the Commerce Clause. Nor does the Court put in doubt the capacity of Congress to institute a national registry of property titles, a uniform law of sales, or a national driver's license—all matters traditionally in state control. On the other hand, there is considerable doubt whether Congress could use the Commerce Clause to mandate a national grade-school curriculum (as opposed to paying federal money to schools that voluntarily adopt one). Congress's authority "though broad, does not include the authority to regulate each and every aspect of local schools." Yet the Court does not go so far as to hold that there are, among "each and every aspect of local schools," some aspects that by their own force can repel an otherwise valid exercise of congressional power. It is just that the national power runs out before it reaches, say, the best method of teaching reading to first graders.

Counterforce: The Tenth Amendment
Counterforce doctrines do, however, also exist to give substance to the federalistic structure discerned by the Court in *Lopez* and *Morri-*

son. One such counterforce doctrine, that of *New York v. United States*[61] and *Printz v. United States,*[62] is still (or again) active. Invoking the Tenth Amendment, the Court has ruled that Congress may not regulate in such a way as to impair the status of the states as independently governing units. This notion is quite different from the one implicit in the old notion of dual sovereignty. It does not deny the extent of the national power to regulate a particular topic, but rather prevents the federal government from interfering with the operation of state *government* in inappropriate ways. The notion is far from clear. It is illustrated by the two cases that gave it prominence, *National League of Cities v. Usery* (1976)[63] and *New York v. United States* (1992).[64] In *National League of Cities,* the Court had held that the extension of federal wages and hours legislation to state and municipal workers violated the Constitution's recognition of state sovereignty by interfering with the states' ability to perform "traditional governmental functions" such as fire and police protection and public health. Practically, it was indeed a burden on local government that it had to pay its firefighters and police officers time-and-a-half overtime pay, whenever they were assigned a tour of duty longer than eight hours, even if the duty included being on call at a fire station during sleeping hours or if the longer tours were interspersed with whole days off so that the total workweek did not exceed forty hours. But the complaint was not that Congress was regulating a purely local activity—it was not questioned that Congress could impose its wages and hours regime on a private security company whose activities were just as local—but rather that such regulation was met by the counterforce of the state's sovereign prerogatives to structure its labor relations as it provided vital governmental functions. The Court then declined to apply this doctrine in a series of cases dealing with federal regulation of local mining practices, a state-owned commuter rail line, mandatory retirement for state police officers, and local utility regulation,[65] until finally, only nine years after *National League* in *Garcia v. San Antonio Metropolitan Transit Authority,*[66] the Court abandoned the doctrine, pronouncing itself unable to define a "workable" line to distinguish regulations impairing essential governmental functions from those where it would permit national regulation.

Seven years after the announced demise of that doctrine the Court partially revived it in *New York v. United States,* but in a very special and limited form. The idea was that even if Congress might regulate a particular subject—in this case the location of low-level radiation disposal sites—it could not do so by forcing the states themselves to enact, or take an active role in, the regulation. The phrase that rings in the ear is that the national government may not regulate a subject by "commandeering" the machinery of state government to do the regulating for it. This limited counterforce doctrine appears to have stuck, having been reaffirmed in 1997 in the *Printz* case, although the unanimous decision in *Reno v. Condon*[67] made it clear that the "commandeering" doctrine did not extend to negative commands, forbidding the states from regulating certain subjects, or regulating in certain ways—a good thing too, for otherwise it is hard to see what would have remained of the doctrine of the supremacy of national law and of federal preemption. Nor did the doctrine extend to regulations that applied generally, to nongovernmental as well as governmental entities. Thus *National League of Cities* was not revived, as the federal wages-and-hours regulation at issue there applied across the board to all employers—public and private. The idea, I suppose, is that only when a state's governmental powers to regulate its citizens' conduct are enlisted is there the particular offense of requiring the state to regulate the primary activity of private citizens according to a national mandate, rather than allowing the state to regulate according to its own policies (so long as they do not interfere with national policies) and making the national government do its own regulating of primary conduct all by itself. (Of course the national government enlists state governments in the administration of federal policies all the time, but only by making their cooperation a condition under which states may receive financial and other assistance from the national government in respect to a particular program.)[68]

Counterforce: Sovereign Immunity

The standing of the states within the national union is protected by another doctrine, which I shall discuss more briefly, because it is exceedingly complicated, because it achieves its purpose in an oddly indirect and incomplete way, and finally because it seems to me so seriously mistaken—both historically and doctrinally—that I can only hope and believe it will sooner or later be abandoned. This is the doctrine that the Eleventh Amendment, and a doctrine of state sovereign immunity extrapolated from it, preclude a state from being sued without its consent in a federal tribunal or even in its own state courts by any party other than the federal government. The Eleventh Amendment, adopted in 1798, reads:

> The Judicial power of the United States shall not be construed to extend to any suit in law or equity, commenced or prosecuted against one of the United States by Citizens of another State, or by Citizens or Subjects of any Foreign State.

The amendment was a direct response to the Supreme Court's decision in *Chisolm v. Georgia*,[69] allowing a South Carolina vendor to sue Georgia in federal court to recover, under common law, payment for blankets, uniforms, and other military supplies sold to Georgia during the Revolutionary War. The Court applied Article III, §2, of the Constitution: "The judicial Power shall extend to . . . Controversies . . . between a State and Citizens of another state; [and] between Citizens of different States" and concluded that there was federal jurisdiction over the suit. The subject of Revolutionary War debts and the states' obligations for them was a particularly touchy one and this decision provoked a furor. After the Eleventh Amendment such a suit could no longer be brought. But what was such a suit? At its narrowest and most specific, such a suit invoked the diversity jurisdiction of the federal courts to bring a common law action not against a citizen of another state but against the state itself. This diversity jurisdiction of the federal courts adjudicating ordinary common law suits was included in the Constitution because of the concern that state courts might be prejudiced against parties from out of state.

In the 1890 case of *Hans v. Louisiana*,[70] the Supreme Court applied the Eleventh Amendment to bar federal jurisdiction in a suit against the state of Louisiana brought by a citizen of that state claiming a federal constitutional violation. The amendment quite clearly does not in terms bar such a suit: it was not brought "by a citizen of *another* state." Nor was it necessary to extrapolate the literal text to this case in order to make sense of the amendment, for here unlike in *Chisolm* the basis for federal jurisdiction was not diversity of citizenship but the separate Article III grounds that this was a case "arising under this Constitution, [and] the laws of the United States." (In modern terminology, Hans invoked not the "diversity" but the "federal question" jurisdiction of the federal courts.) And the reasons for giving federal courts jurisdiction to hear controversies based in federal rather than in state law are stronger than the reasons for giving the federal courts diversity jurisdiction. Not only may federal courts be less biased against one of the parties, they may be more familiar with and readier to apply federal law, and the development of federal law would be more coherent if federal courts had the principal (though not necessarily the exclusive) charge of developing it. The basis for the Court's decision in *Hans* was not the text of the Eleventh Amendment, but what it discerned as a principle behind it: that the amendment was a recognition of the distinct sovereignty of the states, and that it was an offense against that sovereign dignity to allow a private party to bring a state into a federal court without its consent.[71] With complications, qualifications, and exceptions I shall not go into here,[72] this doctrine was definitively reaffirmed only in 1996 in *Seminole Tribe of Florida v. Florida*.[73] This was intended as a strong statement of respect for the dignity and independence of the states. The decision three years later in *Alden v. Maine*[74] was an even stronger such statement, as it precluded a group of Maine citizens, state probation officers, from suing the state even in *state* court for back wages they claimed were owed them by the application of the federal wages and hours laws.[75]

Alden is the case that shows the strengths and weaknesses of the Court's recent Eleventh Amendment jurisprudence. The federal wages and hours laws—like, for instance, federal antidiscrimination laws,[76] many environmental laws,[77] labor laws, bankruptcy laws[78]—rely to a greater or lesser extent for their enforcement on their individual beneficiaries' bringing suit against the subjects of the regulation. *Alden* means that where the regulated entity is a state, private enforcement may be altogether precluded, as there is no court which can be required to hear private complaints. But the United States Department of Labor could still sue Maine to obtain the back pay owed the probation officers and to force Maine to comply with the federal standards in the future. The result is distinctly awkward, because as a practical matter it is hard to see why the dignity of the state—whatever that means—is less offended by a suit brought by federal bureaucrats than by one brought by its own citizens. The clumsiness of this device is particularly salient in light of the fact that the particular federal regulation involved in *Alden* was the same one that had been the subject of earlier cases, in which the proper question had at least been asked: was this regulation an excessive interference with a state's ability to order its own operations of government and thus beyond the power of Congress to impose at all? *National League of Cities* had, I believe, correctly denied Congress that substantive power, but *National League of Cities* had been overruled by *Garcia* before the Court had embarked on its present revival of federalistic limits on the substantive powers of Congress. Evidently the Court lacked the will (or the votes) to revive *National League of Cities*, leaving the strange result that the Court (for the time being) allows Congress the substantive power to order the labor relations of the states as employers, but denies to Congress the usual and most efficient means of exercising that power.[79]

Moving away from the practicalities of this turn in Supreme Court jurisprudence, there are theoretical and methodological considerations that both support and argue against this peculiar body of law. It is certainly true that the doctrine of sovereign immunity—with its roots in archaic and statist conceptions—has played an important role in the development of the law of individual remedies against government, limiting in a variety of complicated ways what courts can do without the benefit of legislation. This has not been an altogether bad thing, because it has encouraged the development of comprehensive legislative schemes like the federal Administrative Procedure Act[80] and the state versions of that act.[81] The upshot of the combination of this legislation and doctrines allowing constitutionally based remedies against government agents[82] has been to produce a situation in which it might fairly be said that the principle of the rule of law—which demands, more or less, that for every wrong by whomever, there be a remedy—has superseded the anachronistic doctrine of sovereign immunity, for that immunity spells the immunity of the government from the rule of law. The sovereign immunity doctrine seems particularly inapt when applied to limit the authority of the national Congress, acting by hypothesis within its assigned powers and pursuant to the Supremacy Clause, to prescribe not only the substantive regime it wishes to impose on the states but the remedies best suited ("necessary and proper") to implement that scheme.

On the other hand, the Court in *Seminole Tribe* did not invent an obstacle to congressional power but rather carried forward doctrines and precedents that lay about, not overruled in the Court's jurisprudence. This is especially so of the century-old precedent of *Hans v. Louisiana*. *Alden* may be said to have done no more than extrapolate from the sovereign immunity principle explicitly embraced in *Hans* to provide that immunity as a shield to actions against the state brought in the state's own courts. But these precedents, and the doctrine derived from them, were neither so well founded nor so solidly entrenched as to require, out of fidelity to *stare decisis,* their recent exhumation. The most powerful reason is that *Hans* itself went beyond the explicit words of the Eleventh Amendment, the occasion for the amendment's adoption, and (what seems to me) its evident purpose as revealed in both: to remove suits by citizens against the states from the federal court's diversity jurisdiction, leaving unaffected the federal court's federal question jurisdiction. The Court would have done better to do its federalism work along the lines of *Lopez* and *Printz.*

The Two Combined: Implementing the Fourteenth Amendment

Gun-Free School Zone legislation and the Violence Against Women Act were such obvious examples of congressional grandstanding and so evidently unnecessary that *Lopez* and *Morrison* caused a stir mainly among constitutional lawyers. Similarly, the commandeering doctrine of *New York v. United States* and *Printz* did not disturb the political waters. But the cases in which the Court struck down aspects of laws addressing religious liberty, and age and disability discrimination, provoked considerable anger.[83] These cases—along with two other emotionally less charged but no less significant cases—grow out of the Fourteenth Amendment, which effected a major shift in the federal-state balance.[84] The unamended Constitution offered few barriers to the exercise of power by the states upon individuals:[85] states might not pass bills of attainder or ex post facto laws, nor laws impairing the obligations of contracts.[86] The Bill of Rights by its text and subsequent interpretation applied only to limit the power of the national government.[87] The Fourteenth Amendment, by sharp contrast, stated broad inhibitions on the power of states to impose on individuals, most notably protecting individuals from denials by the state of life, liberty, or property without due process of law and the equal protection of the laws—the former guarantee eventually coming to incorporate most of the protections of the Bill of Rights. The substance of these protections is the subject of later chapters. Of significance here is the final section of the Fourteenth Amendment, giving Congress the power "to enforce, by appropriate legislation," these protections. Given the breadth and radical nature of the amendment, this enabling provision had the potential to become as open-ended and encompassing a grant of power as the Commerce Clause. Yet here too the Supreme Court both in early and in very recent decisions has devised doctrines that put distinct constraints on that power. The story is complicated and before we reach its denouement we must follow several doctrinal strands, which woven together bind quite tightly.

First, it was decided in 1883[88] that the Fourteenth Amendment only protects against actions by the state and its officials, not against actions by private parties. So private acts of discrimination or of injury to life, liberty, or property did not fall under the amendment's guarantee—it was the domain of (equal and impartial) state laws to protect against these.[89] It was this doctrine that forced the Congress to invoke the Commerce Clause as the source of its power to outlaw in the Civil Rights Act of 1964 discrimination in private employment and places of public accommodation—such as a hotel open to interstate travelers.[90] It was this doctrine that the Court held forecloses recourse to the Fourteenth Amendment. The amendment gave Congress the power to enforce it by appropriate legislation. And the necessary and proper, the Sweeping Clause, applies not only to the original powers, like the commerce power, given to Congress but "to all powers vested by this Constitution in the government of the United States." But, the state action doctrine holds that because the amendment offers no protection against private action, legislation like VAWA is not a measure "necessary and proper for carrying into execution" the promise of the amendment; it is not legislation "appropriate" to enforce its provisions. Once the Court had crossed the bridge to the conclusion that the amendment did not extend to private action, it was not a long step to concluding that this aspect of VAWA was not "appropriate" legislation, however presumptuous it might have seemed to Congress that another branch should hold its action inappropriate. The Court had done no more in deciding in *Marbury v. Madison* that Congress had overstepped its constitutional authority when it gave the Court powers denied it by the Constitution.[91]

The same doctrinal line was invoked in a case that proved even more controversial, *City of Boerne v. Flores*.[92] Seven years earlier, the Supreme Court, in *Employment Division v. Smith*,[93] had held that the Constitution's protection of religious liberty did not extend to laws of general applicability, but only to those that in some way targeted religion. I consider the substance of the *Smith* decision in Chapter 5; here it is sufficient to note that the decision was closely divided and to many seemed at odds with the purpose and traditions of the constitutional guarantee. The decision directly contradicted the test set out in 1964 in *Sherbert v. Verner,*[94] that where government action burdened religious practice it must be justified by a "compelling governmental interest." Congress reacted. The Religious Freedom Restoration Act (RFRA) declared in terms that any national *or state* law that burdened religious practice must meet the test set out in *Sherbert.* Of course Congress has the same power to limit its own enactments in this way as it had to pass the burdening enactments in the first place. To limit the power of *state* governments, however, Congress must point to some explicit constitutional grant of power, and the enforcement clause of the Fourteenth Amendment is the only candidate. The amendment's guarantee of liberty had long ago been interpreted to incorporate the First Amendment's guarantee of religious liberty, but the Court had ruled that *Sherbert* was not the correct understanding of religious liberty. Thus Congress in RFRA would limit the power of the states in the name of enforcing the Fourteenth Amendment according to its own and not the Court's statement of what religious liberty meant. *Boerne* certainly had the effect of protecting state power from constitutionally unauthorized encroachments by Congress: the emphasis in the ensuing debate was not on that federalistic principle but on the Court's claim that it must have the last word when it comes to interpreting the Constitution. This confrontation might have been softened had Congress less baldly purported to overrule the Court's interpretation of the Constitution but instead claimed to be implementing that interpretation by building a remedial hedge around it, as the rabbis sometimes are said to construct a "hedge around the Torah" by proposing broader prohibitions lest those subject to the law be tempted to walk right up to the precise limit and thus risk transgressing it. But here Congress had issued a direct challenge to the substance of the Court's interpretation in *Smith.*

These lines of doctrine—the extent of Congress's substantive powers under Article I, sovereign immunity, and the interpretive hegemony of the Court—came together in the age and disability discrimination cases *Kimel*[95] and *Garrett.*[96] It had been decided as long ago as the labor board cases and affirmed in *Lopez* that the economic nature of the employment relation was a sufficient predicate for congressional regulation under the Commerce Clause. And *Garcia,* which *Lopez* and *Printz* had left standing, had established that regulations of employment relations generally could include regulation of employment by state governments as well. Therefore the laws forbidding age and disability discrimination in employment protected employees of the states. The state of Florida acted unlawfully in discriminating against Mr. Kimel because of his age and Alabama against Ms. Garrett because of her disability. The law gave employees the right to sue for wages they had lost because of discrimination; accordingly had they been employed by private institutions they could have won money damages. But the sovereign immunity doctrine of *Seminole Tribe* appeared to block that relief, with the result that only agencies of the federal government could enforce the law against the states—a prescription either for inaction or for greatly increased federal bureaucratic activity.

The statutes were defended by pegging them not just to the commerce power but also to Congress's power to enforce the Fourteenth Amendment's guarantee of the equal protection of the law, because that power, having been granted later, was not blocked by the Eleventh Amendment's sovereign immunity limitation. And there was no problem of private discrimination here; it was the state that was doing the discriminating. But *Boerne* came in to block that route. The Court had previously held quite firmly—this is discussed in detail in Chapter 7—that while a state may not constitutionally discriminate arbitrarily on the basis of age or disability, such discrimination, unlike discrimination on the basis of race or gender, can be justified quite easily by any legitimate government purpose, such as a rough judgment that distinctions on this basis may reasonably (if incorrectly) be thought to increase the efficiency of the state government's workforce. This conception of what the Fourteenth Amendment offers by way of age or disability discrimination protection is a very long distance from the very stringent protections offered by the federal statutes. So to bring this kind of discrimination under Congress's Fourteenth Amendment enforcement power (and thus escape the sovereign immunity limit) Congress would either have to claim: a different and more generous view of equal protection, which was blocked by *Boerne*; or a remedial power to implement that rather stingy protection by erecting a much wider buffer around that meager protection. This latter remedial route was not blocked here by any candid avowal of a purpose to overturn the Court's substantive constitutional judgment.

And yet the Court balked, sensing no doubt that the remedial/implementation route offered a very short way around the Court's jealously asserted authority to have the last word as to the meaning of the substance of constitutional protections. And it threatened to turn the enforcement power under the Fourteenth Amendment into the general power of government—the power to legislate on any subject as it wished—that the Court had denied Congress when the subject was "effects on commerce" under the Commerce Clause. This time it offered a doctrinal stop far less categorical than the "economic activity" line of *Lopez*—but a line the flexibility and reasonableness of which is less open to charges of arbitrariness and implausibility: Congress has wide discretion to judge which measures are necessary and proper (or "appropriate," to use the amendment's own word) to implement the amendment's protections. But lest that power erase all limits on federal power, these measures must be *congruent* and *proportionate* to the Fourteenth Amendment right these measures are supposed to implement. As the Court put it in *Boerne:*

> While the line between measures that remedy or prevent unconstitutional actions and measures that make a substantive change in the governing law is not easy to discern, and Congress must have wide latitude in determining where it lies, the distinction exists and must be observed. There must be a congruence and proportionality between the injury to be prevented or remedied and the means adopted to that end. Lacking such a connection, legislation may become substantive in operation and effect.[97]

The meaning of this formulation was further elucidated in two far less heated but structurally more troubling cases, in which states were sued for violating the patents and trademarks of private businesses.[98] In the same section as the Commerce Clause the Constitution gives Congress the power to secure "for limited Times to Authors and Inventors the exclusive Right to their respective Writings and Discoveries."[99] No objection was, or could sensibly have been, raised that Congress had violated some prerogative of the states by making them respect this constitutionally authorized property right it created. Indeed, the patent laws explicitly gave states the possibility of patenting the inventions they created and sought to make them liable when they infringed the patents of others. The issue is far from theoretical, as state universities generate and use much patentable and copyrightable material. Because the patent and commerce powers come from the unamended Constitution, they are subject to the Eleventh Amendment so that private individuals are barred from vindicating their intellectual property rights when state governments take that property. As in *Morrison* and the discrimination cases, the states' victims sought to invoke the enforcement clause of the Fourteenth Amendment. This time the substantive violation of the amendment that Congress would be taken to be remedying is the provision that no state shall "deprive any person of . . . property, without due process of law." Here the state offered the patent holders no due process of law. They just took their property, so that subjecting the states to suit for infringement remedied this deprivation. Yet once again the Court held that Congress had gone too far.

In defense of this surprising result it may be said that such a use of the Fourteenth Amendment's due process clause might very well have opened the way for undoing not only recent but all prior Eleventh Amendment jurisprudence. Because any uncompensated tort or breach of contract by a state could be characterized as depriving its victim of "life, liberty, or property," states would be subject to suit by individuals in just the kinds of cases that *Hans*—a suit for recovery of unpaid interest on a state bond—over a century ago had kept out of federal court by reference to the Eleventh Amendment. *Morrison, Kimel,* and *Garrett* fit under the "congruence" leg of the Court's doctrine limiting recourse to the enforcement clause. The Fourteenth Amendment violation Congress purported to remedy was not congruent to the scope of that remedy as defined by Congress: Congress offered a remedy for age and disability discrimination that had a quite different shape from that which the Court had said those wrongs took under the Constitution. VAWA offered remedies for private acts of discriminatory violence, but the Constitution spoke only to such acts by state actors. In the patent and trademark cases the remedy fit perfectly the shape of the wrong: Congress had created a kind of property; the state had deprived its owner of that property; and the remedy gave compensation for just that deprivation. This time the vice of the scheme, according to the Court, was a lack of proportionality. "Congress identified no pattern of patent infringement by the States, let alone a pattern of constitutional violations . . . [so that] the provisions of the Patent Remedy Act are 'so out of proportion to a supposed preventive or remedial object'" as not to justify a recourse to the Fourteenth Amendment's authorization to Congress to enact legislation remedying a state's unconstitutional conduct.

The congruence and proportionality standard is promising just because, while flexible and inviting judgment on particular circumstances, it cannot properly be used to cover any decision at all. We can see how incongruence works in the RFRA, VAWA, and the age and disability discrimination cases. But as to patent and trademark infringement the congruence is perfect, and each case remedies only the violation. Nor is a remedy in state court appropriate, because these are specialized bodies of federal law; indeed patent and copyright law are so specialized that Congress has concentrated all appeals in one specialized circuit court. It counts in favor of the Court's congruence and proportionality standard that it permits lawyerly argument about the validity of particular measures. Such argument leads me to the conclusion that, in spite of the faulty Eleventh Amendment doctrine the standard implements, in all but the patent and trademark cases the Court used the concepts of congruence and proportionality correctly.*

Why Federalism Doctrine?

Herodotus reports that Xerxes, in order to bring his army from Asia for the conquest of Greece, constructed a vast bridge of boats across the Hellespont. A storm came up and scattered the boats. In a fury Xerxes ordered his men to the shore to beat the waters with whips.

---

* In *Nevada v. Hibbs*, 123 S. Ct. 1972 (2003), the Court may have flinched in the relentless extension of its sovereign immunity jurisprudence. In an opinion written by the Chief Justice—the author of *Seminole Tribe*—and replete with affirmations of that jurisprudence, the Court ruled that the doctrine of that case did not preclude a suit against the state for violating a federal statute requiring all employers to grant a period of unpaid leave to employees—man or woman—to care for ailing family members. Because it was claimed that the caregiving role had been stereotypically assigned to women, making them less desirable employees, and because, as is explained in Chapter 7, gender discrimination by the government requires a greater justification than discrimination on grounds of age or disability (as in *Kimel* and *Garrett*), Congress's supposed purpose of alleviating that discrimination by making both classes of employees equally undesirable satisfied the requirements of congruence and proportionality. It seems something of a non sequitur that the heightened scrutiny accorded to gender discrimination should entail a less demanding test of congruence and proportionality for remedies of such discrimination. In any event, religious liberty receives the highest degree of constitutional protection and property is protected from uncompensated government appropriation by specific constitutional command, and yet the claimants in *Boerne* and the patent and trademark cases were denied relief because of the doctrine of sovereign immunity. Moreover, the evidence adduced for intentional discrimination by state governments against women in this regard—the prerequisite for a constitutional violation—was exceedingly thin, thinner indeed than in those other instances.

This, concluded Herodotus, was an impious and un-Greek thing to do.[100] Justice Breyer's remark in his *Morrison* dissent that "judges cannot change the world" may have been uttered in the spirit of Herodotus.

The Court has had relatively little impact on the balance of power between the national government and the states. The early decisions of Chief Justice Marshall set a doctrinal trajectory that got the Court out of the way of politics and economics as the nation found its initial bearings. The biggest fight—over the Bank of the United States—though fought in the language of constitutional principle, actually played out as a political struggle.[101] The Court's aggressive intervention in the late nineteenth and early twentieth centuries to keep Congress from regulating mining, manufacturing, agriculture, and labor relations no more than slowed the increasing national legislative involvement in the inexorably integrating national economy. In this longer context it would be absurd to imagine that the Court's recent doctrinal *démarches* will have a large practical effect. After all, the most powerful lever of national control over local government is fiscal, and doctrine has placed no real impediment to Congress's power to condition the flow of money from the national treasury to the states on their participation in and subordination to national programs.[102] I do not mean to suggest that the Court is quixotic or insincere in its recent statements about the virtues of federalism as the genius of our constitutional structure, but only that the evident realities make it implausible to explain the Court's recent federalism jurisprudence as a political project to shift the distribution of power between the nation and the states.

I suggest instead that this developing jurisprudence reflects the Court's conception of its own function: to decide the cases that come to it according to law, and that means according to a proper conception of the Constitution. The signal case is *Boerne,* in which the Court balked at Congress's claim to overrule the Court's statement of the meaning of the guarantee of religious liberty. At the very beginning of the Court's exercise of judicial review of legislation Chief Justice Marshall declared: "It is emphatically the province and the duty of the judicial department to say what the law is."[103] The recent federalism decisions are best understood as assertions that the Constitution does embody a conception of the relation between state and national power; that that conception can find expression in constitutional doctrine, and that when cases come before it implicating that doctrine it is "the province and the duty of the Court to say what the law is." The energy behind these decisions is the rule of law.

If that is the project, to reverse *not* the course of history but the course of constitutional doctrine's abdication to politics, then the achievement is only as good as the doctrine. And the persistent dissents in these cases can be understood to deny either the correctness of the conception of federalism on which the doctrine builds or the capacity of doctrine to embody such a conception. The recent Commerce Clause cases employ a categorical approach: they allow the regulation of the instrumentalities of interstate commerce, of things or people moving in interstate commerce, and of *economic* activities that have a substantial effect on interstate commerce. Being categorical, these lines have a fair chance of succeeding as doctrinal lineaments. Although it may seem arbitrary to focus on the nature of the activity regulated rather than on the effect that activity produces, the limitation does tend to keep Congress's commerce power from spreading to activities that have been the traditional concern of state government, and so the doctrine is not only workable but more or less apt to embody the conception which is its source.

The Tenth Amendment "commandeering" doctrine of *New York* and *Printz* also has the virtue of embodying in a reasonably determinative way an intuition about the nature of our federalism: that the states should not be mere administrative units of the national government. This thought is captured in the Court's statement that the doctrine helps to preserve the citizens' sense of who is responsible for what government does to them. It helps maintain transparency and lines of political responsibility. The limitation has as much symbolic as practical effect, however, as it does not preclude often achieving the very same results through the use of conditional spending. Nor can the doctrine be allowed to spread so far as to prevent Congress from *forbidding* state governments to *interfere* with federal programs, because this would contradict the clear statement in Article VI that laws made in pursuance of the Constitution "shall be the supreme law of the land." And so the whole doctrinal edifice on occasion will depend on the sometimes fragile distinction between affirmative commands and flat prohibitions.

The doctrine of congruence and proportionality lacks the categorical quality of the previous two and so invites a more imprecise, judgmental intervention, but this may be as much a virtue as a defect. These terms correspond to the concept of proportionality that—as Justice Breyer has noted in another context[104]—has been invoked in European institutional thought, and under the name of the doctrine of subsidiarity has been used to assign control of matters to the lowest reasonably appropriate level, the level closest to the people. It is also a doctrinal device familiar in other areas of constitutional law. For instance, governments sometimes try to avoid the constitutional obligation to pay for property they want to acquire from private parties by conditioning the grant of regulatory permissions on the property owner's "voluntarily" turning over a part of the property government desires. What distinguishes this extortionate from the appropriate use of the regulatory power is a test that may be summed up as asking whether the exaction is congruent and proportionate to the regulatory aim the government invokes to justify it.[105] This kind of cross-reference is a feature of well-functioning constitutional doctrine elsewhere (free speech and religious liberty, for instance). It is good to see its appearance here.

That leaves the textually and historically misbegotten sovereign immunity cases, against which I have already inveighed. What the doctrine enjoys in definiteness it lacks utterly in aptness. By hypothesis, the state has properly been put under an obligation to the citizen, and it is hard to understand what modern conception of the states' dignity is offended by allowing the person to whom this obligation is owed to claim it before an otherwise lawful tribunal. The doctrine is also inapt because it deflects attention from what might be the real source of constitutional trouble, the real indignity: that the authority should not have been conceded to Congress to impose the substantive obligation in the first place. *Seminole Tribe* is such a case and *Alden v. Maine* is another. Thus the Eleventh Amendment doctrine has the vice which is the mirror image of the virtues of the proportionality and congruence test: it inhibits the development of adjacent, sounder doctrines.

CHAPTER THREE

Separation of Powers

Because the Constitution was a new beginning, assigning powers to the various elements of the national government was the framers' necessary task. It is natural today to take for granted not only the existence of the national entity the Constitution established, but also the various organs of its government. The Congress, the presidency, and the Supreme Court and lower federal courts, to which Articles I, II, and III assign the legislative, executive, and judicial power of the new government, were all called into being by the Constitution—unlike the states, whose prior actual and legal existence was assumed. Although the figure of George Washington, say, and the precedent of the state governors and legislatures were surely on everyone's mind, the references to legislative, executive, and judicial power are to concepts and abstract functions—not to preexisting entities that were now being invested with new or altered functions. Whatever form these entities took depended on how they were selected, the powers explicitly granted them, and the conceptual aura that might surround the terms (president, court, chief justice, senator, representative) used to name them.

The Constitution's creativity makes its terms difficult to interpret. When institutions have become associated with and inhabited by real people, those people have interests and dispositions that outrun whatever formal functions are assigned them. An institution long established—a monarchy or a corporate body like the House of Commons—attains a materiality and personality that keep it from being a mere abstraction of political theory. In establishing entirely new, as yet uninhabited offices, the framers necessarily addressed how the officers are chosen, the terms and conditions of their tenure, the tasks they must perform, the way they must perform them, and their relation to adjacent institutions. But as these abstract institutions have had to take on life from the people who inhabited them and the realities they have had to confront, these general prescriptions alone could neither fully explain how the mature government has come to work nor by themselves resolve conflicts among those institutions—just as the framers' text and intent alone could not answer all the questions about the relations between the states and the national government, nor all the questions about limits of all governmental power over individuals. All of these questions have had to be the subject of evolving constitutional doctrine. As Justice Robert Jackson wrote in the single most famous judicial opinion on the powers of the branches of the national government:

> Just what our forefathers did envision, or would have envisioned had they foreseen modern conditions, must be divined from materials almost as enigmatic as the dreams Joseph was called upon to interpret for Pharaoh. A century and a half of partisan debate and scholarly speculation yields no net result but only supplies more or less apt quotations from respected sources on each side of any question. They largely cancel each other.[1]

Any contemporary account of this topic must explain not only what the Constitution's various assignments of powers are, but also whether some general conception may be discerned from those assignments. Without some such conception, there is no guide for extrapolating from the Constitution's terse prescriptions to solving problems in a government far larger and more complex than that imagined at the time of the framing. Perhaps that would not pose a serious problem if, as some have suggested,[2] the Court has no business delving into the Constitution's premises, its role being limited to assuring that none of the document's literal provisions are contradicted. The Court has occasionally been more ambitious than that and sought to enforce a general conception it has discerned from those particulars. This has proved difficult, especially because, acting as a court, it has had to embody that conception in rules and doctrines so as to give generality and predictability to its work. The Court cannot be content just to act as an umpire, calling plays without explanation or rationale.

The traditional rubric under which this development of rules and doctrines has gone forward—and the one chosen to name this chapter—is the separation of powers. Article XXX of the Declaration of Rights, which is the first part of the 1780 Constitution of the Commonwealth of Massachusetts drafted by John Adams, states:

> In the government of this commonwealth, the legislative department shall never exercise the executive and judicial powers, or either of them; the executive shall never exercise the legislative and judicial powers, or either of them; the judicial shall never exercise the legislative and executive powers, or either of them; to the end it may be a government of laws and not of men.

Unlike the Massachusetts Constitution,[3] the federal Constitution does not speak of the separation of powers.[4] Rather, the Constitution provides at the head of each of its first three articles that "all legislative Powers herein granted shall be vested in a Congress," "the executive Power shall be vested in a President," and "judicial Power of the United States, shall be vested in one supreme Court, and in such inferior Courts as the Congress may from time to time ordain and establish." After these three vesting clauses, the Constitution goes about the business of stating how to choose the people to occupy these offices[5] and stating what the powers of those offices are. From this spare material must be deduced the doctrines that structure our government as well as the principles that would guide and rationalize those doctrines.

One Choice among Many

The Constitution might have accomplished its essential task of setting up the national government by granting all power to one institution and letting that institution set up and alter the offices and functions of government. That is, after all, close to what the British principle of parliamentary sovereignty or the autocratic principle of czarist Russia comes to. Apart from the fact that neither of these two regimes has or had written constitutions—what would the text of such a constitution look like?—the great difference between such systems and ours is that in ours, no single person or institution represents the ultimate reservoir of authority.[6] And even in the British system, differentiation by kinds of task has seemed indispensable. The difference between such a system and one with an articulated assignment of powers is that in the latter, the assignment of tasks to particular institutions itself attains constitutional status. In the czarist autocratic example, if the Czar grants appointment power to a prime minister, that assignment is normative with respect to all other actors in the system, but not with respect to the Czar. The same is true if Parliament empowers a particular minister to make certain appointments: the grant is normative against all—binds all—except Parliament itself. So to say that an assignment of powers has constitutional status is to say that it is fundamental in the way that the Constitution itself is: there is no normative appeal against it. Important as that status is, it should not confuse the separate question whether and to what extent such an assignment may be enforced in court, particularly the Supreme Court. It is rather a distinct feature of the assignments of powers in our Constitution that those assignments may sometimes be the subject of court enforcement. Indeed, the courts' availability to hear challenges to official action on the ground that the action somehow outran a constitutional assignment of power is itself a feature of the Constitution's assignment of power—this time to the courts themselves.

In allocating the powers of the national government to people and institutions, the framers were concerned in approximately equal measure with effectiveness in the exercise of those powers and security against their abuse.[7] If separation of powers means clear assignments of responsibility, then that very clarity achieves a measure of efficacy. This is particularly so if the assignment is not only clear but *appropriate,* in the sense that it is granted to the institution best suited to carrying it out. How the separation of powers provides security against their abuse needs a more complicated account. The standard explanation is Montesquieu's[8] by way of Madison[9]: by dividing up the powers of government, power will check power. And if that is the point, then it does not matter so much how we designate the competing powers. In the Roman Republic, for instance, the supreme magistracy was held by two consuls, each of whom could veto any act of the other—although in practice they divided up the tasks of government between them, one taking charge, for example, of military matters abroad, the other of domestic concerns.[10] The division of the legislative branch into two Houses is another example of such a contingent arrangement. It arose by analogy to the two Houses of Parliament. The British structure illustrates another, quite different conception of separation of powers: differentiation in terms of social orders—King, Lords, Commons.[11] Some of this remained in the Constitution of 1789: the House was chosen by direct election and was intended to be the more popular chamber; the Senate, chosen by the state legislatures, was intended to be the more sober and perhaps more aristocratic body—the difference between the two- and six-year terms surely was also intended to effect this differentiation, as was the higher minimum age required for senators, and the assigning to the Senate alone the tasks of ratifying treaties and confirming judicial and executive appointments. Today, this aspect of bicameralism is much attenuated—there have been periods in recent history in which each House has tended to be the more conservative—and the only point that can be confidently made is that bicameralism is a brake on rapid change. If security against government means security against government activity, bicameralism has been an important engine of security and a perfect example of Madison's checking function.

The general goals of efficacy and security against abuse do not obviously dictate either a particular assignment of powers or a particular modality of that assignment. For instance, the rigorous separation prescribed by Article XXX of the Massachusetts Declaration of Rights is but one way that the assignment might be done. There might be more or fewer recipients of government power. So in a parliamentary system, the preeminence of the legislature makes any assignment to either the executive or even the judiciary provisional or customary only. The needs of a modern administrative state require the existence of a large bureaucracy, whose activities and membership may be made dependent on either the executive or the legislative branch, or might be accorded a measure of separateness and even independence from both. It is not fanciful to imagine other divisions of governmental power. For instance, the job of auditing the government's accounts or otherwise assuring regularity and honesty in governmental acts may be assigned to a completely separate branch of government. A special branch might have as its only charge the overseeing and certifying of elections. In a society that highly prizes education, intellectual and cultural attainments may form the academy as a distinct branch of government. And the role of training and certifying people for high office may be entrusted to that branch, or a distinct branch, or it may be parceled out among several of the others.[12] In short, the strictly separated tripartite scheme announced by the Massachusetts Declaration of Rights is but one choice among many.

Inferring Roles from Structure

In its pursuit of efficacy and security, what choices has our constitutional system made? As noted, the Constitution lacks an explicit statement of a separation of powers principle. In establishing institutions that had no prior existence, the Constitution first specifies how the people to inhabit those institutions will be chosen and what their qualifications for and tenure in those new offices will be. Next, the Constitution states what the people in those offices may do and by what procedures they may do it. In drawing inferences from this scheme, the question naturally arises whether the provisions must be read as exclusive. May the Congress exercise its power only on the specifically enumerated subjects? And may it act only in the specified ways? As to the President, Article II sets out a fairly short list of specific powers and duties. Are these his only powers, or is there more implied by the general assignment to him of "the executive Power" and perhaps by the corresponding duty that "he shall take Care that the Laws be faithfully executed"? In both Article I and Article II, considerable weight is borne by the very designations "legislative Powers" and "executive Power." In the case of the Congress, this designation is given specificity by the combination of the wording of the introduction, "all legislative Powers herein granted," together with the detailed list of powers in §8. Those powers mainly refer to regulating, the making of rules for particular subjects—suggesting that the legislative power is the power to make rules. Certain of the enumerated powers, however, are stated in different terms, suggesting action in a more managerial mode: Congress not only has the power to lay but to "collect" taxes, and at several places it is to "provide" for certain ends. These statements have always been taken to designate a congressional power to make rules about how to secure those ends.[13] For instance, the clause giving Congress the power "to provide for organizing, arming, and disciplining, the Militia" means that Congress shall make the rules and appropriate the funds for that end.[14] So not only are the subjects of Congress's power specified, but also how it exercises that power: by making rules. This is made even clearer in the formulation employed in the enforcement clauses of the Civil War amendments: "Congress shall have power to enforce this article by appropriate legislation." Legislating is what Congress does.

It is less easy to discern the roles of the President and the courts from the text and structure of the Constitution alone. Just what are the executive power, the judiciary power? In the case of the latter, the specification of its exercise to "Cases" and "Controversies" helps a good deal.[15] In the case of the former, however, we have only history and context to help us infer what the executive power means—assuming it means more than the power to do the particular things set out in Article II, such as making appointments and treaties and receiving ambassadors.

Separation of Powers and the Modern Administrative State

In a modern state, the doctrine of separation of powers shows up in two principal ways: control over administration and the independence of the judiciary. I turn first to control over administration.

As history shows, whatever the separation of the executive from the legislative may have meant originally, that principle takes on a very different meaning as it is applied in a modern state. As originally conceived, the principle assumed a very limited role for any organ of national government at all. In Britain, local authorities, powerful barons, and private individuals had the greatest responsibility for managing land, trade, and manufacture. Common law and statutory rules were sufficient to coordinate and regulate their activities. In France, the other country in which the separation of powers was urged as a principle, this was far less so, but the principle's first proponents sought a society more like the British. What is everywhere different from that time two hundred years ago is that national governments do vastly more in every area of national life. Our national government is involved in aspects of life that once did not exist—telecommunications, aviation—or that previously had been left to private arrangements, to voluntary associations, or to state or local governments. There are now some 2.5 million federal employees who are involved in neither military nor foreign affairs.[16] In 1800 the number was less than 4,000[17] for a population of 5,308,483[18] and in 1900 around 240,000[19] for a population of 75,994,575.[20] These numbers do not, of course, provide an accurate index of the importance of the federal government's activities in our national life, but they offer a rough idea: all these people are busy administering national programs (or administering people who are). Doctrine about the Constitution's allocation of powers must account for the existence of these people and the programs they administer. They constitute what goes by the name of the "modern administrative state."[21]

The modern administrative state does not fit easily into the Constitution's tripartite scheme, because the officers of administration carry out (execute) the policies of rules made by Congress, make (legislate) their own rules that they then proceed to carry out, and adjudicate disputes (cases and controversies). Here are just some of the things that administrators do: they make rules about how much of which substances may come out of the tailpipes of cars or factory smokestacks, and they decide when those rules have been broken and how much the offender is to be fined for breaking them; they fix the interest rates on federal obligations and so influence the cost of money throughout the economy; they make rules about when a person is too disabled to work and then decide whether a particular person falls under these rules so that he will receive a regular check from the government; they decide what artists, musicians, writers, museums, and theaters will receive a federal subsidy and what projects for scientific research will be funded by the federal government. Where do all these officials fit into the Constitution's allocation of powers; what in the Constitution allows them to do all these things?

The shortest answer is that Congress, using its Article I lawmaking power according to constitutionally prescribed procedures (votes by both Houses, presentment to the President), authorized all of these programs, created the offices to administer them, and specified the powers they exercise.[22] Article II, §2 (the Appointments Clause), provides that the President, with the advice and consent of the Senate, "shall appoint Ambassadors, other public Ministers and Consuls, Judges of the supreme Court, and all other Officers of the United States, whose Appointments are not herein otherwise provided for, and which shall be established by Law. . . ." This expressly acknowledges Congress's function of creating offices "by law,"[23] making explicit what is already implicit in the Necessary and Proper Clause in Article I: that Congress, having the power to accomplish a particular task (for example, to establish post offices), has the power to establish offices in order that its projects be carried out. So the office must be created under a program within Congress's power and the officer must be appointed in accordance with the Appointments Clause. Any limitations on what these officers can do must be gathered from the structure of the Constitution, and within that inference are contained all the issues about the structure of the modern administrative state: how much discretion and what kind may Congress grant these officers; to what extent may the President assume control over them, and having appointed them is he free to dismiss them; are there ways that Congress may control these offices other than by changing the laws under which they operate; and finally what is the nature and function of courts in these arrangements.

These provisions standing alone and looked at one by one suggest a conception that is almost parliamentary in the extent to which the legislature sets the structure and functioning of the national government. Contrary pressures are mainly inferential. In recent years the Supreme Court has applied two related brakes to Congress's supremacy. In *Bowsher v. Synar*, it held that (except where the Constitution specifically provides otherwise—for instance, in the case of impeachments or in matters concerning the internal management of each House) the Congress is limited to the passage of laws.[24] And in *INS v. Chadha* it held that Congress in passing laws must follow the steps set out in clauses 2 and 3 of Article I, §7: identical resolutions must have been voted by majorities in both Houses, presented to the President, and either approved by him or passed over his veto by a two-thirds vote in each House.[25] This is the requirement of bicameralism and presentment. By this doctrine, Congress acts as a corporate body only by passing laws that it must present to the President, and since a corporate body can only effect its resolutions through agents, it must rely on agents provided for elsewhere in the Constitution. This doctrinal inference, read together with the Appointments Clause of Article II, which vests the appointment power in the President—or in the case of "inferior officers" also in the heads of departments or courts of law—creates a legible structure that gives concrete meaning to the principle of separation of powers: the Congress depends, for the execution of its laws and the manning of the offices to execute those laws, on officers appointed by the President (subject to Senate confirmation). The executive power can be identified, then, as the reciprocal of the legislative: it is the power that completes the implementation of laws enacted by Congress. (There is one large qualification: laws—especially those creating private rights—are also often enforced in court actions brought by private parties to compel future compliance or exact damages for past noncompliance. This implicates the third branch of government, the judicial. For the moment I shall put this very large qualification aside, although we must return to it.)

This firm cabining of the legislative power—not in terms of subject matter, as in the vertical separation of powers of federalism, but in its mode of action—is required neither logically nor by historical precedent. As a matter of logic, it would seem that a law establishing a congressional committee to manage some matter—say, the distribution of construction contracts—passed by both Houses and signed by the President complies with the Constitution's literal requirements.[26] And as a matter of history, both the Continental Congress under the Articles of Confederation and the Convention in France conducted government affairs through committees of their members, the best known being the Committee of Public Safety.[27] But the two constitutions in those examples specifically envisioned such arrangements,[28] and they lacked any provision for an executive with distinct powers.[29] Does the logical argument prove too much in that it would allow Congress to transfer all governmental power to a single person?

The perceived need to block such devices, real or hypothetical, shows that something other than the logic of the text (and certainly more than history) is at work to thwart Congress if it grants itself managerial functions or purports to make dispositive declarations other than through Article I lawmaking. I believe this is the basis of the Court's decision in *Clinton v. New York*,[30] the Line-Item Veto case, invalidating a congressional scheme that the Court believed would effectively allow the President to reduce appropriations and tax expenditures without the necessity of further enactment. What is at work is an inference from the Constitution's structure establishing three branches of government.[31]

By confining Congress's effective mode of action to legislation as a corporate body, the Constitution, as interpreted by the Court, not only deprives Congress of the capacity to execute and administer the laws it passes, but it also makes Congress dependent (for the most part)[32] on officers nominated by the President or his subordinates. This limitation, more than anything, creates the structural picture we have of the national government, with the President and his people bringing about the actual results that Congress decrees in its more abstract laws. It is this limitation on Congress that leads us to think that the actual machinery of government is in the hands of the President and his people. It is this limitation that leads one to speak of *his* administration.

Of course, there is more to account for the power and prestige of the presidency. Above all, there is the President's duty to "take Care that the Laws be faithfully executed."[33] From this, some have argued for the existence of an inherent managerial role that empowers the President not only to execute specific laws but also to create and control the general conditions under which the ensemble of laws and offices in the nation may be carried out. This implication was firmly rejected in *Youngstown Sheet & Tube Co. v. Sawyer,*[34] the Steel Seizure case: the President takes care to execute only and just such laws as there are. So was the attempt to draw some such broad authority from the very term "executive" in the Vesting Clause of Article II. As Justice Jackson put it, "I cannot accept the view that this clause is a grant in bulk of all conceivable executive power. . . ."[35] And as to the notion that there must somewhere in the government be a residual power to deal rapidly with emergencies, and that that place must be in the President, Jackson said: "[O]urs is a government of laws, not of men, and . . . we submit ourselves to rulers only if under rules. [As to a claimed power to act as may be necessary in an emergency] such power either has no beginning or it has no end."[36]

Then there are the powers that are specifically assigned to the President. These are few but striking: he is the Commander-in-Chief of the armed forces; it is he who negotiates treaties; it is he who receives ambassadors. Each of these powers is actually circumscribed by Congress. The President is Commander-in-Chief only of such armed forces as the Congress chooses to "raise" and "maintain";[37] and the treaties he may negotiate with the ambassadors he receives must be ratified by two-thirds of the Senate. Still, these powers, circumscribed though they may be, are emblems of prestige. They clothe the President in the uniform of the nation. We are here in the realms of both symbolism and practical power. The Congress might, for instance, stifle the President's advantage with his appointments power by refusing to confirm his nominees or by insisting that they will confirm only those on a slate that they present to him. The only question, then, is whether the Congress can get away with it politically. And the President has tools of retaliation. He may refuse to make appointments at all. He may veto legislation. It is a competition in which each side plays an uncertain hand, but the President has advantages that far outrun the explicit powers the Constitution grants him. Justice Jackson captured this distinct aura:

> Executive power has the advantage of concentration in a single head in whose choice the whole Nation has a part, making him the focus of public hopes and expectations. In drama, magnitude and finality his decisions so far overshadow any others that almost alone he fills the public eye and ear. No other personality in public life can begin to compete with him in access to the public mind through modern methods of communications. By his prestige as head of state and his influence upon public opinion he exerts a leverage upon those who are supposed to check and balance his power which often cancels their effectiveness.[38]

The picture of the administration as being *his* administration is far from complete. Although the Congress has no power of implementation and must leave this to officers whom the President names, the question remains: once in office, are they truly *his* officers? This depends on whether the President may issue orders to them and dismiss them just as he pleases. Early in our life under our Constitution, there was genuine doubt about this. John Adams may have ruined his presidency by hesitating to replace the cabinet members he inherited from Washington.[39] In what has ever since been called the decision of 1789, the first Congress, in setting up the Departments of Foreign Affairs, War, and Treasury, acquiesced in the proposition that the Senate need not give its advice and consent to confirm the dismissal of an officer, as it must when the officer is first named.[40] Had the resolution gone the other way, it would have moved us halfway to a parliamentary system: officers, once confirmed, would not depend wholly on the President. We would have gone far along the rest of the way if the Senate could dismiss—unconfirm, as it were—those to whom it had once consented.

The issue is acute because, as the national government took on any complexity at all, it became impossible for Congress to direct by law every action it wanted the President and his officers to take, although when Congress did make an act mandatory it was early recognized—in *Marbury v. Madison*[41] and *Kendall v. United States*[42]—that the officer has no choice but to carry out that order. Congress is bound to do most of its legislating in general terms; only in that way can it extend its reach. This shows up today for example in environmental regulation. Congress can only accomplish its broad aims by general directions to be carried out by the President's officers. But with the general assignment comes discretion, and with discretion, policy. Each change of administration and administrator brings new policies. Congress is often dissatisfied that its general direction is being grudgingly or even perversely implemented. Sometimes it responds by enacting very specific directives that cannot be evaded; more often it must fight with political weapons.

But this is an old story. It was played out more than 150 years ago in the controversy over the Second Bank of the United States.[43] Chartered by an Act of Congress in 1816, by 1829 the bank had become perhaps the most powerful institution in the nation. It had branches throughout the country, could issue notes which circulated like currency, and had an assured and enormous base derived from the Treasury's use of the bank as the depository of United States funds. Andrew Jackson shared a popular resentment of so powerful an institution, which had public responsibilities but was subject to no public accountability. He determined to destroy the bank. Its partisans in Congress had overplayed their hand and got through a bill to renew the bank's charter some four years before its expiration. Jackson vetoed the bill. Though the bank still had a long lease on life, Jackson sought to kill it. His most effective blow was to withdraw the funds of the United States from the bank. No law required the bank to be the sole and official depository for government funds, but it was assumed that it would be when the bank was set up.[44] By what authority, then, did Jackson pursue a policy at odds with the legislation chartering the bank? As far as Jackson was concerned, his warrants were his electoral mandate and the actual management that he as head of the executive had over the assets of the government.

A far more vicious confrontation took place in 1867–68 and resulted in the impeachment of President Andrew Johnson.[45] Johnson was hostile to the military occupation of the former Confederate states and to the Radical Republicans who imposed it. The President was the Commander in Chief, but acted through his Secretary of War, Edwin Stanton, a Radical Republican inherited by Johnson from the administration of President Abraham Lincoln. Fearing that Johnson would frustrate Reconstruction efforts by dismissing Stanton and other of his cabinet officers, Congress in 1867 passed, over Johnson's veto, the Tenure of Office Act, which forbade the President to dismiss his high officers without the advice and consent of the Senate. Johnson defied the act by dismissing Stanton, and the House responded by impeaching Johnson in 1868. The impeachment failed in the Senate by one vote. Since then the size of the bureaucracy and the complexity of the programs it administers have grown beyond any earlier time's capacity to imagine them and far beyond the Congress's capacity to control them in any but the most general terms. President Franklin Roosevelt thought that this made him "the general manager of the United States"—with the Congress perhaps serving as the board of directors, but without the power except by impeachment to remove the chief executive. Congress has not acquiesced in this conception and has several weapons for maintaining its position in the balance of power. It has the power of the purse ("No Money shall be drawn from the Treasury, but in Consequence of Appropriations made by Law. . . .")[46] and can discipline a headstrong executive by starving his programs of funding and his employees of pay. It can legislate with unevadable particularity, but it lacks the capacity to do that continually or too much. Or—though Congress cannot make the bureaucrats depend directly upon it by exercising a power to dismiss them—it can nevertheless try to drive a structural wedge between the President and his officers. And that is what it has done. Since at least 1820, some offices have been created to be filled by persons appointed for a term of years—sometimes longer than four, so that the appointment may outlast the President who makes it.[47]

Humphrey's Executor, the case in which this potential for conflict played itself out, arose out of President Franklin Roosevelt's attempt to dismiss a federal trade commissioner, writing him that "I do not feel that your mind and my mind go along together on either the policies or the administering of the" Federal Trade Commission.[48] The President's action was an expression of his view that "the plain fact is that the present organization and equipment of the executive branch of the Government defeats the constitutional intent that there be a single responsible Chief Executive to coordinate and manage the departments and activities in accordance with the laws enacted by Congress. Under these conditions the Government cannot be thoroughly effective in working, under popular control, for the common good."[49]

The issue concerned the "independence" of the independent agencies. The first of these was the Interstate Commerce Commission that Congress had established in 1887, mainly to regulate rates and routes in the newly developing national rail system. Other such agencies followed. Among them were the Federal Trade Commission, to investigate and prosecute unfair trade practices; the Federal Reserve Board, to oversee the national banking system and set certain interest rates; the Federal Communications Commission, to license and regulate broadcasting and interstate telephone communications. The members of these commissions all had appointments for a term of years, which provided—under various formulations—for removal for cause. But what exactly were these commissions (and commissioners) to be independent of? The Congress? Politics? The President? Of course they could not be independent of the Congress, in the sense that they could not be independent of the laws it passes. *Marbury v. Madison* established that where the law places a quite definite duty on an officer, a person who would stand to benefit from the duty may sue to enforce it. And if an officer acts to violate a determinate right of an individual, that person may sue to prevent it. Beyond that limit lies the whole realm of policy, of discretion, of judgment, and the question is, whose judgment, whose policy, should that be.

Congress, with some plausibility, thinks its policy should govern. The duty of *faithful* execution of the law that the Constitution places on the executive entails execution in good faith, that is, in the spirit of the enactment. But it is the unexpected, unprovided-for case that tests the proposition—as does the necessity to establish priorities in pursuit of goals that may conflict or compete (if only for resources). The President, particularly but not only, if he is of a party different from Congress, will have different ideas about such conflicts and priorities, and Congress does not want to be at his mercy. By putting some officers beyond the reach of the President's power to dismiss, those officers at least are less likely to pursue only his policies. They might try, for example, to develop an independent sense of some policy implicit in the law itself. This is what judges are supposed to do in interpreting statutes, and it is the stance that independence is supposed to foster. It is a stance that supposes there is indeed such a thing as the implicit rationale of a law or enacted program, which can be discerned by impartial judgment. If Congress must make itself hostage to those who administer the laws, it may prefer to be hostage to bureaucrats who administer the law in that spirit than to the President, who is a rival center of elected political power.

But the independent agencies are only a small part of the government. At the head of most programs are secretaries, assistant secretaries, and administrators who are not protected from dismissal by term appointments and "for cause" dismissal clauses. The federal bureaucracy consists of some 2.5 million persons.[50] The presidential appointees at the heads of departments are in their posts for a relatively short time (an average of 20–22 months),[51] while the programs are exceedingly complex and various. The people who make them work in an orderly way are not officers appointed by the President, but bureaucrats, many of whom serve for decades in their agencies. Where does the Constitution provide for them? They are either employees or the "inferior officers" spoken of in the Appointments Clause, who may be appointed without Senate confirmation by the President or heads of departments. What makes an office an "inferior" office is quite indeterminate, but whenever Congress establishes an office—a deputy assistant secretary in a particular department, to take a frequent example—without requiring Senate confirmation, this assumes (in a circular way) that he or she is an inferior officer. Other people who do important or routine work in the government are designated "employees," and employees may be hired in much the same way that the executive department may enter into contracts: Congress must appropriate money to hire them and may or may not specify how many, at what pay, and what work they may take on. This body of employees is the civil service of the nation, and since the reforms of the Progressive Era at the end of the nineteenth and beginning of the twentieth century, the determination of their qualifications and terms of employment have been increasingly regulated by laws, the result of which has been to keep politics out of their selection and to protect them from politically motivated removal.

The word "politics" in this formulation might refer to patronage—government jobs bestowed as a reward to party faithful and taken away at the change of administration to make room for the new batch—or it might refer to political control, the selection and retention of bureaucrats because of their ability and willingness to carry out the administration's projects. (The two senses are not, of course, unrelated.) It is the unstated premise that in placing civil servants beyond the reach of politics, there is an impartial craft in implementing a wide array of policies and programs. The adept civil servant is like the skillful pianist who can execute the works of many composers under the baton of a variety of maestros. In reality, the civil service develops habits and commitments of its own: at their worst, these fasten on the civil servant's own power, prestige, and even survival; at their best, these commitments are to long-standing, complex, and evolving programs whose good functioning requires familiarity and steadiness. Since these programs are by hypothesis instituted and maintained by congressional enactment, faithfulness to them seems constitutionally appropriate. It is some version of this more neutral stance, where the administrator is an expert in the program, that may be behind Congress's provision of fixed terms and for-cause removal even of certain principal officers, as in the independent agencies. Add to this that many of these officers serve in collegial bodies—like the Federal Reserve Board or the Federal Trade Commission—and the purpose of creating continuity through, and some distance from, presidential administrations is evident.

This conception of the President's appointees and employees conceives of them more as impartial experts, technicians, servants of the laws that they administer, rather than as agents of the President who appoints them. This civil-service, *haut fonctionnaire* conception of the executive establishment accords well with the parliamentary system of government in which it is usually found. Where the executive is an organ of and chosen from and by the legislature, there is not the tension between the legislature's and the executive's policies or politics. There is a seamlessness between the laws and their administration, because the laws that the premier and his ministers execute are those that his government has enacted or chosen to leave in effect. But that is not the case in our system. The two branches are chosen by different constituencies, in different ways and at different times: only one-third of the Senate is chosen at the presidential election, and the entire House must stand for reelection halfway through the President's term. These circumstances alone, quite apart from tradition and the pull of ambition, ensure that there will usually be a gap between the policies of the Congress, which enacted the laws, and those of the President who must execute them. FDR, with his conception of the President as general manager, yearned for the flexibility of a prime minister—but without the discipline of a parliament that could replace him at any time. By putting at least some of his officers beyond the President's reach, Congress subtracts from the power and coherence of presidential management. It also creates power centers not directly responsible to either elected branch. A body of experts appointed by FDR to examine the functioning of government once referred to the independent agencies (and by extension in an attenuated sense the civil service) as the "headless fourth branch of government."[52] Some say that by subtracting that branch from presidential control, Congress necessarily increases its own power. They argue that because the two branches are locked in competition, whatever diminishes one enlarges the other. Others see this "headless fourth branch" as a distinct power center with its own constituencies, of which the Congress is but one, the other constituencies being the particular interests on which this fourth branch operates and the President's establishment with which it must interact.

The Supreme Court and the "Headless Fourth Branch"

The Supreme Court has not offered a clear picture of this articulation of powers. The two major early moments in the struggle over the President's control over his establishment—the Decision of 1789 and the impeachment of President Johnson in 1868—were played out in the congressional arena, the arena of politics. The Supreme Court only once intervened definitively on the side of the President. In *Myers v. United States*[53] the Court in effect ratified the political decisions of 1789 and 1868, holding unconstitutional a statute requiring the Senate's consent to the removal of postmasters—an office of little consequence for policy but rich in political patronage. Chief Justice William Howard Taft's opinion drew from the President's constitutional duty to see that the laws are faithfully executed the implication that he had the power not only of *choosing* (as the Appointments Clause states) but also "of *removing* those for whom he can not continue to be responsible."[54] But this dictum outran the occasion, since the controversy dealt only with the requirement of Senate consent to removal, and not the broader question whether the President should always have the unlimited power to remove—and therefore to control—any officer with whom he is displeased. It is that broader question that asks whether the President is to be constitutionally in control of the whole executive establishment—the conception known as the "unitary presidency"—or whether it may include independent centers of power, a headless fourth branch. The Court's next intervention in this question put the whole issue in doubt. *Humphrey's Executor v. United States,*[55] referred to above, limited the rule in *Myers* to what it called "purely executive officers . . . [who acted] as an arm or an eye of the executive."[56] The commissioner could not be removed by anyone during his prescribed term of years except for "cause," because federal trade commissioners promulgated rules and prosecuted and judged their violation and, therefore, acted "in part quasi-legislatively and in part quasi-judicially."[57]

This reasoning does not make a great deal of sense now, and probably did not at the time of the decision. Much administration inevitably involves rule making, rule enforcement, and the adjudication of rule violation: examples are the Immigration and Naturalization Service, the Social Security Administration, the Environmental Protection Agency, and the Internal Revenue Service, all of which are headed by officers who serve at the President's pleasure. Certainly their functions are subject to judicial review, and the application of penalties may require court enforcement. But that is as true for the National Labor Relations Board—an independent agency—as it is for the Internal Revenue Service. Court review and enforcement are, however, highly deferential to the agency, so that the Court's review is nothing like an original action—say, a criminal prosecution—started in court by the government. Finally, many of these executive branch functions have been subject by statute—the Administrative Procedure Act—to a system of control to assure regularity and a degree of impartiality. For instance, much agency fact-finding and adjudication is first done by a cadre denominated administrative law judges, who, though they do not enjoy the protections of judges appointed under Article III, have significant civil-service-type statutory protections.

It was not until 1988, however, that the Supreme Court explicitly did away with the doctrinal anomaly it had introduced in *Humphrey's Executor* in 1935. *Morrison v. Olson*[58] rejected constitutional challenges to the Ethics in Government Act, which has a federal court instead of the attorney general or President appoint the independent counsel to investigate and prosecute criminal allegations against high executive branch officials (including the President himself). The Court stated: "We undoubtedly did rely on the terms 'quasi-legislative' and 'quasi-judicial' to distinguish the officials involved in *Humphrey's Executor* . . . from those in *Myers,* but our present considered view is that the determination of whether the Constitution allows Congress to impose a 'good cause'-type restriction on the President's power to remove an official cannot be made to turn on whether or not that official is classified as 'purely executive.'"[59]

The decision seriously undermined the claim that the Constitution itself required a unitary presidency. Ruling that the independent counsel is an inferior officer, the Court turned aside the claim that the independent counsel must be appointed by the President and confirmed by the Senate. The Court also turned aside the claim that if an inferior executive officer gained the appointment by a court of law—a cross-branch appointment—that action violated the Appointments Clause.[60] Given the enormous political power the counsel wielded—as was demonstrated several years later by Independent Counsel Kenneth Starr's investigation of President Bill Clinton, which provoked only the second impeachment of a President in our history—the Court's decision appears to leave up to politics how far Congress may put outside the President's control the personnel of the executive branch, giving only a vague hint that the Court will police the far outer limits of this struggle.

Security and Efficacy: Two Justifications for the Separation of Powers

Locke and Montesquieu gave individual security as the reason for keeping separate the legislative and executive powers. And the *Federalist Papers* gave the efficacy of government as a further reason for the independence of the executive from the legislature.[61] How do the current arrangements meet these two concerns of security and efficacy? Here is Montesquieu on the security of the individual:

> The political liberty of the subject is a tranquility of mind, arising from the opinion each person has of his safety. In order to have this liberty, it is requisite that the government be so constituted as one man need not be afraid of another. When the legislative and the executive powers are united in the same person, or in the same body of magistracy, there can be then no liberty: because apprehensions may arise lest the same monarch or senate should enact tyrannical laws, to execute them in a tyrannical manner.[62]

The argument is quite summary. Is it that a decent executive will not "faithfully execute" tyrannical laws; or is it that laws susceptible of tyrannical applications will not be applied that way; or is it that the legislature, knowing that its tyrannical laws will be applied in all cases, including those to which the legislature would not want them applied, will not enact them in the first place? The current arrangement, after *Chadha, Bowsher,* and *Morrison,* certainly protects against government by Congress, but it does not assure the execution of the laws only by the President, leaving an indeterminate but significant amount of governing to the headless fourth branch.

Is this a threat to the security of the individual? Not quite in the way that Montesquieu, Locke, and John Adams—the author of the Massachusetts Declaration of Rights—imagined, but there is a threat nonetheless. Because administration includes rule making, rule application, and adjudication, the bureaucracy unites within itself the three powers that the theorists warned us must be kept separate. When modern citizens complain about the Kafkaesque ubiquity and impenetrability of modern bureaucracy, this uniting of functions might be what they have in mind. The modern response has been to create independent controls on the bureaucracy to assure that it stays within its legislative mandate and complies with fair and open procedures. In the United States, this is accomplished by the Administrative Procedure Act (APA) (which establishes a kind of second-tier separation of powers within some agencies), by judicial review of administrative rule making and application under the APA, and only remotely and rarely by the application of constitutional norms. In France, the same control is entrusted to the administrative tribunals, at the head of which sits the Conseil d'Etat.[63] These control mechanisms may assure regularity within broad limits, but within those limits the bureaucracy is responsible to no one, and particularly not to anyone who might pay a price at the polls for high-handed or unpopular administration.[64] But then that may be just the point.

What about efficacy? That the administrators are independent of the President is another way of saying that the President cannot be sure of enforcing a coordinated policy or set of policies. For instance, whether cost-benefit analysis will be used in the administration of particular programs may depend on whether the program is administered by an independent agency or by an agency headed by a removable presidential appointee.[65] Whether racial and gender preferences will be used, and in what way, will depend, for example, on whether those preferences are used in making grants and contracts out of the Department of Transportation, which is headed by a removable cabinet secretary, or in the grant of broadcast licenses by the Federal Communications Commission, an independent regulatory commission. One may either sympathize with FDR's ambition to be the general manager of the United States or view some degree of disorganization and contradiction as a reasonable price to pay for not putting all our administrative eggs in the presidential basket. In any event, the Court has left this question of degree up to Congress and has refused to impose any limits—though it has vaguely hinted that there *are* such limits—on how much dispersal of the President's power it will allow.

The Judicial Branch as Safeguard of Liberty

The security of the citizen against arbitrary power, whether presidential or bureaucratic, ultimately depends on the courts, and therefore depends on the degree of independence—separation—of the judicial power from the rest of the government. Locke had little to say on this subject, treating the judicial branch as an arm of the executive and laying his emphasis on the separation of that branch from the legislature. Certainly these were the Crown's courts and the Crown's judges, but they had long asserted a kind of professional, moral, and intellectual distinctness. Lord Coke rebuked James I when that king claimed authority over the administration of justice:

> [T]rue it was, that God had endowed his Majesty with excellent Science, and great Endowments of Nature; but his Majesty was not learned in the Laws of his Realm of England, and Causes which concern the Life, or Inheritance, or Goods, or Fortunes of his Subjects, are not to be decided by natural Reason but by the artificial Reason and Judgment of Law, which Law is an Act which requires long Study and Experience, before that a Man can attain to the Cognizance of it. . . .[66]

Montesquieu insisted on the independence of the judiciary as a safeguard of individual liberty, although his account emphasized criminal prosecutions and the lay jury as judges of guilt or innocence.[67] It was once again John Adams, in Article XXIX of the Declaration of Rights in the Massachusetts Constitution of 1780, who stated the modern principle, with its emphasis on the judiciary:

> It is essential to the preservation of the rights of every individual, his life, liberty, property, and character, that there be an impartial interpretation of the laws, and administration of justice. It is the right of every citizen

to be tried by judges as free, impartial and independent as the lot of humanity will admit. It is, therefore, not only the best policy, but for the security of the rights of the people, and of every citizen, that the judges of the supreme judicial court should hold their offices as long as they behave themselves well; and that they should have honorable salaries ascertained and established by standing laws.[68]

The Constitution carried forward the conception without the rhetoric. Article II, §2, gives the nomination of judges to the President, but requires the Senate's "advice and consent," so that federal judges are placed in office pursuant to decisions made by the two other branches of government. Once federal judges gain office, Article III seeks to protect them from further pressures from those who put them there by giving them life tenure (subject only to the cumbersome processes of impeachment) and prohibiting any reduction in salary. To this deliberately insulated situation, Article III effects a corresponding delimitation of the role judges are to play: the judicial power extends to the decision of cases and controversies, and in one of the several strokes of genius in the Supreme Court's early history, the Justices in *Hayburn's Case*[69] firmly stated that the judicial power extended to cases and controversies *only,* refusing to be drawn into the processes of administration as if it were a subordinate agency in the executive department. None of this was inevitable or thought to inhere in the very conception of the judge's office. The British tradition had the judges appointed by the King or his representative, the royal governor. At the other extreme was the movement toward the election of judges, there being a lively controversy whether, as Thomas Passmore, writing in 1803, put it, "there is any analogy between what is called the *independence of the judges* in England, and the independence of the judges in America—and whether making the former independent of the *king* justified the making of the latter independent of the people."[70] Nor was the sharply delimited role of the judge universally assumed; on the contrary, both in Britain and in the states, judges and courts performed a wide variety of functions that quite outran the austere "cases and controversies" designation of Article III.[71]

Although John Adams's conception of a rigid separation of the legislative and executive functions is everywhere obsolete under the pressure of the modern administrative state, the judiciary's independence is everywhere on the rise, and particularly as the world embraces some version of constitutionalism and judicial review.[72] This reliance on the judiciary as the guarantors of individual security can be explained in part in the same structural terms that the *Federalist Papers* used to justify the separation of powers generally: by having "ambition . . . counteract ambition,"[73] no power center can become too menacing, and most essential is that the power centers be kept sufficiently distinct that this function be assured. As I have indicated, the Court has been reluctant to play umpire in maintaining the unitary presidency, although it has been quite firm in insisting that Congress act only as a legislature. When it comes to the powers of the judiciary, however, the competition takes on a different face, because the judiciary *is* the umpire. Nor is the analysis changed if these umpiring decisions are put in the hands of a separate "constitutional court," as is done in Germany and several other countries. On the contrary, the United States arrangement, that—by virtue of the Supremacy Clause (Article VI)—gives this role to every state and federal court in the nation, has the distinct advantage of signaling that there is something special about the office of "judge" that lets its occupants act as umpires (which is, of course, simply another word for "judge").

The independence of the judiciary is the reciprocal of the separation of powers as between the judiciary and the other powers. It asserts that judges must be allowed to do their work free from the interference—direction—of the executive or legislative branch. That work is the deciding of cases and controversies. Countries whose legal system descends from the English common law, and the United States most especially, have a reverence for the judiciary that shuts off—because the answer seems self-evident, while in fact it is merely circular—an inquiry into what is distinctive about the office of judge. A. V. Dicey in the nineteenth century claimed that the common law was the one true manifestation of the rule of law and that continental *droit administratif* was merely a counterfeit, a statist device for imposing the regime's bureaucratic will on its citizens.[74] But the bureaucracy, and the civil service that staffs it, is often more a guarantor than an enemy of the rule of law as Dicey conceived it—that is, the predictable and impartial application of governmental power according to preestablished rules and procedures. When it works well, the political regime determines the policy, makes the rules, and the bureaucracy then applies them to the citizenry. It is Anglo-American parochialism that insists that only if control of the bureaucracy be entrusted to the same tribunals that judge all other disputes—controversies over wills, automobile accidents, criminal prosecutions—will the citizen be assured that the administration will truly be held to account to the law. This conception of control over administration is a matter of culture, tradition, and professionalism. The fear that administrative tribunals will too much view themselves as part of the administrative apparatus, and that they will lack independence and side unduly with their administrative colleagues simply because they view them as their colleagues, is not a necessary fear and cannot be fully guarded against by any institutional device. In common law countries, for instance, where the adjudicative and prosecutorial functions are rigidly separated according to Adams's paradigm of the separation of powers, busy judges in criminal sessions, overwhelmed by huge dockets of cases in which common sense tells you the accused are generally guilty of something (even if not of precisely the crime charged), too often see their task as processing this vast, miserable stream of humanity as quickly as possible. Even the term chosen—"the administration of justice"—reveals the actual similarity to the judges' non–common law counterparts. And finally there is the fact that for over a century we have become accustomed to a variety of administrative tribunals adjudicating disputes arising out of the vast array of programs that make up the modern welfare-administrative state.[75]

What is distinctive about the rule-of-law regime is the discipline and culture of deciding cases according to law. Adams spoke of a government of laws and not men, and of the rule of law, because this is the best (imperfect) guarantee that people will be subject only to rules stated and known beforehand. Deciding according to law is not easy. There is a great deal to know, and the judge must be able to put out of his mind some aspects of the dispute that laymen would consider relevant. The judge must be able to listen to parties and their advocates making unattractive, even implausible, arguments with a mind open to the possibility that they contain some validity, some truth. That is the discipline. Then there is the culture: the forms of argument, the kinds of references and authorities that are or are not traditional. The culture and discipline come together in the courts' development of doctrine, which was the subject of Chapter 1. The details may differ, but in many civilizations there is this conception of the judge as a man apart, a kind of priest. In Islam it is said:

> The just qadi (judge) will be brought on the judgment day, and confronted with such a harsh accounting that he will wish that he had never judged between any two, even as to a single date.

> Judges are three: two in Fire, and one in Paradise. A man who has knowledge, and judges by what he knows—he is in Paradise. A man who is ignorant, and judges according to his ignorance—he is in the Fire. A man who has knowledge and judges by something other than his knowledge—he is in the Fire.[76]

And this is what Jethro said to Moses:

> Moreover thou shalt provide out of all the people able men, such as fear God, men of truth, hating covetousness. . . .[77]

It is foreign to this conception of the judge that he be dependent on the Prince (even an elected Prince, or a whole Congress full of princes). And it should be clear what that independence comes to: the discipline and culture to decide according to the law and only according to the law. Separation of powers, as it applies to the judiciary, thus means that Congress and the President may influence the judge only through the law. (Recall Adams's formulation: "judges as free, impartial and independent as the lot of humanity will admit.") It means that the ultimate adjudication of rights must be left in the courts. Undergirding this statement is the idea that if the judiciary's independence is to be an effective constitutional principle, then only the judiciary may do the judiciary's work. So if Congress pronounces a criminal judgment on someone, it is doing the courts' work, and Congress's judgment is invalid. If Congress overturns a judgment recognizing one man's right against another, it acts like a court of appeals, which it may not do. But if it *defines* property rights for the future, that is its job.

Judicial Review

It is an important feature of our Constitution that the separation of powers and the independence of the judiciary are themselves constitutional, not just political, principles. And since the Constitution proclaims itself to be law, indeed "the supreme law of the land," this has from early in the life of our Constitution implied that the courts must conclude for themselves what the law is. This is the point of Chief Justice Marshall's canonical statement: "It is emphatically the province and duty of the judicial department to say what the law is."[78] The inevitability of that conclusion has also been famously questioned: it is said to confuse the supremacy of the Constitution with the supremacy of the judiciary and to ignore the duty that Article VI places on all officers, state or federal and in whatever branch, to uphold the Constitution. This response to the early Court's and Chief Justice Marshall's claim is too undifferentiated, as that claim itself may be. In the two early cases in which the Justices took it on themselves to judge according to their view of the Constitution and not according to acts of Congress, *Hayburn's Case* and *Marbury v. Madison,* they declined to exercise powers which Congress imposed on them but which the Justices thought were outside the scope of what Article III designated as the "judicial power." It is not, therefore, that the judges were telling the other branches what to do, but that they would not let the other branches tell them what their job was. Consider the outcome of a contrary ruling. The judiciary's independence would be limited to only such independence as ordinary law allowed. This would mean the courts would have to comply should Congress instruct them, as Marshall hypothesized, to judge treason cases on a laxer basis than Article III, §3, requires ("the Testimony of two Witnesses to the same overt Act, or on Confession in open Court"), or should Congress instruct a federal court to enter a judgment for one side in a particular case. These instructions would be laws enacted in due form, and so in a sense the court would judge only according to law, but the judiciary's independence would be reduced to a formality requiring two steps rather than one to evade. The Court assumed a more robust independence than that. The Court concluded that the reach of the judiciary power is defined by the Constitution, and when exercising their powers courts must do so in ways distinctive to courts, ways that are in part explicit in the Constitution (as with trials for treason), or set out in broad terms by it (as with the Fifth Amendment: "No person shall . . . be deprived of life, liberty, or property, without due process of law. . . ."), or perhaps ways inherent in the very notion of a court.

The possibility that judicial independence might become judicial supremacy looms when we recall that the other branches must after all work through the law, and it is emphatically the duty of the judicial branch to "say what the law is." If in the course of saying what that law is a court concludes that an official is acting outside the warrant of the law, the official becomes a private person, and what may otherwise have been a lawful show of authority becomes a lawless act of force. It requires only a short further step to conclude that even a law passed in regular form is deprived of the status of law if it contradicts a constitutional prohibition ("Congress shall make no law . . . abridging the freedom of speech. . . .").[79] In all such cases, judges may be seen as simply refusing to participate in what they see as departures from constitutional forms and limits of law, and thus doing no more than preserving their independence and integrity. But what if they go further, as they sometimes do, and order officers of government to do this or that? At that point do judges go beyond refusing to acquiesce in what seems to them unconstitutional action, and cross over into managing the affairs of government—executing the laws? The first steps in that direction were easy. In *Marbury* itself, Chief Justice Marshall noted that courts in the Anglo-American tradition had long had the authority to order officials to perform certain acts:

> [W]here the heads of departments are the political or confidential agents of the executive, merely to execute the will of the president, or rather to act in cases in which the executive possesses a constitutional or legal discretion, nothing can be more perfectly clear than that their acts are only politically examinable. But where a specific duty is assigned by law, and individual rights depend upon the performance of that duty, it seems equally clear that the individual who considers himself injured, has a right to resort to the laws of his country for a remedy.[80]

The picture Marshall holds up for us is that even in such a politically charged context, courts are acting only in the way that courts have traditionally acted: resolving concrete disputes about rights. That is why in their very first opinion resisting a congressional statute, the Justices in *Hayburn's Case*—then under Chief Justice John Jay—refused to assume an advisory or subordinate managerial role in the administration of a contentious veterans' pension program: "[B]y the Constitution of the United States, the government thereof is divided into three distinct and independent branches, and that it is the duty of each to abstain from, and to oppose, encroachments on either. That neither the legislative nor the executive branches, can constitutionally assign to the judicial any duties, but such as are properly judicial, and to be performed in a judicial manner."[81] This assumes that we have a sense of what is a judicial duty and what is its performance in a judicial manner.

It is a long distance from Marshall's step to the complicated involvement of courts in the management—usually with the assistance of masters, who become a kind of court-appointed and court-supervised bureaucracy—of prisons, mental hospitals, school systems, and other institutions. Perhaps some of that distance might be explained as an alternative, acquiesced in by all involved, to simply shutting down the programs altogether, which would be more in line with the traditional role of judges. At each further step along this long road, the Court has been careful to devise complex doctrines that identify when there is a real dispute to be decided, about matters of legal right, between actual parties, having a concrete interest in the dispute. These doctrines are too complex and technical to set out here, but their aim is to stay within the picture sketched in *Hayburn's Case*. The length of the road traveled should not obscure the constitutional basis of federal court activity in the reciprocal doctrines of separation of powers and the independence of the judiciary, nor should it allow confusion of the supremacy of the law and of the Constitution with some notion of the supremacy of the judicial branch itself.

Horizontal Controls on the "Least Dangerous Branch"

The Constitution does give the other departments some weapons against the judiciary: there is the power of appointment, the power to create or not create lower federal courts, and the control over federal courts' jurisdiction, including that of the Supreme Court. Article III does not require Congress to create lower federal courts at all, and as to the Supreme Court, whose existence the Constitution assumes, Article III gives it appellate jurisdiction "with such Exceptions, and under such Regulations as the Congress shall make." There is a lively debate whether the latter power may be used to keep any and all federal courts from ruling in certain politically charged matters.[82] Even assuming that Congress may enact such "jurisdictional gerrymanders"—for example, for cases involving school busing or abortion—the rule of law is not completely negated as long as the state courts sit. Those courts are courts of general jurisdiction, with authority over everyone in their territory. And state judges are as much bound as federal judges to treat the federal Constitution as the supreme law of the land. Because Congress did not establish the state courts, though it may in the valid exercise of one of its enumerated powers take away their jurisdiction over federal questions and lodge it in federal courts, those courts are free to inquire into whether a congressional attempt to limit them is indeed constitutionally valid.[83] This nice—and happily untested—argument brings to the fore the ultimate dependence of the rule of law on a shared, inherited conception of what courts, state or federal, do, and why courts must not be driven entirely from the scene.[84]

CHAPTER FOUR

Speech

Foundations

The First Amendment's speech and press clauses—"Congress shall make no law . . . abridging the freedom of speech, or of the press"— today strongly protect against government regulation of the obvious objects of the amendment: political speeches and pamphlets, books, and newspapers. But the clauses also protect expression and activities some of which the framers would probably be quite surprised to find sheltered under the amendment: books and pictures explicitly depicting the widest imaginable range of sexual activities, careless libels of public figures, commercial advertising, grossly insulting vituperation, campaign expenditures and (up to a point) contributions, flag burning, and (almost) nude dancing. As elsewhere, what the framers might have envisaged as the application of the broad principles they launched in the document is not at all conclusive of the proper understanding of those principles today. The conception behind the speech and press clauses is contested.[1] The narrowest conception is hardly a conception but more a cramped inference from the historic record: that the First Amendment had as its "main purpose . . . to prevent all previous restraints upon publication . . . and not [to] prevent the punishment of such as may be deemed contrary to the public welfare."[2]

The next narrowest view, which in one form or another enjoys considerable academic support today and has had Alexander Meiklejohn as its signal proponent, sees the speech and press clauses as serving the processes of democratic self-government. According to this view, speech not contributing to the content or quality of political discourse is outside of the clauses' protection.[3] Unprotected speech, on this conception, would include not only obscenity and speech violent and abusive in tone but commercial advertising and perhaps painting, film, poetry, and music, unless they carry a political message. The argument for this political conception of the First Amendment is an argument from democracy. The political conception overcomes a distaste for judicial interference with the political choices of the branches, whose authority is bathed in democratic legitimacy, by the argument that official interference with speech criticizing current policies and officials is a palpable interference with democratic controls over those currently in power.[4] The law has long since moved past this conception. Films, plays, pictures, works of literature (in a very generous sense of that term), advertisements, and sexually explicit and abusive expression are all protected. Some of these forms of expression in some remote sense might be squeezed into the democratic conception.[5] For instance it has been said that even works of fiction of a distinctly gossipy and salacious sort depict different ways of living,[6] and these alternatives may sometime, somehow manifest themselves in political choices. But this is pretty far-fetched, or rather it turns the distinctively Meiklejohnian perspective into something else.

The First Amendment, I show in this chapter, is best understood as protecting a very broad and fundamental liberty—what I call the freedom of the mind. More precisely, it places firm limits on government's power to interfere with my liberty to think as I choose, to express my thoughts to others, and to receive their expressions in turn. I first examine this foundational idea—what it means and why it is important—and then show how First Amendment doctrine may best be understood as embodying it. I certainly do not claim that First Amendment doctrine perfectly embodies this idea, nor even that it sensibly could. The law of defamation, the law of intellectual property, and the law of commercial fraud, for instance, do not entirely accord with that rigorous conception, and perhaps they should not. And yet freedom of the mind is the animating conception behind First Amendment doctrine, the conception that explains the developing trajectory of that doctrine. Finally, I insist that this animating conception is of a limit on government, not of some generalized value of free thought and discourse, because stated in this more general way—as some commentators and Supreme Court justices have—it invites the Court (and courts) to assume a general, managerial role in fostering this value, as they might foster the value of the security of children or the well-being of families. But courts are also organs of government, and assigning such an active, affirmative role to them entails an authority to judge and balance the importance of this value in relation to other values. Such generalized balancing would then be just another interference by government in the freedom of the mind. The conception that I believe animates First Amendment doctrine is quite rigorously negative. First Amendment doctrine places limits on government, including implicitly on courts themselves, to interfere with the liberty of the mind. Doctrine hews to this negative conception by the elaboration of rules, which, more firmly than elsewhere, discipline the temptation of decision makers—including judicial decision makers—to judge and manage the substance of what the rules they administer might bring about.

Freedom of the Mind

It is often said that the First Amendment protects the interests of both speakers and listeners, so that the right of people to annoy others with messages they would rather not hear—as for instance in the case of protesters swarming about the entrances to abortion clinics, or religious or political solicitors ringing doorbells—is just as protected from government interference as the right to read a book or watch a film. The invocation of the listener's interest in enlightenment (political, cultural, or frivolous) cannot be straightforwardly offered as the basis for protecting the speaker to a hostile or indifferent audience. At least some further steps are needed in the argument. Perhaps it might be said that if today the government can stop me from reading a book I do not want to read anyway, then tomorrow it might stop me from reading a book I do want to read. And how can the government know what I might be interested in? Such accounts emphasize the right of an audience to receive messages without government interference, but doctrine recognizes the speaker's right as well and not solely as a corollary to the audience's right. You do indeed have an interest in learning whatever you choose, but I have an interest in trying to instruct or persuade you. So the free speech right protects two distinct rights: my right to expression and your right to be the target of my expression. It protects communication.

Begin with the speaker's interest. Do we, should we, recognize a right to expression apart from the purpose to communicate to another person—a targeted purpose, as in a conversation, or a generalized purpose as with most books? I suppose when I play the piano for myself or dance alone this may be thought of as solitary expression. (What if I am practicing for a recital?) Government interference with such solitary expression is surely a grave offense against individual autonomy, but does the Constitution protect this autonomy? And if so, by what provision? Consider a complementary, less far-fetched form of government interference that hampers the listener's (better yet, learner's) interest in being an audience where there is no speaker or writer—such as when Galileo trained his telescope on the skies and Leeuwenhoek his microscope on droplets of water. A government might very well want to stop that kind of inquiry because it might be the prelude to disturbing communications to others, because what I learn may lead me to act in certain ways the government does not like or to be generally less amenable to follow where it would lead, or finally because what I find out may make me a different person than the government would like me to be. This connects with the situation of the person who speaks (sings, dances) only for herself. The government in her case too may want to control such solitary activity, as that activity may reinforce other dispositions, take time away from what the government considers worthier activity, or again just contribute to making the actor a different sort of person than the government would want her to be. Indeed the two cases come close to being the same thing, as do whatever claims the government has to control these solitary activities.

In the more usual situation covered by the First Amendment, that of a communication between two or more persons, both the individuals' interests and the government's claims are the same as in the solitary cases, although the government's intervention in the solitary cases is bound to be more intrusive. In all of these instances the individual's interest is in the freedom of his mind: to think what he wishes, to learn what he wishes, to hear, read, and see what he wishes—as Justice Louis Brandeis put it, that "freedom to think as you will, and to speak as you think."[7] It is a corollary of that interest that others not be prevented from reaching the mind. Therefore the standard terms, freedom of speech or expression, include both the freedom to express one's thoughts and the freedom to hear, read, and think. These I compendiously call freedom of the mind. The speech and press clauses of the First Amendment protect that freedom against limitation by government.

This broad conception makes sense of the variety of expressions that are sheltered under the First Amendment. The amendment protects you not only against the government's suppressing your thought and its expression, but also against the government's putting words in your mouth, compelling you to print what you do not want to print, affirming what you do not believe. Justice Jackson expressed this last thought in his opinion upholding the right of students to refuse to salute the American flag:

> It is now a commonplace that censorship or suppression of expression of opinion is tolerated by our Constitution only when the expression presents a clear and present danger of action of a kind the State is empowered to prevent and punish. It would seem that involuntary affirmation could be commanded only on even more immediate and urgent grounds than silence.
>
> . . .
>
> If there is any fixed star in our constitutional constellation, it is that no official, high or petty, can prescribe what shall be orthodox in politics, nationalism, religion, or other matters of opinion or force citizens to confess by word or act their faith therein. If there are any circumstances which permit an exception, they do not now occur to us.[8]

As constitutional law after 1937 turned aside from strong protection against government regulation of freedom to engage in most forms of behavior, particularly in the way of business, it recognized expanded protection for freedom of the mind. It might be said that the upshot is to protect the freedoms that matter most to a relatively small part of the population, while giving government freer rein to regulate those, like the use of property or even smoking, that matter to everybody.[9] But there is an important sense in which freedom of thought is the preeminent freedom, different in kind and importance from all others. Philosophers have put this in various ways. Aristotle speaks of man as a rational animal. Kant defines human nature as free and rational. What these formulations claim is that what we desire, do, and experience is organized by our thinking. Our judgment on what comes to us by way of our senses, our choices about what we do, all are backed by thinking. So even before we speak of higher modes of abstract reason we must judge how to make sense of our experience and how to project our actions on the world. Freedom of the mind denies government the authority to control those judgments. John Stuart Mill put it in terms of my ownership of myself—my body and my mind.[10] How I use my body may affect others, and to that extent impinge on their rights of self-ownership. How I use my mind, to the extent that that use affects others through *their* minds, is a matter of my own judgment and that of those whom I may persuade. Mill's claim to ownership of our bodies and the freedom he derives from that claim yield a comparable claim to freedom, but one that is more controversial. It is more controversial because many insist that government rightfully has the authority to control that use: certainly so that I do not harm others, but perhaps also so that I do not harm myself, or even so that I do not lessen my capacity to benefit others. But all of these uses of my physical freedom and the constraints upon them are judged by me. Perhaps my physical freedom may be restrained for the good of others or for my own good, but government must not claim the authority to coerce what judgment I make on those restraints.

There is a political, and therefore a Meiklejohnian aspect to this account. Government's physical authority would be prolonged and extended if government could also control our judgment, so that we ended up not only being physically controlled but liking that control. The claim for freedom of the mind expresses a commitment more fundamental than democracy and self-government. The commitment is to the principle of individuality or self-ownership. It spells the limits of community and its claims. It is what is left of individualism when the force of all the arguments about our obligations to others, our dependence on others, our inevitable impact on others, has been acknowledged.

The roots of this hard core of self-ownership reach into our religious past. Even in the more communitarian, authoritarian tradition of the Roman Catholic Church it has always been a premise that compelled belief is not true faith, that man can come to salvation only if he comes freely, and therefore, in the end, that a man is responsible for his own soul. This element, of course, becomes central in Protestant theology, which emphasizes each individual's personal and unmediated relationship to God. The individual's capacity and therefore right to judge both truth and goodness was a premise of the Enlightenment, most forcefully formulated by Kant. So too the growth of modern science depended on the premise of the individual's ability to judge evidence and argument for himself, free from the authority—though not the argument and evidence—of tradition. The commitment to truth and reason—rationality, for short—entails a commitment to remaining open in principle to persuasion, that is, to evidence and argument. The reverse proposition also holds: rationality is in principle inconsistent with a refusal to consider arguments or evidence—that is, a refusal to allow oneself to be persuaded. Freedom of thought is a regime in which no coercive power may legitimately limit persuasion as persuasion. Thus rationality entails a regime of freedom of mind and provides the Archimedean point for strong First Amendment freedoms. And as we shall see, that leverage once established, the freedom extends beyond rational persuasion to as wide a conception of expression as the concept of the mind itself.

A Right against Government

The text of the First Amendment is a prohibition: "Congress shall make no law. . . ." The right is formulated not in abstract terms[11] but as a limit on Congress, a limit that has been generalized to any prohibition by whatever level of government or its agents. The great principle of freedom of mind reaches beyond government impositions. Philosophers like Kant proclaimed the freedom not only as a right but a duty, so that the individual who ceded that freedom to another—a master, a church, a parent—offended his own person. The Constitution does not compromise the principle by not going that far, but rather respects the limits of its own authority. Indeed, if it tried to assure the freedom of the mind beyond imposition by government, it would run the certain danger of violating the very freedom it protects. A person who allows a family or business or institution to limit what he hears and expresses might be said to do just that, *allow* these impositions, and so may be taken to have made a judgment favoring these impositions. Though his family, say, may forbid his access to certain expressions, it can only maintain that prohibition so long as the individual judges for himself that this prohibition is for the best. If government did try to protect a person against the impositions of, say, his church, that protection would be an imposition on his judgment that his thoughts and choices are better if limited by the church. Government is different. The claims of government are, potentially, total. Government controls even the exit option—exit, it must be said, to the jurisdiction of another government. That fewer governments than once did exert this last, final measure of coercion, just as fewer governments seek to control the minds of their citizens, is a development inherent not in the phenomenon of government but rather in the acceptance of constitutional limitations on the powers of government.

There is a distinct formality to this argument. Some partial institutions—churches, businesses, families—have a stronger hold over their members than some governments. It might be said that this is either because government allows the institutions this power—which may make the state their accomplice—or because they have that power whether the state likes it or not. The latter alternative describes the situation of premodern states, or states in the process of formation or upheaval. Stable modern states enjoy formally, and to a more or less complete degree practically, what Max Weber has called the monopoly of force, because the claims of government potentially blanket the field. Weber did not mean that others do not use force in a modern state, but that all legitimate force is wielded either by the state itself or by its permission or delegation. The state is the ultimate ground on which we stand—there is no further retreat—and so if the state seeks to control our minds, we are caught indeed. (This is a normative, not a factual, monopoly. We may, of course, defy the state; but within the context of law—and that is our context here—we may not do so lawfully.) Of course there is a certain circularity in ascribing to the state the monopoly of force, qualifying that ascription to all legitimate force, and then defining the state as the source of legitimacy. But that circularity describes the juridical theory of the modern state,[12] and First Amendment theory, like constitutional theory in general, is part of the theory of law and of the state.

Constitutional freedom of the mind is freedom from government mind control. It is the axiom of self-ownership asserted against government, which usually defines, adjudicates, and protects ownership rights. It says to the government: however you may ascribe and define ownership in general, my mind is my own.

Theocratic and totalitarian governments have cared what you think, hear, and say because they care what kind of person you are. The Nazi judge told a German aristocrat, a deeply religious man who defended himself saying that he had never in deed or word been disloyal to the regime, that "we Nazis are like your Christian Church: we care not just about men's actions, but about their souls." Modern governments, including ours, rarely make that kind of claim. If they seek to control what you say, hear, or think, if they seek to control your mind, they will claim that it is because they care what you will do.

As we shall see later in detail, there are serious issues about speech which is more signal than a sign, a "lever of action," like the orders to a firing squad: ready, aim, fire. And so also communications in the course of a criminal conspiracy, the words in a contract, or those contained in a threat or a proposal for blackmail.[13] Although these cases must somehow be fit into a sensible legal scheme, they are not the cases that challenge the principle of the freedom of the mind. The great challenge comes from the general claim that speech may be suppressed because those who hear it may act upon it. This claim poses a challenge to freedom of the mind not at its margins but at its core. If it were allowed, nothing would be left of freedom of the mind, because any but the most reflexive action is preceded by thought, and speech communicates and may move thought. The principle implies also the limitation that keeps it from proving too much. The principle of freedom of the mind protects expression just insofar as it works through the mind. It protects expression that seeks to involve itself in the mind, that is, the thought, of another. The principle protects expression insofar as it persuades or instructs another. More fully, the principle protects the thinking audience that may be persuaded or draw instruction just as much as it protects the thinking speaker who seeks to persuade or instruct.

When we return to the details we will have to consider the suggestion that, for instance, some sexually explicit material has its effect neither through persuasion nor instruction, that though it may pass through the eyes or ears, it does not work on the mind. On the other hand the instructions in a criminal plot surely are processed by thought. That we are on the right track, however, is shown by the naturalness of looking for the answer to these difficult cases by asking whether and how they implicate freedom of the mind.

Prohibition and Inhibition

"Congress shall make no law . . . abridging the freedom of speech, or of the press." The meaning of that injunction is clearest when Congress does just that: asserts the right to control the minds of its citizens by prohibiting with its criminal law what they may say or hear. The use of the criminal law makes the imposition palpable, because criminal prohibitions are categorical. The bold, the reckless, or the devious may choose to violate a criminal law and risk punishment, but in doing so they defy the government: by using the criminal law, government intends not just to put a price on conduct but to shut it off altogether. In this respect, the criminal law is like the state in general. As we have seen, the state claims a monopoly of force and that claim is (among other things) what makes it a state, even though in practice a certain amount of force—that is, illegitimate force—will escape its grasp. So also by invoking the criminal law the state deploys that concept which announces its intention that something not happen at all, even though it will not completely succeed in that purpose. And a criminal law that says you may not say certain things, or seek to hear them, is a law that asserts a claim to control your mind. It is the core of what the First Amendment says government may not do.

But government affects thought in many ways other than direct prohibition. First Amendment jurisprudence describes these impositions as burdens on First Amendment rights. Government may be seen as burdening speech along one of two axes. First, government may seek to discourage certain speech or speakers by placing a price on expression. Unlike a criminal prohibition, a tariff by its terms does not propose an absolute bar to the thing priced. On the contrary, a tariff proclaims that the thing is allowed, so long as the price is just. But the price may be very high, and in any event any price discourages to a certain extent.[14] When the state puts a tariff on thought (as such, and not just the materials in which it is embodied or the economic arrangements by which those materials are bought and sold), it asserts authority over thought as it does over most other aspects of the lives of its citizens.

The second axis along which government may burden speech comprehends all those regulations which neither prohibit nor impose a tariff on speech as such, but, in the pursuit of other legitimate ends—keeping streets clear of litter, raising revenue—make the expression or reception of thought more difficult. In these cases government does not drive straight at speech but sideswipes it as it moves along to other goals. A general sales tax makes books more expensive just as wages-and-hours laws may increase the labor costs of newspapers. Indeed, there is little government does that does not under some circumstances, in some degree, burden speech. This is just an entailment of our being material beings and not disembodied minds, so that the regulation of our material circumstances cannot avoid having a pervasive impact on what we think, express, and hear. And instances where government inhibits expression by bestowing some benefit on a broad class of persons but withholds that benefit from those who express themselves in certain ways or on certain topics—no fire protection, say, for newspapers—may be located on either axis: the denial of a generally available benefit is after all a kind of tariff, but if newspapers or chemists offer some peculiar difficulty to the provision of fire protection, then the denial may be viewed as a burden incidental to the provision of that benefit. How do these instances accord with the First Amendment's protection of freedom of the mind, that is, freedom from government imposition on the mind?

It makes no sense to claim that any government regulation that has an impact on the exercise of that freedom is forbidden. A more plausible proposal acknowledges the pervasiveness of government imposition and for that reason makes the prohibition a matter of balance: the weight of the government's purpose against the degree of intrusion. This conception entails a constitutional regime which requires that the importance of the interest in free speech be weighed against any goal at which government aims. This kind of balance is the stuff of politics. It is what legislators and executive officers do. But courts interpreting and applying the Constitution, and particularly a provision as categorical in its language as the First Amendment—"Congress shall make *no* law . . ."—are thought to be doing something different. But what? Is it that courts stand between government and individuals and for that reason are more objective about the importance of both competing interests, while legislators and executive officers after all are the government and thus may tend to overbalance in favor of the government's goals? This explanation is an uncomfortable one for several reasons. First, it does not acknowledge that when government is working well, it is never pursuing *its* interests but the interests of its citizens, so that when government weighs interests it is always weighing the interests of one group of citizens against the interests of others. On this view, the courts just would be doing again what good government has already done. Second, this view casts courts as judges of the importance of the interests on each side of the balance and therefore offends the status of both. It makes courts judge the importance of what government has already decided is an important goal and so offends the democratic authority of legislatures and elected officials. And it makes courts judge the importance of what a particular individual wants to say or hear, and thus offends the conception of individual sovereignty that stands behind the principle of the freedom of the mind.[15] That principle, after all, claims that the individual is free to decide for herself what she will hear and say and so how important those things are.

There is a dilemma about keeping the principle of freedom of the mind from either proving too much or being dissolved by a balancing test. This is an instance of a dilemma that exists whenever rights protect or embody an interest, and the resolution of this dilemma here follows the form that the law takes in many of those other instances. Instead of authorizing a global balance of one value or interest against the other, the law structures the conflict. It organizes the conflict into types and resolves the balance within each type. If the conflict is assigned to one type of category, one or the other of the interests takes absolute precedence over the other. In another category of types the priorities may be softened, so that one or the other of the interests enjoys only a presumptive precedence, and that presumption may be overcome by competing interests of specified strength or type. And finally, a residual category will indeed require an ad hoc balancing, but one that has a limited domain. Thus is the conflict disciplined and balancing limited or eliminated by a system of rules. This is the regime of doctrine.

Many things that government does may impinge on the freedom of the mind, or in the terminology of First Amendment doctrine, may burden freedom of expression. I have already offered examples ranging from criminal prohibitions on saying or hearing certain things to general regimes, like income taxation, that withdraw resources that might be used for, among other things, the dissemination or reception of speech. A person may complain to a court that his First Amendment freedom has been burdened in one of these ways. Assuming that burden can be made out, it is then up to the government to explain its action. The structure of First Amendment doctrine is best revealed by the kinds of explanations that will or will not justify the burden.

IMPERMISSIBLE GOVERNMENT PURPOSES
One whole category of justifications government may offer takes the general form of the government's stating that it has acted just to prevent you from saying or hearing a particular class of things. You may

not say *X;* you may not buy books that say *X*. Of course government will always have a further reason. You may not say or hear *X* because saying or hearing *X* is a precondition to your doing *Y;* or people who say or hear *X* are more likely to do *Y*. Or saying or hearing *X* is bad for you: it makes you feel bad or makes you a worse person. As a first approximation, I offer the proposition that whatever *X* or *Y* might be, a justification in this form is incompatible with freedom of the mind, and therefore with the First Amendment.[16]

It is frequently objected that a rule formulated in terms of government's motives is inappropriate and unworkable. Only individuals, not institutions, have motives. And because institutions are almost invariably inhabited by a number of individuals, often over a period of time, and rarely will all those individuals share the same motives, the attribution of motives to the institution is a logical and factual solecism. The objection is too sweeping, but at any rate it does not apply to the rule as I have formulated it. The rule I offer begins with the speaker's complaint that his speech has been burdened by government action and then asks the government to justify that action. Such a complaint need not refer to the government's motive at all. Or the complaint may itself allege a motive to suppress speech, as when it is argued that some action which does not usually burden speech, such as firing a government worker, was taken as punishment for speaking. It is the government's own stated justification that is the subject of the suit, and it comes into play when the government itself offers a forbidden reason. Of course the government may offer justifications that are not its true reasons but mere rationalizations. It may deny a purpose to retaliate against the government employee, offering instead his record of absenteeism. Or in a time of labor agitation, a municipal government may ban the distribution of leaflets in the streets and offer as its reason a desire to reduce litter.[17] There must, therefore, be ways of sorting out acceptable justifications from those that are rejected as pretexts: more doctrine. For the moment I propose as the first step in the exposition of First Amendment doctrine the rule that government may not justify a burden on speech on the ground that it does not wish persons to convey or receive a particular expression. I call this the ground zero rule.[18]

What, then, of the cases, which must be the most usual ones, in which this justification by government is a step on the way to a further justification: you may not speak (hear) *X* because of the relation between this expression and the doing of Y? For instance, a political pamphlet vehemently criticizing the income tax as legalized theft may be shown to have led some people to cheat on their tax returns. May the government ban the publication (or possession of) the pamphlet on that ground? Certainly the government has the right to collect lawfully imposed taxes and to make tax evasion a crime. And just as certainly government may punish an accountant who advises a client how to conceal income and then prepares and signs a fraudulent return for that client. The prohibition of the pamphlet, however, violates the ground zero rule in that it prohibits the communication of a particular message. We are not presented with the complexity of the case of the antilittering ordinance already mentioned. Here the governmental measure (the criminal prohibition) is a clear statement that the government does not wish a particular message to be spoken or heard. That the government then has a further reason why it does not want that message conveyed does not alter that fact.

The ground zero rule is a direct expression of freedom of the mind. All sorts of other entities try to influence how we use our minds. Churches may go so far as to designate certain thoughts unthinkable and certain books forbidden, but churches are voluntary associations to whose discipline one submits because of an antecedent judgment. Media may pick what they will broadcast because of a conviction about what it is good for people to hear, and employers may restrict the speech and sanction the attitudes of their employees—as may neighbors and friends. But as I have said, these are all partial powers to which we have some choice not to submit. When the government violates the ground zero rule, it alone asserts a claim to control our minds from which it means us not to be able to escape—though like other laws we may violate or evade its prohibition. When government violates the ground zero rule, it asserts a claim which directly contradicts the First Amendment. What is less evident is whether ground zero should encompass the case where government prohibits speech X for the further reason that speaking (or hearing) X makes Y more likely, and Y is not a thought but an action. Yet the inclusion is necessary, not only because this case will be the usual one, so that practically if it is not included there is very little that the ground zero rule will cover. The deeper reason is that the principle of the freedom of the mind not only blocks the ambition of government to shut you off from certain thoughts just because it does not want you to entertain those thoughts (as a church might), but also blocks the government from blocking (or procuring) certain actions by controlling what you will think about performing those actions. Government may try to control what you do—for instance, pay your taxes—by threatening a penalty if you do not pay, and in that way it might be said that it tries to influence what you think about paying your taxes. But it does that by offering you something else to think about—contemplating the chance of paying a fine or going to prison—not by blocking all or part of your thought processes.

PERMISSIBLE GOVERNMENT PURPOSES WITH IMPERMISSIBLE EFFECTS ON SPEECH

Many things that government does will have the effect of making expression more difficult, and everything that government does will make some expression more difficult than some other expression—that is, government will place a greater burden on certain speech. (I shall sometimes call these cases of indirect burden to contrast them with the category just considered, which I shall sometimes call cases of direct burden.) The ground zero rule blocks government from justifying these burdens on the ground that it disapproves of the message or on the ground that it disapproves of what you might do if you think about the message. But many of the justifications government will offer for indirect burdens will not have this form at all, and the alternative justifications may not be pretexts for violations of the ground zero rule. It is these cases that present a difficulty for First Amendment doctrine. They include situations where government regulation may significantly inhibit freedom of the mind, but the invocation of the First Amendment requires the Court to balance against the importance of the government's goal the value of what the speaker wishes to say, and that inquiry offends the principle of the freedom of the mind insofar as the Court—a government agency of sorts—is judging the value of what I want to hear or say. Doctrine may soften such dilemmas by treating them as direct burden cases after all, because the Court either will not credit or will not allow the government's claim that it has something other than burdening speech in mind. But after that there are still many cases that remain to bedevil the law, in which the Court and common sense fully credit the government's nonspeech justification. In some but not all of these cases the Court does engage in balancing, but a balancing disciplined by quite complexly structured doctrine. In other cases the Court does not start down that path at all. As we shall see when free speech doctrine is examined, it is not easy to explain why some cases are treated in one way and some in another.

THOUGHT AND ACTION

The previous category of cases are those where the government's justification for burdening speech points only at a purpose having nothing to do with the prohibition of speech—either as an end or as a means to an end. There are two other categories of cases that test the meaning of freedom of the mind, and they are in a way mirror images of each other. In one a person undoubtedly is restrained or punished for what he says, but the government's justification is that the supposed speech is not speech at all but action. The executioner who calls "Ready, Aim, Fire" to a firing squad or the purchaser who writes his signature or states his acceptance to a proposed contract is undoubtedly just uttering words, but the government rightly claims that these words are no less part of a course of action than, say, the pulling of the trigger is part of firing a rifle.[19] The speech really is just action. The complementary case is one in which action is just speech where the individual utters no words but his actions convey a message as surely as if he did: the protester who draws a flag and then defaces or destroys it in the course of a demonstration against government policy.

The first kind of case—speech as part of a course of action, what Justice William Douglas has called "speech brigaded by action"[20] is sometimes difficult to untangle. "Words are not only the keys of persuasion, but the triggers of action."[21] The principle of freedom of the mind forbids government from interfering with persuasion, but persuasion may bring about action just as surely as a command. In practice the line between the two may be difficult to draw, but at this stage of the inquiry it is important to establish what distinct concepts the line is supposed to separate. I would say that persuasion appeals to judgment. It sets in motion the evaluative powers of the mind. A command, of course, requires understanding, but it is not an invitation to evaluation or reflection. It does not ask you to make what you think best of it. Similarly, other forms of speech—say, a signature on the acceptance line of a contract—are meant to issue directly, without evaluation or reflection, in a concrete effect in the world.[22] The practical difficulties, indeed, are many. Does artistic expression—paintings, music—seek to persuade? What of materials intended to procure sexual arousal? In quite a different vein, computer code both communicates information and operates machinery.[23] The same text in one context may be part of a set of instructions for the making of a bomb as part of a criminal plot and in another context be part of a political argument about how easy (or difficult) it is to make bombs.[24] The principle in all these cases asks the same question: does the communication address some judgment, seeking to persuade or to elicit appreciation or evaluation?

The reverse case—flag desecration—is much simpler and the law protects it. All expression requires some overt manifestation. It would be arbitrary to limit the protection afforded expression and thus the freedom of the mind to spoken or written words or to any other particular overt manifestation. The law speaks of symbolic speech, as if all speech did not make use of symbols in one way or another. In Franz Kafka's story "In the Penal Colony" a device causes a pattern of needles slowly to inscribe in the body of an offender the nature of his offense. Although it is a form of communication, this gruesome practice—if used by a private person on his enemies—surely would not be protected by the principle of the freedom of the mind. Government may prohibit the use of that machine but not the tattooing of a message on your own photograph of your enemy, because the prohibition in the former case focuses on the physical violence done to the victim, whatever may or may not be communicated by that violence, while in the latter case there is little else to prohibit except the communication. Again, at the level of detailed doctrine there will be complex distinctions to be made and nuances to be observed, but the principle is clear.

GOVERNMENT SPEECH

Finally, government prohibits or commands speech in contexts where the speech is attributed to the government itself, rather than to a nongovernmental agency. Government is not a person; it can only speak or act through persons. As an abstract entity, it instantiates the purposes and judgments of the persons who constitute it. There is nothing about the principle of the freedom of the mind, especially as it is asserted in the First Amendment against the government, that is incompatible with the government—either in the person of the particular officials carrying out its functions or as an abstraction—having opinions, judgments, values, preferences, thoughts, and goals. That government is the residual and final authority is why the First Amendment asserts protection of the freedom of the mind against it, but that principle does not preclude those who inhabit government from having convictions and expressing their minds, singly or collectively. True, the governmental judgments, governmental "mind," may have a greater—perhaps even potentially crushing—weight, but that is an important part of the reason why individuals subject to government are protected against it.

Because a democratically chosen government expresses the values of the community it governs, it would be a perverse limitation of that community's aspirations to fashion constitutional doctrines in such a way that the community's manifestation of its (metaphorical) mind is precluded for the sake of protecting the freedom of mind of its citizens. But government cannot express its judgments, its collective mind, without directing the expression of those who are constituted to speak for it. Such directions—any directions—logically entail a range of prohibition. Those who speak for the government, who *are* the government while they speak for it, may not at the same time undermine the very message they convey. For the same reason a citizen may not complain that his freedom has been curtailed because government does not choose to adopt and broadcast his message. Otherwise, at the extreme, government could have no projects, as its ability to carry them out would always be hostage to the claims of whoever came along claiming its facilities for his own projects. To quote Justice Jackson from another context, such a principle "either has no beginning or it has no end."[25]

This analysis, like the analysis of state action and doctrine, only works if government does not engross all the time, facilities, and income of its citizens. Both analyses assume a significant private domain, that is, a domain which is not the government's to command. The existence of some regime and substantial quantum of private property and some general level of discretionary income is a presupposition of the scheme I have been describing. If (almost) everything belonged to the government, then the principle of freedom of mind would require a quite different analysis, and a very precarious one, for it would be far more likely to get the courts into the business not of policing boundaries but rather of assigning particular speech opportunities. And that task could not avoid having to judge the value of a particular expression or of expression in general relative to other uses of (now the government's) resources.

Doctrine

Freedom of the mind is not only a correct principle, it is also the principle that provides energy for much of the intricate structure of First Amendment doctrine. The doctrine does not correspond exactly to the principle. At several points doctrine draws back from fully implementing it—sometimes for historical reasons and sometimes because of the pressure of countervailing considerations. As I shall show, doctrine protects freedom of the mind by placing a very high barrier to the government's justifying a burden on speech if that justification includes a purpose to foreclose or even to burden speech as such or some particular instances of speech. Doctrine also imposes a strong prohibition on compelled speech. Government often offers justifications other than a purpose to foreclose or even burden. In those instances, doctrine insists that the asserted benign purpose be of particular weight and aptness to that purpose. Finally, doctrine makes the principle a limit on government, rather than a right to government's facilitating of speech. Constitutional freedom of the mind is a negative right.

Prohibition: "Prevention and Punishment"

"[T]he constitutional guarantees of free speech and free press do not permit a state to forbid or proscribe advocacy of the use of force, or of law violation except where such advocacy is directed to inciting or producing imminent lawless action and is likely to incite or produce such action. . . ." This sentence from the Supreme Court's 1969 decision in *Brandenburg v. Ohio*,[26] a criminal prosecution for racist words spoken at a Ku Klux Klan rally, is now a canonical statement of First Amendment law. The clearest embodiment of government's burdening speech by foreclosing it altogether or burdening speech for the very purpose of discouraging a message (what I shall call, for the sake of brevity, foreclosure) is a law that makes it a crime to say certain things. Those things may either be designated in terms (which is rare) or by some general description of the forbidden speech. But a more general law—say, one against interfering with the draft—may be applied to speech, so that arguing that the draft violates the Thirteenth Amendment might be taken as an interference with the draft. The criminal prohibition is only the clearest case of foreclosing a message, because a criminal prohibition is intended not to allow an option to disobey it, even if the penalty may be low enough that some may conclude that it is worth paying it. The law may sometimes prescribe no more than a tariff on speech, but if the justification for the tariff is that the law seeks to discourage the particular message, that too would fall under this rule.

Constitutional doctrine does not bar every instance of foreclosure. It has been said that government may foreclose speech if that speech presents a "clear and present danger" of some grave evil the government is entitled to prevent. This formulation has a troubled history and is fraught with difficulties and ambiguities in every direction. It may hark back to a famous passage in John Stuart Mill's *On Liberty:*

> An opinion that corn-dealers are starvers of the poor, or that private property is robbery, ought to be unmolested when simply circulated through the press, but may justly incur punishment when delivered orally to an excited mob assembled before the house of a corn-dealer, or when handed about among the same mob in the form of a placard.[27]

Originally offered by Justice Holmes, the clear and present danger test may have been intended to do no more than sweep speech into the general analysis of ways in which an actor may be punished for conduct leading up to or assisting criminal conduct. Holmes as an author and state court judge had been interested in the law of attempts,[28] and had sought to formulate a test for determining how close an actor might come for his conduct to count as an attempt—scouting a building as a prelude to arson; buying the gasoline and matches; loading them into a truck and driving to the scene. Insisting on a clear and present danger that the ultimate evil will ensue would be one way to designate the required degree of closeness. In the case of attempts, an intent to bring about the harm must also be shown—buying gasoline and matches is not punishable as an attempt at arson unless part of a scheme to burn down a building. When we apply this rule to speech that may, for example, lead citizens to refuse to comply with a call to military service, we say that the speech must be both close to that harm and intended to produce it. In its developed formulation, the clear and present danger test in free speech doctrine adds a further constraint that does not appear in the law of attempts: the evil to which the speech may be a prelude may not be just anything the law designated or might designate as criminal but must itself be judged (by a court, not the legislature) as sufficiently serious to justify this imposition on speech.[29]

The clear and present danger test extends to cases in which the speech produces its effect not as a mere signal—a "trigger of action"—but by its persuasive force. But shutting down persuasion is the central case of interference with the freedom of the mind. Sensing this, the law has gotten itself into a tangle of formulas. Justice Harlan in the *Yates* case sought to discipline the use of criminal prosecutions during the cold war:

> [D]octrinal justification of forcible overthrow, . . . though uttered with the hope that it may ultimately lead to violent revolution, is too remote from concrete action to be regarded as the kind of indoctrination preparatory to action [that may be] condemned. . . . The essential distinction is that those to whom the advocacy is addressed must be urged to *do* something, now or in the future, rather than merely to *believe* in [something].[30]

This has been thought to echo a much earlier formulation by Learned Hand:

> Words are not only the keys of persuasion but the triggers of action, and those which have no purport but to counsel the violation of law cannot . . . be a part of that public opinion which is the final source of government in a democratic state. . . . If one stops short of urging upon others that it is their duty or their interest to resist the law, it seems to me one should not be held to have attempted to cause its violation.[31]

But Holmes pointed out the flaw in this distinction in rejecting the argument that a publisher of a manifesto could be prosecuted for the crime of criminal anarchy because "th[e] manifesto was more than a theory . . . [it] was an incitement." Discarding this distinction, Holmes then wrote, "[e]very idea is an incitement. It offers itself for belief and if believed it is acted on unless some other belief outweighs it or some failure of energy stifles the movement at its birth. The only difference between the expression of an opinion and an incitement in the narrower sense is the speaker's enthusiasm for the result. Eloquence may set fire to reason."[32]

Since the test of propinquity clearly allows punishment of speech identified by its persuasive force, this felt imposition on the freedom of the mind is justified as exceptional because of the immediacy of the danger—when the danger posed by speech cannot be met by "more speech."[33] Even the universal applicability of the clear and present danger test has been questioned. In the *Dennis* case, addressing the menace posed by the Communist Party during the early years of the cold war, Learned Hand reformulated the test: "In each case [courts] must ask whether the gravity of the 'evil,' discounted by its improbability, justifies such invasion of free speech as is necessary to avoid the danger."[34] And, in the Supreme Court, Justice Jackson took up the same thought: "The authors of the clear and present danger test never applied it to a case like this, nor would I. If applied as it is proposed here, it means that the Communist plotting is protected during the period of incubation; its preliminary stages of organization and preparation are immune from the law; the Government can move only after imminent action is manifest, when it would, of course, be too late."[35]

In the end the law has settled upon the *Brandenburg* formulation set out at the head of this section. It requires (i) that the speech to be punished be spoken with the intent to bring about lawlessness, (ii) that it be spoken with the intent to bring it about imminently, and (iii) that it be likely that it will in fact produce that result.[36] The *Brandenburg* test does not perfectly correspond to what I have called the principle of freedom of the mind: it may sometimes allow shutting down a message because of the ideas it conveys, because of its persuasive force. It is not limited to speech as a signal. Justice Douglas's concurrence in *Brandenburg* makes the point:

> Though I doubt if the "clear and present danger" test is congenial to the First Amendment in time of a declared war, I am certain it is not reconcilable with the First Amendment in days of peace. . . . The line between what is permissible and not subject to control and what may be made impermissible and subject to regulation is the line between ideas and overt acts. The example usually given . . . is the case of one who falsely shouts fire in a crowded theatre. This is, however, a classic case where speech is brigaded with action.[37]

But the *Brandenburg* formula does confine the departure within very narrow limits. The Court simply is unwilling here, as in other areas, to foreclose entirely the government's ability to respond with exceptional measures in extreme circumstances. Nor is it correct to say that First Amendment doctrine limits such exceptional measures to the circumstances of war. The clear and present danger test or its variants are applied explicitly or implicitly to civil disturbances and even small-scale street encounters, if the dangers seem both sufficiently great or imminent.[38] There is this nuance: some opinions suggest that the government may not justify silencing a speaker when the disturbance it seeks to avoid would be caused by the hostile and unlawful reaction of the audience to him.[39]

Brandenburg seems to enshrine the clear and present danger test as the sole exception to government's inability to foreclose speech because of what is said. But that is not so. There are other occasions where the Court has allowed speech to be foreclosed just on account of its message. In *Buckley v. Valeo*[40] the Court held that limiting political contributions amounted to "suppressing communication" and yet allowed their regulation because of what it concluded was the important interest in avoiding both the appearance and the fact of political corruption. And in *Burson v. Freeman*[41] the Court allowed a state to prohibit all political speech—including the display of political signs and the distribution of political literature—within one hundred feet of the entrance to a place where people come to vote.[42] Such cases may be distinguished as forbidding only certain modes of speech or restricting it in certain places, but it is striking that the Court did not speak in those terms. Rather it invoked a doctrinal analysis that applies generally to all cases where the government seeks to justify action that is claimed to violate individual rights. This analysis assigns cases to one of three levels of scrutiny: *rational basis,* a level of scrutiny which any interference with a liberty interest must meet, according to which the government need only claim some plausible purpose and some rational connection between the measure complained of and the implementation of that purpose; *strict scrutiny,* which requires the government to convince the court that its interest is compelling and the means chosen to attain it are particularly apt and limited to that end; and *intermediate scrutiny,* in which both the urgency of the government's goal and the closeness of the means-end fit need not be so great as in strict scrutiny. This three-level system of constitutional justification, though now quite general,[43] had not become canonical until after the clear and present danger test and its variants like *Brandenburg* had become a fixed standard for certain kinds of cases.[44] *Brandenburg* may be assimilated to that later system as specifying what in certain circumstances will satisfy strict scrutiny. Both *Brandenburg* and strict scrutiny imply great but not inescapable stringency. The *Brandenburg* test by its terms applies to government measures that "forbid or prescribe advocacy of the use of force or law violation," and so does not reach government action against speech which does not threaten violence or lawlessness (for example, *Burson, Buckley*), nor does it reach government action against speech which does not work by making speech criminal but by burdening it in other ways for the purpose of suppressing it. (I consider that latter class of instances in the section on burdens below.)

Categorical Exclusions

> There are certain well-defined and limited classes of speech, the prevention and punishment of which have never been thought to raise a Constitutional problem. These include the lewd and the obscene, the profane, the libelous and the insulting or "fighting" words—those which by their very utterance inflict injury or tend to incite an immediate breach of the peace.[45]

Justice Frank Murphy was certainly correct about First Amendment doctrine at the time he spoke. And he might have added the category of commercial speech.[46] But by 1976 every one of these categories was at least partially assimilated into the larger body of free speech doctrine, having to pay its way by showing how special treatment of that category could be justified by the principles that govern First Amendment doctrine generally. As a result much expression that in 1942 did indeed fall outside of the bounds of First Amendment protection is now more or less fully protected. Nonetheless these categorical exclusions continue to have some force that needs to be examined and explained.

SEX

Justice Murphy was certainly correct that the "lewd and the obscene" had always been considered outside the protection of the First Amendment. Just what was lewd and obscene had also not been the subject of constitutional doctrine. The famous case which declared that James Joyce's *Ulysses* was not obscene interpreted and applied that term in the Tariff Act of 1930, which forbade the importation of "any obscene book, . . . picture, drawing or other representation. . . ."

Judge Augustus Hand put it this way: "The question in each case is whether a publication taken as a whole has a libidinous effect. The book before us has such portentous length, is written with such evident truthfulness in its depiction of certain types of humanity, and is so little erotic in its result, that it does not fall within the forbidden class."[47] This was a precursor to the definition of obscenity in the American Law Institute's *Model Penal Code:* "A thing is obscene if, considered as a whole, its predominant appeal is to prurient interest, that is, a shameful or morbid interest in nudity, sex, or excretion, and if in addition it goes substantially beyond customary limits of candor in describing or representing such matters."[48]

It was not until 1957 that the Supreme Court in *Roth v. United States* and *Alberts v. California*[49] addressed the issue in constitutional terms. Justice Brennan, who was to wrestle with this topic for the next sixteen years, rejected the argument that the rule limiting prohibitions of speech generally should also limit the regulation of sexually explicit speech. He would allow prohibition not only if there was "proof . . . that obscene material will perceptibly create a clear and present danger of antisocial conduct, or will probably induce its recipients to such conduct," but would also allow prohibition of that "obscenity [that is] utterly without redeeming social importance, . . . [and therefore] not within the area of constitutionally protected speech or press." But he went on to say that "sex and obscenity are not synonymous. Obscene material is material which deals with sex in a manner appealing to prurient interest," specifically endorsing the American Law Institute's test.

This doctrine does not sit easily with the principle of the freedom of the mind. Here is speech addressed to the mind. It is not a signal for action. The principle would not ask, as *Roth* does, whether the speech has any "redeeming social importance." Under *Roth,* the speaker must justify as socially important his thoughts and their expression. This formulation assumes a general power in government over the mind and its expression, and that is just what the freedom of the mind denies. It is the government that should have to justify its deliberate impositions on the mind. Tradition apart—and it is a long and broad one—it is hard to see what that justification might be. Some sexually explicit expression may deepen our sense of that aspect of human relations, and the formulations at least since the *Ulysses* case acknowledge that. But what of less edifying, so-called prurient speech?

Granted that it may aspire to do no more than provide vicarious sexual gratification,[50] nothing should follow as long as we are asking the right question, as long as it is the government that must do the justifying.

Justice Harlan, in *Alberts,* sought to meet this challenge: "[E]ven assuming that pornography cannot be deemed ever to [cause] criminal conduct, [the] State can reasonably draw the inference that over a long period of time, the indiscriminate dissemination of materials, the essential character of which is to degrade sex, will have an eroding effect on moral standards." And Chief Justice Warren, dissenting in *Jacobellis v. Ohio:*[51] "[There is a] right of the Nation and of the States to maintain a decent society." But these effects—the erosion of moral standards, the maintenance of a decent society—come about through the mind, with even more opportunity for contrary messages to counteract them and with a far less precise notion of what harm we are seeking to ward off than in the case of speech advocating political violence and lawlessness. Only if we revert to the notion that the First Amendment protects speech which society judges valuable to its ends—especially the end of facilitating self-government—can this sort of argument gain a footing, and that very claim that society may control (not just contribute to) how we use and affect each other's minds is what I reject. I believe that First Amendment doctrine also rejects it, and thus must deal with the law of obscenity as an anomaly. Alexander Bickel addressed this anomaly:

> It concerns the tone of the society, the mode, or to use terms that have perhaps greater currency, the style and quality of life, now and in the future. A man may be entitled to read an obscene book in his room, or expose himself indecently there. . . . We should protect his privacy. But if he demands a right to obtain the books and pictures he wants in the market, and to foregather in public places—discreet, if you will, but accessible to all—with others who share his tastes, then to grant him his right is to affect the world about the rest of us, and to impinge on other privacies. Even supposing that each of us can, if he wishes, effectively avert the eye and stop the ear (which, in truth, we cannot), what is commonly read and seen and heard and done intrudes upon us all, want it or not.[52]

The argument is not that the state has the right to protect us from the mere thought that others in the society are reading this stuff (much less to close off our temptation to read it ourselves) but that its availability in the market imposes on the public space we all share images and words that we do not wish to encounter there. These are the "other privacies" on which the purveyors of these materials "impinge." This is a serious argument. If sexually oriented materials are not political, then their effect may at least be analogized to the purely aesthetic—that which pleases the eye, ear, or mind, without any claim of an effect on conduct, much less on politics. Although the state has no business telling me what pictures to look at, it may represent the community in constructing a public space pleasing to most. The very sight of so-called adult theaters and bookstores may disturb inhabitants of that public space as much as does the sight of uncollected garbage or dilapidated buildings. But it must be the *sight,* not the *thought,* that disturbs. And so also the prostitutes, drug dealers, and drifters who congregate about such places may disturb the common inhabitants of the public space. But if that is the argument, it implies its own limitations. So long as the bookseller maintains discretion, passersby cannot complain just because they *know* what is being sold inside.[53]

This argument corresponds quite well to how the present law works in practice. With the exception of child pornography, to which I shall come later, discreet sellers of sexually explicit material are not much disturbed, and the private possession of such material seems to be beyond the reach of the law.[54] But nonetheless the argument is disturbing to the principle I have been stating, for it implies that some words, images, ideas may be driven into seclusion, may be denied the right to occupy the same public space as others just because these addresses to the mind are displeasing to a majority of the citizenry. This would not do for the suppression of bookstores selling political tracts, science fiction, books on bridge and solitaire (a more palpable "expense of spirit in a waste of shame"[55] than solitaire cannot be imagined), or reproductions of the art of Rockwell Kent. I agree that much of the material that today falls under what remains of the ban on obscenity is ugly and degrading, and that there are objective standards for despising it, but the principle of the freedom of the mind does not allow government to determine or apply those standards. My objection to the law of obscenity in this regard is greatly strengthened by the First Amendment treatment of descriptions and depictions of violence and cruelty. Nothing that can be said about the degrading and demoralizing effects of obscenity is not at least as true of violent speech, yet no exception to First Amendment doctrine exists to allow the prohibition or limitation of such material. And with good reason. The law is incompetent to distinguish such literary classics as the *Iliad* or Flaubert's *Salammbô*, with their detailed descriptions of extreme violence and exquisite torture, from merely disgusting works that exploit the depraved human fascination with the infliction of pain and suffering.

I reach the same conclusion as Justice William Brennan in his dissent in *Paris Adult Theatre I v. Slaton:*

> But the State's interest in regulating morality by suppressing obscenity, while often asserted, remains essentially unfocused and ill-defined. And, since the attempt to curtail unprotected speech necessarily spills over into the areas of protected speech, the effort to serve this speculative interest through the suppression of obscene material must tread heavily on rights protected by the First Amendment.
>
> . . .
>
> [W]hile I cannot say that the interests of the State—apart from the question of juveniles and unconsenting adults—are trivial or nonexistent, I am compelled to conclude that these interests cannot justify the substantial damage to constitutional rights and to this Nation's judicial machinery that inevitably results from state efforts to bar the distribution even of unprotected material to consenting adults.[56]

The law of obscenity has not in practical effect, however, ended up very far from where Justice Brennan (and I) would have it. The *Miller* case,[57] the companion to *Slaton*, announced a standard for obscenity so demanding that very little sexually explicit speech falls under its ban:

> [S]tatutes designed to regulate obscene materials must be carefully limited. As a result, we now confine the permissible scope of such regulation to works which depict or describe sexual conduct. That conduct must be specifically defined by the applicable state law. . . . The basic guidelines for the trier of fact must be: (a) whether the 'average person, applying contemporary community standards' would find that the work, taken as a whole, appeals to the prurient interest, (b) whether the work depicts or describes, in a patently offensive way, sexual conduct specifically defined by the applicable state law; and (c) whether the work, taken as a whole, lacks serious literary, artistic, political, or scientific value . . . [there being no requirement that the work be] *"utterly* without redeeming social value". . . .[58]

This standard has been further tightened to make clear that there must be considerable if undefined control of a jury's discretion in determining what appeals to prurient interest, what is patently offensive, and what has serious value.[59] And this last determination is to be made by not a local but a national standard.[60] A visit to the "adult entertainment" districts of any large city or to the "adult" movie channels provided in most hotels convinces that the *Miller* test leaves very little indeed to the prurient imagination. On the other hand Justice Brennan's exception to protect juveniles from sexually explicit material may have become if anything more stringent. Not only may the state control the display of such material *to* children (provided the control does not sweep adult audiences within its ban)[61] but also it may forbid sexually explicit depictions *of* children.[62] And the ban may extend beyond the trafficking in such depictions to their possession.[63] Thus it protects children not only from the harm of exposure to the material but also from the more substantial harm to children that comes from being used in the production of such material. By drying up the market, the law hopes to discourage the exploitation of persons too young to consent in a meaningful way to their participation. The logic of this argument does not extend to sexually explicit materials depicting only adult actors portraying children nor to computer-generated depictions of children risking no actual child.[64]

DEFAMATION

Until 1964 a lawsuit brought by one person against another on the ground that what that other had said or written defamed him was a matter of state tort law beyond the reach of the Constitution, just as much as a suit over an automobile accident.[65] Today the law of defamation is hardly taught in first-year courses in tort law, but has become an intricate and much litigated branch of First Amendment jurisprudence. The subject was then and is now hard to fit into free speech theory and hard to leave out. Unlike criminal prohibitions of speech, defamation is a private wrong to reputation for which one person sues another.[66] Yet it counts as the government making a law abridging the freedom of speech because it is the government that has made the law allowing the lawsuit. And that law—unlike the general law of contract, for instance, which I discuss later—is directed specifically at speech. The facts of the case that constitutionalized the tort of defamation, *New York Times Co. v. Sullivan,*[67] make the point. The *New York Times* published an advertisement by a group called

"The Committee to Defend Martin Luther King and Freedom in the South." The advertisement criticized authorities in the South for waging a campaign of terror against civil rights demonstrators, and referred to the action of the police in Montgomery, Alabama. Several local officials, none of whom had been mentioned by name, sued the *New York Times* for defamation in an Alabama court. The plaintiffs proved only that the advertisement was inaccurate in a number of trivial ways, none of which contributed to whatever defamatory sting the text might have had. A local jury awarded each of the plaintiffs $500,000 in "presumed" damages, although none had shown that the publication had hurt them in any way.[68] The Court treated the case as one in which the state had acted—at the instance of a plaintiff suing in his capacity as a private citizen—to penalize the newspaper for its speech in an amount one thousand "times greater than [the fine] provided by the Sedition Act."[69] The Court allowed a public figure to recover only actual damages for defamation and only if the plaintiff proved that the statement was false and uttered with knowledge that it was false or with reckless disregard whether it was true or false.

Why has the Court not gone further to foreclose such lawsuits altogether? It is quite clear that "Congress [could] make no law prohibiting the freedom" to say whatever you wanted—clear and present danger of a grave evil apart—about a political party, welfare recipients as a class, an institution of government, a racial group, the truth of the Holocaust, or the institution of private property.[70] Yet the state may make a speaker pay damages for false statements of fact about an identified living person (in a suit by that person) if the plaintiff can prove that the speaker knew that the statements were false or made them not caring whether they were true or false. Indeed, if the statement is not about a public figure, even careless misstatements may be actionable.[71] A false statement harms its victim by harming his reputation, but that is a harm that comes about through the minds of an audience, by persuading them. However hemmed in by *New York Times v. Sullivan,* this doctrine is directed at the freedom to speak and to listen. The Court noted a "profound national commitment to the principle that debate on public issues should be uninhibited, robust, and wide-open," and that "erroneous statement is inevitable in free debate and [must] be protected if the freedoms of expression are to have the breathing space they need to survive." So why not go the whole way to protect all defamatory statements?

The simplest way to fit this particular body of law within a more general theory of speech is, I must admit, to accept some version of the Meiklejohnian thesis as the core of the subject. If the First Amendment is designed above all to protect public debate on public issues as the central engine of democracy, then allowing citizens to injure each other in their reputations only so far as is necessary to protect that debate makes perfect sense. The *New York Times* case takes as its background the long-standing common law of defamation, which treats injury to reputation as a private wrong, in much the same way that injury to my person or property is a private wrong. It assumes that background and modifies it only so much as is necessary to protect the democratic function of public debate. The exclusion from First Amendment protection of knowing or reckless falsehoods can be explained as a policy of leaving the common law of defamation as little disturbed as possible: the person who knowingly lies or does not care whether he tells the truth or not has no purpose to contribute to the search for truth and understanding through public debate and so cannot claim the benefit of constitutional protection. And this is more or less just what the Court said in the *New York Times* case. But I am not convinced.

There is the whole range of expression—painting, music, poetry, sexually explicit expression—that receives full protection but cannot be fit into the Meiklejohn paradigm. Nor will it do to say that the First Amendment must be taken to pursue many goals and is not reducible to a single theory. True as it may be, this invocation of disparate rationales risks incoherence when their instantiations appear to conflict. It is not that the constitutional law of defamation adds to the protections that can be fit under the theory of protecting the freedom of the mind without being required by that theory. Rather it subtracts from the protections that that view entails. So we must try a little harder before throwing up our hands and admitting confusion.

Let us imagine a world in which there is no liability for defamation. I do not doubt that people may suffer considerable hurt and even financial loss as a result of false statements made about them. Harm comes about because people believe—or at least wonder about the truth of—these falsehoods, and the law of criminal libel seeks to prevent, civil defamation to deter and compensate for those harms. The victims of defamation use the law to achieve vindication. But if the harm could be countermanded at the level of belief, then criminal and civil libel would not be needed.[72] The notorious absence of criminal or civil recourse would itself go some way in that direction, because sophisticated audiences would be on their guard—as against counterfeit money—when they heard scurrilous accusations. (Given the difficulty of legal redress, *very* sophisticated audiences are already on their guard.) But as with counterfeit money, such a regime has costs: it impedes circulation to have to bite every nickel to make sure it isn't wooden, and it impedes discourse to have to investigate the truth of every claim.[73] The defamation system bites the nickel for us—at great cost and with uncertain results—but has two aspects that are in conflict with free speech principles: it works by punishing or preventing speech, and it makes the government the official judge of truth. One alternative would offer the person who feels he has been wronged the right to force the speaker to publish his victim's side of the story. This device has been correctly condemned as violating what might be called the passive freedom of the mind: the right not to have speech put into your mouth.[74] But the state could provide a forum for vindication in which injured persons could proclaim their innocence and voluntarily submit to an official evaluation of their claims. The speaker would be free to enter the forum and contest the complaint. Each side would bear its own costs. The speaker would, of course, run the risk of being officially called a liar, but that designation would have as much sting as the public cared to attach to it.[75]

I bring up this fanciful possibility because it suggests to me that the present contours of the law of libel might best be understood as a historical evolution, out of earlier means of personal vindication toward a legal regime that in many situations offers very little opportunity for vindication at all. Of course the law of defamation is to some extent anomalous and unsatisfactory. But I do not offer the principle of the freedom of the mind as an axiom from which the whole body of the law can be deduced. No existing regime—moved as it is by practical considerations, history, and powerful countercurrents—can be expected to conform to principle in this way. Rather the principle informs, criticizes, explains, and perhaps offers a trajectory for the law.

INSULTS, HARASSMENT, AND "FIGHTING WORDS"

Women's groups and minority groups have succeeded in procuring legislation, ordinances, and regulations to punish (or allow a lawsuit for) speech offensive to their members. The law has not yet come to rest in its response to this set of politically highly charged prohibitions of speech. As in the case of sexually explicit and defamatory speech, the point of departure is Justice Murphy's list of speech that he said was altogether beyond the protection of the First Amendment, which includes "the profane . . . and the insulting or 'fighting' words."

The Court has never subjected the category of "fighting words" to the kind of explicit analysis and limitation that it has bestowed on two other of Justice Murphy's categories: the obscene and the libelous. In all of the more recent cases in which the "fighting words" category was in play, the Court was willing to assume the viability of the "fighting words" exception for the sake of argument, but found some reason to decide the case in favor of the speaker without addressing what the category covers and whether it is compatible with the development of First Amendment law. A number of these cases involved language as offensive and provocative as could be imagined.[76]

The concept of "fighting words" belongs to an earlier stage in the development of free speech doctrine. The analysis which places the categories of the "lewd and obscene, the profane [and] the libelous" categorically outside the scope of the First Amendment has, as we have seen, been superseded by one that gives them varying degrees of protection. (As we shall see, the same is true of the previously excluded category of commercial speech.) The exclusion of fighting words is particularly anomalous as the harm it aims at is exactly that of imminent disturbance, as to which *Brandenburg* seemed to settle the law. The most likely explanation of the Court's reluctance to eliminate fighting words as a distinct category is that it simply particularizes—with a familiar and vivid phrase—a case of the general concept of speech which threatens and is intended to produce imminent (if often only small-scale) violence.[77] And where the supposed "fighting words" do not produce imminent violence, the Court finds one way or another to give them First Amendment protection. Two suggestions might find a distinct use for the category. First, in the words of John Ely, these words are "a quite unambiguous invitation to a brawl."[78] Perhaps the Court is unwilling to protect such an invitation without pressing the inquiry whether there is sufficient likelihood that the invitation will be taken up to satisfy *Brandenburg*. If so this is a small and perhaps practically useful departure.

More potentially fruitful—and disturbing—is the suggestion Justice Murphy himself makes in *Chaplinsky*: that these are words that "by their very utterance inflict injury." This second point has been taken up in the literature to argue for the exclusion from First Amendment protection of racial slurs and insults directed against a person based on—variously—that person's religion, gender, sexual orientation, or several other attributes or group memberships thought to be particularly likely to cause distress or a sense of exclusion.[79] The usual designation for this kind of insult is "hate speech." My general analysis, protecting speech that achieves its effect by persuasion or by affecting beliefs or attitudes, would seem to cover hate speech as well. To escape this conclusion several arguments are offered. It is said that such insults are not communications of ideas intended to persuade—after all they are often addressed to the object of the insult—but assaults intended to injure. Or it is said that such speech may be prohibited because it tends to silence or drown out its victim's own speech. These are not arguments at all but metaphors. Of course the words do not literally inflict wounds upon the body of their victim ("sticks and stones . . ."), nor do they make their victim's words actually inaudible. Insults may cause the victim to think less well of himself or convey to him that he is despised by the speaker, and maybe by others. This is painful. And such insults may lead to the sense that what he has to say will not be valued, perhaps that what he says has no value because it comes from him, and that therefore it is not worth speaking. In this sense he is silenced. But the mechanism of the harm is solely through the mind: what the victim is led to believe about himself and his standing in the community. That this is speech protected by freedom of expression is evident because the same or worse injurious effects may be inflicted by calm and quiet speech that purports to prove that intellectual and moral characteristics are correlated with race or gender or that, for instance, the Holocaust is a myth propagated by Jews to gain the advantages accruing to victim status. Indeed in nations in which the community is ceded a larger authority over the lives and thoughts of its members than do our constitutional traditions, the prohibition of hate speech extends to just such statements.[80] Quoting Justice Jackson again out of context, such a justification "either has no beginning or it has no end." Of course, if the insult indeed presents a clear and present danger of an imminent violent response, it may be prohibited for that reason. That is because of what the person to whom the insult is addressed may *do*—right away, before there is a chance to restrain him. The Supreme Court has never quite closed off this claimed exception to the *Brandenburg* rule, but neither has it affirmed it.

A difficult variant of the "hate speech" argument has been successfully invoked under the rubrics of racial or sexual harassment, which, while not prohibited as a crime, carries severe consequences. An employer who is himself guilty of such harassment, or whose employees or even customers engage in it, may be taken to have created a "hostile work environment" for the employee.[81] If the employee falls within one of a number of protected classes, such a conclusion may make the employer liable for damages or subject to an injunction. Not only are employees in the workplace protected from such harassment, but students on school and college campuses,[82] and customers at places of public accommodation like restaurants, hotels, and theaters are also protected.[83] The Supreme Court has never confronted a challenge to antiharassment regimes on First Amendment grounds, although it has turned aside challenges on other grounds[84]—from which some draw the conclusion that the Court has tacitly accepted that this category of speech is exempted from First Amendment protection.[85]

The speech that has been held to constitute such harassment does not always fit easily within the *Chaplinsky* categories. The most egregious instances may be taken as examples of "insulting or 'fighting' words."[86] But many are the kinds of things that are unpleasant, demeaning, and if continued over a long period of time can make somebody not want to go to work where they must be endured, but they do not come near being fighting words. For instance, the speech and symbols granted constitutional protection in *Brandenburg* or in the American Nazi Party march through Skokie, Illinois,[87] would in a workplace easily qualify as unlawful harassment. The standard example is a workplace with pinups of nude women in provocative poses.[88] If an employer kept the work space of only his women employees at uncomfortable temperatures, this would constitute illegal sex discrimination, but many women would find a shop floor decorated with such calendar art, especially if accompanied by sly remarks, as unpleasant a place to work as one which was too cold in winter or too hot in summer.

It does seem that harassment law has been the occasion for governments (usually through state antidiscrimination agencies, which tend to see their mission as enforcing norms of equality to the exclusion of all other considerations) to impose significant restraints on what in other contexts would be clear examples of speech protected by First Amendment principles.[89] At least in employment contexts, however, it might be said that harassing speech may be assimilated to commercial speech in the sense that what is said in the workplace is an aspect of the commercial relation between employer and employee.[90] This is most palpably the case where the speech would drive a reasonable person subject to it out of a job in which the law protects the employee from sexually or racially motivated discharge.[91] And the employee might argue that the workplace is different from other contexts in which speech is protected—streets or parks, where everyone has a right to be—or from blanket prohibitions of certain messages, no matter where or how they are conveyed. After all, you may not give a political speech in my living room against my will, for reasons having to do with my privacy and property interests and nothing to do with speech. The harasser in this setting is at least as much an intruder on my privacy as the beggar who corners me on a lonely subway platform.[92] A rule against this sort of harassment, if it is not directed at speech as such, much less at particular messages, protects against nonconsensual intrusions upon one's right to be in a public or other place in relative tranquility. Now the workplace is not quite your home, but neither is it Speakers' Corner in Hyde Park. For reasons that do not relate to speech at all the law might assign me a right to limit the intrusions I must endure at work to those that relate to my work—this could cover as well loud noises, bad air, or uncomfortable temperature. The same is true of a college dormitory and some parts of a campus. People should no more be free to pursue me into my dormitory than into my apartment-house lobby.[93]

COMMERCIAL SPEECH

"Commerce is intercourse," Chief Justice Marshall pronounced.[94] Whatever that means, it is quite clear that commerce involves communication and communication involves speech. Perhaps at their most primitive level, manufacture, mining, and agriculture might go on without communication, although if a man collaborates with even one other in these endeavors, there must be communication between them. Trade, commerce, cannot ever take place without communication. Even the most primitive barter requires a communicated understanding of the respective intentions of the trading partners. Come to agreements of any complexity at all and the point is obvious.

Until 1976 it was assumed without much discussion that commercial speech was categorically beyond the bounds of First Amendment analysis.[95] The exclusion saved a great deal of trouble. Application of the increasingly rigorous First Amendment standards would threaten to inhibit the corresponding increasing appetite for economic regulation. Advertising is speech. So are fraud and every kind of false advertising. The offer and the acceptance that together make a contract are speech. So are agreements (conspiracies) in restraint of trade. The various regimes controlling what is communicated in the marketplace—the antitrust laws, consumer protection laws, compelled disclosures in securities prospectuses, and food and drug laws—are at the very heart of economic regulation. As we have seen, the general free speech regime assumes that the contents of speech must be free of prohibition or compulsion unless government can come up with a compelling and narrowly drawn justification, which the Courts will scrutinize with a gimlet eye. From the latter part of the nineteenth century until the "turn" of the New Deal cases after the election of 1936, economic regulations had to justify themselves to courts in much these terms.[96] *Lochner v. New York*[97] is the notorious example of this earlier approach to economic regulation. Since the turn, of course, those subject to economic regulation may still demand that government justify its impositions, but that demand can easily be met by a mere showing that the regulation is a plausible means for accomplishing some not illegitimate end (rational basis review). By putting the regulation of commercial speech out of the range of First Amendment scrutiny, the Court sought to preclude the reemergence of *Lochner*-like scrutiny of economic regulation.

But the move was too crude and the specter could not forever be kept at bay. First, the boundaries of the category are quite unclear. Certainly it is untenable to mark the distinction by the speaker's motive to make money. Most publishers exist to make money. Some speakers and publishers make money from the sale of the communication itself. Others make money by persuading members of the audience to spend their money on buying goods or services or contributing to charitable causes. The subject of the *New York Times* case was a paid advertisement by civil rights organizations seeking contributions to fight segregation in the South. Often the two ways of making money are inextricably intertwined.[98] Airline magazines and specialized magazines for gardeners, audiophiles, auto enthusiasts, and the like are often nothing but compendia of materials touting certain products and these magazines may garner the bulk of their revenue from their advertisers.[99] If commercial speech "did no more than propose a commercial transaction,"[100] this could mark a usable boundary. Commercial speech might then be conceived as an example of the class of performative utterances that produce an effect rather than convey information apart from that effect, as when the groom says "I do," the officer issues an order to fire, or a merchant makes or accepts an offer to conclude a contract. But most of what today counts as commercial speech—that is, advertising for commercial goods and services—goes well beyond such bare-bones utterances. Advertising is intended to inform rational decision and to stimulate demand. Much speech is intended to accomplish this, sometimes for altruistic ends and sometimes for ends that are distinctly self-serving and even mercenary. By allowing the state to close off an avenue of information and persuasion, the government manipulates the minds of its citizens, and this is what the First Amendment forbids.

Second, it is not any longer tenable to argue that the First Amendment has no concern with such government regulation because commercial information and persuasion relate not to political issues but to matters of consumer choice. The confinement of First Amendment protection to distinctly political discourse—the Meiklejohnian thesis—is quite incompatible with the development of free speech doctrine, as the protection accorded sexually explicit speech shows. Commercial advertising is much more about informing and influencing choices than is the sexually explicit expression in books, pictures, films, and live performances[101] sheltered under the umbrella of the First Amendment. As Justice Harry Blackmun put it in a case striking down a state prohibition of accurate advertising of prescription drug prices, the case that put commercial speech squarely on the map of free speech: "Our pharmacist does not wish to editorialize on any subject, cultural, philosophical or political. . . . The 'idea' he wishes to convey is simply this: 'I will sell you the X prescription drug at the Y price.' . . . [T]he particular consumer's interest in the free flow of commercial information . . . may be as keen, if not keener by far, than his interest in the day's most urgent political debate."[102]

In a later case, the Court struck down a Rhode Island statute forbidding the advertising of liquor prices, and Justice Clarence Thomas characterized this and the drug price case as cases in which "the government's asserted interest is to keep legal users of a service or product ignorant in order to manipulate their choices in the marketplace."[103] It is only an irrational aversion to interfering in what is, though clearly a manipulation of the mind, also economic regulation—what I would call being spooked by the ghost of *Lochner*—that would deny these cases First Amendment protection. The haunting is quite obvious in that some of the legislation in which the *Lochner* principle was rejected involved similarly motivated economic regulation: the filled milk and artificially colored margarine prohibitions[104] allowed in post-*Lochner* days were clearly cases of legislation detrimental to competition and harmful to the public enacted at the behest of politically powe rful special interests. In the commercial speech cases too, small retail pharmacists and local liquor merchants used their political influence to reduce price competition so they might continue to gouge the public. This was a fight the Court had not wished to be drawn into. Somehow it was not quite politically correct to use the Constitution to protect the free market, but the Court in these price-advertising cases saw that there was a crucial difference between frank market regulation—as by mandating minimum retail prices for liquor or prescription drugs—and achieving similar economic effects by keeping consumers ignorant of facts bearing on their choices.[105]

The Court's movement in this regard is a triumph for the principle of the freedom of the mind. But the triumph is not total. The Court has not given commercial speech the full-strength protection that it accords to speech generally. Just how far it is willing to go in that direction is not clear. In *Central Hudson Gas v. Public Service Commission,* a case in which the Court struck down a state agency regulation that public utilities may not advertise in order to encourage the use of electricity, the Court laid down this test:

> At the outset, we must determine whether the expression is protected by the First Amendment. For commercial speech to come within that provision, it at least must concern lawful activity and not be misleading. Next, we ask whether the asserted governmental interest is substantial. If both inquiries yield positive answers, we must determine whether the regulation directly advances the governmental interest asserted, and whether it is not more extensive than is necessary to serve that interest.[106]

Some of the intricacies of this test are likely of passing significance,[107] but in the *Posadas*[108] case, for what proved to be an instant, the Court suggested that suppressing demand for a lawful product (casino gambling) might be such a substantial government interest

as to justify suppressing advertising for that product. Of course such
an interpretation could destroy the protection for commercial speech,
and the Court in the *44 Liquormart* case, in effect, abandoned
Posadas and applied a strongly speech-protective test to regulations
that do their work by keeping consumers ignorant of fairly presented,
true information.[109] What is significant is that in any event commercial speech only attains constitutional protection if it is true, not mis-
leading, and is not directed to promoting illegal activity. This is quite
different from the general case of speech prohibitions, where only a
compelling interest will justify suppressing speech, true or false. It is
more like the law of defamation, where truth is and must be an absolute defense, so that it is only false defamatory statements that must
justify themselves—although the path to justification is easier than
even for true commercial speech. This limitation of First Amendment
protection of commercial speech can best be understood as drawing
on the connection between commercial speech and the performative aspect of contractual utterances generally. A false representation
about the quality of goods sold is often treated as a contractual term,
a promise (warranty) that the goods are indeed as represented. There
is no First Amendment problem with holding the promisor to the
terms of his bargain, or else the law of contracts as a whole violates
the First Amendment. It is a short step from there to treat obtaining
value (or trying to) by such false assurances as a kind of theft (fraud).
And why, then, do we not punish false statements in political campaigns,[110] in newspaper stories and editorials, in history books, and in
scientific articles? Because none of these is assimilable (except by a
more or less strained metaphor) to theft by deception.[111]

Burdens—In General

In my analysis of First Amendment doctrine, the government has to
account for itself when an individual complains that something government has done burdens his ability to express himself or to access
the expression of others. In the preceding section I have considered
categories of cases all of which share the characteristic that the government's justification includes a reference to the substance of what a
person wants to say (show) or hear. In those cases it is fair to charac-
terize the government's purpose as mind control—the government
seeks to accomplish its goal by suppressing speech. But a great deal of
what the government does may burden speech, and the justification

for those burdens may have little or nothing to do with the suppression of expression or of ideas, but rather with the suppression of noise (as much from motorcycle exhaust as from sound trucks) or the taxing of businesses (any businesses) or the setting of minimum wages and maximum hours for employees (whether musicians, coal miners, or newspaper reporters). As my discussion of foundations in the first section sets out, applying a regime of any stringency to this category of government actions in general would lead either to paralysis or to a practically intolerable general supervisory role for the courts of all governmental business.

The regime I have been examining for cases in which the government does frankly justify its imposition as a suppression of certain expressions because they are dangerous or offensive *as expression* might be quite sufficient to assure the freedom of the mind if the government could be counted upon to offer such a justification whenever it was the real basis for its action. But that is expecting too much. Governments are not always sincere. Nor do they have an incentive to put forward justifications that will severely limit their discretion when they can plausibly offer other, more anodyne justifications. And, of course, it is not even clear what insincerity on the part of an institutional entity means. So, in addition to the doctrines that weigh the sufficiency of the government's justification when it frankly sets out to burden speech because of what it expresses, there has grown up a doctrinal structure for cases in which the government asserts a justification for burdening speech that does not refer to the danger or offensiveness of the ideas expressed. This structure, which has only been fully elaborated in the last decades or so, distinguishes between regulations that are or are not "content-neutral" and, among those that are content-neutral, those that are "viewpoint-neutral." Content-neutral regulations are easier to justify than those that are content-specific and viewpoint-specific regulations are harder to justify than those that are viewpoint-neutral, though content-specific. As I shall show, these categories are not always clear and their application in particular cases is quite controversial.[112] But what this branch of the doctrine seeks to accomplish accords with my general analysis: in these burden cases the law seeks to avoid engaging in a case-by-case balancing of the importance of the government's asserted purpose relative to the degree of burden imposed on free speech "values." Rather the doctrine seeks to impose a structure of categorical rules to smoke out (or construct) a speech-suppressing purpose when none has been asserted.

Laws punishing incitements to violence or obscene publications are drawn in terms of the content of what is expressed, and they are strictly limited by First Amendment doctrine. By contrast, general and nondiscriminatory taxes which make publishing more expensive,[113] or wages-and-hours laws which may increase publishers' labor costs,[114] are content-neutral and escape First Amendment restriction entirely. To these must be added the general regimes of property, tort, and contract law. The issue does occasionally come up and is taken seriously where the application of such general regimes focuses in tightly on speech activities. Such a case was *Cohen v. Cowles Media Co.*[115] A newspaper had promised anonymity to the source of a story but later published his name because it judged his identity was relevant to a full understanding of the story it was reporting. The Court ruled, without embarking on balancing or deploying any of the doctrines I consider below, that the First Amendment did not require that an exception be made to the general promissory regime simply because its application would in effect make the newspaper pay damages for speech that was clearly protected by the First Amendment. Publishers are regularly liable for damages when they breach contracts to publish certain material, or publish it in certain forms, even though the law cannot force a newspaper to publish a reply by a person who believes he has been unfairly criticized.[116] The difference in the defamation and right-to-reply cases is that the laws invoked there make specific reference to speech as the occasion for liability or regulation, so the government cannot plausibly deny that its justification for the law addressed the substance of the speech. (There is no problem in such cases about inferring the government's true purpose: it appears on the face of the law.)

The categories are not, however, entirely clear. A law prohibiting all speech on certain days, or by particular persons, or by a particular medium,[117] or in the extreme all expression altogether may be content-neutral but would still be subject to the strictest constitutional scrutiny. The term *content-neutral* is unfortunate in this regard, because it suggests that a prohibition or frank burden on a category of speech or all speech might be justifiable so long as it does not refer to a particular subject matter. But my examples must fall, even though they do not target a particular subject matter—religion, for or against, free sex—because on their face their purpose is to suppress expression. That they target too much expression hardly makes them better. The doctrine is further complicated because, as we shall see, some content-specific regulations may survive constitutional scrutiny—a government's limitation of the use of its facilities only for educational purposes, or only for lectures on mathematics—but may not survive scrutiny if the limitation is also viewpoint-specific, as when lectures espousing general relativity are allowed, but those questioning it are not.[118] But the line between content-specificity and viewpoint-specificity is not always clear. Depending on how a subject matter is identified, a limitation may be characterized as simply excluding discussion of that subject matter or as silencing a particular viewpoint. *Rust v. Sullivan* was such a case. The Court analyzed a restriction on providing advice regarding abortions in a government-funded prenatal care program as permissibly limiting speech to the particular purpose of the program and not as limiting speech in terms of a viewpoint on the subject of abortion. Or in *Police Department v. Mosley*[119] the Court struck down as "content control" an ordinance forbidding picketing within 150 feet of a school, excepting peaceful picketing of a school involved in a labor dispute. Since only one side in such a dispute is likely to engage in picketing, the ordinance may just as well have been characterized as viewpoint-specific.

In general, the category of content-neutrality/specificity comes into play when government claims that it has only sideswiped speech, not deliberately run over it—that is, when it seeks to justify some burden it imposes on speech in terms that make no reference to the substance of the expression (in contrast to regulations of incitements to violence, obscenity, defamation, or commercial speech). In such cases content-specificity is a powerful indication that the claim is a pretext, that government really had speech in its sights after all, and so must justify the regulation as a suppression of speech. This claim must be tested particularly in two kinds of cases: where conduct and speech are closely related and the government purports to regulate only the conduct, and where government claims the authority to regulate only the time, place, and manner of speech. I consider those two kinds of cases in the two sections below. Viewpoint-specificity only becomes an issue in situations—as in government-funded programs—in which government's authority to limit the subjects of speech, and thus to regulate speech as such, to some extent is conceded. Total prohibitions, irrespective of content (and therefore, of course, of viewpoint), on their face suppress speech and therefore must find their justification accordingly.

THOUGHT AND ACTION

Government makes it a crime to burn the American flag.[120] Is that a "law abridging the freedom of speech"? It will not do to answer no, it is a law abridging the freedom to burn the American flag. Recall the argumentative structure I have proposed for deciding whether the government's purpose or justification is one of controlling the mind—blocking the uttering or receiving of expression: the person who claims that his ability to speak or listen has been abridged forces the government to explain itself, and if that explanation refers to the suppression of a message, the First Amendment has been violated. Of course, to start the process this person must come up with a plausible claim that what government has done somehow does inhibit his freedom of speech, and not just in the way that the background law of contract, torts, property, taxes, and so on may on some particular occasion inhibit him.

In the flag case, the speaker can indeed come up with such a plausible claim: "I burn the flag as a way of expressing my disgust with what the flag stands for. To the extent that the flag is more than an indeterminate piece of material—to the extent that it is a *flag*—it is, after all, itself a message. I use that message to send my message." The government must now come forward with a justification for this restriction on liberty that does not depend on blocking the message that the demonstrator wishes to send. For the government to respond that it is not interested in silencing the message of disgust with its policies, but only in prohibiting this particular way of sending the message, simply invites the further question why it chooses to block what is now conceded to be a way of conveying a thought—just as much as the flag itself is a way of conveying a whole set of thoughts. At this crux the government must either concede that it chooses to block this medium of delivering a message because of the color the medium adds to the message and lose its case, or it must come up with a reason that is unrelated to the message.[121] Well, what might such a reason be? The dangers of fire, of smoke inhalation, atmospheric pollution? All of these are perfectly acceptable, content-neutral purposes. They are just not believable as the grounds for this law. If that were the point of the law, why does it forbid burning flags and not newspapers, charcoal, or autumn leaves? And why is the prohibition framed in terms of desecration and disrespect?[122] To refuse to be taken in by such obvious pretexts is not to psychologize about the subjective intentions of lawmakers, but rather to seek the intent or purpose of legislation by what can be inferred from its text and context on the assumption that there is some rationale that may be discovered. This is to do nothing other than engage in the familiar interpretive exercise necessary to discern the intent of any statute so as to apply it appropriately. And if that exercise comes back to a purpose that would suppress speech, then the law must fail.

The canonical formula for this exercise is taken from *United States v. O'Brien,* the 1968 case in which the Court (quite unconvincingly) found a proper, content-neutral purpose in a law forbidding the destruction of Selective Service registration certificates (draft cards):

> We cannot accept the view that an apparently limitless variety of conduct can be labeled "speech" whenever the person engaging in the conduct intends thereby to express an idea. . . . This Court has held that when "speech" and "nonspeech" elements are combined in the same course of conduct, a sufficiently important governmental interest in regulating the nonspeech element can justify incidental limitations on First Amendment freedoms. . . . [A] government regulation is sufficiently justified if it is within the constitutional power of the Government; if it furthers an important or substantial governmental interest; if the governmental interest is unrelated to the suppression of free expression; and if the incidental restriction on alleged First Amendment freedoms is no greater than is essential to the furtherance of that interest.[123]

This is the doctrine. The most important term in it is the requirement that the governmental interest invoked to justify the prohibition be "unrelated to the suppression of free expression." Any regulation that fails this condition cannot claim whatever comfort *O'Brien* might otherwise offer. Fail that condition and the regulation is exposed to the full rigor of the First Amendment.

The *O'Brien* test appears, however, to go further in protecting speech than my analysis. It also requires that government regulation unrelated to an interest in suppressing speech is allowed to burden (place "incidental restrictions on") speech only if it is justified by an interest that is "substantial," and that the burden be "no greater than is essential to the furtherance of that interest." Recall the *Cowles* case, which was an instance of the application to speech activities of the general regimes of tort or contract law; the same analysis would obtain in the application to speech activities of the background regimes of property, tax, labor, or other regulatory laws. In none of these does the Court apply the *O'Brien* analysis. A striking example was *Arcara v. Cloud Books, Inc.*[124] An "adult" bookstore used for encounters between prostitutes and their customers was closed down, as would be a hotel, bar, or any other commercial establishment which had in effect become a place of prostitution. The Court noted the "crucial distinction between the circumstances presented in *O'Brien* and the circumstances of this case: unlike the symbolic draft card burning in *O'Brien,* the sexual activity carried on in this case manifests absolutely no element of protected expression." The regulation was neutral, indifferent to speech, and that is the end of the question. (Of course the regulation must satisfy the rational basis test, but any restriction of any liberty must do that. It is a test that it is almost impossible to fail.) And it is not at all clear that the *O'Brien* test, if it were applied, would always be satisfied in these cases. Just how "substantial" is the interest, and if substantial, is it clear that the restriction is no "greater than essential" to its furtherance? The word "essential" looks quite constraining, and suggests an intrusive role for the Court in reviewing an indefinite and far broader range of government action than actual practice supports.

The mystery lifts to a degree if we pay close attention to the introductory terms of the statement of the *O'Brien* rule. It applies when "the person engaging in the conduct intends thereby to express an idea [, . . . and] 'speech' and 'nonspeech' elements are combined in the same course of conduct . . . ," and the regulation, rather than a very general one like the law of tort or contract, focuses more narrowly on the very conduct that is used to carry the message. The focus is on what is called in the jargon of constitutional doctrine "symbolic speech," and the very conduct subject to regulation is the embodiment of the communication. So O'Brien, like the flag burners, claimed that his act *was* his message. Consider two other striking examples: *Barnes v. Glen Theatre, Inc.*[125] and *Clark v. Community for Creative Non-Violence.*[126] The first involved the application of a municipal ban on public nudity to nude dancing performances in an "adult" theater; the second, the application of a regulation against sleeping in certain parks in central Washington, D.C., to an encampment in Lafayette

Park erected to protest government policies on homelessness. In both cases the regulations were subjected to the *O'Brien* test: in the first because the nudity added an undoubted extra charge to the erotic message the dance expressed; in the second, because the sleeping was the chosen method of dramatizing the political message, much like burning a flag.

In both cases the regulations survived the test because, though they clearly restricted the medium with which the message was inextricably bound up, the government could (convincingly) offer a justification that had nothing to do with suppressing either the message or the particular medium *as* the chosen way for embodying the message. The Park Service had a long-standing and readily accepted purpose to keep the small, meticulously maintained, and heavily visited parks in the center of Washington from being used as campgrounds, with the attendant clutter and sanitary problems. And the state in *Barnes* had a general statute against public nudity—for whatever reason and in whatever public place. The second leg of *O'Brien* was also met in each case by the government. The Park Service allowed the protesters to erect temporary tents to make their point; they just could not stay in them overnight. And the dance was allowed so long as the dancers wore "pasties and G-strings." Thus the regulations were narrowly tailored so that "the incidental restriction on alleged First Amendment freedoms [was] no greater than is essential to the furtherance of [the asserted] interest."

There is still something left over. In *Minneapolis Star & Tribune Co. v. Minnesota Commissioner of Revenue*,[127] Minnesota imposed a tax based on the cost of ink and paper used in the production of publications, exempting the first $100,000 consumed by a publication in any year. Here was a law that did not prohibit or regulate any message or speech, but it was directed at, and just at, one of the principal ways that speakers reach their audiences. The *O'Brien* analysis is quite inapposite to what was wrong with this tax, and the Court struck it down without invoking it. Rather it emphasized its discriminatory nature.

> [T]he States and the Federal Government can subject newspapers to generally applicable economic regulations without creating constitutional problems. . . . [and a]ny tax that the press must pay, of course, imposes some "burden." . . . The cases approving such economic regulation, however, [have] emphasized the general applicability of the challenged regulation to all businesses. . . . When a State so singles out the press, the

political constraints that prevent a legislature from imposing crippling taxes of general applicability are weakened, and the threat of burdensome taxes becomes acute. That threat can operate as effectively as a censor to check critical comment by the press, thus undercutting the basic assumption of our political system that the press will often serve as an important restraint on government. . . . Further, differential treatment, unless justified by some special characteristic of the press, suggests that the goal of the regulation is not unrelated to suppression of expression, and such a goal is presumptively unconstitutional.[128]

But this emphasis on discrimination shares an underlying rationale with my general analysis. Taxes and regulations discriminate—or to use a less pejorative term, make distinctions—all the time. Cigarettes are heavily taxed; milk is not. In some states sales of clothing under a certain dollar amount are exempt from sales tax. Marijuana use is prohibited; alcohol and tobacco use is not. But in the case of First Amendment freedoms the burden must be justified, and the discriminatory nature of the burden undermines a justification that in the case of a tax or other law of general applicability would be quite sufficient. The labor laws protect worker rights to unionize, but if they applied only to book publishers that explanation would lack plausibility. So emphasis on the difference between discriminatory laws and laws of general applicability smokes out what is—or may be taken to be, absent some very good explanation—the forbidden purpose to regulate or burden speech because it is speech.

TIME, PLACE, AND MANNER RESTRICTIONS

It is sometimes said today that government has a general authority to impose reasonable regulations on the time, place, and manner of speech, although not on its content. It has never been doubted that, as to my own property, the government may insist that I obey fire ordinances that limit the number of people who may be allowed to assemble there—for speech or prayer or any other purpose. And the government may protect my neighbors from excessive noise my guests may make at odd hours of the day or night.[129] If I own a bookstore, the state may require that I comply with zoning laws regarding commercial uses of property and with any generally applicable regulations of opening hours for commercial establishments. In much the same way the government has authority over the holding of protest marches and assemblies in city streets and parks.

When originally formulated, the time, place, and manner doctrine was used to describe the government's authority to limit speech in public places. Here is a classic statement of the doctrine:

> The authority of a municipality to impose regulations in order to assure the safety and convenience of the people in the use of public highways has never been regarded as inconsistent with civil liberties but rather as one of the means of safeguarding the good order upon which they ultimately depend. The control of travel on the streets of cities is the most familiar illustration of this recognition of social need. Where a restriction of the use of highways in that relation is designed to promote the public convenience in the interest of all, it cannot be disregarded by the attempted exercise of some civil right which in other circumstances would be entitled to protection. One would not be justified in ignoring the familiar red traffic light because he thought it his religious duty to disobey the municipal command or sought by that means to direct public attention to an announcement of his opinions. As regulation of the use of the streets for parades and processions is a traditional exercise of control by local government, the question in a particular case is whether that control is exerted so as not to deny or unwarrantedly abridge the right of assembly and the opportunities for the communication of thought and the discussion of public questions immemorially associated with resort to public places.
>
> . . . If a municipality has authority to control the use of its public streets for parades or processions, as it undoubtedly has, it cannot be denied authority to give consideration, without unfair discrimination, to time, place, and manner in relation to the other proper uses of the streets.[130]

The law relating to the government's right to regulate speech on its own property has grown up separately from the doctrine recognizing the applicability of general background law to regulate speech generally. I can call the police to throw you out of my home because I don't like what you are saying.[131] But a city cannot give that same reason for chasing you off your soap box in a public park. It is far less clear, however, that it may not give that reason for chasing you out of the employee's cafeteria in a city office building or out of your classroom and off your job in a public high school.[132] I start with the distinctive regime that assigns to public authorities the control of the exercise of First Amendment rights in public places.

I have already, in my discussion of government speech in the first section, explained that government may, consistent with the principle of freedom of the mind, choose to address messages to its citizens. In framing and delivering those messages it must be able not only to control its chosen (willing, not conscripted) messengers but also the context—that is, the place—of their delivery. And it may also choose not to associate itself with certain messages and therefore, just like a private person,[133] may deny others its platform for the delivery of unwanted messages. This becomes complicated because, as a matter of background law (with exceptions irrelevant here),[134] it is government that holds title to streets, parks, and public buildings.

Constitutional doctrine long ago rejected[135] the conclusion that Holmes, when a state court judge, drew from the intersection of the regime giving a property owner the right to control activities (including speech and assembly) on his property and the assignment to government of the property right over public places: "For the Legislature absolutely or conditionally to forbid public speaking in a highway or public park is no more an infringement of the rights of a member of the public than for the owner of a private house to forbid it in his house."[136] Constitutional doctrine rejected this analysis, but not for the reason that public property is just that: *public* property, so that regulation of that property must answer to First Amendment norms just like any other government regulation. That would be an argument that proves too much, subjecting government's capacity to shape and deliver messages to pervasive court supervision. But so does Holmes's analysis prove too much. I may be free by virtue of the First Amendment to say whatever I want to whomever I want, but only if I can find my intended audience at home, or on the telephone, or in a book or newspaper they buy and read, or in a broadcast to which they choose to listen. But my message may be general, my audience may be strangers, and no bookshelf, newsstand, or air time may be available to me. Even then constitutional doctrine will not allow me to go unheard:

> Wherever the title of streets and parks may rest, they have immemorially been held in trust for the use of the public and, time out of mind, have been used for purposes of assembly, communicating thoughts between citizens, and discussing public questions. Such use of the streets and public places has, from ancient times, been part of the privileges, immunities, rights, and liberties of citizens.[137]

Thus is created an irreducible space, the "public forum," in which citizens may try to find an audience, buttonhole their fellows, speak and perhaps be heard—what Harry Kalven has called a First Amendment easement.[138] The streets, after all, are the place where (at least until very recently, with the advent of computers and the Internet) almost everyone had to venture from time to time in pursuit of business, food and drink, company, or amusement. They were the indispensable place of common resort, and this doctrine reserved them as a place of individual liberty rather than of pervasive public regulation.[139] (This liberty almost certainly extends not just to speech but to movement as well,[140] but that is not my subject in this chapter.) It is to regulation of this "public forum" that the phrase "time, place, and manner" properly applies. Starting with the premise of liberty, it recognizes a need to adjust its exercise to prevent speakers from stepping on each other's toes (as when two groups seek to assemble and march along the same route), from preempting the other public function of streets as places of communication in the sense of movement, and finally from not intruding on the rights of those who are not in the streets but in the buildings that line them. In this spirit we have regulations requiring parade permits,[141] limiting the volume of sound equipment,[142] or allowing distributors of literature to ring doorbells unless the "householder . . . has appropriately indicated that he is unwilling to be disturbed."[143]

It is these regulations of the public forum that the classic "time, place, and manner" doctrine constrains. Here is the canonical statement of that doctrine:

> In such places, the government's ability to permissibly restrict expressive conduct is very limited: the government may enforce reasonable time, place, and manner regulations as long as the restrictions are [1] content-neutral, are [2] narrowly tailored [3] to serve a significant government interest, and [4] leave open ample alternative channels of communication.[144]

The first three elements of the test we have already encountered in the context of commercial speech. They give assurance that the justification (the "significant government interest") is not a pretext for the suppression of speech.[145] The key I have offered to resolving the conflict between the burdens government inevitably imposes on speech as it goes about its regular and necessary business and the imperative that government not seek to regulate the minds of its citizens has been to force government to justify those burdens by some purpose other than the desire to suppress speech. Doctrine forces those justifications and makes it more or less easy for government to justify itself. Content-neutrality is less a disciplining device than the simple expression of the principle itself:[146] a justification that refers to the content of the speech is a justification in terms of regulating messages as such, and this is just what the principle forbids.

> The central problem with Chicago's ordinance is that it describes permissible picketing in terms of its subject matter. . . . [T]he First Amendment means that government has no power to restrict expression because of its message, . . . or its content. . . . The essence of . . . forbidden censorship is content control.[147]

Narrow tailoring (the second prong of the test) imposes additional discipline. It is not sufficient that government has offered a proper and "substantial" purpose: prevention of littering[148] or preservation of quiet in residential areas or near schools, for example. Doctrine insists that the regulation be so carefully drawn that if at all possible it does not sideswipe speech on its way to its proper destination, and if it must, that it do as little damage as possible. Narrow tailoring goes further than content-neutrality, preferring the individual interest in speech over a conflicting but content-neutral public purpose: even if burdening speech is necessary to government's accomplishing a proper end, it must find some way to leave generous scope for the individual interest in speech.

These prongs of the test may be understood in two ways: as devices to smoke out public claims that are pretexts for the forbidden purpose of regulating speech,[149] or as the institution of an affirmative obligation to make public provisions for furthering the private interest in speech. The first explanation makes the doctrine a hedge around what is still essentially a negative right—as certain rabbinical rules are said to be a "hedge around the Torah." The second begins to transform it into a positive right, like a right to a subsidy for speech. Narrow tailoring may plausibly be construed in line with the former conception. The last prong, requiring government to leave open "ample alternative channels of communication," hardly so. Although the *O'Brien* test and the time-place-and-manner test are virtually identical in their first three prongs (and similar to the test for commercial speech as well), the last is articulated only as part of the public forum doctrine,[150] but that may be because in the *O'Brien* context there will almost always be alternative ways of expressing the same message. The public forum, I have explained, is the place where an individual, even if she has no other means of reaching an audience, has a right to look for and is likely to find one. The requirement that there be "ample alternative channels" is essential to maintaining the speech easement in the public forum. An equivalent general provision outside of the context of public forum doctrine would work a significant change in the conception of free speech.[151] It would place a general obligation on government to offer individuals opportunities to listen, to speak, and maybe even to be heard.[152]

Such an obligation may seem generous to speech rights, but would have troubling implications. For such affirmative provisions cannot be made up to the full amount of each individual's claim to them. There must be a budget, and that entails not only an overall limit but a method for allocating public resources among individual claimants. Constitutional doctrine can sensibly impose content-neutrality on such allocations within very discrete and limited contexts. The public forum is one such context. But if free speech generally is to rely on government provision, if government must assume a general obligation to underwrite the speech rights of its citizens, then in short order what government—quite reasonably—decides is good and bad, worthy and unworthy speech will determine that allocation. For constitutional doctrine to dictate otherwise would defeat government's obligation to represent the majority of citizens whose votes put that government in office. The state-action limitation of the free speech right (that it is a right against the government) assumes that not only the general background law but the availability of disposable income in the society will assure most individuals (singly or in groups)[153] some scope for the exercise of that right, if only government does not get in their way. The generalization of the public forum—the baseline guarantee that speech will be heard—to all contexts would disturb that assumption and turn the First Amendment into a positive rather than a negative right. In a sense, the content-neutrality of general background law and economic holdings may be conceptualized as a sort of content-neutral pervasive public forum.

These considerations also raise the stakes in deciding just what counts as a public forum. It may seem mindless to leave the designation to tradition: "streets and parks . . . use[d] . . . time out of mind . . . for purposes of assembly, communicating thoughts between citizens, and discussing public questions."[154] There is attraction to the argument that a large metropolitan airport is today's equivalent of the traditional public forum, having "broad, public thoroughfares full of people and lined with stores and other commercial activities,"[155] so that denying its designation as a public forum "has no warrant in a Constitution whose values are not to be left behind in the city streets that are no longer the only focus of our community life."[156] The danger in such a functional analysis is that it moves toward—without quite embracing—the quite different doctrine that government has an affirmative obligation to provide some public space for free communication and that that space must be one in which the effort to attract an audience is likely to be effective. It cannot be denied that with changing circumstances the significance the doctrine gives to streets and parks may seem quite archaic. If people use the streets only to move from destination to destination in enclosed vehicles, so that the chance of their encountering each other there face-to-face are rare and aberrant, the purpose I have identified for the doctrine will have withered away. Some substitute for it must be found. Perhaps there always will be such places; if not streets then airports, shopping malls, or bus and train terminals. (I discuss the Internet in the next section.)

On the views I have quoted it is function and circumstance that designate these new venues as public fora. The elaboration of public forum doctrine has proposed complicated nuances to account for the difficulties in this doctrine. At the furthest remove from the public forum is, say, the back office of a social benefits office where clerks file claims and calculate benefits, or a judge's office where he does his studying and writing. Some of the cases speak of the government's acting in a proprietary capacity in those places,[157] but that does not offer the correct distinction, since what goes on there is certainly the public's business. It is just that that business could not get done if such places were also places of open public resort. The uneasy and no doubt temporary resting place on which doctrine has settled puts it this way:

> [In addition to parks and streets, the traditional public fora], a second category consists of public property which the State has opened for use by the public as a place for expressive activity. The Constitution forbids a State to enforce certain exclusions from a forum generally open to the public even if it was not required to create the forum in the first place. Although a State is not required to retain indefinitely the open character

of the facility, as long as it does so it is bound by the same standards as apply in a traditional public forum. Reasonable time, place, and manner regulations are permissible, and a content-based prohibition must be narrowly drawn to effectuate a compelling state interest.

Public property which is not by tradition or designation a forum for public communication is governed by different standards. We have recognized that the First Amendment does not guarantee access to property simply because it is owned or controlled by the government. In addition to time, place, and manner regulations, the State may reserve the forum for its intended purposes, communicative or otherwise, as long as the regulation on speech is reasonable and not an effort to suppress expression merely because public officials oppose the speaker's view. As we have stated on several occasions, the State, no less than a private owner of property, has power to preserve the property under its control for the use to which it is lawfully dedicated.[158]

This statement is now canonical. Unfortunately, in respect to the second and third categories it is circular: a place takes on the character of a public forum if it is so designated—that is, so long as the government opens it up to the full range of expressive activities. Where it has not done so, government retains discretion akin to that of any proprietor. In that third category, however, the government's proprietary interests may include inviting some members of the public to speak on designated topics. For instance, a school auditorium may be opened for a lecture series on the dangers of alcohol or tobacco, or for a festival devoted to the plays of Shakespeare.[159] Has the government designated the auditorium as a public forum and then unconstitutionally limited the speech there by its content? Or does the limitation require the conclusion that government has not made that designation?

The muddle is deepened by cases that propose yet another category, that of the limited public forum,[160] in which government is taken to have opened up its property for expressive activities, but only on a particular subject. In those cases it is said that while government may impose regulations that do refer to content (that is, the speakers must stick to the subject), it must not limit what the speaker says about the subject—in the jargon of this sub-sub doctrine, the regulations may be content-specific but must be viewpoint-neutral.[161] This just subdivides without solving the difficulty. Government cannot sensibly be wholly deprived of the authority in some settings to specify not only the subject of speech but its point of view as well—indeed it must be able to write the very script its chosen spokesman recites.[162] Otherwise the axiom that the government must be recognized as one speaker among many would be violated and the government would not be able to perform its representative functions. Doctrine has a way to go before it sorts out the conflicting premises as they intersect in these cases.

Finally, there is a reverse side to this doctrine: may government seek to accomplish its purposes by declining to communicate, keeping secret, what it knows—even when that information is crucial to the lives and decisions of its citizens? Does the freedom of the mind encompass a right to know? First Amendment doctrine protects only against state action, but does it protect against state inaction? Does the First Amendment ever imply a right to find out what others do not want to tell you? What the government does not want to tell you? Certainly the political, Meiklejohnian conception of the First Amendment might readily be thought to imply a right to know, at least against the government, and several constitutions express such a right[163]—as does much federal and state legislation.[164] But the embodiment of that affirmative right in the First Amendment carries the difficulty that attends all positive rights: the need to strike a balance which must be carefully and continuously administered by the courts. The more categorical regime of First Amendment negative rights will not do to define when government and government officials may keep their secrets or even just maintain their privacy. Must the President live his life on continuous CSPAN? Must the conferences of the justices, or their conversations with their law clerks, be recorded and published?[165] Yet the denial of access to the workings of government may make the freedom to criticize government quite useless. The Court has trod very lightly here, leaving it to legislation to define the limits of government's obligations of disclosure. The closest the Court has come to connect such a right to know with the First Amendment was in *Richmond Newspapers, Inc. v. Virginia, Inc.,*[166] where it announced a constitutional right of public access to criminal trials in a case in which both the prosecution and the defense would have preferred a closed trial. And even then the Court did not squarely locate this right in the First Amendment and thus pointedly avoided announcing a generalized "right to know" component to the First Amendment. Rather, reviewing the history of public trials in England and the United States, the Court discerned an "unarticulated" right "not explicitly defined" but "implicit in enumerated guarantees," concluding that the right "to attend criminal trials is implicit in the guarantees of the First Amendment; without [that right], which people have exercised for centuries, important aspects of freedom of speech and of the press could be eviscerated." But it has never generalized this right beyond the context of criminal trials and related proceedings.

Speech and New Technologies

First Amendment doctrine has a certain quaintness to it. Its frequent images are of pamphleteers like John Peter Zenger, street-corner orators, face-to-face encounters. If the doctrine does not retain its explanatory power or even its plausibility in modern economic circumstances, or when applied to contemporary technological contexts, such as broadcasting or the Internet, then this undermines my argument for that doctrine, and for the principle I claim that doctrine embodies. The greatest pressure is applied to the concepts of the public forum and of state action.

It was not until 1969, in *Red Lion Broadcasting Co. v. FCC*,[167] that a unanimous Supreme Court considered and approved the frank content regulation imposed by the Federal Communications Commission under the regulatory authority granted it by the Communications Act of 1934. In allocating licenses to use the airwaves, the commission was to consider "public convenience and necessity"—the standard formula used in delegating authority to allocate franchises and regulate the rates and practices of railroads, urban transportation companies, public utilities, and the like. The commission from the start took that phrase as a mandate to consider what kinds of programming applicants for broadcast licenses would offer, to extract commitments on that score, and (in the regulation at issue in the *Red Lion* case) to impose a right to reply far more intrusive than that rejected in the newspaper context in *Tornillo*.[168] The Court reasoned to its conclusion from two premises: that there must be some kind of broadcasting regulation, if only to prevent interference of broadcasters with each other's signals; and that the number of broadcast channels was limited. Along the way it noted that the regulations did not contradict but served the First Amendment value of "protecting and furthering communication" by preventing the "monopolization" of the "marketplace for ideas" by the necessarily restricted number of licensees. Further invoking the language used to justify economic regulation of monopolies, utilities, common carriers, professions, and even hotels and restaurants, the Court spoke of the broadcast licensee as having "fiduciary obligations" to "share" his facilities and present the views of the "community" which he serves. The Court continued this line of reasoning in its approval of a 1971 act of Congress obliging broadcasters to give or sell "reasonable amounts of time" to candidates for federal office.[169]

The casual deployment of these analogies and metaphors threatens to unravel the doctrinal framework I have offered and with it the conception of free speech rights that underlies it. First, the public utility, monopoly, and antitrust-regulatory analogies cannot be confined to the broadcasting media as they existed in the early seventies. The newspaper market in most large cities is less open to competition than the broadcasting market. In many major markets there may be only one or at most two or three major daily newspapers, with very high barriers to entry by new competitors. Even in 1969 the broadcast market was quite rich by comparison: many AM and FM radio stations, and a large number of UHF and VHF television stations. Yet only academic commentators have suggested that the *Red Lion* analysis be extended to the print media.[170] The Court's analysis does suggest a distinction between the two markets, which has some resonance in antitrust law: the concentration in the print media is the result only of economic factors, while in broadcasting the government allocates a naturally, not economically, scarce resource. This might be thought to justify the different First Amendment treatment just because of the government's inevitable role in managing broadcast spectrum scarcity. That justification might invoke two familiar First Amendment doctrines: state action and the public forum. Neither will do the job without serious stretching. It is standard doctrine that status as a franchised, regulated monopoly or a licensed supplier of a controlled good or service does not make the franchisee or licensee a state actor such that the state is responsible for its actions or that constitutional obligations are imposed upon it.[171] If broadcast licensees were indeed state actors, this would impose far more onerous constitutional restrictions than were contemplated in *Red Lion*. For instance, religious broadcasting would be barred by the Establishment Clause. As state actors, broadcasters would have to be classified either as government speakers—like the Voice of America or the Armed Forces Network—or as providers of some sort of public forum. But were broadcasters in charge of a public forum (by designation—the second of the two categories set out above), neither they nor the government would be constitutionally allowed to engage in just the kind of content regulation that is the essence of what broadcasters refer to as their editorial judgment. Editorial judgment is simply a name for a speaker's First Amendment right to say what he wishes and not to say what he does not wish. This suggests still a third analogy, which becomes more plausible in the case of cable and Internet providers: that these entities are not speakers at all but more like common carriers—say, the telephone company—which must carry any lawful message that comes along provided its sender pays the posted tariff.[172]

The invocation of these analogies is a sign of a doctrine in trouble. The trouble technology created, technology might also alleviate, and the advent of cable, satellite, and Internet technology offer the occasion to reconsider *Red Lion*. These media undermine the scarcity/monopoly rationale because they compete directly with broadcast signals, and also because they offer hundreds of additional channels. The Supreme Court first acknowledged[173] and then confronted the inappositeness of the *Red Lion* analysis to cable in the *Turner Broadcasting* cases[174] and *Denver Area Educational Telecommunications Consortium, Inc. v. FCC*.[175] In the *Turner Broadcasting* cases the Court considered the "must-carry" provisions of federal law, requiring cable operators to include, in the large array of channels they offer their subscribers, channels dedicated to stations that transmit their signal over the air. At the time 60 percent of American homes had cable service. The stated rationale for the regulation was that without such a requirement the cable operators might decide not to offer some of these stations—most notably the major network affiliates and public television stations; these stations would not be able to survive on only the broadcast audience; as a result the homes without cable would be deprived of valuable programming. The Court bravely marched up the hill, proclaiming that whatever the initial validity of *Red Lion*, it had no applicability to a medium with a practically limitless number of channels, so that cable regulation must be measured by the full rigors of First Amendment doctrine. In particular the Court acknowledged that the First Amendment distinction between content-based and content-neutral laws must apply, specifically adverting to *Miami Herald v. Tornillo*.[176] The Court then marched down the hill again: the cable operator has a "chokehold monopoly" over what channels enter the viewer's home. This fact was said to render the must-carry rules content-neutral, designed as they were—so the Court said—not to favor any particular content, but rather to overcome the cable operators' "bottleneck, or gatekeeper, control" over access of the broadcast stations to the cable customers. The regulation, on the Court's own analysis, is not content-neutral as that term has been used in the doctrine. The Court and the government spoke about the importance of keeping the local broadcasters from going out of business because of the services—particularly programs of local community interest and the programming of public television—that they offered. This may or may not be a viewpoint-neutral consideration. It certainly is not content-neutral.

The Court's analysis is troubled for two reasons. First, cable operators essentially run two businesses: they deliver programming from many originators—CSPAN, MTV, the Home Shopping Channel, the Discovery Channel, the Weather Channel, and so on—and they themselves originate some of this programming. Indeed, many cable operators have been buying or consolidating with programmers. This dual function does not make the operators more susceptible to control. The *Reader's Digest* conveys the work of other publishers. A bookstore rarely publishes any of the books it sells. Yet the First Amendment protects to the hilt their decisions about what to publish, what to sell—sometimes under the rubric of editorial discretion. The Court purported to honor this same editorial discretion—to offer some but not other channels—in the *Turner Broadcasting* cases, but then qualified it in a way that the standard use of that term would not support.

Second, although the number of channels cable may bring into a home is very large indeed and in this it resembles a bookseller, the number of cable operators that may serve a particular viewer is severely restricted. The operators must use the public streets to lay or string their cables, just like the telephone company. If the operators could direct their signals to a receiver without using the public streets (as in satellite broadcasting) and without using a part of the limited electromagnetic spectrum, then the regulatory claim would have far less purchase—but then the operators would not be *cable* operators.[177] Also the provision of cable service, if not exactly a natural monopoly, is close to it: there are physical limits to how many cable companies the streets of a community can support without introducing unbearable clutter and congestion.[178]

There is no obvious reason in doctrine or principle why government at whatever level should have to treat the laying or stringing of cables under or over the streets as an instance of speech in the public forum.[179] True, the cables carry speech, but cables do not use the streets in the way that a pamphleteer, solicitor, or street-corner orator does. Cable is a permanent physical occupation of the street that is incompatible with similar occupation by more than one or two other rivals. I do not see why the law did not ignore the fact that cable operators are also message originators, and treat the cabling part of the operation as a distinct enterprise, a regulatable public utility like the telephone company. Government could require cable operators to make their wires available for a fee to competing message suppliers in much the same way that, under deregulation of local telephone service, the owners of telephone wires and switching facilities are required to make those facilities available to competing suppliers of telephone services. The consumer would pay one fee to the cable company for the connection and another to the content providers, who would pay the cabler for the use of its cables. Government might choose to assure that those who wanted to transmit over the system could do so without discrimination, just as in the case of telephones— except the fee would necessarily be much higher, and the cable speakers would recoup that fee either from advertisers or from subscribers.

Instead of this straightforward analysis, the Court has muddied the waters sufficiently that Justice Breyer in another cable case, *Denver Area,* speaking for a plurality, could quite plausibly urge abandoning the use of the standard categories as they "import law developed in very different contexts into a new and changing environment."[180] This seems quite unexceptionable, except that Justice Breyer went on to raise a plea for "the flexibility necessary to allow government to respond to very serious practical problems without sacrificing the free exchange of ideas the First Amendment is designed to protect." As he has urged in other contexts,[181] Justice Breyer would step away from First Amendment doctrine to a direct scrutiny of what he has called "First Amendment interests."[182] But this tactic is more perilous for free speech than an effort to apply the more categorical, formalist (if you will) rules of existing doctrine, in that it invites government in the first instance and courts thereafter to engage in an ad hoc determination of which government regulations will or will not further free speech in a particular circumstance.[183] Although, of course, there are values and there are principles that stand behind First Amendment doctrine and its formalisms, the very point of doctrine in this area is to put the question of the value of speech on particular occasions and in particular contexts beyond the reach of government decision makers, including courts. It is only if that doctrine manifestly breaks down that we should be driven to judge directly in terms of those values. I have tried to show that in respect to cable no such calamitous breakdown has been demonstrated.

It is the Internet that has been invoked as a radical, indeed terminal threat to the established concepts and categories of First Amendment doctrine.[184] I am not at all convinced. Indeed, the Internet is on the verge of solving the cable television conundrum on exactly the lines I have proposed, without doing any violence to doctrine. Like broadcasting or publishing, the Internet delivers more or less identical messages to large audiences. The delivery is almost instantaneous and may reach hundreds of millions of people everywhere in the world. At the same time the Internet is like the telephone or the post in that it is the medium of communication between individuals. And it is everything in between: all sorts of speakers, speaking to every conceivable subset of potential recipients. Also the transmission on the Internet requires a complicated array of entities and technologies. Individual speakers and audience members must have (or have access to) a machine capable of originating or receiving the ultimate message. These machines, now relatively inexpensive, may be analogized to pen and paper, typewriters, or perhaps eyeglasses. These machines must be connected to one another, and that introduces considerable complexity. The connections may be by wire, although they are also wireless. In this respect the medium of connection is similar to that of telephone communication. But the essence of the Internet is the virtually instantaneous switching of messages from the sender to any recipient or set of recipients. Ordinary telephone connections cannot accomplish that; nor can they accomplish it for the lengthy and data-rich messages (texts, images—moving and still—and sound) available on the Internet. You can send a fax to one or several recipients, but just as with telephone messages, the ability to send them broadcast is quite limited. The Internet's distinct capability depends on the way in which messages are coded near their source, routed, and then decoded near their destination. These tasks are performed by Internet service providers who code and route the messages along networks of communication channels (the Internet's "backbone"), collecting and decoding them at the other end.

The service providers in this and many nations are private companies. In the United States the backbone communication channels are privately owned as well, just as are telephone and cable television lines. It is quite in accord with standard doctrine to treat all of these entities just as we do providers of telephone services: as public utilities required to carry the messages of all without discrimination. Unlike the case of cable television, these channels can accept and deliver a virtually unlimited number of messages, so that even the degree of scarcity that constrains cable is lacking. There is no more need to pick and choose among Internet messages than there is among telephone messages—indeed at the end of the line an Internet message often just is a telephone message. Some Internet enthusiasts see such a regime of open access as constitutionally required, claiming that the Internet is a new kind of public forum. This is wrong. Since the entities are privately owned, there is no public anything. And for that reason the First Amendment does not directly compel such open access. But neither are these providers speakers. They are channels for other people's speech. Government may, should, but need not require open access. The First Amendment only comes into play if government imposes that obligation in a way that seeks to regulate speech, to pick and choose which messages may, must, or must not be carried. (It may, for instance, allow or require carriers to exclude obscene speech, but such speech—properly defined—is not protected by the First Amendment in any event.) Nor should these entities be allowed to get out from under such regulations by (as have cable television providers) originating as well as transmitting messages. They may not be prohibited from doing so, but on the same terms as any other originator. Federal Express, for instance, could not escape regulation as a common carrier by delivering books, even books published by Federal Express.

I do not mean to suggest that there are not important challenges in applying First Amendment doctrine to the Internet, nor even to predict unequivocally that doctrine will be equal to the task. Ingenious people have raised a host of questions.[185] Some of the most interesting arise out of the application of copyright law to the Internet.[186] That challenge is why law is fun—and important. And for success to be an accomplishment there must be the chance of failure. I argue only that any cry of failure is wildly premature and that the price of failure for freedom of the mind may be very great indeed.

*   *   *

An afterword on intellectual property: In discussing defamation I explained that we must not expect too much from theory, nor expect doctrine always to hew closely to the principle of freedom of the mind. The regime encompassing patent and copyright law offers another example of how refractory reality may be to theory. The law of intellectual property, and especially copyright law, quite frankly limits what speech may be published, and regularly even authorizes injunctions (prior restraints) against publication.[187] It is no answer to the trouble this raises to say that this regime is just a branch of property law, which in turn is a regime of general applicability that incidentally burdens speech in particular cases.[188] Copyright is more like defamation, which constitutional law finally took in hand in the *New York Times* case. It is a set of doctrines that is specifically about limiting speech. Copyright law is like defamation in another respect: it is a well-elaborated body of law that grew up in isolation from the general elaboration of First Amendment doctrine. Indeed, unlike the case of defamation law, the Constitution contains a specific authorization that Congress "promote the Progress of Science and useful Arts by securing for limited Times to Authors . . . the exclusive Right to their . . . Writings. . . ."[189] The provision is unusual in that it states its purpose and the statement is frankly instrumental. In its development copyright law has not been insensitive to what Justice Breyer calls "First Amendment values." First of all, the very purpose stated in the Constitution is a purpose to promote speech by offering incentives for its creation. But this is an approach quite at odds with the general regime of First Amendment doctrine, which is rigorously negative out of a sense that the greatest danger inheres in government's regulating the area at all, however benignly. And the law of intellectual property has itself reflected concerns that are similar to those of First Amendment doctrine. For instance, the regime has from the start distinguished between ideas—ideas may not be copyrighted (though they may sometimes be patented)—and what in the arcane terminology of copyright law is called "expression," which is the form of words or images in which an idea is embodied and may be copyrighted.[190] There is also the "fair use" doctrine, which allows limited use of actual pieces of text for specified purposes, such as criticism or comment.[191]

Under the pressure of the wide new opportunities for publication offered by the Internet, the First Amendment has been invoked to challenge the constraints copyright law imposes on the freedom to speak.[192] In *Eldred v. Ashcroft,*[193] the Court's most recent foray into the relation between copyright law and the First Amendment, it almost casually brushed aside a free speech challenge to the latest of a series of congressional enactments that have extended the term of copyright protection to a length of time that threatens the meaning of "limited times" in the Constitution's Copyright Clause.[194] It is uncertain whether as the Supreme Court continues to address copyright in First Amendment terms it will leave the present regime wholly untouched.

CHAPTER FIVE

Religion

The Dilemmas of the Religion Clauses

"Congress shall make no law respecting an establishment of religion, or prohibiting the free exercise thereof." This is the opening of the First Amendment. Its prominence reflects the importance of religion in the history of our country—from its settlement, to the writing of the Constitution, and on into the present. Many came to this continent to escape religious persecution or to found religious communities. The role of religion in public life was intensely debated throughout our early history and particularly around the time of the writing of the Constitution. In the early years of the Republic, there existed the widest variety of relations between religion and government. In some of the colonies and new states there was great tolerance for differing religious views and (to a lesser extent) even of irreligion. In others there were established churches and serious persecutions of sects that dissented from official orthodoxies. In Virginia, Baptists were persecuted and imprisoned.[1] Pennsylvania was particularly tolerant to all.[2] But everywhere the subject was of general and urgent concern.

Today the situation is quite different. First, the variety of beliefs that count as religion has greatly expanded to include views that may not include belief in a God at all, or may include a belief in several gods. At the time of the framing there was probably little thought given to Islam, much less to Buddhism or Santeria; Native American religions did attract some interest. Although the United States may be one of the most churchgoing nations in the world, still there are many people today who profess themselves strangers to religion, and in many important contexts—for instance, in the faculties and student bodies of the leading law schools—an individual's religious commitment is treated very much as a personal matter, not decently to be inquired into or discussed. We may be a religious people, as Justice Douglas once wrote,[3] but we are a secular state and a secular society.

In understanding the constitutional doctrine on religion today, history is more than usually important. Of course, it is always important to know the history of a constitutional doctrine, if only to get a sense of its trajectory. Also in a number of contexts contemporary doctrine makes explicit reference to, and so requires detailed inquiry into, the historical situation at the time of the framing.[4] But history is not important to contemporary religion clause doctrine only in that way. Indeed, as a matter of history, the Establishment Clause certainly was intended only as a limit on the *national* government's power to pass laws "respecting" the establishment of religion—that is, establishing a national church or disestablishing the churches established in several of the original states—a conception that was left in the dust a half century ago[5] in favor of some kind of principle of separation of church and government at whatever level. The relevance of history to an understanding of present religion clause doctrine is much more elemental than that. The history of the religion clauses explains the great energy behind the subject, an energy that infuses doctrine today, even apart from the seriousness with which religion is taken in contemporary society. People care about the subjects of religious freedom and of the separation of church and state today because those concerns are part of our history, of who we are as a people. It was not the original purpose of the Establishment Clause to keep all levels of government separate from religion, but even in those states where government supported religion—especially Virginia—the subject was one of intense controversy.[6]

It is this special energy—the combination of an intensely engaging subject and a connection to a long history of engagement—that makes today's religion clause jurisprudence more tense and unstable than free speech doctrine, which textually is separated from it only by a semicolon. Why does there even need to be a separate clause protecting the free exercise of religion, given the very broad conception of expression in contemporary free speech jurisprudence? What exercise of religion could not be understood as speech, including symbolic speech? After all, is there a great difference between freedom of conscience, which is said to animate the Free Exercise Clause, and freedom of the mind, which I have maintained stands behind the Speech Clause? The generalization of speech doctrine is a product of only the last sixty or so years. At the time the First Amendment was written the expressive and symbolic aspects of religious exercise might not have been thought to be covered as speech and so required special mention. But what of today's doctrine? Does free exercise disappear into free expression, or is something left over? The same question might be put in respect to the Press Clause. Given a narrow original conception of speech, the separate mention of the press may have been necessary, but today—when films and television broadcasts count as speech—is the mention of the press superfluous? There are two possible answers: to treat the clauses as presently redundant, remaining only for emphasis and to remind us of their history; or to insist that they confer some further and distinct protection on the press or on religious exercise. In the case of the Press Clause that latter, expansive tendency has had little effect on doctrine.[7] In Free Exercise Clause jurisprudence, however, the present trouble and controversy may be located just there.

The Establishment Clause is unproblematical if it is taken as it was originally meant. In its current interpretation—having been incorporated against the states by the Fourteenth Amendment—it stands out as removing a potentially large subject from the reach of *any* level of government. The contrast to speech and the press is striking. Although government may not silence speakers or shut down a newspaper because of what it says, government certainly is free to speak and publish as it chooses and make its judgments the basis for all kinds of laws, in effect establishing its point of view. (For instance, governments conduct antismoking campaigns, restrict the sale of tobacco products, and impose heavy taxes on cigarettes.) By contrast the prohibition in the Establishment Clause accords religion a very special place—it would seem a very specially disfavored place—in the constitutional scheme: as the sole subject on which government may not have a point of view, and certainly may not make that point of view an explicit basis for taking action. It is also striking that of the many countries that have adopted new constitutions since World War II—

including many like Germany and South Africa that are strongly protective of individual rights—only India has instituted anything like the regime of separation that obtains in present constitutional doctrine.[8]

How shall we understand this special place set for religion in constitutional law? What conception of religion is implicit in it? Does it suggest a conception of the relation between the state and the individual? Or is it a historical artifact, deposited in the text and continuing to radiate its energy into the present and therefore requiring some conscientious acknowledgment even if no satisfactory answer can be made to those more general and theoretically ambitious questions? There is no doubt that at the time of the framing many cared more about their churches, their religion, and their relation to God than they did about anything else, and so it seemed a prudent proviso to the new social compact to leave religion out of the reach of the new national government altogether. Many may still have those views, and in any event viewing the Constitution in part as a compact, the present generation is bound to keep faith with that original arrangement. But even if the Constitution is judged against a standard—drawn from Rawls and more remotely Kant—that asks what would reasonable people, not knowing their actual disposition (religious or irreligious), agree to as a just constitutional arrangement, religion may require special attention.

Religion is not thought to be a matter of taste or preference. A religious person does not choose his religion; it might rather be said to choose him. It is in the nature of religion that its claim on adherents is strong and all-encompassing. Religion includes an account of the nature and origins of everything there is; it is a source of value and joy; it offers moral codes governing behavior toward other persons, toward nature, and toward oneself; it often prescribes rites, rituals, and routines that structure the religious person's days and the basic functions of life. Reasonable people would insist that religion receive special treatment in recognition of the distinct dilemma in which religious persons find themselves when confronted with competing religious and civil obligations, and of the particular offense that they may feel when compelled to endorse or contribute to a religion which they do not share.

That a reasonable person might well acknowledge all this does not yield an unequivocal measure of what the special place of religion should be. After all, it is often the case that an exemption for persons with religious commitments increases the burdens on those who do not receive the exemption. The person who stands outside any religious commitment, though acknowledging that the insider claims the priority of religious over secular commitments, points out that so do those who are insiders to many other sorts of commitments, personal or shared. For instance, many believe that their commitments to their family or friends have priority over their obligations to the state. And many who have strong moral or political convictions believe that those commitments stand in judgment on and therefore are superior to the demands of the state. The outsider to religion may have some such moral or political convictions and be prepared to act upon them, but few outsiders would agree that anyone inside any such commitment—whether to a person, a group, or a moral belief—should enjoy the same exemptions from the obligations to the state that are claimed by religious insiders. Many religious persons acknowledge and respect the fact that they live in a society where others do not share their, or perhaps any, religious commitments, and they may even acknowledge a moral—perhaps a religious—obligation to accommodate in various ways the differences between them and their fellow citizens. "Render therefore unto Caesar the things which are Caesar's; and unto God the things that are God's." But this only pushes the difficulty back one level, for there remains the need for doctrine to define the boundary between the two realms. And whose perspective—the religious insider's or the outsider's—should determine that adjudication?

Michael McConnell has suggested that at the time of the founding the dilemma was not so acute and the religion clauses could be seen as but a vivid expression of the period's Lockean ideal of limited government:

> The "whole jurisdiction" of government, Locke wrote, is confined to "civil concernments," which consist of protecting the "life, liberty, health, and indolency of body; and the possession of outward things, such as money, lands, houses, furniture, and the like. . . ." In the Second Treatise . . . Locke insisted that the "great and chief end" of government is the protection of "property," which he defined as including "life, liberty, and estate." When government is confined to this end, freedom is secured. In Lockean theory, there was no tension between liberalism and religious freedom: they were essentially the same. They meant government limited in its powers.[9]

But McConnell goes on to acknowledge that this easy equivalence of limited government with an ample and secure place for religion—an equivalence that embraces both the free exercise and the nonestablishment principle—no longer obtains in the modern welfare/administrative state. The modern state goes far beyond protecting life, liberty, and property to concern itself in one way or another with every aspect of its citizens' well-being.

One view would solve these dilemmas by in effect treating the religion clauses as an anachronism, and folding them into the speech and association clauses of the First Amendment. On the same view, the Establishment Clause would require only that religion and its churches be treated neither more nor less favorably than other doctrines and groupings. Philip Kurland has argued that the two clauses mean that government must be "religion blind"—neither burdening nor benefiting religion as such. This proposes a coherent scheme but does not accord with the importance the clauses attach to religion. It would forbid any accommodation of religion, such as exemptions from military service for religious conscientious objectors, while requiring benefits to religious organizations, especially religious schools, on the same terms as other entities—private schools or hospitals.[10] At the other extreme are the views Justice Brennan expressed over a quarter of a century: not only beliefs and professions but conduct motivated by religious conscience enjoy a high degree of immunity from civil control under the Free Exercise Clause; while his view of the Establishment Clause requires that churches be ineligible for many of the cooperative interactions with government enjoyed by other groups in civil society. Both views are unstable, and constitutional doctrine oscillates uneasily between them. Kurland's is unstable because it ignores the special place assigned to religion by the constitutional text and confirmed by its historical context; Brennan's, because his strong view of the Establishment Clause conflicts with his strong view of the Free Exercise Clause. Kurland places the floor of free exercise very low and the ceiling of establishment very high, with a great deal of room for the government to maneuver in between. Brennan leaves almost no room between the ceiling and the floor—indeed sometimes the floor seems to be higher than the ceiling. McConnell would have high free exercise protections and a very high Establishment Clause ceiling. This greatly favors religion. And Justice Stevens has favored a low establishment ceiling and a low free exercise floor, disfavoring religion top and bottom.[11] The uncertainty of religion clause doctrine and its trajectory reflects these tensions and dilemmas.

Doctrine

Nothing shows more vividly the fundamental confusion in constitutional doctrine about religion than the absence of any secure identification in constitutional doctrine of what counts as religion, such that interference with its free exercise or its establishment is forbidden. I postpone consideration of that issue until the end of the chapter. It casts a shadow backward over everything that I will have said, and definitively blocks the student of constitutional law from believing that we have encountered a topic the foundations of which may be clearly discerned and confidently extrapolated to new problems. On the contrary, a wise reading of the material compels the conclusion that the law has more or less come to rest—to the extent that it has— on a collection of compromises that roughly correspond to the historical commitments and present experiences of our heterogeneous population.

The Free Exercise Clause

The two poles between which free exercise doctrine moves are marked by *Sherbert v. Verner*,[12] decided in 1963, and *Employment Division v. Smith*,[13] decided in 1990. Ms. Sherbert, a Seventh-Day Adventist, was discharged because she declined on religious grounds to work on Saturdays, when her employer, a textile mill, changed from a five- to a six-day week. Because of her conscientious scruple, she was unable to find other work and filed for state unemployment benefits. These were denied in a state administrative proceeding on the ground, set out in the state statute, that she had "fail[ed], without good cause, to accept 'suitable work when offered. . . .'" Justice Brennan for the Court acknowledged that this was not a case of government regulation of religious beliefs as such, against which "the door of the Free Exercise Clause stands tightly closed."[14] Rather, as in the case of regulations that merely sideswipe speech,[15] the state had imposed an indirect burden on Ms. Sherbert's exercise of her religion, "forc[ing] her to choose between following the precepts of her religion and forfeiting benefits, on the one hand, and abandoning one of the precepts of her religion in order to accept work, on the other hand."[16] Such an "incidental burden on the free exercise of appellant's religion may [only] be justified by a 'compelling state interest in the regulation of a subject within the State's constitutional power to regulate.'"[17] The Court concluded that government action that even incidentally burdens the exercise of one's religion must meet strict scrutiny: the regulation must be narrowly tailored to a compelling governmental interest. This is extreme.

We saw that incidental burdens, like income taxes on authors' income or real estate taxes on bookstores and publishers, are generally not subject to heightened scrutiny at all. Only if the regulation interferes with use of a public forum or where government seeks to regulate conduct that is closely intertwined with expression is there heightened scrutiny, and even then it is not at the pitch that Justice Brennan proclaimed in *Sherbert*.[18] Although ministers of some religions might object to paying income tax on their salaries or having to obey parking regulations on the street in front of their church, they rarely bring these objections to court, and when they do they are usually brushed aside as cranks.[19] The Supreme Court has never honored such far-fetched claims. Indeed there were few religion clause claims at all until the middle of the twentieth century, largely because the clauses had not been thought to be incorporated against the states in the Fourteenth Amendment and there was little regulation bearing on religion at the federal level. *Reynolds v. United States*[20] is the leading early case. The defendant claimed that polygamy was a religious duty enjoined upon him by the teachings of the Church of Jesus Christ of Latter-Day Saints (Mormons), and therefore the application to him of federal legislation making bigamy a crime in the territories was a prohibition of the free exercise of religion. The claim was rejected: "Congress was deprived [by the First Amendment] of all legislative power over mere opinion, but was left free to reach actions which were in violation of social duties or subversive of good order. . . . To permit [this claim] would be to make the professed doctrines of religious belief superior to the law of the land, and in effect to permit every citizen to become a law unto himself."[21] *Employment Division v. Smith* is the contemporary statement of that polar doctrine set out in *Reynolds*. Smith and another had been discharged from their jobs as drug rehabilitation counselors because their possession of peyote in connection with the rituals of the Native American Church violated Oregon criminal law. That law made no exception for such religiously motivated possession. The applications for unemployment compensation were denied, because they had been discharged for job-related misconduct. Justice Antonin Scalia, writing for the Court, stated the position clearly:

> We have never held that an individual's religious beliefs excuse him from compliance with an otherwise valid law prohibiting conduct that the State is free to regulate. . . . Conscientious scruples have not, in the course of the long struggle for religious toleration, relieved the individual from obedience to a general law not aimed at the promotion or restriction of religious beliefs. The mere possession of religious convictions which contradict the relevant concerns of a political society does not relieve the citizen from the discharge of political responsibilities. . . . [T]he right of free exercise does not relieve an individual of the obligation to comply with a valid and neutral law of general applicability on the ground that the law proscribes (or prescribes) conduct that his religion prescribes (or proscribes).[22]

The extreme quality of *Sherbert* may be thought to be matched by the harshness of *Smith*. Both engendered strong dissents, heated controversy, and *Smith* evoked an act of Congress, the Religious Freedom Restoration Act, that purported to overrule it and was in turn ruled unconstitutional for that reason.[23]

First the absurdity of *Sherbert*. The exercise of religion may be narrower in its subject matter than expression in general, but it is also broader, because the *exercise* of religion calls to mind not only profession of belief but conduct in accordance with religion. The range of conduct may be as narrow as simply the participation in ritual gatherings, the speaking of prayers and singing of hymns, or the performance of ritual gestures. All of these may be comprehended under the concept of expression: they are speech, association with others for expressive purposes, performance of symbolic, expressive gestures. There is no question that they are all protected. But there is much more to exercise: it includes the widest range of required conduct and abstentions. Some of the incidental burdens on speech—like general tax and labor regimes—also apply to religious expression, but laws prohibiting child abuse and mayhem, zoning laws[24] and building codes, and laws and regulations prescribing standards of dress and grooming[25] may and sometimes have interfered with the exercise of religion. So also the government's management of its own property has been claimed to burden the exercise of religion by impinging on religious claims on that property.[26] Because courts are forbidden by religion clause jurisprudence from undertaking an independent evaluation of how important to a particular religion a particular prohibition or requirement may be,[27] by the *Sherbert* test a person with religious scruples may force government to show how almost any law serves a compelling interest and is narrowly tailored to that interest. Failing in that justification, government must grant that person exemption from the law. In rejecting this possibility, *Smith* appears to go no further in protecting religion than the speech clause goes in protecting expression.

Practices (that is, conduct) also may not be forbidden for the purpose of harassing religion. A clear case of such a "religious gerrymander"[28] was the ordinance in *Church of the Lukumi Babalu Aye, Inc. v. City of Hialeah*,[29] that forbade killing animals within the city limits, but with so many exemptions that the Court concluded the ordinance might as well simply have forbidden the killing of animals as part of a religious ritual. This is a significant protection. Government regularly burdens or prohibits conduct altogether just because it does not like the particular conduct or the kind of people who engage in it. But it may not forbid conduct—for example, female circumcision—just because it disapproves of the religion that enjoins it or only as a religious practice. The government must have a religion-neutral purpose in mind. This prohibition accords with *Smith,* because such religion-focused laws are not laws of general applicability. It might also be said that such religious gerrymanders fail the *O'Brien* test discussed in Chapter 4, because the conduct constituting the practice is expressive of the religion and the targeted prohibition of that conduct is directed not against that conduct generally (for example, outdoor fires) but against that conduct just because it is religious expression (as burning a flag expresses a point of view). This is not to say that a law would count as a religious gerrymander if it was enacted because a religious practice had brought it to legislative attention, although as enacted it applied as well outside that religious context. Female circumcision again may be an example of such a practice.

The laws that make the life of religious persons difficult are rarely designed just to hurt them. Certainly the laws that chafed Sherbert or Smith did not have that intention. Neither do laws requiring military service, or school attendance by children, or vaccinations. Those who object may often be put into a cruel squeeze, and the *Smith* rule offers them no relief. Although for some thirty years *Sherbert* was the explicit constitutional rule, still the Supreme Court applied it to strike down legislation in only five cases: three unemployment compensation cases similar to *Sherbert*,[30] a case invalidating the application to the Old Order Amish of a law requiring school attendance until age sixteen,[31] and a case striking down a state constitutional provision disqualifying clergy from serving in the state legislature.[32] The last of these would probably have been struck down under *Smith* as well. But a wide range of laws escaped invalidation on a variety of rationales: because of special contexts like prisons[33] and the military,[34] because the action related to the government's management of its own resources,[35] or because the rule was thought necessary to the accomplishment of a compelling state interest.[36] The government resources cases depend on an argument that undermines the premise of *Sherbert:* that the regulation of government resources is different from government regulation of private conduct. But government resources are public resources and their management in a way that burdens some because of their religious commitments is a burden on the fulfillment of those commitments. In *United States v. Lee*[37] the requirement that social security taxes be deducted from wages paid by and to Old Order Amish survived strict scrutiny, even though "the Amish believe it sinful not to provide for their own elderly."[38] The compelling interest that moved the Court was the need for regimes like social security and the income tax to operate universally, without the need to inquire into the validity and urgency of particular exemptions. While this is undoubtedly a real need, it is but a particular instance of the very argument against allowing "every citizen to become a law unto himself"—the basis of the decision in *Smith*. It is true of a large number of laws in the modern welfare-regulatory-administrative state that disregarding the noncompliance of a few persons will make no noticeable difference in the laws' satisfactory implementation, but that the moral hazard of openly allowing such departures may cause the schemes to unravel. If sincerity alone could be the test of a claim for religious exemption,[39] the moral hazard would be significant and the administrative difficulties in patrolling it great. That is not to say that constitutional doctrine might not conclude that the hazard is worth encountering, but the reasoning in *Lee* implies that it is not. The same might be said for *Bowen v. Roy*,[40] in which Roy's religious scruples about allowing the federal welfare bureaucracies to assign his infant daughter, Little Bird of the Snow, a social security number as a condition of her receiving benefits were not respected, even though this one child's account might without great expense have been handled out of the ordinary course.

On the other hand, the claim in *Smith* that *Sherbert* was an anomaly, departing from a long line of contrary doctrine, does not entirely hold up. For instance, there was noticeable equivocation in *Braunfeld v. Brown*,[41] on which *Smith* leans heavily. *Braunfeld* rejected a free exercise claim by an Orthodox Jew for exemption from a Sunday closing law that he said forced him to close his retail business for two days on the weekend, while his competitors lost only one. Justice Brennan, anticipating in dissent his opinion for the Court two years later in *Sherbert,* argued that the law "put an individual to a choice between his business and his religion."[42] Chief Justice Warren's plurality opinion[43] was not an unequivocal embrace of *Reynolds:*

> To strike down, without the most critical scrutiny, legislation which imposes only an indirect burden on the exercise of religion, i.e., legislation which does not make unlawful the religious practice itself, would radically restrict the operating latitude of the legislature. . . . [I]t cannot be expected, much less required, that legislators enact no law regulating conduct that may in some way result in an economic disadvantage to some religious sects and not to others because of the special practices of the various religions.

This was the rule the opinion announced:

> If the purpose *or effect* of a law is to impede the observance of one or all religions or is to discriminate invidiously between religions, that law is constitutionally invalid even though the burden may be characterized as being only indirect. But if the State regulates conduct by enacting a general law within its power, the purpose and effect of which is to advance the State's secular goals, the statute is valid despite its indirect burden on religious observance *unless the State may accomplish its purpose by means which do not impose such a burden.*[44]

This is not the rigorous law-of-general-applicability standard announced in *Smith*. First, the preface to the rule appears to limit it to cases where the indirect burden is economic, excluding those where the law of general applicability makes "unlawful the religious practice itself," as was the case both in *Smith* and *Reynolds* before it. Then, the formula excludes not only laws whose *purpose* is to burden religious practice, as in the *City of Hialeah* case, but also those whose *effect* is to impede religious observance. But surely the Sunday closing laws, like the disqualification for unemployment benefits in *Sherbert* and the drug laws in *Smith,* have the effect of impeding religious observance. Finally, the concluding formulation of the "general law" rule is itself qualified: the imposition on religious observance is justified only if government cannot accomplish its purpose by some less burdensome means. It may be that the purpose of providing the general calm resulting from a common day of rest could not be accomplished by exempting Sabbath observers, but it is a fair question whether the rigor of the drug laws would have been significantly loosened by exempting ritual use of certain substances, as many states and the federal government in fact do.

It is a powerful argument against *Sherbert* that it makes the courts the final arbiters, unconstrained by doctrinal guidance, of the importance of almost any law regulating conduct and of the appropriateness of fashioning exemptions for an indeterminate class of persons and claims. Yet, in responding to *Sherbert,* the *Smith* formulation seems less generous than American traditions of special concern for religious freedom.[45] It is less generous even than the protection accorded to expression under the speech clause, because, as noted, the *O'Brien* and public forum doctrines offer some measure of protection against indirect burdens. Religion has sometimes sheltered under those doctrines to the extent that the exercise of religion has also been an exercise of expression.[46] Similarly the substantive constitutional protection accorded to parents to direct the education of their children has extended just as much to providing that education in religious settings[47] as it has to including in that schooling instruction in a foreign language.[48] But just as the generality of law and its administration would be too far hampered if we gave the *Sherbert* burden test full force against exercise as conduct, so too to the extent that the Free Exercise Clause protects religious exercise (that is, religiously based conduct and abstentions), the *Smith* rule gives too little—really hardly anything at all, since the religious gerrymander would in any event be excluded as a denial of equal protection.

So there is considerable tension in this branch of doctrine and some yearning for a middle way, but no one has pointed to what that middle way might be other than ad hoc balancing unguided by formula or doctrine. Justice Scalia, like Justice Harlan before him, argued that the rigor of the law-of-general-applicability doctrine is considerably mitigated by the American tradition of legislating exemptions for religious observers—pointing to legislated exemptions for the sacramental use of wine or peyote, and from the obligation to swear an oath or to perform military service. Reliance on legislation to resolve the dilemma of the religious certainly absolves the courts from the uncomfortable task of assigning weights to publicly proclaimed policies and determining just how much those policies would suffer if religious exemptions were granted. But this way out has its own inconveniences. First, it puts religious freedom in part at the mercy of majority forbearance, and that forbearance is less likely to be shown to minority, unfamiliar, or uncongenial religious sects. Second, such legislated exemptions have been claimed to amount to exactly the favoritism toward religion that is condemned by the other religion clause, the Establishment Clause.[49]

The Establishment Clause

The text and history of the Establishment Clause make it even harder to arrive at a clear and compelling understanding of this religion clause as it is used in contemporary doctrine. Instead we have a set of phrases and a striking metaphor: the wall of separation between church and state.[50] It must be reported that there is at present a canonical test, promulgated in *Lemon v. Kurtzman*,[51] for compliance with the Establishment Clause:

> First, the statute must have a secular legislative purpose; second, its principal or primary effect must be one that neither advances nor inhibits religion; finally, the statute must not foster "an excessive entanglement with religion."

The test is virtually useless in deciding difficult cases. For instance, the Free Exercise Clause itself, and government action taken to comply with it, would seem to violate the first prong. For this reason the common accommodations of religion like the inclusion of churches among educational and charitable institutions entitled to exemption from a variety of state, local, and national taxes, exemption from military service, or released time for religious instruction are described in the *Lemon* cases not as special privileges for religion, which they plainly are, but as measures to further the supposed secular goal of social harmony.[52] Nonetheless the *Lemon* test continues to be invoked, surely not for its explanatory power but rather as a symbol of the Court's wish to maintain the appearance of continuity and consistency in a jurisprudence marked by inconsistency, incoherence, and shifting bare majorities.[53] The best way to understand this unedifying muddle is to display, along one axis as it were, the range of underlying positions taken up by the justices and sometimes by the Court as a whole, while arraying on the other axis the types of cases in which Establishment Clause claims are raised. A rough pattern and a possibly temporary trajectory emerge.

The strictest separation position, held most consistently by Justice Brennan and held today in a perhaps somewhat softened version by Justices John Paul Stevens, David Souter, and Ruth Bader Ginsburg, would search out and invalidate any action which aligns the state with religion and treats with extreme skepticism any action that channels government resources to religion. Of course, it is not possible to condemn all actions favoring religions without contradicting the Free Exercise Clause and long established practices. Justices Brennan and Stevens were ready—in dissent—to condemn the opening of legislative sessions with prayer by a government-paid chaplain, but one doubts if they would have extended their disapproval to chaplains in the military or in prisons. Nor have they gone so far as to condemn the device "In God We Trust," on the national currency, or the opening of sessions of the Supreme Court with the invocation "God save the United States and this honorable Court."[54] It is not easy to say what explains these stopping places. Assuming that the Establishment Clause is not to be confined to its original and textual meaning as an assignment of all matters "respecting an establishment of religion" to the states,[55] the other extreme is also hard to pin down. Michael McConnell in numerous writings and in several arguments before the Supreme Court has proposed a rule that the Establishment Clause simply forbids government action that accords special privileges or benefits to religion but does not prohibit actions that aid religion so long as secular entities or persons defined by secular criteria also benefit.[56] (We have seen that as a matter of free exercise McConnell insists on considerable exemptions and privileges for religion.) This criterion would allow state subsidies to parochial schools, so long as the subsidy is similarly available to secular private schools. This would be no more generous to religion than the practice in a number of liberal democracies with strong commitments to religious liberty.

But it is anathema to those who proclaim that the contemporary Establishment Clause embodies the principle, attributed to Jefferson, that it is tyrannical to impose any tax, however small, for the support of another man's religion—or even for the support of a man's own religion.[57] Before proceeding further, therefore, I shall set out the elements on the other axis of the relation between religion and government.

Close to the zero point of the axis are cases where government appears to allow itself to be associated with religion in some symbolic way, as when it allows a private group to place a Christmas display in a public park. Although some issue of principle may be implicated in these cases, it is hard to take seriously a doctrine that distinguishes between two Christmas crèches on the ground, among other things, that one included figures of Santa Claus and reindeer drawing sleighs and the other did not.[58] At the other extreme are school prayer cases, such as *Engel v. Vitale*[59] in which the state board of regents composed a prayer and a school board directed that it be recited at the start of each school day. (Unwilling children were not required to join in.) In between are cases in which public funds go to churches or church-related organizations to assist them in providing services—medical care, education at all levels, adoption services, child care, and care for the elderly are among the examples—that government might otherwise provide directly. This in-between category comprises programs that are less coercive, less intrusive than the school prayer in *Engel,* but it is where all the heat is concentrated. For good reason: large amounts of money are potentially at stake, and more importantly church-related schools are a significant competitor to public schools for children from less affluent families, and if the cost advantage of the public schools were lessened by public subsidies, the government's near monopoly of primary and secondary education would be threatened, and with it powerful political and ideological interests. The intricacy crossing over into incoherence of much Establishment Clause doctrine may perhaps be explained by how high the stakes are for some of the participants in the debate.[60]

In recent years several justices have been willing to press the analysis beyond the repetition of slogans like the "wall of separation" or the invocation of the meaningless *Lemon* test to consider what underlying principles Establishment Clause jurisprudence should serve. (It is no good to turn away from such analysis with the cry that, like it or not, this is just what the Constitution requires, because—as we have seen—recourse to the text or the original meaning of the clause is wholly unavailing here. It is doctrine or nothing.) There has been some progress in clarifying the terms of the debate, if not the doctrine itself. One line of analysis, urged by Justice Scalia and Michael McConnell,[61] would see the Establishment Clause as a further safeguard of freedom of conscience: government action violates the Constitution to the extent that it coerces an unwanted religious affirmation—on analogy to the flag salute in *West Virginia Board of Education v. Barnette,* a free speech case.[62] Similarly, the prohibition on entanglement of government with religion, set out in the third prong of the *Lemon* test, may be seen as protecting the liberty of religious persons to associate in churches defined by their own, not anyone else's, notion of orthodoxy.[63] The virtue of this conception of the Establishment Clause is also its obvious defect: it appears to do no work that cannot be done by the protection of freedom of expression or of the free exercise of religion. To escape this objection the concept of coercion might be expanded beyond the kind of coercion exemplified by the flag salute case, in which children who would not participate in the exercise were dismissed from school and their parents charged with contributing to their truancy. In *Lee v. Weisman*[64] the Court struck down the practice of including a nondenominational prayer in a junior high school graduation, a ceremony at which attendance was not compulsory. The Court spoke of a "particular risk of indirect coercion," the appearance to the nonbeliever or dissenter of "an attempt to employ the machinery of the State to enforce a religious orthodoxy," and of "public pressure, as well as peer pressure, ... though subtle and indirect, ... as real as any overt compulsion" at least to stand and maintain a silence that might seem to the unwilling participant as a form of participation rather than just a respectful attitude toward the views of others.[65] (That holding has since been extended to student-led prayer at high school football games.)[66] Justice Scalia's dissent contrasted the history of palpable and sometimes bloody compulsion, against which the Establishment Clause meant to guard, with the amorphous and subjective conception of peer pressure on which the Court relied. And indeed it may well be said that to account for the perplexities of Establishment Clause doctrine in terms of so flaccid a conception of coercion is to explain the obscure by the more obscure.

Justice Sandra Day O'Connor, more often in dissenting or concurring opinions,[67] has urged a related test:

> The Establishment Clause prohibits government from making adherence to a religion relevant in any way to a person's standing in the political community. Government can run afoul of that prohibition in two principal ways. One is excessive entanglement with religious institutions, which may interfere with the independence of the institutions, give the institutions access to government or governmental powers not fully shared by nonadherents of the religion, and foster the creation of political constituencies along religious lines. The second and more direct infringement is government endorsement or disapproval of religion. Endorsement sends a message to nonadherents that they are outsiders, not full members of the political community, and an accompanying message to adherents that they are insiders, favored members of the political community. Disapproval sends the opposite message.[68]

According to Justice O'Connor, whether government action is such an impermissible endorsement must be judged by the response to that action of an "objective observer" subject to it.[69] Though no less vague than the "psychological coercion" criterion offered in *Lee,* the endorsement test has the virtue of attempting a distinct account of what establishment doctrine should be seen as trying to accomplish and invites measuring government action against that account.

As a framework for discussion, the endorsement test is most useful in cases of symbolic actions, which invite interpretation of the meaning of the government's involvement in allowing religious words or symbols on public property and in public ceremonies. It is less useful, because more indeterminate, when applied to the crucial school funding area. It is possible, however, to discern certain features of the developing Supreme Court jurisprudence in this area—subject to the possibility of a change of course with a change of personnel.

The most uncompromising modern statement against material support to religious institutions came in the course of an opinion upholding, over four vigorous dissents, a New Jersey statute allowing school districts to pay for the transportation of children to any not-for-profit school, including public and church-related schools: "No tax in any amount, large or small, can be levied to support any religious activities or institutions, whatever they may be called, or whatever form they may adopt to teach or practice religion."[70] As I have indicated, this statement cannot be taken to the limit of its logic. Not even Justice Brennan, the strongest opponent of state aid to church-related schools, has indicated opposition to police and fire protection for those schools, nor to their exemption from property and other taxes.[71] Indeed the Court has never even considered whether the widely used charitable deduction from the federal income and estate taxes for contributions to religious institutions amounted to an establishment of religion. Only when the deduction was directed specifically to expenses incurred in sending children to parochial schools did Justices Brennan, Marshall, and Stevens conclude (in dissent) that those deductions violated the "no tax" principle.[72] It is also significant that all challenges to the several state[73] and federal programs[74] of assistance to church-related colleges and universities, all of which contained some form of restriction that the money not be used for religious purposes, have been rejected. In fact one of the most successful government programs for assisting the higher education of large numbers of citizens, the G.I. Bill and similar programs, has always without challenge allowed recipients to attend private and church-related institutions.

An almost comically complicated body of law exists to confine the kind of nonfinancial assistance government may lend to church-related primary and secondary schools. The loan of secular textbooks to parochial school students is permissible.[75] The loan of instructional materials is not,[76] nor is the reimbursement to the schools of the cost of such materials.[77] Yet the state may provide these schools with computers and other educational materials.[78] Government may reimburse church-related school the cost of administering state-prepared examinations,[79] but not the cost of administering teacher-prepared examinations.[80] Only rarely has the Court admitted to such inconsistency in these precedents as to require explicit overruling.[81] It is not easy to distinguish the higher education cases from those in which similar assistance to primary and secondary church-related schools has been held to violate the Establishment Clause, except on pragmatic grounds. It is said that college and graduate students are better able to come to their own conclusions about the teaching to which they are exposed.[82] What has been left unremarked in Court opinions is the fact that in higher education there never has been the near-monopoly of government-run primary and secondary schools, and so such programs of public support did not represent a threat to entrenched interests. Indeed it is hard not to see this area of law as a tug between those who seek to find some way to support church-related primary and secondary education and those who are committed to maintaining the government monopoly.

The current scene of struggle is over programs that would give financial assistance not to the institutions but to the parents and students who would attend them. The strongest statement against such assistance is Justice Lewis Powell's opinion for the Court in *Committee for Public Education and Religious Liberty v. Nyquist*,[83] which invalidated a New York State program providing a reimbursement of from $50 to $100 to low-income parents paying tuition to nonpublic schools and allowing moderate-income parents a credit of up to $1,000 a child against state income tax for tuition paid to nonpublic schools.[84] Reciting the *Lemon* test, the Court ruled that

> [i]t is precisely the function of New York's law to provide assistance to private schools, the great majority of which are sectarian. By reimbursing parents for a portion of their tuition bill, the State seeks to relieve their financial burdens sufficiently to assure that they continue to have the option to send their children to religion-oriented schools. And while the other purposes for that aid—to perpetuate a pluralistic educational environment and to protect the fiscal integrity of overburdened public schools—are certainly unexceptionable, the effect of the aid is unmistakably to provide desired financial support for nonpublic, sectarian institutions.[85]

Ten years later, in *Mueller v. Allen*,[86] Justice William Rehnquist, who had dissented in *Nyquist,* wrote for the Court approving a Minnesota statute allowing parents to deduct up to $800 from their state income taxes for expenses for textbooks, transportation, and tuition incurred in sending their children to public or private primary and secondary schools. Applying the second prong of the *Lemon* test and winding his way through the precedents like a skier on a slalom course, Justice Rehnquist concluded that the statute "bears less resemblance to the arrangement struck down in *Nyquist* than it does to assistance programs upheld in our prior decisions and those discussed with approval in *Nyquist.*"[87] Of particular significance were the factors that "the deduction is available for educational expenses incurred by *all* parents, including those whose children attend public schools and those whose children attend non-sectarian private schools or sectarian private schools,"[88] and "that, by channeling whatever assistance it may provide to parochial schools through individual parents Minnesota has reduced the Establishment Clause objections to which its action is subject. It is true, of course, that financial assistance provided to parents ultimately has an economic effect comparable to that of aid given directly to the schools attended by their children. It is also true, however, that under Minnesota's arrangement public funds become available only as a result of numerous, private choices of individual parents of school-age children."[89] The dissent, which curiously did not include the author of *Nyquist,* pointed out that in *Nyquist* too the aid came to the church-related school "only as a result of numerous, private choices of individual parents."[90]

In the years since *Mueller* the Court, usually by closely divided votes, has been increasingly hospitable to programs that put public resources into church-related schools. The most important decision—practically and doctrinally—came in 2002 in *Zelman v. Simmons-Harris.*[91] The Court rejected an Establishment Clause challenge to an Ohio program giving students in failing Cleveland public schools financial grants ("vouchers") that they might use to help gain access to public or private schools—including religiously affiliated schools. An earlier dramatic turn away from the rigorous anti-aid doctrine of *Nyquist* occurred in *Agostini v. Felton,*[92] one of the rare cases in which the Court explicitly overruled one of its precedents in this tangled area. The Court approved a federal program that sent public school teachers into private, including church-related, schools to provide remedial instruction to disadvantaged children. In *Witters v. Washington Department of Services for the Blind,*[93] the Court had a few years earlier approved—again applying the second prong of the *Lemon* test—payments under a state vocational rehabilitation program to allow a blind student to continue his studies for the ministry at a sectarian college. And in 1993 in *Zobrest v. Catalina Foothills School District*[94] the Court ruled that the public provision of an interpreter to a deaf student attending Catholic high school did not violate the Establishment Clause. These programs had the features that were emphasized in *Mueller:* the funds are available for use in public and private schools, and "public funds become available only as a result of numerous, private choices of individual parents of school-age children." But all of these programs touched only a few children and were directed—as was the program in *Agostini*—at children with special needs. Given this welter of irreconcilable precedents and the lack of any clear doctrine, the decision in *Zelman* was doctrinally decisive. Chief Justice Rehnquist—who for decades, first as a dissenter, but since *Mueller* in 1983 with more success, had been pressing for a more accommodating doctrine—was able to declare:

> [T]he Ohio [voucher] program is entirely neutral with respect to religion. It provides benefits directly to a wide spectrum of individuals. . . . It permits such individuals to exercise genuine choice among options public and private, secular and religious. The program is therefore a program of true private choice. In keeping with an unbroken line of decisions rejecting challenges to similar programs, we hold that the program does not offend the Establishment Clause.

The stakes could not have been higher, for unlike the limited and rather sympathetic contexts of aid to students with disabilities, voucher programs represent the possibility of a fundamental restructuring of the way in which the state provides for the universal education of children, potentially turning over a significant part of that function to a variety of private organizations which are not organs of the state but are at most under its regulatory control.

The decision in *Zelman* is doctrinally decisive in the sense that it announces a crisp and readily applicable rule in a critical context, but it may be a precarious precedent. There were four dissenters, who gave every indication of a determination to abandon this rule at the first opportunity and return to the pre-1983 "no-aid" doctrine of *Nyquist.* Justice David Souter could not have been more emphatic: after reviewing the whole course of decisions since 1947, he characterized everything from *Mueller* onward as a period of decline and concluded that "doctrinal bankruptcy has been reached today." Such a condemnation, carrying as it does an implicit commitment to overrule almost twenty years of precedent, is unusual. It casts a deep shadow over the stability of doctrine in this area.[95]

Concluding Reflections

Can anything be said to bring order to this jumble of doctrine, conflicting precedents, and uncertain principles, while not departing too far from the constitutional texts, the legal materials, and our national traditions? Like the other clauses of the First Amendment it is best to see the religion clauses as part—to borrow a phrase from Friedrich Hayek—of our constitution of liberty: liberty of conscience, liberty from state-imposed orthodoxy, liberty for and from churches. A second guiding maxim takes account of the special place that religion plays in the lives of (some) believers. The depth of the claims religion makes upon its adherents and for itself counsels government to keep a prudent distance from religion: not crowding believers unless it has to and not taking sides for or against religious belief. The First Amendment in all its parts is a manifestation of respect for the autonomy of the individual, of the notion that government does not own him. This simple perspective might suggest some way out of the doctrinal tangles of the religion clauses.

I start with the Establishment Clause. Justice O'Connor's no-endorsement principle quoted above has the virtue of connecting the Establishment Clause to conceptions of mutual respect. Even where government endorsement may not, without an implausible stretch, be said to coerce outsiders, such endorsement does make the outsider a stranger in his own land more than does the government's espousal of secular policies he does not share: it is of the nature of religion that it is not the subject of conclusive demonstration, nor yet of choice, so that government's alignment with one or another religion excludes the nonbeliever in a particularly definitive way. In this respect endorsement is like government action that divides us into castes or races.[96] Such actions immobilize individuals in the social space in which we all choose, and submit to, the state. Inevitably, the no-endorsement principle has a certain indefiniteness. It is to a degree subjective. Extreme touchiness on this score, an over-readiness to take offense, where government has become so pervasive, deprives members of the majority of opportunities for expression that it may be awkward to find outside of official settings. Free speech public forum doctrine has something to teach here: where the inclusion of a religious message occurs in a setting where many views may be expressed and the government provides no more than a forum, it is churlish and coercive of the minority to read into that inclusion a message of official endorsement. And the Court has regularly taken the position that religious expression in these contexts does not violate the Establishment Clause, turning aside the argument that such expression may (or must) be limited lest the Establishment Clause be violated.[97]

So also does it seem perverse to require, in the name of liberty of conscience, the exclusion of religious entities from participating in general programs designed to provide benefits—like education, health care, and social services—defined in general and neutral terms. A few cases in the 1970s, like *Nyquist,* drawing on the rhetoric (though not the result) of *Everson,* had been allowed to set a tone of dogmatism and extremism in this regard that is quite at war with constitutional provisions intended to foster tolerance and accommodation. Fortunately, subsequent developments have shown a halting progress to a more moderate and reasonable approach, in keeping with the inevitably approximate nature of what can be accomplished and enforced in this regard. Halting progress is all we should ask for. The notions of endorsement and respect are in part conventional. What counts as an imposition contrasted to what calls for no more than tolerant—perhaps courteous, perhaps ironic—indifference is a matter of custom and habit. It is, therefore, important that Supreme Court precedents not outrun social practices. I suggest that at its most extreme and rigid, in the 1970s, Supreme Court doctrine had lost touch with the community sensibilities that give these concepts much of their substance.

In respect to free exercise also, the Court went off the rails in the *Sherbert* case and cannot have meant what it said there. On the other hand the *Smith* rule is so stingy to religious practice that it seems to deny the nation's and the Constitution's historical special concern for religious commitment. I suggest that free exercise claims should generally not be entertained when the state's actions, rather than prohibiting, discriminating against, or seeking to discourage religious practice, have an indirect and unintended disadvantaging impact on an individual's choice to engage in a particular religious practice. Even in such cases of indirect and incidental disadvantaging, a free exercise claim should be considered, however, if the state's action bears so heavily on an individual's choice as to have virtually the preclusive effect of a direct prohibition. Such an imposition would have then to pass some level of heightened scrutiny.[98] Courts would still have to make the judgment that a particular imposition has this extreme effect, but at least it is a frank exercise of something like a dispensing power where the law has to an extreme degree failed to show the forbearance and decency that is the animating spirit of the Free Exercise Clause. By contrast *Sherbert* requires a balance in every case, and on the standard of strict scrutiny.

This less rigorous stand is particularly appropriate because that animating spirit of respect, decency, and forbearance has from the beginning of our nation shown itself not in the intricate legalisms of the last half century's religion clause jurisprudence, but in statutory and discretionary accommodations of religious conscience: from the early exemptions of Quakers from the requirement to take oaths and to perform military service to the contemporary exemptions for the sacramental use of peyote for Native American religions, the accommodations of those religions in the American Indian Religious Freedom Act,[99] or the exemption of religious employers from the prohibition against discrimination on the ground of religion.[100] Of course such legislated accommodations do not blanket the field of what the virtues of decency and forbearance require: they respond to particular instances that capture the legislative attention. As we have seen, the search for a more rigorous doctrinal formulation that will allow the courts in an entirely predictable way to impose those virtues has proved to be a will-o'-the-wisp, offering only a semblance of regularity. In the end, religion clause doctrine should leave considerable distance between the floor of free exercise and the ceiling of establishment. In contrast, some of the more extreme doctrines—such as *Nyquist* and *Sherbert*—not only leave no room between the ceiling and the floor but sometimes set the floor above the ceiling.

Finally, an overly rigid doctrinal scheme that constitutionalizes—either as an infringement on free exercise or as an establishment—a large part of the space that any government involvement with religion might occupy, is inappropriate because of the evident inability of the Court to offer a convincing (or even a coherent) conception of what is to count as religion for these purposes. The only Supreme Court cases to address the question have parsed the terms of statutory exemptions from military service, and have not done a very good job of it. One case asked whether a "belief that is sincere and meaningful occupies a place in the life of its possessor parallel to that filled by the orthodox belief in God"[101]—a more evident example of explaining the obscure by the more obscure cannot be imagined. Indeed, as Justice Harlan concluded, the very attempt to draw such a line may itself violate the Establishment Clause.[102] The commentators have not done much better. Jesse Choper has urged that the concept be limited to belief systems that teach the possibility of "extratemporal consequences."[103] This suggestion has some affinity with Hobbes's argument about the futility of punishing actions that save one's own life—except in this case the actor's calculus would make the law's threat even more futile. This proposal is obviously inadequate. Some religions do not include doctrine about an afterlife. Also the proposal has little relevance to the use of the term in the Establishment Clause. But more deeply, it misses the reluctance—born of decency, forbearance, and tolerance—to compel our fellow citizens to humiliate themselves by betraying their own consciences, even if we can tighten the screws enough to make them do it. This broader notion, however, once more casts us adrift, because philosophical and cultural commitments,[104] or loyalty to friends or family, may pose similarly cruel dilemmas.[105] And to argue for the religious exemption on the ground that its compulsions are different or greater is evidently to argue in a circle. Kent Greenawalt has sensibly suggested, drawing on the concept of "family resemblance" in Wittgenstein and H. L. A. Hart,[106] instead of attempting a definition of the term by necessary and sufficient conditions of its application,

> [a] more fruitful approach to understanding and employing the concept of religion is to identify instances to which the concept indisputably applies, and to ask in more doubtful instances how close the analogy is between these and the indisputable instances. Such an approach can yield applications of the concept to instances that share no common feature, a result that the dictionary approach precludes.[107]

That approach might work quite well for the legislator or common law judge devising an exemption for a particular class of cases. Although constitutional law also develops by something like this tentative crablike movement, it is under greater pressure to account for itself in terms of underlying principle. Its conclusions are more permanent and preclusive. Unlike legislation, it cannot easily be taken back. Unlike common law doctrine, it cannot be overruled by legislation. And Supreme Court decisions must provide guidance to courts, lawyers, and legislators throughout the country. The constitutional judge must explain what it is about certain instances that makes them "indisputable," if his extrapolation from them is to be convincing and useful beyond just disposing of the case at hand. It will not do simply to list these instances—Buddhism, Christianity, Islam, Judaism—for that list will not tell us what characteristics a belief system must have to be analogous to them.

What comes to mind about these indisputable instances are that they implicate belief in some entity or forces the existence of which is not demonstrable by usual evidentiary and argumentative means (what for brevity I call the supernatural). Any narrower generalization risks excluding beliefs—like those of Native American groups—that are unfamiliar or have a small number of adherents. This identification in terms of belief in and duties to the supernatural also suggests a basis for such special consideration as the law may grant religion: the believer is in some sense beyond the reach of the wider community that deliberates about and enacts its forms of organization in a general conversation available to all. To the extent that the belief system is within the general conversation, it can ask only for such immunity as we argue for and grant to expression—that is, speech—generally. And of course religious persons often do participate in that general conversation, and when they do they may identify the special sources of their convictions, but they cannot expect special treatment *in the conversation* for beliefs that they are bound to decline to submit to it.[108] This leaves any special privileges of religion a matter of humanitarian grace by those who are in the conversation but not in the religion. That so many in our country have been and are outside the conversation in this way—but not all in the same or even similar places outside it—makes them more responsive to this call on their generosity, but should not be the sole basis for it.

This conception accords quite well with religion clause doctrine. Certainly it explains why it is offensive to equal, common citizenship for government to establish religious beliefs and practices, as recent doctrine conceives establishment. It also explains why the law must be careful in excusing from common burdens those who claim exemption because of special religious sensibilities to those burdens. St. Paul wrote that Christianity is foolishness to the Greeks.[109] In respect to civil society we are all Greeks, although many of us may also be Christians—or Jews, or Muslims, or Buddhists.

CHAPTER SIX

Liberty and Property

The constitutional doctrine of free expression comes as close to the libertarian ideal as it is sensible to wish. The mind is free. It does not belong to the state, the government, the community—whatever your preferred locution—but is solely the property of the individual to use as she wishes. The limits on that use—with some exceptions like obscenity—are, in general, the necessary implications of preventing adjacent uses of that freedom from interfering with each other, and, because the mind and its products are nonexclusive goods, these limits are remarkably broad. This regime stinks in the nostrils of the children of Rousseau, today called communitarians, who wish to lay claim to the mind—perhaps above all to the mind—for communal projects in the name of higher goods: salvation, equality, brotherhood, human perfection, national glory. And one of their ruses is to analogize the domain of discourse to the physical domain and thus to press the conclusion that the realm of the mind is also the realm of limited resources, for attention is not infinite and the dissemination of speech costs money.[1] By and large, as Chapter 4 shows, constitutional doctrine has resolutely resisted this attempt at socialism of the mind.

But liberty of action is quite another matter. It is one of the defining characteristics of the world we live in that material resources are limited. Indeed physical proximity is not simply an inevitable but an unfortunate constraint on liberty of action; it is a necessary condition for many kinds of desirable human interactions. Confinement of space and limited resources not only constrain our liberty but place conditions on what we can achieve. And it is a nice question whether the constrained material world or the unlimited realm of the mind is primary. So much of what we express and think is about what we would do in the material world: from building monuments, to curing the sick, to the act of love. The material world is the scene of limitation on our liberty of action and on our use of tangible resources. This is the domain of generalized liberty of action and of property. That is why the Constitution speaks of liberty and property in the same breath. And our constitutional texts, traditions, and doctrine are much more ambiguous in their rejection of the communal claim over space and material goods than they are in respect to liberty of the mind. The claim that material resources are communal resources in the first place, allotted to individuals in accordance with the interests of the community, has a far greater plausibility. Frederic Bastiat's dictum, that "the state is the great fictitious entity by which everyone seeks to live at the expense of everyone else,"[2] thus may seem to be nothing but a sour expression of a necessary truth, a truth which some say might as well be proclaimed in a joyful tone. The contrary posture, that the axiom of self-ownership extends to the "world and the fullness thereof"—implicit in the writings of classical liberals from Locke, to Kant, to Nozick—has been notoriously difficult to work out in concrete detail, and yet it is a persistent tendency in our traditions and law. One reason for this persistence may be the realization that the material world is the necessary scene in which freedom of the mind is played out.

The Texts: Takings, Contracts, and Due Process

The Fifth Amendment provides that "no person shall . . . be deprived of life, liberty, or property, without due process of law." The Fourteenth Amendment applies that limitation on the actions of the national government to the states: "[N]or shall any State deprive any person of life, liberty, or property, without due process of law. . . ." The history of the term "due process" and the placement of the clause in the Fifth Amendment after the several guarantees of rights in criminal proceedings strongly suggest that it was meant to stand as a general guarantee of procedural regularity in legal proceedings that might result in fines, confiscations, imprisonment, or sentences of death.[3]

Perhaps the guarantee was meant to apply also to civil proceedings in which a person might be deprived of his property, but civil proceedings are addressed specifically in the Seventh Amendment, which erects as its sole protection the right to a jury trial.[4] Government action against private interests outside the criminal context is addressed in the provision, immediately following the Fifth Amendment's Due Process Clause, that "private property shall not be taken for public use, without just compensation." This shifts the focus away from criminal proceedings and forfeitures. Whether the government simply grabs the property or institutes some kind of proceeding to seize it, the taking must be for a public use and accompanied by the payment of just compensation. The wording of the Takings Clause and its placement after the Due Process Clause, which addresses not takings but deprivation, further suggests that the Due Process Clause was written with criminal or punitive or penal deprivations in mind. Enactments that directly work a deprivation of life have never been an issue in the United States. In England legislative enactments forfeiting a person's life were not unknown, but they are specifically provided against in the unamended Constitution, which forbids bills of attainder.[5]

In spite of the textual focus of the Due Process Clause on deprivations in criminal proceedings, the argument was put forward, and in the notorious *Dred Scott* case[6] carried the day, that the Due Process Clause protected against substantive impositions and not just against defects in the procedures in which they are applied. Scott, a slave in Missouri, had been brought by his master, an army surgeon, to Fort Snelling in the territory of Upper Louisiana, in what was later to be the state of Wisconsin. Slavery was forbidden in that territory by the Missouri Compromise.[7] Scott brought suit for false imprisonment against his master in federal court after his return to Missouri (a slave state). He claimed his sojourn in those free lands had made him a free man and that he should not be considered to have again become a slave upon his return to Missouri. The Missouri Compromise had certainly been "duly" enacted into law. Nonetheless the Court denied Scott's claim.[8] The conclusion was infamous and its consequences disastrous, but the reasoning of the Court to that conclusion rests on (the misapplication of) a principle that continues to have resonance. Even in a territory not yet a state, "the power of Congress over the person or property of a citizen can never be a mere discretionary power." In passing laws for the governance of a territory, Congress is no less limited by the Bill of Rights and could not, for instance, "make any law in a Territory respecting the establishment of religion, or prohibiting the free exercise thereof, or abridging the freedom of speech, or of the press. . . ." The opinion continues:

> These powers, and others, in relation to rights of person . . . [are] denied to the General Government; and the rights of private property have been guarded with equal care. Thus the rights of private property are united with the rights of person, and placed on the same ground by the fifth amendment of the Constitution, which provides that no person shall be deprived of life, liberty, or property, without due process of law . . . And an Act of congress which deprives a citizen of the United States of his liberty or property, merely because he came himself or brought his property into a particular territory of the United States, and who has committed no offense against the laws, could hardly be dignified with the name of due process of law.[9]

What is significant about this passage—and the decision which it supports—is the firm but unargued assertion that the Due Process Clause judges the substance of law and not just the procedures by which laws are applied in particular circumstances. Consider a tax on incomes, or on incomes of a particular sort or level, or on inheritances: using Taney's phrasing, might one say that the exaction worked by such a tax "could hardly be dignified with the name of due process of law"? It is not *process* at all. It is a law, and the process comes later, when it is determined whether a particular instance falls under it. The Court did not say that the processes by which it was determined that Scott had entered and remained in a free territory were flawed or gave his master insufficient opportunity to show that he had never taken Scott into free territory. The Court's judgment was on the legislative end the law sought to serve, not on how fairly and accurately the processes for applying it served that end.

The same form of argument was used by the Court some fifty years later in the quite different context of a New York State law setting maximum hours for bakery workers. In *Lochner v. New York*[10] the Court held that "the general right to make a contract in relation to his business is part of the liberty of the individual protected by the 14th Amendment of the Federal Constitution." The Court went on:

> It must, of course, be conceded that there is a limit to the valid exercise of the police power by the state. There is no dispute concerning this general proposition. Otherwise the 14th Amendment would have no efficacy and the legislatures of the states would have unbounded power,

and it would be enough to say that any piece of legislation was enacted to conserve the morals, the health, or the safety of the people; such legislation would be valid, no matter how absolutely without foundation the claim might be. . . . In every case that comes before this court, therefore, where legislation of this character is concerned, and where the protection of the Federal Constitution is sought, the question necessarily arises: Is this a fair, reasonable, and appropriate exercise of the police power of the state, or is it an unreasonable, unnecessary, and arbitrary interference with the right of the individual to his personal liberty, or to enter into those contracts in relation to labor which may seem to him appropriate or necessary for the support of himself and his family? Of course the liberty of contract relating to labor includes both parties to it. The one has as much right to purchase as the other to sell labor.[11]

The case is different from *Dred Scott* only in that the New York statute was held to have deprived bakers and their employers of liberty, while the Missouri Compromise would have deprived Scott's master of his property. Both cases assume that the Constitution protects against deprivations of property or liberty even by the procedurally fair application of general laws. And both cases encounter the same textual and conceptual problems. But whatever the original, textual meaning of the Due Process Clause, this has long been accepted as its proper reach. As Justice Brandeis remarked in 1927, "[d]espite arguments to the contrary which had seemed to me persuasive, it is settled that the due process clause of the Fourteenth Amendment applies to matters of substantive law as well as to matters of procedure."[12]

The conceptual problem, however, is fundamental. All law in some way or another affects liberty or property. The background regimes of property, tort, and contract law both institute and limit what is to count as property and what may be considered an interference with liberty. As Holmes once put it, "your right to swing your arms ends just where the other man's nose begins."[13] The property and liberty interests seem so obvious in that example that we do not even notice that law establishes, or at least confirms them. But where is the line between my liberty interest in driving down the highway (at what speed?) and yours to walk along or to cross it? And that is a relatively simple line to draw. Nor have these background regimes been static. So if the Constitution really is to judge when *law* wrongly deprives a person of liberty or property, then constitutional law judges ordinary law.

But by what criteria? Archimedes, articulating the physics of the lever, is reported to have said: "Tell me where I might stand—*pou sto*—and I can move the earth." Where is the necessary constitutional *pou sto?* Even the apparently simpler—and constitutionally unavoidable—question of what constitutes *procedural* due process entails that constitutional law will judge ordinary processes to decide if they are indeed "due." And in that regard, from time to time, it has been claimed that the benchmark for what counts as due process might be found in the procedures and practices that obtained at the time of the framing of the Constitution,[14] except as the Constitution itself specifically lays out more stringent or different procedural requirements. But that view has not prevailed, yielding instead to vaguer, more general notions of procedural fairness in cases for which the Constitution does not specifically provide.[15] Criminal punishments may be imposed only after a jury trial, in which the accused has had the right to the assistance of counsel and to confront the witnesses against him. These and other procedural protections are what count as due process in the circumstances because the Bill of Rights says so.[16] But a person may be deprived of his liberty in proceedings that are not adjudications of guilt: there is preventive detention of those who are charged with crimes, and who pose a danger if left at large.[17] Some persons pose a sufficiently grave danger that they may even be detained after the conclusion of their sentences.[18] A criminal fine may only be imposed in proceedings that meet the standards of due process for criminal proceedings generally, but punitive financial exactions are imposed in civil proceedings and private tort suits.[19] Such noncriminal deprivations of liberty or property must require procedures fair enough to be called "due process," but no constitutional text establishes what process is due. Nor has constitutional doctrine accepted that there is some privileged historical moment, such as the time of the framing, which sets out the benchmark against which future procedures are to be measured. If that is so in respect to procedure, how much more difficult will it be to establish the constitutional *pou sto* from which to judge whether legislative changes in *substantive* rights work a deprivation of liberty or property?

Constitutional doctrine must judge ordinary law as a matter of course—whether the subject is federalism, separation of powers, speech, or religion—but in each of those subjects there is a constitutional text somewhere in the vicinity to offer guidance (or at least cover) for the development of doctrine. Due process is cut adrift from such textual guides. As for procedural due process, it will not do to treat it as simply a shorthand reference to the explicit procedural safeguards of the Bill of Rights (grand jury indictment, trial by jury, and the like), because this would make the reference to due process redundant. Still there is some guidance for the Court from the practices that the lawyers and judges over time have come to consider as fundamental aspects of fair procedure: most inescapably, the opportunity to present arguments and evidence to a decision maker who does not have a personal stake in the outcome,[20] and depending on the nature of the proceeding and what is at stake,[21] other safeguards as well, for instance, the assistance of counsel, perhaps even at government expense.[22] Even in Great Britain, which has no written constitution and no judicial review, the norms of something called natural justice are deployed to judge the fairness of administrative procedures, so long as other procedures are not clearly mandated by statute.[23] These minimum standards are also invoked in international law, as in the treatment of unlawful combatants otherwise not accorded the protections of the Geneva Conventions.[24] But when due process becomes a rubric for judging the *substance* of law, the guidance of professional norms arising out of the practice of adjudication is no longer available and the judges appear to many to be cast adrift on a sea of subjective preference and unbounded speculation.

For a time it was suggested that this unease might be quieted by treating the substantive application of due process simply as a convenient way of incorporating against the states the substantive protections of the Bill of Rights—for instance, First Amendment protections of speech and religion. This position has the signal virtue of tying substantive due process firmly to a constitutional text, but it has not prevailed. Indeed it would be odd, in the name of textual discipline, to do such violence to the text of the Constitution. After all, there is a due process clause in the Fifth Amendment too, and that can hardly be viewed as incorporating the rest of the Bill of Rights against the national government, since it is the national government alone that the Bill of Rights constrains. In the *Dred Scott* case, the Court did not even pause over this possibility, but used the clause as a further substantive constraint on the power of Congress. And in less notorious cases the Court has regularly gone beyond this incorporationist function to invalidate on substantive grounds both state and national government actions.

Embarrassed by these difficulties, commentators and judges, who do not like such apparently untethered judicial power, have proposed another standard for the exercise of this substantive judicial power: government action (legislative, administrative, executive) is unconstitutional if it can be shown to have no rational relation to a legitimate governmental end. So here we meet again the most permissive test of constitutionality: rational basis review, which asks only, Does the government seek to accomplish a permissible end, and are its means rationally related to its accomplishments? As permissive as this is, it is significant that it does assume the person subject to a law may challenge it as unreasonable. In other words, it is not true that government may do anything it wishes so long as it complies with formalities of enactment and there is no specific constitutional bar to that action. Seen from the perspective of rights, this proposition may be restated as a general right of the individual to be free of governmental imposition, if no reason for that imposition can be shown. It is the individual's right to be free from "arbitrary impositions and purposeless restraints."[25] Liberty is the default position. This liberty embodied in substantive due process is sometimes called negative liberty, or the liberty of the moderns[26]—that is, freedom from constraints by the state. Thus we have two competing default positions. The first acknowledges all government power, except as it is excluded by some explicit constitutional limitation; the second makes liberty the default position, and government power must always explain itself when it seeks to limit it.[27]

Some say this latter notion is incoherent, because all the conditions of ordinary civilized life depend on government constraints of some sort at some level, so that the absence of a particular constraint simply leaves in place the underlying net of government constraints. For instance, the absence of a rule preventing employers from requiring their employees to agree not to join a union[28] leaves in place the regime of legal constraints that would enforce such agreements. On this view government constraint is everywhere and it makes no sense to speak of more or less constraint, but only of the quality of one constraint (or system of constraints) relative to another.

Taking and Contracts

The concept of negative liberty depends on some background state of affairs, free from government constraint, from which every new constraint is a departure—a constitutional *pou sto*[29] that privileges this background state and the legal rules that embody it. Although such a privileging is a theoretically radical step, affirming as it does some set of legal rules as having a status that transcends ordinary law, it accords with an assumption in the profession (and beyond) that there is such a set: violence to the person is an actionable wrong, as is violent or fraudulent dispossession of property; agreements should be carried out.[30] So long as the background law is seen as embodying in one way or another these principles, departures from them by the government may be judged as government deprivations of "life, liberty, or property." But what of adjustments, dealing with such inevitable nuances as rules defining negligence or self-defense and specifying the types of agreements that will be enforced and under what circumstances, what counts as property, what as possession, and what as violent or fraudulent dispossession? Just as it is plausible to assign a transcendent status to the basic principles underwriting the security of the person, so it is implausible to assign such status to the details of the particular regimes embodying them. This explains why the decision in *Lochner* was implausible, enshrining a particular status quo in the regime of contract. But it also suggests why *Dred Scott* was not only implausible but wrong: it gave the details of a preexisting, contingent property regime (chattel slavery) a privileged position, while disregarding entirely the contrary, more fundamental claim of Scott himself to the basic protections of the security of his person—a disregard that reveals that even within the vague concepts of the background regimes of person, property, and agreement there is a certain structure and hierarchy.

The difficulty in specifying some background set of rules of liberty, property, and contract is matched by the serious constitutional embarrassment that arises from failing to make such a specification. The Constitution itself seems to require that doctrine find a way out, because it commands that private property not be taken for a public purpose without just compensation[31] and that states may not pass "any . . . Law impairing the Obligation of Contracts."[32] If law defines what does and does not count as a property right or the obligation of contract, then these constitutional guarantees appear to be caught between the extremes of vacuity (any governmental action in regular form counts as a redefinition of property or contract rights rather than their impairment) or paralysis (no change in law is allowed that disadvantages some property or contractual right). The principal strands of the resolution consist in a protection of generalized expectations against a too abrupt, too narrowly focused defeat of expectations and in the unstated but palpable assumption that there are property rights that are necessary to the very notion of having a system of property law.

The first of these strands is illustrated by *Eastern Enterprises v. Apfel*,[33] in which the Court invalidated federal legislation compelling certain businesses to make large annual payments to fund health benefits for retired coal miners, as the legislation was applied to businesses that had not been in the coal business for years and that had long ago fully discharged any obligations they had undertaken to their miners. This legislative imposition might have been analyzed as an impairment of the obligation of the original contract of employment between the miners and their employers, or as the "taking" of the money the former operators were obliged to pay the miners' fund, or as a deprivation of property without due process. The first of these was not readily available, because the impairment clause of the unamended Constitution applies only to the states, so that the force behind the clause must be incorporated—if at all—in the Fifth Amendment's protection against deprivation of property without due process of law.[34] The Takings Clause is an awkward fit too, because the just compensation in this case would simply be the return of the very money the operators had been forced to pay. The Takings Clause originally had in mind a kind of forced sale, allowing the government to get the property it believes it needs, leaving the owner no worse off with its monetary equivalent. Here the just compensation would lead not to increased social value after compensating the former owner, but rather simply to the negation of the scheme. So it was no wonder that, though a majority of the Court believed something was wrong about this imposition, it could not settle on a rationale: four justices plunked for the takings analysis, awkward though it was, while a fifth—emphasizing the violent retroactivity and obvious unfairness of the scheme in that it sought to solve a problem of national scope by recruiting a convenient but remotely related set of interests to bear a disproportionate part of the burden—argued that this was that rare case of legislation that worked a deprivation of property without due process.[35]

An example of the government's trying to solve a problem by redefining a property right out of existence is *Hodel v. Irving*.[36] At the end of the nineteenth century, Congress, pursuing a policy of assimilating Indians to the surrounding legal and social regime, allotted communal Indian reservation land to individual tribal members, on whose death it passed to their heirs. After several generations the original parcels were held in undivided interest by dozens and sometimes hundreds of owners. To solve the obvious and compounding difficulty of this development, Congress in 1983 sought to extinguish the most minuscule fractional interests, which yielded only nominal income, by causing those interests to revert to the tribe. So here a property right created and defined by statute would have been redefined out of existence as a result of a quite reasonable conclusion that it had led to an absurdity. Nevertheless the Court held the statute unconstitutional:

> [T]he character of the Government regulation here is extraordinary. . . . [T]he regulation here amounts to virtually the abrogation of the right to pass on a certain type of property—the small undivided interest—to one's heirs. In one form or another, the right to pass on property—to one's family in particular—has been part of the Anglo-American legal system since feudal times. . . .
>
> . . .
>
> In holding that complete abolition of both the descent and devise of a particular class of property may be a taking, we reaffirm the continuing vitality of the long line of cases recognizing the States', and where appropriate, the United States', broad authority to adjust the rules governing the descent and devise of property without implicating the guarantees of the Just Compensation Clause. The difference in this case is the fact that both descent and devise are completely abolished; indeed they are abolished even in circumstances when the governmental purpose sought to be advanced, consolidation of ownership of Indian lands, does not conflict with the further descent of the property.[37]

This analysis acknowledged the conventional nature of property rights and the government's power to unmake or modify what it has created—up to a point. Where what is created resembles a traditional right in property, then the traditional incidents of that right may be modified but may not be abolished without compensation. So without explicitly recognizing a Lockean natural right to property, constitutional doctrine comes close to that by affirming as the constitutional baseline—the conceptual *pou sto* of property—the long-established, traditional sense of property. Constitutional doctrine has been keen in its positivistic denial that there is some general, federal common law,[38] derided as a "brooding omnipresence in the sky."[39] Nonetheless, in deciding when governments have gone beyond simply adjusting the common law, takings law has assumed some underlying (or overarching) conceptual scheme of basic property law and then has taken it as a point of departure.[40] It could not be otherwise, if the clause were not to be read out of the Constitution.

Now it might be said that there is an alternative analysis that maintains the rigorously positivistic nature of property law regimes: there is no common ground, no underlying basis for property; it is all the contingent creature of state law. So the only inhibition can be that state law not change, or at least not change too much, too quickly, or in too narrowly focused a way. The very breadth of a revision is some guarantee that it is not being used to pick on some vulnerable or arbitrarily selected segment of the population.[41] But how much is too much, how fast too fast, are judgments that themselves suppose some accepted background of relatively stable concepts. Making every tenant the owner of what he rents, for instance, would be so radical as to require compensating the previous owner.[42] Converting a nine-hundred-and-ninety-nine-year lease into full ownership is a less compelling case of a taking, although even there the Indian allotment case suggests that some nominal compensation might have to be paid.[43] Authorizing the public to pass over a strip of your land is a taking, because it snaps into conceptual focus as the creation of an easement, which is a traditional interest in land; but a restriction on the use of property—if part of a general scheme as in zoning—may or may not be a taking because it does not fall under such a familiar conceptual rubric.[44]

The Court has been much more cautious about the Contracts Clause, which makes analogous theoretical demands on constitutional doctrine: unless there is some stable core to what the obligations of a contract are, constitutional doctrine has no way of concluding that those obligations have been "impaired." But the Contracts Clause has the potential to be much more constraining on government action than the Takings Clause. It is unconditional: it does not allow impairments at all, rather than—as in the case of the taking of property—requiring that the government make compensation for the loss inflicted. More important, property regimes come in preset packets of typical property rights (for example, leaseholds, fee simple ownership, easements), which are then bought, sold, traded, inherited, or given away. Contract, however, is a very general framework according to which two or more (perhaps very many more) individuals may structure relationships in the widest possible ways for what may be very extended periods. At its outer limits, contract has the potential to organize an entire alternative state. (This is the fantasy behind social contract theories.) Even much less extensive contractual arrangements offer a powerful alternative to the state's regulatory projects, while at the same time relying on the state's commitment to enforce contracts. I suggest this is the reason that constitutional doctrine has been much less rigorous in enforcing the Contracts Clause than the Property Clause. But it has not read the clause out of the Constitution altogether. Since the New Deal, doctrine has suggested greater scrutiny of government interventions that are designed to get it out of its own undertakings than of those that interfere with the obligations that private parties have undertaken to each other.[45] The test for interventions in the latter category is extremely forgiving.[46] And where the impairment may be seen as an incident of a general regulatory regime as that happens to impinge on such private arrangements, the rule is that the Contracts Clause does not apply at all. The state cannot be stopped from making and enforcing the legislative judgment that commercial gambling or the trade in intoxicating liquor is to be forbidden by the fact that all sorts of contracts in those businesses must as a result be abrogated.[47]

Liberty

But what of liberty? There is no liberty clause outside of the mention of liberty in the Due Process Clauses. Yet we are told that liberty has substantive meaning, and that that meaning is not exhausted by the liberties—for example, freedom of speech and religion guaranteed by the First Amendment—set out elsewhere in the Constitution. There are then two ways to give the concept of substantive liberty determinate content: either some process of constitutional speculation and doctrinal development may identify particular aspects of liberty that are sufficiently salient to attract substantive due process protection, or liberty may be conceived in general terms as absence of governmental restraint. Constitutional doctrine has done both. It embraces the libertarian premise that in principle any imposition must justify itself. In this respect the argument of *Lochner* and *Dred Scott* survives, but, like a vaccine, in radically attenuated form: government answers a challenge based on what is called a generalized liberty interest by showing that (1) its impingement on that interest is for a permissible end, and (2) the impingement on liberty is rationally related to the accomplishment of that end. In other words, government must always explain itself, but any explanation will do that is at all plausible and does not admit to seeking to accomplish what government, for other reasons, is not allowed to do.[48] This is the rational basis test, and it is so easily satisfied that one commentator has quipped that it describes "the Supreme Court as lunacy commission."[49] At the same time *Lochner*'s use of stricter scrutiny has been so discredited that its name stands as the apothegm for a whole basket of arguments against constitutional scrutiny of legislation. Indeed even when that scrutiny is not based on what might be called the Liberty Clauses but on some of the more explicitly constraining provisions of the Constitution, such as the Commerce Clause or the First Amendment, that scrutiny is derided as a reversion to the practice of which *Lochner* is the emblem.[50]

Liberty, as I have said, is negative liberty, and every government constraint impinges upon that to some extent, so that there must be some criteria for judging when those impingements are or are not constitutionally permissible. But this generalized concept of liberty— much more than the concepts of property and contract—lacks a firm textual or doctrinal basis from which to elaborate those criteria. In *Lochner* and similar cases the courts assumed that paternalism (sometimes)[51] and redistribution of bargaining power and resources were illegitimate governmental purposes. But as Holmes in his celebrated dissent in *Lochner* pointed out, that judgment was not so obviously correct that it could stand as the basis for overriding, in the name of the Constitution, the decisions of the democratically elected branches of government. If there is something wrong the Court must be able to say what it is, and what it says must allow principled distinctions to be made between instances in which these invalidating strictures do and do not apply. Apart from an expressed distaste for what was seen as incipient socialism, the Court was unable to offer such distinctions. *Lochner* was abandoned in *West Coast Hotel Co. v. Parrish*[52] at the beginning of Franklin Roosevelt's second term. Yet emphatic as that repudiation was, the Court never went the whole way to assert that apart from procedural defects and incorporation of explicit constitutional protections in the Bill of Rights, the Liberty Clauses afford no basis for invalidating government action. At least government must always explain itself.

Fundamental Rights

What has kept the Liberty Clauses alive has not been this largely symbolic and admonitory residual function, but their service as a font for the elaboration of a few but very powerful protections of several particular liberties. Two recent cases illustrate the interplay between these two functions of the clauses. In *Lawrence v. Texas*[53] the Supreme Court overruled its decision seventeen years earlier in *Bowers v. Hardwick*,[54] to the effect that there is no "fundamental right to engage in homosexual sodomy," and held that a statute criminalizing that very conduct was an unconstitutional infringement of liberty.

Washington v. Glucksberg, decided six years before *Lawrence*, offers the negative example. A person suffering from a painful, disabling, and terminal illness complained that he was prevented from receiving his doctor's help in ending his life because state law made the doctor's assistance a crime. The patient sought a judgment that this application of the law was an unconstitutional deprivation of liberty. The Court did not turn the complaint away on the ground that there is no explicit constitutional "right to die." Rather it acknowledged that the patient had a "liberty interest" in getting this help and for that reason the state had to offer a justification for this imposition on him.[55] The state's interest in protecting human life was held to be that sufficient justification. The Court was not clear whether this justification extended even to persons who did not wish to live or whether instead such persons' wishes were justifiably sacrificed in favor of a general rule that would protect people who might be incompetent to make such a choice or who might be pressured into making it. The Court also emphasized the traditional ban on suicide in the law of most states, as if a purpose that government has proclaimed generally and over a long period of time must for that reason be taken as legitimate. The concurring opinions displayed an alternative approach; each with various emphases acknowledged that, in an appropriate case, this generalized state interest would not be sufficient to overcome the individual's liberty interest: one justice wrote that if a person was in terrible pain and nothing short of death would end that pain, then the generalized state purpose might not be sufficient to justify depriving him of assistance in seeking to end his life.[56] Several others emphasized that this generalized interest would not be sufficient to justify withholding medication to alleviate pain, even if that medication would hasten death.[57] There was common ground in this spate of separate opinions: although the patients could cite no particular constitutional right that the government not prevent physicians from assisting them in committing suicide, all the justices granted that the patients at least had a liberty *interest* that the State of Washington law constrained. Although the burden of demonstrating unconstitutionality rested with the complainants, they were able to take the first step toward meeting it by showing that their liberty had been limited; it was then up to the state to offer some justification for that constraint.

In *Glucksberg* two quite different claims about liberty were in play. The most sweeping, which all the justices rejected, argued that a person's liberty to control the time and circumstances of his death could only be limited for some very good reason, a reason the Court should scrutinize closely. The concurring justices were concerned to save from that rejection the more focused claim to what may be the only means of surcease from extreme pain. For them, that liberty interest could not be so easily overridden by the invocation of a generalized state interest in protecting human life or perhaps not even by a more pointed concern that vulnerable persons not be pressured into ending their own, sometimes inconvenient, lives. The concurring justices assumed that some liberties, though not mentioned in the constitutional text, stand out from the undifferentiated background of liberty interests to receive a greater measure of protection than the rational basis test offers.

Glucksberg gives a vivid sense of how such liberties emerge. Their first statement must not be overly broad and abstract—as, for instance, a generalized right to control the shape of one's own life story, to write one's own ending to that story. Rather, a quite concrete situation evokes the reaction: that's monstrous; they can't do *that!* In these intimate matters the *fons et origo,* to which justices continually repair, is Justice Harlan's dissenting opinion in *Poe v. Ullman,*[58] in which he concluded that the application to a married couple of a Connecticut statute making the use of contraceptives a crime violated substantive due process. A majority of the Court ruled that the case was not justiciable, because there appeared to be no realistic prospect of its ever being enforced. Justice Harlan dissented from that threshold ruling and went on to explain why the statute was a deprivation of liberty without due process of law. Although that opinion is often cited as support for an expansive and indeterminate conception of substantive due process, the reasoning in that case was quite carefully limited to that specific application.

> I believe that a statute making it a criminal offense for married couples to use contraceptives is an intolerable and unjustifiable invasion of privacy in the conduct of the most intimate concerns of an individual's personal life. I reach this conclusion, even though I find it difficult and unnecessary at this juncture to accept appellants' other argument that the judgment of policy behind the statute, so applied, is so arbitrary and unreasonable as to render the enactment invalid for that reason alone.
>
> . . . Precisely what is involved here is this: the State is asserting the right to enforce its moral judgment by intruding upon the most intimate details of the marital relation with the full power of the criminal law. Potentially, this could allow the deployment of all the incidental machinery of the criminal law, arrests, searches and seizures; inevitably, it must mean at the very least the lodging of criminal charges, a public trial, and testimony as to the corpus delicti. Nor could any imaginable elaboration of presumptions, testimonial privileges, or other safeguards, alleviate the necessity for testimony as to the mode and manner of the married couples' sexual relations, or at least the opportunity for the accused to make denial of the charges. In sum, the statute allows the State to enquire into, prove and punish married people for the private use of their marital intimacy. This, then, is the precise character of the enactment whose Constitutional measure we must take.[59]

It is in this context that the opinion acknowledges that, while state legislation enjoys a presumption of constitutionality, that presumption is not so strong as to justify—quoting from an earlier case[60]— "arbitrary impositions and purposeless restraints." Nor is the discouragement of sexual immorality—Harlan instances fornication, adultery, homosexuality, and abortion—ruled out as a proper state purpose. What makes the case against the Connecticut statute is the concrete way in which its prohibition would work out in practice. "Though the State has argued the Constitutional permissibility of the moral judgment underlying this statute, neither its brief, nor its argument, nor anything in any of the opinions of its highest court in these or other cases even remotely suggests a justification for the obnoxiously intrusive means it has chosen to effectuate that policy."

So the heart of the matter is a *frisson* of disgust at what the state threatened to do. Justice Harlan underscored this aspect of his decision by his reliance on an earlier procedural due process case, *Rochin v. California.*[61] Police officers had forcibly entered the bedroom of a suspected drug trafficker and, when he swallowed two capsules on a nightstand, first jumped on his stomach and then removed him to a hospital where they had his stomach pumped out to retrieve the evidence. Justice Frankfurter declined to find a violation of any specific provision of the Bill of Rights, which had at that time not been incorporated against the states through the Due Process Clause of the Fourteenth Amendment. Rather, he fastened on the particulars of the case:

> This is conduct that shocks the conscience. Illegally breaking into the privacy of the petitioner, the struggle to open his mouth and remove what was there, the forcible extraction of his stomach's contents—this course of proceeding by agents of government to obtain evidence is bound to offend even hardened sensibilities. . . . Due process of law, as a historic and generative principle, precludes defining, and thereby confining, these standards of conduct more precisely than to say that convictions cannot be brought about by methods that offend a sense of justice.[62]

The difficulty with this explanation is that it seems both highly subjective and episodic. How much more serious is this complaint when the Court acts not against a particular act of official misconduct to overturn a particular conviction but invalidates a general enactment, as Harlan would have in *Poe;* that is, when it passes from procedural to substantive due process. Yet Harlan did not shrink from making that passage, and quoted from Frankfurter's defense against the charge of subjectivity:

> The vague contours of the Due Process Clause do not leave judges at large. We may not draw on our merely personal and private notions and disregard the limits that bind judges in their judicial function. Even though the concept of due process of law is not final and fixed, these limits are derived from considerations that are fused in the whole nature of our judicial process. . . . These are considerations deeply rooted in reason and in the compelling traditions of the legal profession.

Constitutional adjudication is a kind of common law adjudication, in which courts proceed by way of analogy from particular to particular, invoking traditions, precedents, and professional intuition. As Frankfurter referred to the privilege against self-incrimination in *Rochin,* so Harlan pointed to specific provisions in the Bill of Rights—for instance, the Third Amendment's prohibition against quartering of soldiers in private homes in peacetime (a rare invocation of that provision) and the Fourth Amendment's protections against unreasonable searches and seizures—not as controlling constitutional texts, but as evidence of the "compelling traditions of the legal profession":

> It is this outlook which has led the Court continuingly to perceive distinctions in the imperative character of Constitutional provisions, since that character must be discerned from a particular provision's larger context. And inasmuch as this context is one not of words, but of history and purposes, the full scope of the liberty guaranteed by the Due Process Clause cannot be found in or limited by the precise terms of the specific guarantees elsewhere provided in the Constitution. This "liberty" is not a series of isolated points pricked out in terms of the taking of property; the freedom of speech, press, and religion; the right to keep and bear arms; the freedom from unreasonable searches and seizures; and so on. It is a rational continuum which, broadly speaking, includes a freedom from all substantial arbitrary impositions and purposeless restraints.

The Harlan opinion also found support in *Pierce v. Society of Sisters*[63] and *Meyer v. Nebraska,*[64] two decisions from the days before the Court had repudiated *Lochner* and similar cases. In *Pierce* the Court struck down a state law requiring children to attend only public schools, and in *Meyer* the Court struck down a statute forbidding instruction of young children in foreign languages. In neither case could the laws be characterized as "arbitrary impositions and purposeless restraints." Nor could it be said that these laws were not rationally related to a legitimate government interest. On the contrary, both laws had in view the similar, substantial government interest in providing a unifying common experience to young children as a prelude to one conception of common citizenship. The Court based its decisions on the guarantee of substantive liberty in the Due Process Clause, writing that "it denotes not merely freedom from bodily restraint but also the right of the individual to contract, to engage in any of the common occupations of life, to acquire useful knowledge, to marry, establish a home and bring up children, to worship God according to the dictates of his own conscience, and generally to enjoy those privileges long recognized at common law as essential to the orderly pursuit of happiness by free men." There is no doubt that these cases would come out the same way today and perhaps the Court might find some way to fit them under the speech, association, and religion clauses of the First Amendment, but it seems closer to the truth that the offense is to a generalized notion of liberty. By citing them, Harlan makes his point that generalized substantive due process liberty comes into sharper focus in the vicinity of explicit constitutional guarantees, which lend force and warrant to what might otherwise seem untethered speculation, but he also makes the point that there are liberties—and urgent ones at that, deserving more than mere rational basis scrutiny—outside the explicit scope of particular constitutional provisions. *Meyer* and *Pierce* have continued to be cited for just those propositions ever since.

But as the masters of the exposition of the common law have shown,[65] particularistic decisions, moved by the force of urgent specifics, may for a time exert their influence in a case-by-case accretion of precedents in similar circumstances, but their influence cannot forever be exerted in this sideways fashion. Eventually they either run out, or, if potent, they invite courts to move to higher levels of abstraction, where more general propositions are announced, and it is these that begin to take over some of the work of deciding cases. So it was with the Harlan dissent in *Poe* and substantive due process. As a first step, four years later, in *Griswold v. Connecticut*,[66] the Connecticut anticontraception statute was once again before the Court and this time the Court reached the merits in a welter of opinions, none of which had the sweep and majesty of Harlan's original dissent in *Poe*. The opinion of the Court did pick up on Harlan's reference to several provisions of the Bill of Rights and argued that, though not specifically controlled by them, the case fell in the penumbra of each. (I suppose, continuing the optical metaphor, that where several penumbra intersect they darken to a determinative holding.)

In *Poe*, Harlan also emphasized the concept of privacy as it appears in several contexts in the law:

> Although the form of intrusion here—the enactment of a substantive offense—does not, in my opinion, preclude the making of a claim based on the right of privacy embraced in the "liberty" of the Due Process Clause, it must be acknowledged that there is another sense in which it could be argued that this intrusion on privacy differs from what the Fourth Amendment, and the similar concept of the Fourteenth, were intended

to protect: here we have not an intrusion into the home so much as on the life which characteristically has its place in the home. But to my mind such a distinction is so insubstantial as to be captious: if the physical curtilage of the home is protected, it is surely as a result of solicitude to protect the privacies of the life within. Certainly the safeguarding of the home does not follow merely from the sanctity of property rights. The home derives its pre-eminence as the seat of family life. And the integrity of that life is something so fundamental that it has been found to draw to its protection the principles of more than one explicitly granted Constitutional right. Thus, Mr. Justice Brandeis, writing of a statute which made "it punishable to teach (pacifism) in any place (to) a single person . . . no matter what the relation of the parties may be," found such a "statute invades the privacy and freedom of the home. Father and mother may not follow the promptings of religious belief, of conscience or of conviction, and teach son or daughter the doctrine of pacifism. If they do, any police officer may summarily arrest them. . . ." This same principle is expressed in the *Pierce* and *Meyer* cases. These decisions, as was said in *Prince v. Commonwealth of Massachusetts,* "have respected the private realm of family life which the state cannot enter."

Griswold picked up on this and spoke of marriage specifically as a "relationship lying within the zone of privacy created by several fundamental constitutional guarantees." From this the Court drew two potent general concepts: that certain aspects of liberty are "fundamental" and that those aspects may be captured in the notion of a "right to privacy." A few years later, in *Eisenstadt v. Baird,*[67] *Griswold* was extended in a strikingly offhand way to strike down a Massachusetts law forbidding the distribution of contraceptives, as applied to unmarried persons. Justice Brennan's opinion for the Court brushed aside the heavy emphasis on the traditional special protection for the marital relationship in both the *Poe* dissent and *Griswold:*

> If under Griswold the distribution of contraceptives to married persons cannot be prohibited, a ban on distribution to unmarried persons would be equally impermissible. It is true that in Griswold the right of privacy in question inhered in the marital relationship. Yet the marital couple is not an independent entity with a mind and heart of its own, but an association of two individuals each with a separate intellectual and emotional makeup. If the right of privacy means anything, it is the right of the individual, married or single, to be free from unwarranted governmental intrusion into matters so fundamentally affecting a person as the decision whether to bear or beget a child.

I have said that the common law method, which the Court appears to have adopted here and in other areas, does include an eventual passage from the random walk of decisions on particular, often striking facts to some greater degree of generality. But the move from *Griswold* to the pronouncement in *Baird* was quite a leap. It proclaimed two generalizations, neither of which was by any means implicit in the earlier decisions. *Poe, Griswold,* and *Eisenstadt* itself all involved only contraception. The phrase "the decision whether to bear or beget a child" casually slips in the word "bear," and so alludes to the quite different and much more controversial issue of abortion. The issue is different because, of course, the kind of intrusion on privacy—marital or not—that Harlan found so offensive in *Poe* is not present with respect to a surgical procedure. And it is more controversial because contraception involves only a judgment on the voluntary conduct of the persons involved, while the energy in the opposition to abortion comes from the claim that it involves killing what is referred to as the unborn child, an innocent third party. There is much to be said on both sides of this concern, but Justice Brennan's phrase disposes of the issue as if it did not exist. That what is involved here is a "right of privacy" and that this right is a right to be "free of unwanted governmental intrusion into matters so fundamentally affecting the person" point even further beyond the facts of this case to suggest a very general principle of liberty in respect to "matters fundamentally affecting a person."

And it was only one year later that the subterranean passage Justice Brennan had dug between contraception and abortion made possible the decision in *Roe v. Wade,*[68] in which the Court pronounced that the right to privacy under the liberty clauses of the Fifth and Fourteenth Amendments included the right to choose an abortion virtually free of any substantial government regulation, at least in the first three or six months of a pregnancy. (In the first three months, the only permissible regulations require that a doctor be consulted and that he supervise the procedure. In the next three months, the state may intervene a bit more, but only so far as is necessary to protect the health of the mother.) The opinion explaining this important conclusion is quite cursory. The Court rejected the claim, pressed by some who submitted briefs in the case, "that one has an unlimited right to do with one's body as one pleases." The Court instead stated that the right of privacy "founded in the Fourteenth Amendment's concept of personal liberty . . . is broad enough to encompass a woman's decision whether or not to terminate her pregnancy." To deny a woman that choice would in some cases cause "direct harm medically diagnosable." The birth of the child "may force upon the woman a distressful life and future. . . . Mental and physical health may be taxed by child care. There is also the distress, for all concerned, associated with the unwanted child." And there is the "continuing stigma of unwed motherhood." The seriousness of these detriments led to the conclusion that the woman's liberty interest to be free of them is "fundamental," with the entailment that the state can overcome it not with just any legitimate governmental purpose but only with one that is "compelling." The Court recognized two legitimate government interests in regulating abortion: the health of the mother and the "potentiality of human life" that the pregnancy presents. It is in balancing these legitimate state interests with the woman's fundamental liberty interest that the Court came up with its trimester formulation: in the first trimester the interest in the woman's health can only justify insisting that abortion be a matter between the woman and a physician. In the second trimester the opinion allows only such additional regulation as is necessary to assure that any abortion at this medically somewhat riskier stage is performed in a way that will safeguard the mother's health.

This much is straightforward. The difficulties arise from the recognition of a legitimate governmental concern in "the potentiality of human life." The very formulation of that interest is oddly, even coyly abstract. Opponents of abortion, of course, claim that the fetus is not potential but actual human life—a person. But the Court emphatically rejected that claim, pointing to the lack of a consistent history in the common law of treating the unborn as persons, to the dispute among scientists, moralists, and theologians on the point, and to the lack of a definition of the term "person" in the text or the background materials of the Fourteenth Amendment.[69] To have decided otherwise might have implied, as the German Constitutional Court concluded, that permissive abortion laws not only are not constitutionally required; they are constitutionally forbidden.[70] The difficulty deepened when the Court ruled that the state's legitimate interest in potential life is compelling, but only in the third trimester of the pregnancy. Roe held that at that late stage it is not the woman's liberty interest, but only the life or health of the mother, that can overcome the state's interest in potential human life. But why then, or only then? The Court offers without any elaboration the reason that it is in the third trimester that the fetus becomes viable, that it is in theory capable of life outside the womb. Because, standing alone as it did, this seems a total non sequitur, one is driven to seek the explanation elsewhere. I find the explanation in the intuition that at that late stage the fetus is more palpable to us as a baby. We can imagine its separate existence in a crib or incubator, so that allowing it to be killed seems too much like infanticide. If it "shocks the conscience" to force a woman pregnant for a few weeks to carry that pregnancy for the next eight months although relief is medically an easy matter, so I suppose it may shock the conscience to allow the abortion of a baby a few weeks or days short of its birth in the ordinary course. And of course it is true that every late pregnancy is preceded by an early one, during which time the pregnancy could have easily been ended. But these intuitions seem a very slim and doubtful basis for a set of constitutional rules promulgated in the face of strong differences not only in the public mind but also among the legal regimes in the several states—some quite permissive and others allowing little or no room for abortion. And all this is a long way from the truly anomalous Connecticut statute in *Griswold.* Just what authority the Court was claiming for itself in *Roe v. Wade* and in the name of what doctrine is hard to tell.

In 1994 in *Planned Parenthood of Southeastern Pennsylvania v. Casey,*[71] the Court reconsidered and, in a much more elaborate set of opinions than in *Roe,* reaffirmed what the principal opinion called *Roe*'s "essential holding."[72] That opinion took into account the generation of criticism and analysis since the original decision. For instance, there was explicit recognition of the claim that the ready availability of abortion had had a large impact on women's ability to plan their lives and careers and thus removed a barrier to equality between the sexes. And less was made of the earlier touchstone in the notion of a right of privacy. Rather, recalling a phrase in Justice Brennan's *Eisenstadt* opinion, there was a suggestion of a far more comprehensive and generative conception of liberty:

> Our precedents "have respected the private realm of family life which the state cannot enter." These matters, involving the most intimate and personal choices a person may make in a lifetime, choices central to personal dignity and autonomy, are central to the liberty protected by the Fourteenth Amendment. At the heart of liberty is the right to define

one's own concept of existence, of meaning, of the universe, and of the mystery of human life. Beliefs about these matters could not define the attributes of personhood were they formed under compulsion of the State.

This concept of liberty recalls the very strong First Amendment concept of liberty of the mind, but goes beyond it to comprehend as well restrictions on conduct that only by a stretch can be described as communicative—although sexual intimacy comes closer to fitting under that rubric than does abortion. Of course, any conduct may be considered expressive, but only in the sense that much of what one does issues from one's desires and beliefs, and in that sense expresses them. Indeed one wag has defended the decision in *Lochner* as upholding the right of competent adults to engage in consensual economic relations without the interference of the state—which is very close to what the Court held in *Lawrence,* changing only one adjective. Clearly the *Casey* opinion did not intend to embody John Stuart Mill's principle that "the only purpose for which power can be rightfully exercised over any member of a civilized community, against his will, is to prevent harm to others. His own good, either physical or moral, is not a sufficient warrant." It is doubtful if the law has even come close to so rigorously an antipaternalist rule, and at any rate it is not difficult to identify some spillover effect from almost all adult consenting conduct, say, which courts would then have to accept as satisfying Mill's principle, if indeed they did adopt it as the meaning of the Liberty Clauses. Thus by the Court's own reasoning abortion limitations are not just "purposeless restraints," but they consider the "harm" to society that comes from the destruction of what the Court called potential life—as well as the harm that comes from the disappointment of whatever hopes and claims the father of the child may entertain. The "mystery of life" passage, therefore, promotes certain liberties to a level where government intrusion is excluded in spite of legitimate governmental concerns. Why the decision to "bear . . . a child"—as profoundly as it may color the rest of a person's life—should be promoted to this level, but the decision to control the circumstances of one's death should not, can only be explained in terms of practical and political concerns and not in terms of the vague general principle offered in *Casey.*

The strong reaffirmation of *Roe* in *Casey* put considerable pressure on *Bowers v. Hardwick,* the 1986 decision in which the Court in a strikingly cursory and disdainful opinion dismissed the notion that "any kind of private sexual conduct between consenting adults is constitutionally insulated from state proscription." If abortion is an intimate, private choice such that its prohibition "shocks the conscience," as would the prospect of mounting a prosecution of a man and woman for using contraceptives, then surely so is the prosecution of two men observed by sheer chance as they engaged in sexual relations behind what they thought was a closed bedroom door. The Court in *Bowers* noted that here there was no "connection between family, marriage, or procreation" and homosexual sodomy. And it recurred to Justice Harlan's criteria for discerning fundamental rights in the absence of some warrant in the constitutional text: "those fundamental liberties that are implicit in the concept of ordered liberty such that neither liberty nor justice would exist if they were sacrificed," or "those liberties that are deeply rooted in the Nation's history and tradition."[73] Because proscriptions on homosexual conduct have been long-standing and quite general, the Court held that the complainant Hardwick's claim was implausible. The same argument was deployed in *Washington v. Glucksberg,* that laws against suicide or assisting it have been so long-standing and general that a contrary liberty could not be claimed to be "deeply rooted in the Nation's history and tradition." Yet the general principle and its expanded conception of privacy stated in *Casey* would seem to apply quite directly to Bowers— indeed even more than to the abortion decision. Sexual orientation, and the organization of sexual expression and the conduct of one's life it may entail, fit far more closely than does the decision to have an abortion the notion of "attributes of personhood" that should not be "formed under the compulsion of the state."* As the Court put it in *Lawrence:*

---

* Indeed, the dissents in *Lawrence* quite clearly derive their energy from the dissenters' expressed strong antipathy to the abortion decisions, in which both practically and morally they believed a great deal more was at stake than in the Texas sodomy case. Justice Thomas, for instance, called the Texas statute "uncommonly silly" and stated that as a legislator he would vote to repeal it. *Bowers* was decided after *Roe* but before the reaffirmation of *Roe*'s "central holding" in *Casey* seven years later. Thus *Bowers* may have been viewed at the time as a stalking horse for the reconsideration of *Roe*, and this may account for the harshness of the Court's opinion, the author of which was one of the principal dissenters in *Roe.* The decision in *Bowers* was closely divided, and only the concurrence of Justice Powell, one of *Roe*'s most consistent supporters, prevented a contrary result. After his retirement in 1987 Justice Powell stated publicly that he regretted his vote in *Bowers.*

The statutes [in this case and in *Bowers*] . . . seek to control a personal relationship that, whether or not entitled to formal recognition in the law, is within the liberty of persons to choose without being punished as criminals.

This, as a general rule, should counsel against attempts by the State, or a court, to define the meaning of the relationship or to set its boundaries absent injury to a person or abuse of an institution the law protects. It suffices for us to acknowledge that adults may choose to enter upon this relationship in the confines of their homes and their own private lives and still retain their dignity as free persons. When sexuality finds overt expression in intimate conduct with another person, the conduct can be but one element in a personal bond that is more enduring. The liberty protected by the Constitution allows homosexual persons the right to make this choice.

The Court's conclusion moves beyond the particulars that first moved Justice Harlan to bridle at the Connecticut birth control statute and to refer there to a right to privacy, and embraces a far more general and fecund conception of privacy, a conception that, as I have said, bears a close resemblance to the principle of freedom of the mind:

Liberty protects the person from unwarranted government intrusions into a dwelling or other private places. In our tradition the State is not omnipresent in the home. And there are other spheres of our lives and existence, outside the home, where the State should not be a dominant presence. Freedom extends beyond spatial bounds. Liberty presumes an autonomy of self that includes freedom of thought, belief, expression, and certain intimate conduct. The instant case involves liberty of the person both in its spatial and more transcendent dimensions.

Although the decision does not quite embrace the Millian principle, it comes close:

The present case does not involve minors. It does not involve persons who might be injured or coerced or who are situated in relationships where consent might not easily be refused. It does not involve public conduct or prostitution. It does not involve whether the government must give formal recognition to any relationship that homosexual persons seek to enter. The case does involve two adults who, with full and mutual consent from each other, engaged in sexual practices common to a homosexual lifestyle.

If liberty is the default position, then this statement may be taken to deny that widely shared moral disapproval standing alone is a sufficient ground for government's restriction of liberty. "The issue," said the Court in *Lawrence,* "is whether the majority may use the power of the State to enforce these [moral and religious] views on the whole society through operation of the criminal law. Our obligation is to define the liberty of all, not to mandate our own moral code." Justice Harlan, by contrast, endorsed the community's moral judgments as a ground for curtailing liberty—citing laws on "marriage and divorce, adult consensual homosexuality, abortion and sterilization, or euthanasia and suicide." In this respect, *Lawrence* moves quite close to Justice Brennan's views on obscenity, discussed in Chapter 4.

And the principle enunciated in *Casey* and carried forward here also greatly attenuates Justice Harlan's other disciplinary caution: that substantive due process must be referable to the customs and traditions of the law and the legal profession. The Connecticut statute was a distant outlier. The Texas statute, while representing a distinct minority position and one with dwindling support, certainly has roots in public morality and its legislated embodiment.* Justice Scalia, having failed to uproot substantive due process altogether, would have formalized the disciplining authority of tradition invoked by Harlan by staying with the most particular traditional judgment and moving to a higher level of generality only when history does not speak to the particular practice before the Court.[74] But in interpreting tradition, as in interpreting the First Amendment or the structural provisions of the Constitution (or the Eleventh Amendment), the Court has been willing to look behind the established particulars to discern principles that may outrun the specific applications that were originally contemplated. Once again, as the Court put it in *Lawrence:*

> Had those who drew and ratified the Due Process Clauses of the Fifth Amendment or the Fourteenth Amendment known the components of liberty in its manifold possibilities, they might have been more specific. They did not presume to have this insight. They knew times can blind us

---

* For the first time, the Court in *Lawrence* drew on a decision of the European Court of Human Rights. That court had held that laws of Northern Ireland criminalizing consensual homosexual conduct violated the European Convention on Human Rights. The Court in *Lawrence* said that this "decision is at odds with the premise in *Bowers* that that claim put forward was insubstantial in our Western civilization."

to certain truths and later generations can see that laws once thought necessary and proper in fact serve only to oppress. As the Constitution endures, persons in every generation can invoke its principles in their own search for greater freedom.

In these leading cases it was not a generalized conception of liberty that carried the day but a notion of fundamental rights. Nor has this notion been limited to abortion and sexual practices. Several cases have relied on the substantive due process concept of liberty and on the opinions in *Poe, Griswold,* and *Casey* to protect the right of a grandmother to live with her two grandchildren—cousins, not brothers—in a "single-family" unit,[75] the right of a divorced father to marry without satisfying a court that he could meet his obligations to the children of his prior marriage,[76] the right of a prisoner to marry without the prison superintendent's permission,[77] and in *Troxel v. Granville* a widow's right to limit her dead husband's parents' access to her children in spite of a state statute and a court order granting visitation to the grandparents.[78] In that last case the opinion affirmed the "fundamental" substantive due process right of a fit parent "to make decisions concerning the care, custody and control of their children."

These decisions—and especially the ones concerning abortion and homosexual relations—have been controversial and have attracted powerful dissents. And indeed it is difficult to discern a principle that would make coherent the pattern of decision. If abortion is an intimate, private choice such that its prohibition "shocks the conscience" as does the prospect of prosecuting a man and a woman for using contraceptives, or two adult men engaging in sexual relations in private, and if making choices that define the shape and meaning of one's life dictates a right to choose abortion or to engage in homosexual practices, then why does it not follow that a terminally ill person who is in extreme pain may not choose to end his life a few days or weeks earlier than would inevitably happen? How are these lines drawn? A strong and general version of the Millian presumption of liberty is not at work. Only "fundamental" rights are protected. Nor are the traditions of the common law and the legal profession doing the work: certainly the Connecticut contraception law was an anomaly, but laws regulating abortion more stringently than the *Roe/Casey* line would allow were standard in the country and still are in many nations, including liberal democracies.[79] Tradition may be a guide, but its teach-ings are nuanced and require interpretation. Justice Harlan in *Poe* cited traditions of respect for the institution of marriage, and the Court in *Moore* referred to a tradition of the family and the home that not only included a mother, father, and children but extended connec-tions, as to grandparents. As suggested above, even the concept of pri-vacy as developed in *Lawrence* might be said to have some traditional force behind it.

But the task is difficult and uncertain. After all, though the grand-parent won in *Moore*, the grandparents lost in *Troxel*, the grandpar-ents' visitation rights case. There are reasons why those cases do not contradict but support each other: in both cases the Court would not allow the state to interfere with family arrangements. It might be said—as has been said in respect to negative liberty in general—that in *Troxel* leaving in place the mother's de facto control over access to her children is to sanction a governmental judgment about the family too. We must refine further and notice that *Troxel* depends on the judgment that a fit parent should be left in charge of determining the shape of her child's situation without splitting that authority with more distant relatives. And by this more nuanced use of tradition, *Bowers* was wrongly decided and did not survive, insofar as it applies to consensual adult sex, but that conclusion may have uncertain en-tailments for issues like same-sex marriage and adoption by same-sex couples, and discrimination against homosexuals by the military or educational institutions.

This uncertain picture shows how perilous it would be for the Court to assign itself the task of policing the whole universe of laws, regulations, and administrative and executive actions in the name of the Liberty Clauses and substantive due process. Although the Court has declined to deny itself such a role in principle—all government acts are subject at least to rational basis review—or even to restrict it to the incorporation in constitutional liberty of the specific liberties set out in the Bill of Rights, still by the doctrine of fundamental rights it has limited its effective role to a few topics, roughly relating to is-sues in and around the family and to intimate associations which the law should blush to interfere with. Other aspects of liberty are covered quite robustly in the expansive understanding of the First Amendment's protection of expression and association.

What is left uncovered is the important area of economic liberty, which the Takings and Property clauses protect only partially. This is an artifact of history and of a kind of allergic reaction to the Court's activities in the *Lochner* area. For some people liberty as it touches their work and property is as important as their family and sex life. For not a few people who work, profession and property may involve "choices central to personal dignity and autonomy, [that] are central to the liberty protected by the Fourteenth Amendment. At the heart of liberty is the right to define one's own concept of existence, of meaning, of the universe, and of the mystery of human life." The best that I can say to explain and perhaps to justify this uncertain body of law is to relate it to the principle of freedom of expression and association that the Court has elaborated in the name of the First Amendment. Matters of sex are forms of expression after all, and, like family groupings, forms of association. If in the future the Court is pressed to use these decisions to declare a right to same-sex marriage, to adoption by same-sex couples, perhaps even to plural marriages, the line may once again be drawn in terms of liberty: the state need not recognize same-sex couples as married, but it must leave them alone and not interfere with how they conduct their relations. Perhaps even adultery may not be prosecuted as a crime, while the state may decline to recognize plural marriage and grant adultery as a grounds for marriage's dissolution. So far the Court has not gone too far in its protection of liberty under the Due Process Clause. Perhaps it has not gone far enough.

Pervasive Procedural Protection

The preceding sections dealt with limits on government's substantive power to deprive persons of life, liberty, or property—no matter what procedures it followed. To complete the account of due process doctrine, I consider the amorphous domain of limitations on government power which address not what deprivations it may impose, but what procedures it must observe when it does so. In *Board of Regents v. Roth*[80] a state university teacher with a one-year contract complained that he had been given no reasons why his contract was not renewed at the end of his term and therefore he had been denied property without due process of law—that is, without fair procedures having been followed. The Court denied the claim because state law, which had created the position, had created no entitlement beyond the one-year term and so no property interest beyond that term. The state could decline to renew the appointment without following any procedures at all. Justice Marshall in dissent gave a very broad statement of the opposite position:

> Every citizen who applies for a government job is entitled to it unless the government can establish some reason for denying the employment. This is the "property" right that I believe is protected by the Fourteenth Amendment and cannot be denied "without due process of law." And it is also liberty—liberty to work—which is the "very essence of the personal freedom and opportunity" secured by the Fourteenth Amendment.

This very proposition could not have been confined to the circumstances of Roth's case, for the same could be said of persons who seek government contracts or benefits of any kind. Such a conclusion would have constitutionalized a vast range of state and federal government decision making, giving the federal courts a general supervisory authority over much of government at all levels. Nor is the proposal less sweeping for being limited to its insistence only on procedural regularity in all such decisions, for if courts have the constitutional mandate to insist that government give reasons for all actions someone finds detrimental, then it is hardly any step at all for courts to infer a responsibility to decide what amounts to a good reason. After all, a court that followed Justice Marshall's conception should not be satisfied with the reason "because we felt like it," or "because it was for the good of the service."

The Court has stated it is quite unwilling to assume such a role as guarantor of administrative regularity and rationality for all government action in which review would pass from process to substance.[81] But neither has it closed the door entirely on assuming some such role. Just two years before *Roth* it had held in *Goldberg v. Kelly*[82] that New York violated due process when it removed a person from the welfare rolls without first offering an opportunity to appear in person and contest the denial of eligibility. (The system did allow a fairly full opportunity to contest the termination in writing and then granted a full personal hearing, but only after termination.) The Court emphasized that the denial of a benefit to which a person may be entitled by law was the kind of deprivation that required procedural safeguards. Justice Black's dissent is instructive:

I would have little, if any, objection to the majority's decision in this case if it were written as the report of the House Committee on Education and Labor, but as an opinion ostensibly resting on the language of the Constitution I find it woefully deficient. Once the verbiage is pared away it is obvious that this Court today adopts the views of the District Court that to cut off a welfare recipient in the face of . . . brutal need without a prior hearing of some sort is unconscionable, and therefore, says the Court, unconstitutional. The majority reaches this result by a process of weighing the recipient's interest in avoiding the termination of welfare benefits against the governmental interest in summary adjudication. Today's balancing act requires a pre-termination evidentiary hearing, yet there is nothing that indicates what tomorrow's balance will be. Although the majority attempts to bolster its decision with limited quotations from prior cases, it is obvious that today's result does not depend on the language of the Constitution itself or the principles of other decisions, but solely on the collective judgment of the majority as to what would be a fair and humane procedure in this case.

This decision is thus only another variant of the view often expressed by some members of this Court that the Due Process Clause forbids any conduct that a majority of the Court believes "unfair," "indecent," or "shocking to their consciences."

. . .

The procedure required today as a matter of constitutional law finds no precedent in our legal system. Reduced to its simplest terms, the problem in this case is similar to that frequently encountered when two parties have an ongoing legal relationship that requires one party to make periodic payments to the other. Often the situation arises where the party "owing" the money stops paying it and justifies his conduct by arguing that the recipient is not legally entitled to payment. The recipient can, of course, disagree and go to court to compel payment. But I know of no situation in our legal system in which the person alleged to owe money to another is required by law to continue making payments to a judgment-proof claimant without the benefit of any security or bond to insure that these payments can be recovered if he wins his legal argument.[83]

What is the difference between *Goldberg* and *Roth*? Is it the urgency of the need—the welfare recipient who has been cut off is desperate, the college teacher is just out of a job? The Court in *Roth* made the point that the very government program on which the teacher relied, far from establishing an entitlement to future employment, explicitly limited the position to one year. There was no such limit in the welfare program. So perhaps the two cases illustrate yet again the same point that appeared in the takings cases: property is a creature of law, and government cannot be charged with "taking" an interest that it had not first established as a property interest.[84] Might it not be said that the procedure for contesting a denial of welfare was part of the very entitlement the claimant was insisting upon and that the claimant must "take the bitter with the sweet"?[85] That approach would limit procedural due process claims to those in which government officials failed to comply with the terms of the very statute establishing the program: the constitutional dimensions of the claim would drop out, and the claimant would be left in every case with nothing but a claim under the very law establishing the program. The Court has explicitly rejected this line of argument:

> [I]t is settled that the "bitter with the sweet" approach misconceives the constitutional guarantee. . . . The point is straightforward: the Due Process Clause provides that certain substantive rights—life, liberty, and property—cannot be deprived except pursuant to constitutionally adequate procedures. The categories of substance and procedure are distinct. Were the rule otherwise, the Clause would be reduced to a mere tautology. "Property" cannot be defined by the procedures provided for its deprivation any more than can life or liberty. The right to due process is conferred, not by legislative grace, but by constitutional guarantee. While the legislature may elect not to confer a property interest in [public] employment, it may not constitutionally authorize the deprivation of such an interest, once conferred, without appropriate procedural safeguards.
>
> In short, once it is determined that the Due Process Clause applies, the question remains what process is due.[86]

And the answer to that question is, in Judge Friendly's phrase, "some kind of hearing."[87] What kind depends on the circumstances: the intensity of the interest, the likelihood that a more or less formal procedure would contribute to an accurate result.[88] But the Court's resounding rejection of the "bitter with the sweet" is not entirely satisfactory. Whether the legislature has indeed determined to confer a property interest may sometimes be gathered from the procedures it has provided for its protection, and then the two questions the Court would treat as logically distinct begin to come together.[89]

Justice Black, in the dissent quoted above, was not far off the mark. The same methodology that moved from the *Poe* dissent to *Griswold* to *Roe* and *Casey* could be invoked whenever government did something that "shocked the conscience"—substantively or procedurally. But for one reason or another mistakenly holding a suspect in prison for several days pursuant to a valid but mistaken warrant,[90] carelessly sending a municipal maintenance worker to his death in a noxious sewer,[91] accidentally killing and maiming innocent bystanders in a high-speed chase of escaping suspects,[92] returning a child to his father's custody in the face of knowledge that he was prone to beat the child,[93] and posting the names of "active shoplifters"[94] all failed to count as actions denying the victims life, liberty, or property without due process of law. In the last of these cases the Court concluded that a person's interest in reputation does not count as property or liberty protected by the Constitution. This is a step beyond *Roth,* because the common law, the background state law, by granting a tort cause of action for defamation recognizes just such an interest. The explanation offered is that the Constitution must not be allowed to become a "font of tort law." The Court thus refused to go down a path of substituting redress on constitutional grounds for the ordinary processes and remedies of state law—with whatever particular gaps and limitations state law may display[95]—except sometimes: for instance, when the state tort violation also violates the Fourth Amendment's protection against unreasonable searches and seizures.[96]

This uncertain and theoretically unsatisfactory relation between constitutional protections and background state law is well illustrated by *Flagg Bros., Inc. v. Brooks.*[97] State law (indeed the Uniform Commercial Code, which codifies state law uniformly) allows a warehouseman, after sending proper notice and demands, to sell the goods of a person who fails to pay the set storage fee. This is similar to laws that allow sellers of goods—usually cars, appliances, and furniture—to repossess them if the buyer fails to make the agreed installment payments. Mrs. Brooks was evicted from her apartment for nonpayment of rent. So that her furniture would not simply lie in the street it was removed to the Flagg Brothers warehouse, which charged a standard rate for storage. She did not pay the storage charges and her property was sold to satisfy them. Mrs. Brooks complained that the sale of her property without a prior judicial determination of delinquency deprived her of her property without due process of law—of the procedural variety. The Court accepted Flagg Brothers' response that the Constitution was not implicated at all because its action was that of a private party and not of any government official; the Constitution protects only against "state [not private] action."[98] It is the dissent that displays what is at stake. The dissent did not conclude that Mrs. Brooks was entitled to relief, but only that the Court should have considered the merits of her claim: the state action was the state statute authorizing the sale. Nothing less was at stake than the possibility that all the ordinary background law governing relations between private parties should be the subject of Supreme Court supervision—at the instance of a disappointed private litigant—on the ground that that background law was in one way or another unfair, or that it "shock[ed] the conscience." It may in some common sense of the word be "unfair" for a private employer to fire an employee because the employer wants to give the job to his brother-in-law, or for a business to transfer its custom for the same reason, or for a landlord to refuse to renew the lease of a business because he is offered more by the renter's competitor, or for a lender to refuse a loan to an individual because he doesn't like him or because he is African-American, or for a publisher to decline a novel because he finds the hero distasteful.

These "injustices" happen because the background law is quite general in allowing private parties to make what arrangements they wish and then in enforcing those arrangements. There may be specific laws enacted to guard against some of these actions: there are laws in some jurisdictions against unfair termination of employment; racial discrimination by private parties is in some contexts forbidden by statute. But there are reasons why statutory and common law does not forbid such unfairness wholesale or why courts do not undertake to do so in the application of background law. This is the battleground of ordinary legislative and common law/interpretive struggle. The dissent's proposal in *Flagg Bros.* would open all of these questions for Supreme Court review on constitutional grounds. This is the intersection with the *Roth* line of cases, as Justice Black's dissent in *Goldberg* anticipated: the state college's failure to rehire Roth was certainly state action, but the Court concluded that whether Roth had a right to the job, such that it had to accord him notice, a hearing, and reasons when not rehiring him, was a matter of the state law's defining the job. Under the dissent's view in *Flagg Bros.*, whether even a private employer owes his employee due process before firing him would also be a question not just of the state law of contract and employment but of federal constitutional law's passing judgment on that background state law regime.

This was an expansion of its authority the Court was quite unwilling to assume. That may have been a prudent reluctance, but the dissent pushes the point by asking whether the Court would really be prepared to accept a state law regime that, for instance, assigned the property right to whoever could assert control over the property by force. And if it would not permit that, why in principle does it shrink from assuming a watching brief over the fairness of all background state laws—at least to assure that they do not "shock the conscience"? The only reasonable answer to the dissent is that such a shocking law would be so far off the beaten track of the ordinary Anglo-American background legal regime that we cannot imagine it as a part of the law of one of our states. (The legal rule in *Flagg Bros.*, far from being an anomaly—like the Connecticut statute in *Poe*—is general in the United States not only as to warehousemen but as to a wide range of self-help measures.)

And here we come back to the problem we faced with the Takings and Contracts clauses: if the Constitution protects against the uncompensated "taking" of property, the "impairment of the obligations of contracts," and deprivations of liberty and property without fair procedures, then contract, liberty, and property are concepts that cannot be left entirely to state definition and redefinition; these concepts must have some core meaning as a matter of constitutional background law, neither created by the state nor freely abrogable by it. It is only because this background is largely unquestioned that constitutional doctrine can afford to pretend it is not there as part of its own working grammar.

CHAPTER SEVEN

Equality

The Declaration of Independence offers as its first "self-evident" truth that "all men are created equal." This statement raises the large and enduring questions of the meaning of equality. In the eighteenth-century context of the Declaration the meaning was political: equality of political right, the denial of politically conclusive classes and castes[1]— a very great irony, as the phrase came from the pen of a slave owner.[2] For some time now the claims of equality have widened to include claims—contested claims, to be sure—to some degree of equality of total life situation, and especially of material goods. The Constitution's textual commitment to equality is more modest. Not until the Fourteenth Amendment does the Constitution speak of equality at all and then only once: "[N]or shall any state . . . deny to any person within its jurisdiction the equal protection of the laws." That this promise bound only the states and not the national government was an embarrassment that elicited the doctrinal response—at the beginning of the Court's project finally to dismantle the system of legally mandated segregation—that "discrimination may be so unjustifiable as to be violative of [the Due Process Clause of the Fifth Amendment]," because it "would be unthinkable that the Constitution would impose a lesser duty on the Federal Government."[3] What the promise of equality means and how far it extends beyond the area of race and, particularly, beyond dismantling the legal disabilities imposed on African-Americans were not settled then and are not settled now. One theorist has argued that equality is the sovereign virtue and the ultimate constitutional command, which entails all others.[4] And at the other extreme the claim has been made that the promise of equality has no meaning at all, beyond simply assuring the substance of whatever rights are accorded by other provisions of the Constitution or the law.[5] Apart from disappointing the expectations that attach to the rhetoric of equality, that last argument is wrong. Understanding the difference between the guarantee of substantive rights—which have been the subject of the three previous chapters—and the guarantee of "equal protection" (if not of equality) goes a long way to introducing the fundamental concepts of the Constitution's approach to equality.

Equality in General

Equality of application is indeed a necessary entailment of recognizing a constitutional, or any, legal right. Your right to speak freely is the same right enjoyed by (roughly speaking) all persons, so that denying that right to some is a violation of the right itself. This is the sense in which equality is just another name for the rule of law: equal justice under law is justice under law. Regularity implies equality, but it does not exhaust equality. Consider the case of voting in elections for members of the state judiciary, judges being elected in many, but not all, states and not at the national level. Neither the text of the Constitution nor constitutional doctrine grants a right to vote in state judicial elections, as it does in elections for United States senators.[6] What constitutional equality has been held to require is that if any citizen gets to vote for judges in the state, then all must. (It would not be allowed, for instance, to limit that vote only to members of the bar or to graduates of accredited law schools.)[7] This distinct aspect of constitutional equality is more comprehensive than the system of substantive constitutional rights: it applies potentially to any right, benefit, or detriment provided for in ordinary law. Equality judges all ordinary law, and it judges it not only for the regularity of its application, but for the fairness of the classifications it sets up. So if a state really did limit voting in judicial elections to members of the bar, it would raise a question of constitutional equality, even if the state scrupulously applied its law and accorded this right to vote to every member of the bar. Of course, if a law violates a substantive right, this complaint swamps any complaint that the classification by which that law disadvantages some but not others is a violation of equal protection; it does not matter who else is or is not hurt by the classification. Equal protection, therefore, is a more general, less pointed source of constitutional concern.

But the idea of a perfectly neutral law is nonsense. All law classifies, makes distinctions, so the attack that a law is insufficiently general in conferring a benefit (unjustly excluding the complainant) or excessively general in imposing a burden (unnecessarily including the complainant) is in theory always available. Equal protection judges the constitutionality of classifications. It is like substantive due process in that it must judge ordinary law, and not just the regularity of the law's application. It needs an external criterion—a constitutional *pou sto*—by which to judge ordinary law. And it is like substantive due process also in that that criterion—absent special circumstances, like race or gender, where most of the action is—is mere rationality: in making a classification (the inclusions and exclusions), is the law seeking to further a purpose that is legitimate for the government to pursue, and does that classification bear a rational relation to that purpose? Is the end a legitimate one, and are the means rationally related to it?[8]

Rationality review was not at all constraining in substantive due process. It is a little more constraining in equal protection, so that even in recent times a law has occasionally failed this most lenient test. There is a reason for that: substantive due process attacks often focus on the legitimacy of the purpose government purports to serve. Equal protection cases by contrast generally grant the legitimacy of that ultimate purpose, and perhaps the rationality of the means chosen to serve it, but ask how a particular *classification* serves that end. In other words, the complainer may be taken to say: This is a possible end, and even the means of getting to it are reasonable, but why (not) me? This is an inquiry that has far less chance of setting the Court adrift on the seas of boundless speculation about the value and legitimacy of a purported governmental objective. Justice Jackson offered the classic statement of the point in *Railway Express Agency, Inc. v. New York:*[9]

> Invalidation of a statute or an ordinance on due process grounds leaves ungoverned and ungovernable conduct which many people find objectionable. Invocation of the equal protection clause, on the other hand,

does not disable any governmental body from dealing with the subject at hand. It merely means that the prohibition or regulation must have a broader impact. I regard it as a salutary doctrine that cities, states and the Federal Government must exercise their powers so as not to discriminate between their inhabitants except upon some reasonable differentiation fairly related to the object of regulation. . . . The framers of the Constitution knew, and we should not forget today, that there is no more effective practical guaranty against arbitrary and unreasonable government than to require that the principles of law which officials would impose upon a minority must be imposed generally. Conversely, nothing opens the door to arbitrary action so effectively as to allow those officials to pick and choose only a few to whom they will apply legislation and thus to escape the political retribution that might be visited upon them if larger numbers were affected.

There are really two arguments nestling here. First, a gross lack of fit between the purported aim of the law and the classification of persons whom it affects is an indication that some more sinister, perhaps illegitimate purpose lurks behind the legislation, and insisting on a better fit would smoke this out.[10] Second, by insisting that the burden of the legislative pursuit fall generally, government cannot, by sloughing the burdens off on a disfavored few without adequate explanation, avoid the issue whether the balance of benefits and burdens really is in the interest of all. This second justification is at the heart of the concept of equality, "the sovereign's duty to govern impartially."[11]

Both aspects of equal protection are illustrated by *United States Department of Agriculture v. Moreno*.[12] As originally enacted, the food stamp program, designed to offer food assistance to low income persons, determined need by household income and defined a household as "a group of related or non-related individuals, who are not residents of an institution or boarding house, but are living as one economic unit sharing common cooking facilities and for whom food is customarily purchased in common." A later amendment changed that definition to exclude "any household containing an individual who is unrelated to any other member of the household." The Court concluded that this classification was a denial of equal protection. The classification was "irrelevant" to the originally stated purpose of assisting the needy to meet their nutritional needs. As to the purpose of minimizing the risk of fraud, suggested by the government in the litigation, the Court again concluded that—especially in the context of the program's specific provisions penalizing abuse—"the 1971 amendment excludes from participation in the food stamp program, not those persons who are 'likely to abuse the program,' but, rather, only those persons who are so desperately in need of aid that they cannot even afford to alter their living arrangements so as to retain their eligibility. Traditional equal protection analysis does not require that every classification be drawn with precise 'mathematical nicety.' But the classification here at issue is not only 'imprecise,' it is wholly without any rational basis." The Court also noted that

> [t]he legislative history . . . indicates that that amendment was intended to prevent so-called "hippies" and "hippie communes" from participating in the food stamp program. The challenged classification clearly cannot be sustained by reference to this congressional purpose. For if the constitutional conception of 'equal protection of the laws' means anything, it must at the very least mean that a bare congressional desire to harm a politically unpopular group cannot constitute a legitimate governmental interest.

So while the classification bore no rational relation to any legitimate government interest, it fit an illegitimate interest like a glove. This is a prime example of robust rational basis analysis—robust in the sense that the Court will not allow itself to ratify an argument that no serious person could consider persuasive, compared with a mode of analysis that will accept any assertion at all of some relation to a plausible government interest. The case illustrates the several functions of equal protection analysis: preventing the government by inadvertence or bureaucratic stupidity from pointlessly prejudicing some group of its citizens; smoking out an illegitimate governmental purpose; and putting government to the choice between depriving everyone of a benefit (or subjecting everyone to a detriment), with all the attendant political consequences, or offering the benefit even to politically less popular or powerful groups. Thus is Justice Jackson's characterization of rational basis equal protection vindicated.

This robust conception of equal protection corresponds to the robust conception of substantive due process, according to which government might in principle be called to account for every impingement on liberty in principle. But as we have seen in Chapter 6 discussing substantive due process, since the "turn" of the New Deal Court, the Court has found very little that fails the minimal rational basis test in that regard. Instead it has discerned a number of fundamental aspects of liberty, limitations on which it subjects to heightened scrutiny. As *Moreno* illustrates, claims that a classification fails rational basis equal protection have fared somewhat better. In *Romer v. Evans*[13] the Court struck down an amendment to the constitution of Colorado precluding the legislature or any level of state government from adopting a rule specifically protecting persons from discrimination on grounds of sexual orientation. *Eisenstadt v. Baird*,[14] discussed in Chapter 6, was similarly stated to be an equal protection case. The Court has also struck down a local method of valuing property for tax purposes that reassessed property only when it was transferred, creating gross disparities between equally valuable properties depending on the date of the last sale.[15] And, remarkably, the Court has struck down on equal protection grounds the demand of village authorities for unusually burdensome conditions on a single, unpopular homeowner seeking connection to the village water supply.[16] These are slim pickings, and they are even slimmer when one considers that both *Romer* and *Eisenstadt* touched on areas that implicate what the Court in substantive due process cases has called the fundamental right to privacy (although in *Romer* the Court did not purport to modify—it did not even cite—its earlier decision in *Bowers*).[17] And even *Moreno*, having to do with living arrangements, bears a resemblance to *Moore v. East Cleveland*, which struck down on due process grounds a local ordinance forbidding persons not closely related (cousins living with their grandmother) from occupying the same housing unit.

Race

The development of Equal Protection Clause doctrine only begins with the fact that the clause was so much the child of the post–Civil War settlement and the Reconstruction Congress's determination to achieve full citizenship for the emancipated slaves and their descendants in the face of fierce recalcitrance in the southern states. As the Court put it in the *Slaughter-House Cases:*

> Among the first acts of legislation adopted by several of the States in the legislative bodies which claimed to be in their normal relations with the Federal government, were laws which imposed upon the colored race onerous disabilities and burdens, and curtailed their rights in the pursuit of life, liberty, and property to such an extent that their freedom was of

little value, while they had lost the protection which they had received from their former owners from motives both of interest and humanity.

They were in some States forbidden to appear in the towns in any other character than menial servants. They were required to reside on and cultivate the soil without the right to purchase or own it. They were excluded from many occupations of gain, and were not permitted to give testimony in the courts in any case where a white man was a party. It was said that their lives were at the mercy of bad men, either because the laws for their protection were insufficient or were not enforced.[18]

Thus the Court had no difficulty turning aside an equal protection challenge to a law establishing a monopoly on the business of slaughtering meat in New Orleans: the "one pervading" purpose of the Reconstruction amendments was "the freedom of the slave race, the security and the firm establishment of that freedom, and the protection of the newly-made freeman and citizen from the oppressions of those who had formerly exercised unlimited dominion over them. . . ."

Although this was certainly the occasion for the Fourteenth Amendment and for the Equal Protection Clause, the amendment and its clauses were deliberately drawn in general terms, in contrast to the Fifteenth Amendment, which provides that "the right of citizens of the United States to vote shall not be denied or abridged by the United States or by any State on account of race, color, or previous condition of servitude." Both in the congressional debates and in subsequent early cases, official action disadvantaging not only African-Americans but other racial groups was acknowledged to be within the clause's reach. Of particular significance were early decisions that corporations were "persons" within the scope of the Due Process and Equal Protection clauses, but not "citizens" for the purposes of the Fourteenth Amendment's clause that "No State shall make or enforce any laws which shall abridge the privileges and immunities of citizens of the United States."

Moving away from the historical occasion for the Equal Protection Clause to its more general application raised the nest of theoretical difficulties that the rational basis test was designed to untangle. No such test was needed or appropriate in one of the early equal protection cases, *Strauder v. West Virginia*,[19] which invalidated the murder conviction of an African-American because state law limited jury service to "white male persons." If this obvious case were run through the doctrinal machinery used in rational basis cases, the outcome would not be at all certain. It counts as a legitimate purpose that government should want guilt or innocence to be decided as reliably as possible, and because reliable decision making correlates with levels of education and because, at the time of the *Strauder* case, African-Americans as a group may have been less well educated than whites, the state's classification might be thought to be rationally related to that end. It is also true that whites may be less sympathetic to claims made by African-Americans, but that is an objection that goes only to how well education correlates with a disposition to judge reliably, and rational basis analysis does not require that all factors that correlate with the government's end be taken into account. It is also true that in West Virginia in 1880 there were quite a few African-Americans who were better educated than quite a few whites, but rational basis analysis does not demand anything like a close correlation between the classifications a law uses and the purposes it serves. Finally, it is certainly the case that the prior institution of slavery was the overwhelming reason for the educational disparity, but that too would be irrelevant in rational basis analysis. Of course none of these arguments worked, because the amendment was aimed against just such legal incapacities. Curiously, the Court went on to say that it would be a palpable denial of equal protection if white men or "Celtic Irishmen" were excluded from juries, even though prejudice against them—and as to the latter, prejudice certainly did exist—was not at all the occasion for the amendment.

It is a premise of the *Strauder* decision that classifications disadvantaging by race are illegitimate. Translating that into the means/end analytic structure I have been using: either the end of disadvantaging individuals classified by race is illegitimate, or attaining a legitimate end (and I have posited such an end) by a racially disadvantaging classification may be a rational means to an end, but is not a permissible means. *Strauder* does not go into such detail. It notes the historical purpose of the amendment and "that the very fact that colored people are singled out and expressly denied by a statute all right to participate in the administration of justice, by law, because of their color [is] practically a brand upon them, affixed by law, an assertion of their inferiority, and a stimulant to that race prejudice which is an impediment to securing [equal justice] to individuals of the race." Sixteen years later, in the notorious case of *Plessy v. Ferguson*,[20] the Court upheld a state statute mandating race segregation in railroad carriages because African-Americans were allotted carriages from which whites were excluded; there may have been separation but there was equality—unlike *Strauder* in which only whites were allowed to serve on juries. What the Court waved aside was the stigma implicit in segregation. The Court saw no stigma in separation, except as African-Americans chose to put that construction on it. The first Justice Harlan's dissent from that callous assertion in *Plessy* laid the ground for a new and fertile understanding of racial equality under the Constitution: that the Constitution does not allow the law to create a system of castes,[21] with that term carrying the further implication of permanent subordination of one group to another.

This conception of the permanent, institutional subordination of blacks to whites is the theme in the single most important equal protection case, *Brown v. Board of Education*.[22] For the Court in that case did not denounce all classification by race; nor even did it denounce the separation of the races as such. Rather it famously based its decision on what it took to be the implicit social message of inferiority in school segregation and its practical effect in maintaining that inferiority: not only did black children not learn as well because of that message, but, because they did not learn as well, their continued subordination was assured. Soon after *Brown* the Court expanded its doctrine to strike down all laws that in their terms required segregation of the races. The cases covered golf courses,[23] parks, beaches, buses, and restaurants. These extensions—mandated but not explained by the Court—put some strain on *Brown*'s original rationale, which emphasized the effect of segregation on children and education, but are quite consistent with it if seen in the light of the dismantling of a legally enforced caste system, with its implication of racial subordination.[24]

Loving v. Virginia,[25] the case which struck down laws against interracial marriage, enlarged and clarified this project.[26] From the perspective of the interracial couple, antimiscegenation laws (as they were styled in the South) were a violent restriction of the fundamental liberty regarding marriage and intimate relations that was soon to be recognized in substantive due process cases like *Griswold, Moore, Zablocki, Turner, Casey,* and *Lawrence*.[27] The government's stated purpose, to preserve the distinctness of the several races, even if conceded to be legitimate, could hardly survive strict scrutiny when the purposes offered in *Griswold* and the cases subsequent to it could not.

But the Court treated *Loving* as an equal protection case—perhaps because substantive due process doctrine was not yet well developed—requiring analysis in terms of the *classification* and not the imposition as such. And in those terms the classification seemed perfectly symmetrical: the restriction imposed on one half of the couple is exactly the same as that imposed on the other, and with no inequality, there seemed to be no basis even for invoking the Equal Protection Clause. When "separate but equal" was announced and denounced, it could be said that what was claimed to be equal never was in reality: the facilities for whites were always better,[28] and only if blacks and whites were required to share schools, public facilities, railway carriages, and so on could equality in fact be assured. But no such argument applied to antimiscegenation laws. A different rationale needed to be found if they were to be struck down in the name of the Equal Protection Clause. The most straightforward was that these laws were part of a system meant to maintain the superior position of whites, a system that would be confused and eroded by intermarriage and mixed-race children. To a lesser extent the same would be true if blacks and whites could mingle freely in general, because—as the segregationists often said—such mingling, in schools, parks, places of amusement, and elsewhere, would make it harder to discourage more intimate relations between the races. But the Court in *Loving* did not pause at that explanation. Rather, it recalled a more fundamental rationale still: that all racial classifications are inherently suspect.[29] The principle is different from the antisubordination principle, because in theory at least—and in some societies perhaps in practice—racial or group separation may be not only compatible with equality of situation and respect, but perhaps a practical condition for it.[30]

In invoking equality the *Loving* Court meant more than equality: it meant a kind of unity of basic civic situation. We are not only equal before the law, but one before it. This is the best meaning to be attributed to the first Justice Harlan's dictum in dissent in *Plessy* that the Constitution is "color-blind." So the notion certainly entails equality, but goes beyond it to assert a principle not just of *equal* but of *single* citizenship.

This conclusion entails a whole basket of questions with which constitutional doctrine has tried to cope. Is race a forbidden category that the law may never acknowledge, or does it refer to a forbidden end, which the use of that perhaps permissible category may not serve?[31] That end might be antisubordination, but I believe it is the different and more ambitious one of forbidding a segmented citizenship—requiring, as I have said, a single citizenship. But it has been plausibly argued that antisegmentation as much as antisubordination may justify taking account of race as a means to its achievement; that is the crux of the affirmative action debate.[32] But beyond questions of race, what does unity of citizenship mean? All law classifies. So what other categories or classes threaten the principle of single citizenship? Ethnic and national origin are so close to race (which in any event is a dubious and imprecise concept)[33] that they were early equated with it.[34] So was religion with its powerful capacity to divide; indeed the Establishment Clause, as generalized to the states, has often been explained in part by this purpose to preserve a unity of citizenship.[35] Gender, as we shall see, has been very difficult. Differences of age and ability threaten to divide us. And so, of course, do differences of wealth, occupation, and social status. How many of these differences does the antisegmentation or the narrower antisubordination principle reach? And—history apart—why do they apply with such rigor to race? Finally, the Fourteenth Amendment promises only that "No *State* shall . . . deny to any person within its jurisdiction the *equal protection* of the laws." This raises questions cutting across all those about which are the forbidden ends or categories: To what extent does the Constitution forbid discriminatory *private* action sheltering behind neutral, general laws—for instance, contracts or wills in proper form making such discriminations? And related to those questions, how far does the Constitution require positive steps to remove or alleviate conditions of inequality?

Gender and Other Classes

It has become a cliché of equal protection doctrine that the Constitution offers special protection only against measures disadvantaging "discrete and insular minorities." This phrase is drawn from a footnote to Justice Harlan Stone's opinion in *Carolene Products Co. v. United States,*[36] a case from the 1930s ratifying a nasty piece of special interest legislation prohibiting the interstate shipment of "filled milk"—skimmed milk "filled" with nonmilk fats. It is not entirely clear that such legislation, evidently designed to protect dairy interests against competition and at the expense of the public,[37] would survive even under rational basis scrutiny, given the somewhat more robust conception of that standard discussed earlier in this chapter. As John Hart Ely has pointed out, the footnote was intended as a capsule theory:[38]

> Ours is above all a democracy. There are no objective bases for political choices and when courts intervene to make them, they merely substitute their own for the legislators' policy predilections. The Constitution does appear, however, to demand such interventions. These can be understood as protecting democracy rather than substituting for it. Speech is protected so that today's majority cannot entrench itself by closing down criticism that might lead to democratic change. And the equal protection clause protects against the inevitable win-some-lose-some aspect of politics only those groups whose more or less permanent minority status—a status moreover that extends over a wide range of interests—precludes them from hoping for a share in the spoils of politics.

This theory, a manifestation of the disdain for the *Lochner* era, conveniently allowed only those court interventions that would promote and not hinder a "progressive" agenda.[39] It is hardly in accord with modern substantive due process and free speech doctrine, especially modern commercial speech doctrine,[40] yet it is regularly invoked to explain which of the inevitable classifications law must make require special scrutiny under the Equal Protection Clause. Racial, ethnic, and religious minorities that have suffered from a history of prejudice and isolation fit the theory perfectly, as they were meant to. But what of women? First, they are not a minority. Second, though discrete (if this means distinct), their insularity, if it exists, must be of a different sort from that of isolated racial groups, since every man has had a mother, and many a woman companion, daughter, or sister, so that there would seem to be a wide identity of interest between men and women. Add to this the Nineteenth Amendment's guarantee to women of the right to vote and the fact that women do vote in large numbers[41] and it is understandable that not until 1971[42] were constitutional complaints concerning legislation disadvantaging women (not to say simply treating them differently and perhaps more favorably)[43] taken seriously. But after only a few years, in the 1976 case of *Craig v. Boren*,[44] the Court determined to accord heightened, though not the highest, level of scrutiny, to legislation making distinctions on the basis of gender.[45] Strikingly, this *Brown v. Board* of gender discrimination invalidated an Oklahoma statute giving women the right to buy 3 percent "near beer" at the age of eighteen, while men had to await their twenty-first birthday to enjoy that privilege. The Court reached its conclusion in spite of statistics showing a far greater incidence of young men than young women driving while drunk.[46] The case illustrates the difficulties of applying equal protection analysis to questions of gender. It is plausible to see the role of equal protection as negating the disadvantages imposed on women by laws and custom—analogous to the "Black Codes" that were the target of the Reconstruction amendments—that denied women the right to vote, to exercise certain professions,[47] and imposed upon them a wide variety of disabilities.[48] The Nineteenth Amendment, giving women the vote, makes the analogy even closer.[49] But how, then, does a law disadvantaging men relative to women come into the sights of this project? Another example is the definition of statutory rape that punishes the man but not the woman who engages in sexual relations when the woman is under the age of eighteen—whatever the man's age.[50] There are several arguments available. Closest to the antisubordination principle is the argument, often repeated in the cases,[51] that such measures perpetuate stereotypes of women as less capable, or in the case of the Oklahoma law, less vigorous, aggressive—less, well, masculine. But there is another explanation: whether or not such laws subordinate one gender to the other, they have the effect of segmenting the citizenry into two groups and thus denying the common humanity and citizenship of each with the other.[52]

Given that all law classifies, either explanation, however, raises the question of why classifications according to gender should call down the heavy constitutional artillery of heightened equal protection scrutiny. A history of subordination and disadvantage is one reason. That a person does not move in and out of the category—voluntarily or, as with age, naturally—but is fixed in it through life, and that it is a sharply binary characteristic[53] make the risk of making a caste of the class (as it is in some cultures) much greater. In the language of doctrine, gender is a "fixed and immutable" characteristic.[54] Further difficulty arises because there are differences between men and women the recognition of which need not be attributed to the reinforcing of false and subordinating stereotypes nor to the impulse to separate and divide the citizenry. What these differences are is a matter of debate, but the most salient has to do with the fact that only women bear children. In contrast, there are few such differentiating characteristics between blacks and whites that are not the product of the very social segmentation the doctrine is meant to overcome, and those few—like a differential susceptibility to certain diseases—if recognized and acted upon have little or no potential for a subordinating or segmenting effect. With gender the opposite is the case, for family relations and the social consequences of child bearing are at the very heart of the difficulty. Similarly, a certain degree of separation—as with bathing and health facilities—although culturally determined may at once seem benign and equally desired on each side. The whole business of sexual attraction is in play here. Modesty and separation are conditions for voluntary mingling of the most intimate kind. Yet it is exactly these kinds of separation that in the case of race have been the most harmful and insulting. It is in recognition of these distinctions, I suggest, that constitutional doctrine has stopped short of making gender as suspect a classification as race, according gender classifications what is called intermediate scrutiny—that is, there is a wider range of valid ends which such classifications may validly serve.[55] Some have chafed at this lesser degree of protection. One bad reason, I believe, for equating race and gender and for according highest scrutiny to the latter as well would be the symbolic effect of such an equation as a pledge of allegiance to the cause of gender equality in the teeth of the analytic unsoundness of such a doctrinal move: doctrine as billboard. Another bad argument would acknowledge the occasional need to make distinctions of gender, but would celebrate the transfer of the power to make these distinctions to courts (and lawyers) and away from legislatures.

This analysis of race and gender equality explains why the Court has consistently refused to treat classification by age as deserving any heightened scrutiny,[56] but what of disability and especially permanent, life-long disabilities such as mental retardation? The Court has given its answer twice, in *Cleburne v. Cleburne Living Center*[57] and *Board of Trustees of the University of Alabama v. Garrett:*[58] classifications according to disability are not inherently suspect and do not invoke heightened scrutiny; it is sufficient that they be rationally related to a legitimate government purpose. The first case is the more revealing. A local ordinance allowed group living arrangements for the elderly and former prisoners—but not mentally retarded persons. The Court concluded that the classification was so ill suited to any of the proffered purposes—supposedly to do with the safety of the residents themselves—that it could only be explained by irrational prejudice.

And catering to such prejudices for the sake, for instance, of preserving property values did not justify this irrationality.[59] At the same time the Court for two reasons emphatically denied any special constitutional protection to disability as such. First, the concept itself was too broad and indeterminate. There are all kinds and degrees of disability which justify the widest variety of differential treatment. The concept lacked the on-or-off quality that attaches objectively to gender and—often by absurd and incoherent social convention—to race. (The defendant in *Plessy v. Ferguson,* for example, was only one-eighth black.) In the language of the *Carolene* footnote, mentally retarded persons are not a *discrete* minority. Second, nor are they insular: circumstances have shown that their family and other ties have provided them with powerful and effective advocates drawn from every stratum of society.[60] Such advocacy has led to potent legislative protections at all levels of government for disabled persons.

Poverty and Fundamental Rights

That leaves the poor. Differentiation by class has been claimed by socialists for the last century and a half to be the most powerful dividing and subordinating of social forces. It is perhaps as much a political as a factual claim that class is not a discrete and immutable characteristic, that ours is as much a socially as a geographically mobile society. But even if this widely shared article of American faith were more myth than reality, it would still be very difficult to see how constitutional doctrine could make the Equal Protection Clause an engine of economic equality.[61] For a brief time in the late 1960s and early 1970s occasional dicta in Court opinions flirted with some such project. It is not a fantastical project, since something like a promise of (a degree of) economic and social equality is enshrined in a number of post–World War II constitutions. The German constitution makes it a first principle not only that Germany is governed by the rule of law *(Rechststaat)* but also that a certain measure of social solidarity and support are at its foundation *(Sozialstaat).*[62] The South African constitution makes a similar promise.[63] Such very general principles are usually accompanied by more specific guarantees of housing, education, health care, family support, and even employment. Although these are not guarantees of equality, they may be seen as guarantees against serious inequalities.

And that is how the occasional flirtation with this notion in Supreme Court dicta appeared. Perhaps the closest approach was a reference by Justice Brennan in *Shapiro v. Thompson* to "the ability of the families to obtain the very means to subsist—food, shelter, and other necessities of life."[64] But the context of this remark precluded it from offering any such general assurances. California had sought to deny for one year its generous welfare benefits to recent arrivals from other states, fearing that it would become a magnet for poor people from stingier states. The case turned, therefore, not on an absolute right to these, or any, social welfare benefits but on their denial to the class of recent arrivals. Such a classification burdens the liberty to move about freely, to migrate from one state to another, and this liberty, the case held, is a "fundamental right" that may not be burdened except for a compelling state interest. So the recent immigrant's wish to move to a more generous locality and to make a better life for her family may not count against her. But had California denied benefits to everyone, *Shapiro* would offer no doctrinal grip for an argument to relieve that deprivation.

A quite unambiguous denial that equal protection offers the leverage to make ours a *Sozialstaat* came a few years later in *San Antonio Independent School District v. Rodriguez*.[65] The decision turned aside a challenge to the system for financing public primary and secondary education in Texas, which relied heavily on local taxes and resulted in large disparities in per pupil funding from district to district. Stating that education was not a fundamental right (as is the right to travel) such inequalities need only—and could easily—satisfy rational basis scrutiny. The only mild note of qualification was the statement that this was so only so long as the system provided each child with "an opportunity to acquire the basic minimal skills necessary for the enjoyment of the rights of speech and of full participation in the political process." But whether even that would call for constitutional intervention is not clear, as who knows what these basic minimal skills are and whether it would ever be politically feasible to deny these in a whole district. (In fact many state constitutions—including that of Texas—guarantee a free public education as a basic right and have been interpreted by their state courts as demanding a serious measure of interdistrict equality.)

By way of coda, the Court a decade later denied that the denial of free transportation to public schools for certain rural children violated equal protection, even though it was claimed that this sometimes made attendance virtually impossible.[66] What held for education was said also of housing[67] and health care.[68] The one exception to this current of denial has been in access to certain aspects of the justice system. Indigent defendants must be offered a lawyer at public expense in felony cases, as must parents in certain child custody cases.[69] These cases might, however, be seen as of limited significance, certainly not promising a principle of government-assured social equality, because it is the government in a criminal proceeding that is trying to do something to the defendant, which as a matter of due process it may not fairly do unless the defendant has had the assistance of counsel.

There is, however, a sense in which the *Shapiro* case illustrates a limited commitment by constitutional doctrine to alleviate the unequalizing effects of poverty. *Shapiro* spoke of a fundamental right to travel and of the constitutional wrong in penalizing that right on account of poverty. Like race and the few other suspect classifications, measures that burden fundamental rights are subject to strict equal protection scrutiny. What are these fundamental rights? Rights guaranteed by the First Amendment are fundamental, as are the right to a trial by jury and several others expressly provided for in the text of the Constitution. But to guarantee their enjoyment against improper classifications under the Equal Protection Clause seems redundant. If I am denied a right to speak, then I have a First Amendment claim, whether or not others suffer the same denial. To condition my right to speak in a public forum on the payment of a fee violates the First Amendment even if the fee is waived in the case of indigency.[70] True, equal protection and substantive protections come together in this sense: as we have seen,[71] a discriminatory denial of the right to speak (and almost all are discriminatory in one way or another) may undercut the claimed justification for the denial. A prohibition on picketing in a residential neighborhood except in connection with a labor dispute shows the ordinance not to be content-neutral and invalidates it for that reason.[72] But in *Police Department of City of Chicago v. Mosley*[73] a similar prohibition on picketing near a school building was struck down on equal protection grounds as an unjustifiedly unequal burden on a fundamental right. Six of one, half dozen of the other. Now apply this reasoning to an implied fundamental right, such as the right to travel offered in *Shapiro*. Surely this is not just an equal protection right: it is a substantive right. A state may not burden it (without a compelling reason) even if it burdens it equally for all—for instance by requiring a five-year waiting period before allowing entrance into the state or residency there. This was part of Justice Harlan's complaint against the decision in his dissent in *Shapiro*. He went on to doubt that the denial of welfare benefits amounted to a burden on that right, although there doctrine had turned definitively against him: the denial of a benefit because of the exercise of a constitutional right counts as a burden on that right that requires justification.[74]

But what of rights that are fundamental only in the equal protection context: rights that need be granted to none, but if granted to some must be granted to all? There are very few such rights. The most important is the right to vote. *Harper v. Virginia State Board of Elections*,[75] the case invalidating a $1.50 poll tax, announced this "new" equal protection.[76] But in spite of statements in the opinion,[77] the case was not so much about wealth classifications as about deliberately imposed burdens on the right to vote. Though a less trivial sum today than in 1966, it was hardly a frank exclusion of the poor from the ballot. Such a nominal fee as a condition for speaking in a public forum or at a private meeting, for printing and passing out leaflets, for displaying a sign, or for holding a worship service would clearly violate the First Amendment. (Imagine a nominal fee for invoking the Fifth Amendment privilege against self-incrimination or for the right to conceive or bear a child.) Nor would the justifications proffered for the poll tax work better in any of those other instances: that the payment of this small sum was a token that the voter was undertaking this civic duty with some seriousness, or perhaps that it went some way toward defraying the expenses of running an election. It is none of the state's business to create tests for the earnestness of a qualified voter's intentions, any more than it is to assure seriousness in the exercise of First Amendment rights. So this is not really about wealth as an improper classification, as would be property qualifications for voting or holding office—measures once familiar but gradually eliminated in most districts because of changes in theories of popular representations, and not seen since.[78]

Voting as an equal protection fundamental right came most dramatically into its own in the reapportionment cases from the mid-1960s onward.[79] These cases changed the political landscape of the country. For decades state legislatures had not altered state or congressional districts to reflect the accelerating population movement from rural to urban areas, with the result that in some cases a state legislator in an urban district represented more than twice as many voters as a legislator from a rural area. Rural areas tended to be more conservative and less prone to competitive races, with the result that both in state legislatures and in the House of Representatives, conservative, almost feudal baronies reigned. The Court took this on as a violation of the right of each individual voter to have his vote count equally with that of all other voters. Surely, the Court reasoned, a rule frankly assigning some classes of voters two or more votes in the same election would violate equal protection, and that was malapportionment's effect. The Court brushed aside arguments based on preserving the need for representation of historically distinct constituencies or of groups and areas with distinct interests in danger of being swamped in a simply majoritarian arrangement, arguments that had resulted in the constitutionally mandated disproportionate representation of less populous states in the Senate, the House of Representatives, and the Electoral College.[80] The Court's reasoning was breathtakingly summary: "Legislators represent people, not trees or acres."[81] With an inexorable logic the principle was extended to every kind and level of election: for instance, the Board of Estimate of the City of New York (a city made up of the joining of separate jurisdictions) could no longer legitimately recognize through disproportionate representation the distinct interests of the several boroughs.[82] Nowhere in constitutional doctrine is there a more emphatic affirmation of the conception of United States citizenship as individualistic, atomized, mobile, and free from the permanent ties of group, history, interest, or place.

Intents and Effects

The reapportionment cases are firmly established in constitutional doctrine, so much so that after every decennial census there is a swell of litigation insuring fidelity to the one-man-one-vote principle. Yet there is a sense in which they stand as an anomaly in equal protection doctrine. It is a firmly established axiom of equal protection doctrine—one that the partisans of equality have never accepted[83]—that only government measures that intentionally impose inequalities, not those that "merely" have the effect of bearing unequally on different classes of citizens, violate the equal protection clause. More than anything else, it is this axiom that prevents the clause from working as an affirmative engine of equality.

Jefferson v. Hackney,[84] the case that first explicitly announced this doctrine, also best illustrates it. The state of Texas offered far less generous welfare payments to poor families with dependent children than it did to blind and disabled persons. There was evidence that the former group, consisting largely of single-parent families, was disproportionately black, while blindness and other disabilities were randomly distributed across the population as a whole. A measure explicitly directed at disadvantaging single-parent families or a racial group would violate equal protection, but the Court held that there was no such intent here. These were two distinct programs, enacted at different times under distinct impulses. If the practical effect of any two such enactments could be calculated, compared, and found defective because they bore unequally on different groups and classes, then the Court would be in the impossible position of having continuously to measure and adjust the entire collection of laws according to their frequently changing differential effects. To appreciate the vastness of the undertaking, consider that there would be no reason in principle to leave out the whole body of private law—of property, contract, and tort—which, as it works out in practical circumstances, may bear very differently on various groups. The job would be difficult enough if only the burden on racial groups, who receive heightened scrutiny, were considered. It would be impossible, unless the Court were simply to replace the rest of the government, if the differential effect on different levels of wealth and poverty had to be considered. For instance, every government service offered for a uniform fee would be suspect. And because the laws of property, tort, and contracts are, after all, *laws* so also would the right of shopkeepers to charge identical prices for food to the rich and the poor; rent control would be constitutionally mandated, as would limits on the rights of inheritance.

But is not malapportionment sometimes the result merely of the failure of legislatures to adjust district lines in the light of changing population patterns rather than of some intention to favor some class of voter? The tension with the intents test of *Jefferson v. Hackney* cannot be escaped by arguing that in malapportionment the legislators who should make the adjustment are the very ones who benefit from failing to do so, because all legislation balances the interests of contending groups and legislators are well aware that if they alter the balance of benefits and burdens they affect the situations of the various groups they represent and who elect them. Nor can the anomaly be escaped by pointing out that districting regimes are instituted all at once in a single comprehensive law, while the kind of effect complained of in *Jefferson* was the result—perhaps unintended—of a whole congeries of laws enacted at different times with different intentions.[85] *Jefferson* has not been limited in this way. The very next year, in *Washington v. Davis*,[86] the Court invoked the intent requirement to turn aside a challenge to a civil service examination that had the effect but not the (claimed or demonstrated) purpose of producing a disproportionate number of successful white applicants.[87] In the end, voting rights are a kind of doctrinal singularity, best explained by the argument that voting determines all other legal (though not constitutional) rights: whatever is not controlled by the Constitution itself is controlled by law, and that should be the product of democratic choice.

Affirmative Action

This account of equal protection doctrine lays a foundation for understanding the perplexities of its treatment of what goes variously by the designation of affirmative action or—to those more hostile to it—reverse discrimination. As was illustrated by *Strauder* and *Brown*, racial classifications disadvantaging the descendants of slaves, whose equal citizenship was the principal end of the Reconstruction amendments, were so deeply suspect that a close connection to a compelling state interest that might justify them could hardly ever be found.[88] But what of laws classifying by race for the purpose of *advantaging* the former victim group, even if at the expense of other groups in the population as a whole?

With the sense that the elimination of formal barriers to racial equality still left blacks far behind by every measure of status and well-being and that they were almost entirely absent from all the seats of honor, power, and privilege, public and private steps were taken to accelerate an equality in fact that might otherwise take generations to achieve. The strongest steps were in the public schools, where *Brown* had first decreed an end to segregation but which a decade later still remained racially distinct in practice. Southern school districts, acting in obvious bad faith, tried a variety of measures that while dismantling formal segregation were designed to maintain it in fact: "freedom of choice" plans which supposedly allowed parents to place their children in any school they wanted;[89] maintaining school district lines that tracked racial residential patterns;[90] and most desperately simply closing altogether a system that could find no other way of keeping black and white children from going to school together.[91] The Court was united and relentless in waving aside such devices. Formal abandonment of segregation was not enough. Where there had previously been a dual system mandated by law, local government had to act affirmatively to come as reasonably close as possible to achieving what was called a unitary system, even if this meant ignoring established attendance zones and busing children across town to achieve some semblance of racial balance.[92] Where governments had deliberately violated the Constitution, the courts' remedial powers extended beyond ordering the end to the illegal practice: they would fashion remedies designed to reverse even the "lingering effects"[93] of this illegality.

But the lesser life chances, lower income, worse status, and almost total absence of blacks from elite institutions and positions of power led many institutions—public and private—that had never practiced discrimination to take what was called affirmative action to include blacks, who because of lower income, worse education, or habits of isolation had been absent from their midst. Only in the last generation has the Court taken up the constitutional issue this raised—most recently in the Michigan affirmative action cases decided in June 2003—and its decisions have been so closely divided ever since and the opposing camps so firm that even now the answer is unstable and could be reversed with the change of heart or replacement of even a single justice.[94]

The case that set the terms of the subject ever since was *Regents of University of California v. Bakke.*[95] In *Bakke,* a white applicant to the University of California at Davis medical school brought an equal protection challenge against the school's admission program, which explicitly set aside sixteen of a hundred places in an entering class in order to ensure the admission of a significant number of students from specified minority groups. For reasons that are more complicated than they are interesting, what has ever since been taken to be the controlling opinion in that case[96] was written by Justice Powell and joined by no other justice. It was nonetheless a deep and magisterial pronouncement, proclaiming that "racial and ethnic distinctions of any sort are inherently suspect." Justice Powell rejected the dissent's contention that racial preferences, when "benign," should be evaluated under a lower level of scrutiny. Powell said that the effect of such "benign" preferences may be simply to "reinforce common stereotypes holding that certain groups are unable to achieve success without special protection." And while Powell embraced measures designed to ameliorate or eliminate the effects of identified illegal discrimination, such as those taken in the school desegregation cases, he feared that the more "amorphous" goal of remedying "societal discrimination" would be "ageless in its reach into the past." Those who advocate for preferences have held on to *Bakke* for its acceptance of diversity as a "constitutionally permissible goal for an institution of higher education." Powell's reasoning, however, limits his holding to educational institutions, for which academic freedom and the ability to select students who will contribute most to "a robust exchange of ideas" is a paramount First Amendment concern. The diversity rationale for racial preferences is therefore hardly applicable outside this educational context. Justice Powell affirmed strongly that whatever its historical occasion, the Equal Protection Clause affirmed that the Constitution protected the situations of individuals, not groups,[97] and assured only that each person be judged—whether to his advantage or his disadvantage—on his own action and merit and not as a member of a racial group.

Justice Marshall's dissent stated the opposite position with unmatched bluntness and power: Justice Powell wanted blacks and whites to stand before the law as individuals, but this ignored the fact that centuries of slavery and generations of legalized discrimination had left their mark on every black person on account of his race and so every black individual was both black and an individual. Justice Marshall was as much an individualist as Powell. He had led the legal crusade for integration, and he surely never for a moment believed that race was an intrinsic and ineradicable distinguishing feature. In this he was different from latter-day black separatists and "multiculturalists."[98] Rather, history had promoted what might otherwise have been a legally insignificant characteristic into a mark fixed on every single black person, something they shared whatever differences there might be between them. "It is unnecessary in 20th century America," wrote Justice Marshall, "to have individual Negroes demonstrate that they have been victims of racial discrimination; the racism of our society has been so pervasive that none, regardless of wealth or position, has managed to escape its impact." For that reason the University of California's system was an appropriate response to an evident fact, and Justice Powell's prescription was as unrealistic as it was indeterminate. It was necessary to bring black people into positions of power and prestige everywhere so that they and whites could get used to their being everywhere and the mark of subordination finally erased. As Justice Blackmun put it in his dissent, "In order to get beyond racism, we must first take account of race."[99]

Justice Brennan's dissent announced a position—more subtle and supple—from which he would not deviate for his next twenty years on the Court[100] and which still is the doctrine to which four members of the Court continue to stick, in spite of the fact that only once since *Bakke* has a majority taken it up.[101] Race, he agreed, is a suspect classification, but different uses of it give rise to different levels of suspicion. (It was Justice Brennan, after all, who in *Craig v. Boren* more or less invented the doctrinal category of intermediate scrutiny, when a majority could not be found to accord gender classification strict scrutiny.) There were racial classifications which were "benign" because designed to further racial equality and others whose purpose—or effect?—was to institute or maintain racial subordination.[102] As Justice Stevens—in dissent—put it almost twenty years later, the Court's affirmative action jurisprudence "disregard[s] the difference between a 'No Trespassing' sign and a welcome mat."[103] On this view, laws that classified by race to favor blacks would still have to account for themselves, but they would not be limited to a few compelling justifications, nor would the means have to be as closely tailored to their proper ends as strict scrutiny would demand.

The difference between these two standards was illustrated by *City of Richmond v. J. A. Croson Co.*[104] The Court, using strict scrutiny, struck down an ordinance requiring all contractors on city construction jobs to let at least 30 percent of its subcontracting work to minority subcontractors, defined to include those who are "Black, Spanish-speaking, Oriental, Indian, Eskimo or Aleut." Richmond's history as capital of the Confederacy, the fact that less than 1 percent of the city's construction contracts had been awarded to minority-run businesses between 1978 and 1983, and perhaps the Court's own experience with the construction industry and construction unions as die-hard racists[105] led the dissent to conclude that there was reason enough for this racial set-aside. The majority specifically rejected the notion that there was such a thing as benign discrimination which would justify a lower level of scrutiny. Using strict scrutiny, it noted that there had been no proof of actual discrimination by the city in its

contracting practices or even by the city's contractors, so that no remedial purpose could be invoked. And echoing Justice Powell in
Bakke, the Court rejected the goal of remedying the societal discrimination that might well explain the underrepresentation of black contractors. Indeed, in a much controverted phrase, the Court suggested
that only the purpose of remedying identified discrimination would
satisfy strict scrutiny.[106] But even if a compelling interest could be
found, the Court concluded with particular emphasis and effect that
the means chosen to serve it were far from carefully and closely
enough matched to it to meet strict scrutiny. The beneficiaries of the
ordinance included Native Americans and Aleuts, neither of whom
were claimed ever even to have worked or lived in Richmond. The 30
percent figure seemed to have been pulled out of thin air.[107] But perhaps most important, the city had not tried any race-neutral measures, such as assisting new entrants into the industry to find work or
adjusting bonding and other barriers that were likely to have an
exclusionary effect. It was this casual and unmodulated recourse to
racial quotas that condemned the measure in the Court's eyes.

As definitive as the *Croson* decision appears to have been, the
Court's stance on affirmative action is even now not settled. For many
years, in spite of conflicting and confused decisions in the lower
courts, the Supreme Court continued to avoid cases that would clarify
the status and meaning of Justice Powell's lone opinion in *Bakke,* and
this would explain the apparent discrepancy between that opinion
and its reference to diversity as an additional compelling interest justifying the use of race and *Croson,* which appeared to allow only the
remedying of identifiable past discrimination. In June 2003 in *Grutter
v. Bollinger*[108] and *Gratz v. Bollinger,*[109] the University of Michigan affirmative action cases, the Court finally revisited *Bakke* and made Justice Powell's opinion the basis for its decisions. Nonetheless, the law
of affirmative action remains confused and indefinite. Before considering the Michigan cases in detail and their impact on affirmative action doctrine, it is necessary in order to complete the picture to set out
another line of cases, those dealing with the equivalent of affirmative
action in drawing voting districts.

The voting rights story as it relates to race is as confused as it is
complicated. One place to begin is with *Mobile v. Bolden.*[110] The city
of Mobile, Alabama, had long chosen its three city commissioners
in an election in which the voters of the city, which was not sepa-

rated into districts, voted at large for each member of the commission. The black population was about 40 percent, but even after the Voting Rights Act of 1965 and open registration gave voting power to blacks, no black was elected. A phenomenon called racially polarized voting guaranteed that the council would remain all white, so long as white voters refused to vote for a black candidate, no matter what that candidate's party or program. If, however, the city were divided into single-member districts (or if some other scheme, like proportional representation, were adopted) the council might more nearly reflect the city's racial composition. A lawsuit under the Fourteenth Amendment, the Fifteenth Amendment guaranteeing the right to vote without regard to race, and the 1965 Voting Rights Act failed. The Court applied its established equal protection doctrine to conclude that the original voting scheme had been in place long before blacks had gained voting rights and so it could not have had as its purpose the exclusion of blacks from the effective power to choose representatives of their choice. And the mere failure to change that scheme because it now had that *effect* was not a violation of law or of the Constitution. Multimember districts were a common phenomenon in the South, being used—generally with a racially exclusionary effect—to choose state legislators and even members of Congress. Congress determined to do something about the *Mobile* decision. But what? A law frankly requiring proportional racial representation was too much like decreeing a racially balkanized republic to be acceptable. Yet something like that was what many wanted, and in a sense if all barriers truly disappeared then the law of averages suggested that some such result is what one might expect in the long run. The deliberately ambiguous formula adopted by the Voting Rights Act of 1982, section 2, in response to the *Mobile* decision provided:

(a) No voting qualification or prerequisite to voting or standard, practice, or procedure shall be imposed or applied by any State or political subdivision in a manner which results in a denial or abridgement of the right of any citizen of the United States to vote on account of race, or color . . .

(b) A violation of subsection (a) is established if, based on the totality of the circumstances, it is shown that the political processes leading to nomination or election in the State or political subdivision are not equally open to participation by members of a class of citizens protected by subsection (a) in that its members have less opportunity than other members of the electorate to participate in the political process and to elect representatives of their choice. The extent to which members of a protected class have been elected to office in the State or political subdivision is one circumstance which may be considered: Provided, That nothing in this section establishes a right to have members of a protected class elected in numbers equal to their proportion in the population.[111]

Under that provision (and section 5, which I will not go into here)[112] courts and state legislatures were moved to fashion what are called majority-minority districts: districts which are so drawn that they sweep in enough minority voters to guarantee them a majority in that district, even if it means bleeding them out of adjacent districts. And it worked. Especially after the 1990 census the number of black members of Congress and state legislators increased substantially.[113] But there was a price. The districts were sometimes bizarrely shaped, defying the usual notion that legislative districts should be continuous, compact, and follow historical political divisions such as city, county, and town lines.

Legislatures have been gerrymandering districts since the beginning of the Republic in order to achieve political ends: usually to guarantee or deny representation to a particular interest or party, or to punish or reward a particular candidate.[114] Perhaps some of these gerrymanders were as extreme as the one the Court struck down in 1993 in *Shaw v. Reno*:[115] North Carolina's District 12, for example, was "approximately 160 miles long and, for much of its length, is no wider than the I-85 corridor. It [wound] in snakelike fashion through tobacco country, financial centers, and manufacturing areas 'until it gobble[d] in enough enclaves of black neighborhoods.'" One state legislator remarked, "[I]f you drove down the interstate with both car doors open, you'd kill most of the people in the district." The fact that the district line divided the population by race was crucial to the Court's decision in *Shaw*. And what of it? Where was the inequality? Who was treated unfairly? Before the reapportionment cases, country people sometimes had twice the voting power of city dwellers. In *Mobile v. Bolden,* the multimember district—intentionally or not—denied a minority any chance at representation. But in the gerrymander, while blacks are fenced in to win in one district, they are fenced out of the adjacent districts. Something other than notions of numerical equality is at work in *Shaw:* it is not a matter of unconstitutional subordination of one group to another, but of offensive segmentation by race. "A reapportionment plan that includes in one district individuals who belong to the same race, but who are otherwise widely separated by geographical and political boundaries, and who may have little in common with one another but the color of their skin, bears an uncomfortable resemblance to political apartheid."[116] The assumption of this "benign" racial gerrymander was that blacks deserved representation as such, not as individual citizens; that yesterday's politicians would decide how today's citizens should arrange themselves to choose tomorrow's politicians; and that that arrangement should be along racial lines. Yet, as the dissenters—who from the outset have been four and unbending—keep pointing out, district lines must be drawn on some basis, those bases have always been political, and at their best have tried to group together citizens with similar interests, so that, say, rural voters have a voice, so that people from fishing communities have a representative who knows their interests and will speak for them. Yes, but for the majority that was just the point: it was offensive to assume that far-away rural blacks have the same interests as urban blacks just because they were of the same race, and if there were some truth to this assumption, institutionalizing it and giving political leaders a vested interest in it would simply dig it in and make permanent a racial divide whose importance should diminish. It was *Bakke* all over again.

There is a particular instability to this part of the story, because the dissenters are surely right that district lines must be drawn somehow and the Court had no appetite for the business of policing them in general.[117] The uneasy compromise in the most recent cases is that only if the lines are drawn on predominantly racial grounds, to the exclusion more or less of other traditional political grounds, is there a violation of the Constitution. So, for instance in the latest iteration of the *Shaw* case itself, the Court concluded that the gerrymander was permissible because among its justifications was the protection of incumbents.[118] The question is further confused because one member of the slim majority, Justice O'Connor, who was indeed the author of *Shaw v. Reno,* has suggested that just the kind of racial gerrymander she deplored in that case might survive strict scrutiny because a state legislature's purpose to comply with the 1982 Voting Rights Act may be sufficiently compelling to survive that highest standard. The suggestion is puzzling: in a case dealing with federal racial set-asides in public works contracting, that same justice insisted that Congress was subject to the same equal protection strictures as had been imposed on the city of Richmond in the *Croson* case.[119] And generally the Court has been reluctant to show much deference to Congress when, in exercise of its enforcement powers under the Fourteenth Amendment, it applied a different substantive constitutional standard than the Court itself had announced.[120] Does it make a difference that in voting rights the Fifteenth Amendment is also in play, or are these just Justice O'Connor's worried second thoughts?

When the Court finally decided to hear two affirmative action cases involving the University of Michigan, there was hope that it might resolve some of the muddle which had characterized doctrine in this area since *Bakke.* Indeed this expectation was heightened by the Court's unusual action of granting review in the undergraduate admissions case *(Gratz),* even though the court of appeals had not yet decided that case, and setting it for argument with the law school admissions case *(Grutter).* The Court upheld the law school's program and ruled the undergraduate admissions program violated equal protection. The opinions for the Court in both cases purported to apply Justice Powell's lone opinion in *Bakke,* and so it may be said that that opinion now enjoys a firm doctrinal footing. But at the same time only four justices fully endorsed that opinion: Justices Scalia and Thomas indicated that strict scrutiny did not admit something so vague as a compelling governmental interest in diversity, and four justices would allow far more scope for benign uses of race, just as Justice Brennan had urged in *Bakke.*

The undergraduate admissions program awarded a set number of points for a variety of factors—high school, grades, the difficulty of the courses and the reputation of the high school, extracurricular activities, and the like. One hundred and fifty points virtually guaranteed admission, and membership in one of three "underrepresented" minority groups—African-American, Hispanic, and Native American—automatically entitled the applicant to twenty extra points. Competition among nonminority applicants who could do the work was quite fierce. But, in practical effect, any applicant with qualifying grades and test scores received enough points for that reason that the addition of twenty points more for minority status virtually assured admission. And indeed a few years earlier, before the institution of the point system, any preferred minority applicant who could be predicted to be able to do the work had been automatically admitted.

The law school, by contrast, in choosing among about 3,500 applicants for 350 places—in contrast to the far larger number of applicants and places to be filled in the undergraduate program—was held by the Court to use no such mechanical system, but rather to consider each applicant individually and in comparison to all others as the rolling admissions proceeded. The law school had, however, formally committed to attaining what it called diversity, and accordingly to admitting members of underrepresented minorities in "meaningful numbers" so as to assure more than a token presence of such students in the classroom—what the law school policy termed a "critical mass." This commitment entailed admitting preferred minority applicants with significantly lower academic credentials. The drafters of the formal policy and the law school's witnesses had obviously studied Justice Powell's opinion well, for they explained the virtues of diversity as adding to the richness of the classroom experience, and—going Powell one better—explained that they did not assume that all minority students entertained the same views or had had similar experiences: on the contrary, one of the valuable classroom lessons to be learned is just that there are as many points of view within these groups as in others, and thus the tendency to think about members of these groups in stereotypical terms would be erased. As the Chief Justice pointed out in his dissent, this more individualized review regularly yielded minority admittees in close proportion to their numbers in the applicant pool and, even more tellingly, the "critical mass" for Hispanics was far smaller than that for African-Americans but greater than that for Native Americans. Moreover, as the rolling admissions reached its completion, admissions officers received daily tabulations detailing the numbers of minority and nonminority applicants and admittees. If this had been evidence presented against defendants in an antitrust case, few would contest Justice Scalia's conclusion that "the University of Michigan Law School's mystical 'critical mass' justification for its discrimination by race challenges even the most gullible mind. The admissions statistics show it to be a sham to cover a scheme of racially proportionate admissions." Only the far smaller numbers involved saved the law school from having to adopt something like the undergraduate program's more mechanical system. As Justice Ginsburg, dissenting in the undergraduate case, put it: "If honesty is the best policy, surely Michigan's accurately described, fully disclosed College affirmative action program is preferable to achieving similar numbers through [the Law School's system of?] winks, nods, and disguises."

That the Court's split decision could be so convincingly attacked from both sides is a sure sign of the unresolved tension—not to say incoherence—in the doctrine the two cases announced. Justice Powell's notion of individualized judgment, where race may come in as one of any number of factors, may make some sense: one should remember that he is the author of the Court's opinion in *McKleskey v. Kemp*,[121] rejecting statistical evidence that juries in certain states are more likely to condemn to death black murder defendants or at least murderers of white victims. Powell explained that jury decisions are individualized judgments, by large and uncoordinated groups, acting under proper instructions to weigh a variety of factors. But this distinction makes no sense at all as applied to an administrative process, with a single set of decision makers, dealing year after year with large numbers of applicants and charged with coming up with "meaningful numbers" and a "critical mass." And yet such a numerical goal is an entirely plausible entailment of the diversity rationale itself. A further incoherence is introduced by Justice O'Connor's enthusiastic endorsement—elicited by amicus briefs on behalf of large corporations, business leaders, and retired military officers—of affirmative action as a way of supplying trained minority group members to take up leadership positions in the corporate world and the officer corps:

> The Law School's claim is further bolstered by numerous expert studies and reports showing that such diversity promotes learning outcomes and better prepares students for an increasingly diverse workforce, for society, and for the legal profession. Major American businesses have made clear that the skills needed in today's increasingly global marketplace can only be developed through exposure to widely diverse people, cultures, ideas, and viewpoints. High-ranking retired officers and civilian military leaders assert that a highly qualified, racially diverse officer

corps is essential to national security. Moreover, because universities, and in particular, law schools, represent the training ground for a large number of the Nation's leaders, . . . the path to leadership must be visibly open to talented and qualified individuals of every race and ethnicity. Thus, the Law School has a compelling interest in attaining a diverse student body.

Justice Powell in *Bakke* had rejected an analogous argument—that the medical school's program was justified by the need to train doctors to serve minority communities—in favor of emphasizing simply and only the educational benefits that diverse viewpoints brought to the classroom. This was an academic judgment with which he said courts should be reluctant to interfere, in deference to the First Amendment value of academic freedom. And Justice O'Connor in the law school case gave great emphasis to this academic freedom rationale. Yet the quoted passage suggests a place for just this kind of program by employers and governments everywhere, although Justice O'Connor herself was the author of vigorous opinions denying the applicability of the diversity rationale in government contracting and the award of broadcast licenses.

In the end, I suggest that the Court has not yet emerged from the muddle first offered in *Bakke*. The number of voices raised in favor of separation and race consciousness for its own sake as the means for overcoming the inequality created by slavery and segregation are louder and more numerous than they were at the start of the desegregationist project. But they have no respectability in constitutional doctrine. The issue now, as at the time of *Bakke,* turns on the best way to achieve a society free from racial segmentation—in law and in fact. At the outset of that project many believed in jump-starting integration with affirmative steps that made what should be the conclusion of the process seem a little closer to realization than might occur if all barriers were removed and events were allowed to take their course. In the course of the justices' confidential discussion of *Bakke* in their conference prior to voting, Justice Stevens said that racial preferences might "be acceptable as a temporary measure but not a permanent solution." Justice Powell agreed. But when Justice Stevens suggested that, "[p]erhaps . . . blacks would not need these special programs much longer," Justice Marshall interrupted to say that it would "be another hundred years." Powell's biographer reports that "this remark left Powell speechless . . . [H]e recoiled from the prospect of generation upon generation of racial quotas."[122]

That is where we are now. Progress has been made, but there is reason to worry that if affirmative action is abandoned, it will be undone.[123] What caused Justice Powell to recoil—rightly, I believe—is more threatening now than at the time of *Bakke*. We have had another generation of racial classifications and preferences. A whole elite cadre depends on racial division for its constituency and its position. Justices Powell and Marshall agreed that a single, unsegmented nation, where race did not matter, was the goal. But if we continue indefinitely to divide ourselves by race, to make race legally dispositive in all sorts of contexts (with the ugly necessity of formally assigning individuals to particular racial groups), then the time will soon come—I hope it is not already here, I hope the entrenched interests have not become too strong—when this new form of racial segmentation will become permanent, that the ideal of each person's being judged as an individual and not as a member of a group to which he is assigned by somebody's "public policy" will no longer be possible. It seems to me that the way to honor this ultimate goal while acknowledging the real concern about resegregation is not by the vague, indeed incoherent distinction between individualized judgment and "mechanical" criteria—imagine anything like such a distinction being applied by the military or any other large, bureaucratic organization—but by a firm commitment to call a halt to racial preferences after a finite, definite period. Justice O'Connor made something of this point:

> We are mindful, however, that "[a] core purpose of the Fourteenth Amendment was to do away with all governmentally imposed discrimination based on race." . . . Accordingly, race-conscious admissions policies must be limited in time. This requirement reflects that racial classifications, however compelling their goals, are potentially so dangerous that they may be employed no more broadly than the interest demands. Enshrining a permanent justification for racial preferences would offend this fundamental equal protection principle. We see no reason to exempt race-conscious admissions programs from the requirement that all governmental use of race must have a logical end point. The Law School, too, concedes that all "race-conscious programs must have reasonable durational limits."
>
> In the context of higher education, the durational requirement can be met by sunset provisions in race-conscious admissions policies and periodic reviews to determine whether racial preferences are still necessary to achieve student body diversity.

Justices Ginsburg and Breyer, concurring in the law school case, agreed, and with additional emphasis:

The Court's observation that race-conscious programs "must have a logical endpoint," accords with the international understanding of the office of affirmative action. The International Convention on the Elimination of All Forms of Racial Discrimination, ratified by the United States in 1994, . . . endorses "special and concrete measures to ensure the adequate development and protection of certain racial groups or individuals belonging to them, for the purpose of guaranteeing them the full and equal enjoyment of human rights and fundamental freedoms." But such measures, the Convention instructs, "shall in no case entail as a consequence the maintenance of unequal or separate rights for different racial groups after the objectives for which they were taken have been achieved."

Unfortunately these ringing statements, like the Court's overall message in these two cases that race-conscious affirmative action is permissible but only sometimes, come to very little. (One is reminded of Gerald Gunther's remark about Alexander Bickel in an entirely different context: "He is one hundred percent for principle, eighty percent of the time.") For this is how Justice O'Connor concludes:

It has been 25 years since Justice Powell first approved the use of race to further an interest in student body diversity in the context of public higher education. Since that time, the number of minority applicants with high grades and test scores has indeed increased. We expect that 25 years from now, the use of racial preferences will no longer be necessary to further the interest approved today.

This is no limitation at all. Fifty years are long enough to make dividing us up by race a habit, to create a practically and politically unshakeable sense of entitlement in those who think they benefit from such schemes and in the racial entrepreneurs who know they do. And even Justice O'Connor's too distant end point is expressed only as an expectation. It may be that the only way to get beyond racism is just to stop using race—not today or tomorrow but with all deliberate speed, in, say, five or seven years. Only with such a determinative end point will institutions have the incentive to confront the political pressures arrayed against a truly unitary concept of citizenship. I believe the Court should have allowed both programs to continue, but only on condition that the university revise them to state a fixed, determinate period of years after which they would come to an end.

Afterword

In the first chapter I left open whether doctrine is possible for the controverted and difficult questions of constitutional law and whether the Court is in fact constrained by doctrine. If the answer to these questions is no, then there is no constitutional law; there are only constitutional decisions. The chapters that followed displayed those decisions as if doctrine is possible and—what comes to the same thing—as if doctrine does guide the Court. I have proceeded almost as if politics did not exist, almost as if justices were not appointed by Presidents and confirmed by senators who cared a great deal how the nominees will decide cases. Some justices have been appointed mainly because of their competence and professional reputation as lawyers and jurists (one thinks of Holmes, Hughes, Cardozo, the second Justice Harlan, Stevens, Breyer), or to satisfy regional or demographic concerns. But John Marshall, Taney, the first Justice Harlan, Stone, Black, Frankfurter, Douglas, Thurgood Marshall, Rehnquist, and Scalia were chosen as much for what they thought as for how well they thought. These appointments were made with the hope—only sometimes realized—that they would change the course of the Court's decisions. If politics—in the high sense of policies championed out of a commitment to a controverted conception of the public good—ruled the Court, then each new appointment would be like a new election, with decisions determined by party platforms.

The work of the Court has not been like that. It would take Olympian confidence in one's own powers of discernment to wave aside as so much high-blown rhetoric the elaborate doctrinal structures I have displayed in this book—rhetoric that digs no channels to confine the flow of decision. A law professor or political scientist may be tempted to such an Olympian stance. But I have worked not only as a scholar and teacher but as an advocate before the Court. An advocate may only rarely and discreetly allow himself to urge his case in political terms. Almost the whole work of the advocate is to take doctrine seriously and to show how the position he urges fits into existing doctrine, or occasionally how the advocate's position may be adopted by the Court so that it will work as doctrine and precedent into the indefinite future. I have also worked as a judge of the highest court of my state, and that work consisted of deciding cases in ways that can be explained in opinions—decisions that will "write"—opinions that can persuade enough of one's colleagues to make up a majority. Those opinions are responsible to the past and hostages to the future, as Chapter 1 explains. So I have presented an insider's view of constitutional law—an insider not in the sense that I offer private information or pungent gossip, but in the sense that I write from within the discipline of law, not from above or outside it. If that discipline were a delusion and what was really going on were wholly determined by interest and politics, I would hope I would have noticed and not tried to reassure myself by capturing you, my readers, within my delusional system. Whether I am right is a judgment I invite you to make for yourselves.

The insider's perspective does not blind one to reality nor does it require the belief, in the words of the Lord Chancellor in *Iolanthe,* that "the law is the true embodiment of everything that's excellent. It has no kind of fault or flaw." Religion Clause doctrine, I argue in Chapter 5, has at several points attained a measure of incoherence. In Chapter 2, I insist that the Court's escalating Eleventh Amendment doctrine is wrong. But even as to doctrines that are clear and coherent, the intelligent observer must understand that some are highly controverted and hang on a single vote. The Court's 2002 voucher decision (discussed in Chapter 5) certainly was clear enough and connected in a standard way to a long course of Religion Clause jurisprudence, but four dissenters stated such emphatic disagreement that a single new appointment might spell its reversal. Similarly precarious are not only the misbegotten Eleventh Amendment decisions but also the much better founded decisions limiting the scope of Congress's powers under the Commerce Clause and the enforcement clause of the Fourteenth Amendment and protecting the states' internal processes from being swallowed up by federal commands. (These are discussed in Chapter 2.) Finally, the whole course of doctrine subjecting to strict and skeptical scrutiny race-conscious measures intended to improve the situation of historically disadvantaged groups—in voting, in the economy, in education—has attracted vehement dissents from four justices. (This subject is taken up in Chapter 7.)

In all of these areas the close division is vulgarly described as between liberals and conservatives, but such labels hardly designate a recognizable, coherent jurisprudential or political program. Nor does the distinction between activist and restrained justices explain anything at all, because, depending on the subject, justices on both sides of the divide are ready to insist on their own conceptions of what the Constitution requires and thus to override the judgments of elected officials and legislators. Party labels and the identity of the Presidents who appointed the justices do little to explain the divide. Nor can we map the split onto a coherent political vision. Such a vision might work to explain what appears to have been the project of the Warren Court carried forward with great skill and persistence by Justice Brennan over his thirty-four years on the Court: to institute via the Constitution and under the supervision of the federal courts something that would look more like a redistributionist social democracy of the sort found in Northern Europe,[1] what in American politics is associated with the Progressive tradition. During that time the Court established a remarkable number of new constitutional doctrines in a wide range of areas: criminal procedure, substantive criminal law, the role of the federal courts in supervising the states' administration of criminal justice, the rights of noncitizens, defamation and free speech law in general, the constitutionalizing of the basic protections of a civil service system, redistricting, desegregation, affirmative action, reproductive rights. If one counted the projects that failed by one or two votes, the list would be much longer, including perhaps a constitutional right to minimal provision of the basic necessities of life at government expense and certainly the abolition of the death penalty. The scope of the project surpasses anything else in the Court's history, with the possible exception of Chief Justice Marshall's firm establishment in constitutional doctrine of the main outlines of our federal system.

The best I can do to explain the present voting blocs is to see the recent decades as a reaction to that program, with a majority today more or less inclined to dismantle large parts of it and a minority maintaining a reflexive but waning loyalty to at least the spirit of that time. It is not remarkable—nor perhaps even inappropriate—that the Court should in part be ruled by its past. But when that past is represented by atmospheric loyalties forged in battles long since won or lost, that atmosphere is bound to dissipate over the years and new reflexes and loyalties are bound to develop, especially as new justices come to the Court. The last decade has been a period of unusual stability for the Court. The last new appointment, Stephen Breyer, was made in 1994, and he replaced Harry Blackmun, from whose general dispositions he does not greatly differ. But given the average age of the justices, there are bound to be several new appointments in the coming years. Whoever they are, it is unlikely that they will cause an abrupt reversal in doctrine, even if their sympathies lie more with the dissenting four than with the five. The institutional inertia of stare decisis would pull powerfully against any wholesale course of reversals.

Justice Souter, one of the most persistent of the dissenters, joined (and perhaps wrote) a strong affirmation of stare decisis in the joint opinion in *Planned Parenthood of Southeastern Pennsylvania v. Casey*,[2] declining to overrule *Roe v. Wade*:

> The obligation to follow precedent begins with necessity, and a contrary necessity marks its outer limit. With Cardozo, we recognize that no judicial system could do society's work if it eyed each issue afresh in every case that raised it. Indeed, the very concept of the rule of law underlying our own Constitution requires such continuity over time that a respect for precedent is, by definition, indispensable. At the other extreme, a different necessity would make itself felt if a prior judicial ruling should come to be seen so clearly as error that its enforcement was for that very reason doomed.
>
> Even when the decision to overrule a prior case is not, as in the rare, latter instance, virtually foreordained, it is common wisdom that the rule of *stare decisis* is not an "inexorable command," and certainly it is

not such in every constitutional case. Rather, when this Court reexamines a prior holding, its judgment is customarily informed by a series of prudential and pragmatic considerations designed to test the consistency of overruling a prior decision with the ideal of the rule of law, and to gauge the respective costs of reaffirming and overruling a prior case. Thus, for example, we may ask whether the rule has proven to be intolerable simply in defying practical workability; whether the rule is subject to a kind of reliance that would lend a special hardship to the consequences of overruling and add inequity to the cost of repudiation; whether related principles of law have so far developed as to have left the old rule no more than a remnant of abandoned doctrine; or whether facts have so changed, or come to be seen so differently, as to have robbed the old rule of significant application or justification.

Few of the many five-to-four decisions of the past two decades meet those criteria for overruling. It is particularly unlikely that a new majority, if there should be one, would reverse a large number of precedents—no matter what the justices believed personally—on the ground that those precedents had "come to be seen so clearly as error that [their] enforcement was for that very reason doomed." As I explain in Chapter 6, the overruling of *Bowers v. Hardwick* by *Lawrence v. Texas* is the rare case that best fits under this last rubric.

A more realistic possibility is that over time different ways of thinking about constitutional doctrine might influence how existing precedents would be applied, extended, or confined. Justice Thomas has often but not regularly expressed an inclination to see constitutional law move in a direction at once more libertarian but also more rigidly simple and direct. Justice Breyer by contrast has articulated on a number of occasions the view that in many areas current constitutional doctrine is too rigid, too legalistic for the practical ends he believes all law is meant to serve. Thus he would reorient free speech law away from rules and doctrinal categories toward an avowedly pragmatic approach that recognizes and seeks to balance the general free speech "values" implicated in many difficult controversies,[3] the control of modern means of mass communication,[4] the clash between privacy and freedom to speak,[5] the regulation of campaign finance and electoral processes generally.[6] Breyer has also urged the consideration of materials from other constitutional democracies and their constitutional courts, a suggestion that would have implications for the development of the law in respect to the death penalty, hate speech, the regulation of political campaigns, and federalism.[7] Only in the *Lawrence* case have such materials been allowed to play a role in the opinion of the Court.

If one of these or some other new approach were to take hold, it would over time change the nature of constitutional law. The change would not be sudden, but it would be more profound than an occasional overruling, because less hemmed in by stare decisis. Stare decisis requires respect for past decisions, but not for ways of thinking about those decisions, for ways of thinking about stare decisis itself, and for ways of thinking about the nature of constitutional law in general.

Notes

1. Doctrine

1. *See* generally Richard H. Fallon, Jr., *Implementing the Constitution* (2001); Charles Fried, "Constitutional Doctrine," 107 *Harvard L. Rev.* 1140 (1994). My argument in this chapter owes a debt to the writings of Ronald Dworkin, from which I have learned over the years.
2. 531 U.S. 98 (2000). *See* Richard Posner, *Breaking the Deadlock* (2001); *Bush v. Gore: The Question of Legitimacy* (Bruce Ackerman ed., 2002).
3. *Terminiello v. City of Chicago,* 337 U.S. 1, 11 (1949) (Frankfurter, J., dissenting).
4. Montesquieu, *The Spirit of the Laws* (David W. Carrithers ed., 1977) (1748).
5. Richard H. Fallon, Jr., " 'Rule of Law' as a Concept in Constitutional Discourse," 97 *Colum. L. Rev.* 1 (1997).
6. Mark Tushnet, *Taking the Constitutional Away from the Courts* 28 (1999); Duncan Kennedy, "Freedom and Constraint in Adjudication: A Critical Phenomenology," 36 *J. Legal Educ.* 518 (1986).
7. U.S. Const. art. VI. The philosophers will point out that this requirement, enjoined by the text itself, makes this argument circular.
8. *See, e.g.,* Robert H. Bork, *The Tempting of America* 155–56 (1990); *Planned Parenthood of Southeastern Pa. v. Casey,* 505 U.S. 833, 943 (1992) (Rehnquist, C.J., concurring in the judgment in part and dissenting in part) (arguing that courts should prefer "a proper understanding" of the Constitution to mistaken constitutional interpretations enshrined in precedent); *Wallace v. Jaffree,* 472 U.S. 38, 110 (1985) (Rehnquist, J., dissenting) ("These difficulties arise because the *Lemon* test has no more grounding in the history of the First Amendment than does the wall theory upon which it

rests. The three-part test represents a determined effort to craft a workable rule from a historically faulty doctrine. . . ."); *see also Albernaz v. United States,* 450 U.S. 333, 343 (1981) (stating that the doctrine in the double jeopardy area is "a veritable Sargasso Sea which could not fail to challenge the most intrepid judicial navigator"); *Graves v. New York ex rel. O'Keefe,* 306 U.S. 466, 491–92 (1939) (Frankfurter, J., concurring) ("[T]he ultimate touchstone of constitutionality is the Constitution itself and not what we have said about it.").

9. Sanford Levinson, "Political Implications of Amending Clauses," 13 *Const. Commentary* 107, 110–11 (1996).

10. Martin Shapiro, *Courts: A Comparative and Political Analysis* 135–36 (1981); John Henry Merryman, *The Civil Law Tradition* 47 (2d ed. 1985). There are grounds for skepticism. Continental judges do refer to the writings of respected scholars and to consistent courses of decision, all of which make up what is called jurisprudence, so that prior decisions do in fact bear on new cases either directly or indirectly. And the newer constitutional courts in Germany, South Africa, and elsewhere as well as the European Courts of Justice and of Human Rights use precedent in a way quite similar to that of the Supreme Court of the United States. *See* Donald P. Kommers, "German Constitutionalism: A Prolegomenon," 40 *Emory Law J.* 837, 840 (1991); "Developments in the Law—International Criminal Law," 114 *Harvard L. Rev.* 2049, 2060 n.66.

11. Originally, Supreme Court justices each delivered individual opinions, separately or seriatim—a practice derived from the English common law courts. Chief Justice Marshall was concerned about the ambiguous precedential value of these decisions, and instead established the practice of writing a single opinion for the Court.

12. I come back to this question after twenty-five years and find that the solution that applies to this very public manifestation of the paradox is very much along the lines I sketched then. See Charles Fried, *An Anatomy of Values: Problems of Personal and Social Choice* 26–40 (1970)—perhaps a manifestation of the very argument I have in mind here.

13. *See* Cass R. Sunstein, "Routine and Revolution," 81 *NW. U. L. Rev.* 869, 884–85, 887 (1987) ("[I]t is difficult to imagine what a world of genuine fluidity would look like. Indeed, part of individual autonomy might be thought to consist of the ability to have a measure of narrative continuity over time. . . .").

14. *Cf.* K. N. Llewellyn, "The Constitution as an Institution," 34 *Colum. L. Rev.* 1, 37 (1934) (noting that the day-to-day ideology of the Court includes an assumption of past infallibility).

15. 5 U.S. (1 Cranch) 137 (1803).

16. 14 U.S. (1 Wheat.) 304 (1816).

17. L. Wittgenstein, *On Certainty* 506–17 (1969).

18. *See* generally, Richard H. Fallon, Jr., *Implementing the Constitution,* ch. 5

(2001); Charles Fried, "Types," 14 *Const. Commentary* 55 (1997); Eugene Volokh, "The Mechanisms of the Slippery Slope," 116 *Harv. L. Rev.* 1026 (2003).

19. Occasionally opinions are unsigned and published *per curiam.* Usually these unsigned opinions deal with less important or routine cases or housekeeping matters. Occasionally, however, a very important decision will appear *per curiam. Buckley v. Valeo,* 424 U.S. 1 (1976), which placed severe free speech limits on campaign finance regulations, was such a case.

20. 198 U.S. 45 (1905).

21. *See, e.g., West Lynn Creamery, Inc. v. Healy,* 512 U.S. 186, 207 (1994) (Scalia, J., concurring in the judgment) (disagreeing with the Court's "broad expansion" of the Dormant Commerce Clause); *44 Liquormart, Inc. v. Rhode Island,* 517 U.S. 484, 517 (Scalia, J., concurring in part and concurring in the judgment) (sharing the Court's "aversion towards paternalistic governmental policies," but cautioning that "it would also be paternalism for us to prevent the people . . . from enacting laws that we consider paternalistic, unless we have good reason to believe that the Constitution itself forbids them.").

22. *See, e.g., General Elec. Co. v. Gilbert,* 429 U.S. 125 (1976) (Rehnquist, J.).

23. *Orozco v. Texas,* 394 U.S. 324, 327 (1969) (Harlan, J., concurring). And then there are the permanent dissenters. *See* Charles Fried, "Five to Four: Reflections on the Voucher Case," 116 *Harv. L. Rev.* 163 (2002).

2. Federalism

1. Jack N. Rakove, *Original Meanings* 170 (1996).
2. *See* Daniel A. Farber and Suzanna Sherry, *A History of the American Constitution* 34–36 (1990).
3. Herbert Wechsler, "The Political Safeguards of Federalism: The Role of the States in the Composition and Selection of the National Government," 54 *Colum. L. Rev.* 543 (1954).
4. For a thorough review of the objections to Wechsler's argument and a suggested reconstruction, see Larry D. Kramer, "Putting the Politics Back into the Political Safeguards of Federalism," 100 *Colum. L. Rev.* 215 (2000).
5. *National League of Cities v. Usery,* 426 U.S. 833 (1976).
6. Learned Hand, *The Spirit of Liberty* (3d ed. 1963); Wechsler, *supra* note 3.
7. *New York v. United States,* 505 U.S. 144, 168 (1992) (O'Connor, J.) ("Where Congress encourages state regulation rather than compelling it, state governments remain responsive to the local electorate's preferences; state officials remain accountable to the people.").
8. Richard L. Revesz, "Rehabilitating Interstate Competitions: Rethinking the 'Race-to-the-Bottom' Rationale for Federal Environmental Regulation," 67 *N.Y.U. L. Rev.* 1210, 1218 (1992); Edmund W. Kitch, "A Federal Vision of the Securities Laws," 70 *Va. L. Rev.* 857 (1984).

9. Larry D. Kramer, "We the Court," 115 *Harvard L. Rev.* 4 (2001); see also "Putting the Politics Back into the Political Safeguard of Federalism," 100 *Colum. L. Rev.* 215 (2000).

10. The phrase comes from Virgil, who used it to praise the return of the golden age: *"Ultima Cumaei venit iam carminis aetas; magnus ab integro saeclorum nascitur ordo"* (Now comes the last age of Cumaean song; the great series of ages is born anew). Virgil, *Eclogue IV,* II.4–7, at 10 (Oxford Univ. Press 1969) (*cited in* Charles McC. Mathias, Jr., "Ordered Liberty: The Original Intent of the Constitution," 47 *Md. L. Rev.* 174, 174 n.1 (1987)). The phrase also appears on the reverse of the seal that the United States Treasury prints on the back of every dollar bill, and it is the title of an excellent study of the Constitution's development. *See* Forrest McDonald, *Novus Ordo Seclorum: The Intellectual Origins of the Constitution* (1985).

11. Gordon S. Wood, *The Creation of the American Republic, 1776–1787,* at 562–64 (W. W. Norton 1969, 1972); *see* Bruce Ackerman and Neal Katyal, "Our Unconventional Founding," 62 *U. Chi. L. Rev.* 475 (1995); Charles Fried, "The Supreme Court, 1994 Term—Foreword: Revolutions?," 109 *Harvard L. Rev.* 13, 20–27 (1995).

12. The Twenty-fourth Amendment abolishes the poll tax in elections for national office and gives the Congress the power of enforcement by appropriate legislation.

13. Rakove, *supra* note 1, at 163–80.

14. 17 U.S. 316 (1819).

15. Gordon Wood has noted how this reference to conventions was itself a radical step, since it bypassed the ordinary organs of state government—the legislatures and governor—in favor of an institution that did not exist in state law and was called for by the Constitution itself. Gordon S. Wood, *The Creation of the American Republic, 1776–1787,* at 339–43 (1969).

16. *McCulloch v. Maryland,* 17 U.S. (4 Wheat.) 316, 403 (1819).

17. Rakove, *supra* note 1, at 163–64. He continues, "The same uncertainty over where Pennsylvania would intersect Lake Erie still existed; it was an open question too, whether New York even had a western boundary, or whether its legal right to an eastern border at the Connecticut River would prove persuasive to the armed residents of Vermont. But along the seaboard, where most of the population resided, there was no doubt where the jurisdiction of one state ended and another began."

18. The Constitution does refer to the states at many places. It assigns the states particular roles in the national government (e.g., as the units from which senators and members of the House of Representatives are chosen). It guarantees their representation in Congress—two senators and at least one representative—and offers other immunities from national action. And it specifically prohibits the states from certain actions—e.g., concluding treaties with foreign powers, making compacts among themselves without the con-

sent of Congress, or passing any law impairing the obligation of contracts or denying to any person due process or equal protection of the law. But all these references assume the existence of the states and of their general powers of government.

19. 514 U.S. 549 (1995).
20. 505 U.S. 144 (1992).
21. *Bd. of Trustees of the Univ. of Ala. v. Garrett,* 531 U.S. 356 (2001).
22. *See* 3 *Debates on the Adoption of the Federal Constitution* (Jonathan Elliot ed., 2d ed., Philadelphia, J. B. Lippincott 1888).
23. "If [federal lawmakers] were to make law not warranted by any of the powers enumerated . . . it would be considered by Judges as an infringement of the Constitution which they guard." Larry D. Kramer, "The Supreme Court 2000 Term—Foreword: We the Court," 115 *Harvard L. Rev.* 4, 70 n. 272 (quoting speech by John Marshall at the Virginia Ratifying Convention (June 20, 1788) in 10 *The Documentary History of the Ratification of the Constitution* 1430–31 (Merrill Jensen ed., 1976).
24. Rakove, *supra* note 1.
25. Articles of Confederation, §2.
26. Eighteenth-century usage lends support to this interpretation of the word "necessary." Much more telling is Marshall's point that when prohibiting a state from imposing levies on imports and exports it exempts only such as may be "absolutely necessary for executing [that state's] inspection laws." U.S. Const. art. I, §10.
27. 22 U.S. 1.
28. *United States v. E.C. Knight Co.,* 156 U.S. 1 (1895); *Hammer v. Dagenhart,* 247 U.S. 251 (1918); *United States v. Butler,* 297 U.S. 1 (1936).
29. *Wilson v. Blackbird Creek Marsh Co.,* 27 U.S. (2 Pet.) 245 (1829).
30. *See, e.g., Bibb v. Navaho Freight Lines, Inc.,* 359 U.S. 520 (1959) (Illinois required contour mudguards on trucks, while Arkansas required straight mudguards and prohibited contour mudguards).
31. *Champion v. Ames,* 188 U.S. 321 (1903).
32. I exaggerate: the eggs were "preserved" and not properly labeled. *Hippolite Egg Co. v. United States,* 220 U.S. 45 (1911).
33. *Hoke v. United States,* 227 U.S. 308 (1913).
34. *United States v. E.C. Knight Co.,* 156 U.S. 1 (1895).
35. *Northern Securities Co. v. United States,* 193 U.S. 197 (1904).
36. *Swift & Co. v. United States,* 196 U.S. 375 (1905).
37. *Stafford v. Wallace,* 258 U.S. 495 (1922).
38. *Houston E. & W. Texas Ry. Co. v. United States* (The Shreveport Rate Case), 234 U.S. 342 (1914).
39. *See Southern Ry. v. United States,* 222 U.S. 20, 26–27 (1911).
40. *Hammer v. Dagenhart,* 247 U.S. 251 (1918).
41. *See* Chapter 6.
42. 301 U.S. 1 (1937).

43. The workers whose discharge was the subject of the complaint before the board were a tractor driver, motor inspectors, a washer in a coke plant, crane operators, and laborers in the Aliquippa plant.
44. *NLRB v. Fruehauf Trailer Co.,* 301 U.S. 49 (1937).
45. *NLRB v. Friedman-Harry Marks Clothing Co.,* 301 U.S. 58 (1937).
46. *Associated Press v. NLRB,* 301 U.S. 103 (1937).
47. The Court cited *In re Debs,* 158 U.S. 564 (1895), a labor injunction in the Pullman strike.
48. See most notably *Perez v. United States,* 402 U.S. 146, 157 (1971) (Stewart, J., dissenting); *Daniel v. Paul,* 395 U.S. 298, 309 (1969) (Black, J., dissenting).
49. 317 U.S. 111 (1942).
50. 395 U.S. 298 (1969). This was just too much for Justice Hugo Black, who dissented.
51. 514 U.S. 549 (1995).
52. 529 U.S. 598 (2000).
53. 18 U.S.C. §922(q)(1)(A).
54. *Lopez,* 514 U.S. at 581.
55. There may be one or two states in which marital rape is not actionable as an assault. I believe that the objection to such an exclusion from the general law could successfully be carried to the Supreme Court as a violation of the Fourteenth Amendment's guarantee of the equal protection of the law.
56. Richard H. Fallon, Jr., "The Conservative Paths of the Rehnquist Court's Federalism Decisions," 9 *U. Chi. L. Rev.* 429 (2002); Catharine A. MacKinnon, "Disputing Male Sovereignty: On United States v. Morrison," 114 *Harvard L. Rev.* 135 (2000); Cass R. Sunstein, "Foreword: Leaving Things Undecided," *Harvard L. Rev.* 4, 23 (1995). John T. Noonan, Jr., *Narrowing the Nation's Power: The Supreme Court Sides with the United States* (2002).
57. 392 U.S. 183, 201 (1968). Only Justice Douglas dissented in *Wirtz,* because he believed the Court disregarded Harlan's caveat in that case.
58. Justice Clarence Thomas was willing to entertain the possibility:

> At the time the original Constitution was ratified, "commerce" consisted of selling, buying, and bartering, as well as transporting for these purposes. *See* 1 S. Johnson, *A Dictionary of the English Language* 361 (4th ed. 1773) (defining commerce as "Intercourse; exchange of one thing for another; interchange of any thing; trade; traffick"). . . .
>
> As one would expect, the term "commerce" was used in contradistinction to productive activities such as manufacturing and agriculture. . . . Moreover, interjecting a modern sense of commerce into the Constitution generates significant textual and structural problems. For example, one cannot replace "commerce" with a different type of enterprise, such as manufacturing.
>
> When a manufacturer produces a car, assembly cannot take place "with a

foreign nation" or "with the Indian Tribes." Parts may come from different States or other nations and hence may have been in the flow of commerce at one time, but manufacturing takes place at a discrete site. Agriculture and manufacturing involve the production of goods; commerce encompasses traffic in such articles. . . .

United States v. Lopez, 514 U.S. 549, 586–87 (1995) (Thomas, J., concurring). See generally, Randy E. Barnett, "The Original Meaning of the Commerce Clause," 68 U. Chi. L. Rev. 101 (2001).

59. *Heart of Atlanta Motel, Inc. v. United States,* 379 U.S. 241 (1964).
60. The economic impact of school violence on education was argued on the basis of numerous governmental and nongovernmental reports collected by Justice Breyer. The economic impact of violence against women was stated as a finding in the legislation itself, summarizing the conclusion of congressional hearings.
61. 505 U.S. 144 (1992).
62. 521 U.S. 898 (1997).
63. 426 U.S. 833 (1976).
64. 505 U.S. 144 (1992).
65. *EEOC v. Wyoming,* 460 U.S. 226 (1983); *FERC v. Mississippi,* 456 U.S. 742 (1982); *United Transp. Union v. Long Island R.R. Co.,* 455 U.S. 678 (1982); *Hodel v. Va. Surface Mining & Reclamation Assoc.,* 452 U.S. 264 (1981).
66. 469 U.S. 528 (1985).
67. 528 U.S. 141 (2000).
68. *See, e.g., South Dakota v. Dole,* 483 U.S. 203 (1987) (states must enact twenty-one-year drinking-age requirement as a condition of receiving full amount of federal highway assistance).
69. 2 U.S. (2 Dall.) 419 (1793).
70. 134 U.S. 1 (1890).
71. The *Hans* Court concluded that this extrapolation was necessary to avoid a constitutional anomaly. It rejected the alternative, more modest interpretation I suggest in the text as a way of escaping that anomaly, because it believed it foreclosed by "several recent cases," in which the amendment was held to preclude a federal court suit against a state by a citizen of another state even though "the case is one arising under the constitution or laws of the United States."
72. *Ex parte Young,* 209 U.S. 123 (1908).
73. 517 U.S. 44 (1996).
74. 527 U.S. 706 (1999).
75. In *Federal Maritime Comm'n v. South Carolina State Ports Authority,* 122 S. Ct. 1864 (2002), the Court extended this doctrine even further to bar a proceeding against a state brought before an executive branch regulatory agency.

76. *See Kimel v. Fla. Bd. of Regents,* 528 U.S. 62 (2000). However, for laws aimed at remedying judicially recognized Fourteenth Amendment problems—for example, race or gender discrimination under Title VII—Congress may abrogate state sovereign immunity if its intention to abrogate is clearly stated, *Fitzpatrick v. Bitzer,* 427 U.S. 445 (1976).

77. *Pennsylvania v. Union Gas Co.,* 491 U.S. 1 (1989).

78. The Circuits are split on whether the Eleventh Amendment bars recovery from states in bankruptcy proceedings. *See, e.g., In re NVR, LP* 189 F.3d 442 (4th Cir. 1999) (Eleventh Amendment does not bar monetary recovery from states); *Sacred Heart Hospital v. Pennsylvania,* 133 F.3d 237 (3d Cir. 1998) (Bankruptcy Clause does not give Congress power to abrogate states' immunity; *see also* Kenneth Klee, James O. Johnston, and Eric Winston, "State Defiance of Bankruptcy Law," 52 *Vand. L. Rev.* 1527 (1999).

79. *See* Ernest A. Young, "State Sovereign Immunity and the Future of Federalism," 1999. *Sup. Ct. Rev.* 1.

80. 5 U.S.C. §551 et seq.

81. *See* Arthur E. Bonfield, *State Administrative Rulemaking* 12–16 n.20 (1986) (listing states that have enacted an APA based on the original Model State Administrative Procedure Act (MSAPA)).

82. *Bivens v. Six Unknown Named Agents of Federal Bureau of Narcotics,* 403 U.S. 388 (1971).

83. John T. Noonan, "Religious Liberty at the Stake," 84 *Va. L. Rev.* 459 (1998).

84. *Fitzpatrick v. Bitzer,* 427 U.S. 445, 455 (1976) (Rehnquist, C.J.).

85. U.S. Const. art. I, §10.

86. Prohibitions on import and export duties also limited the states' power to impose on individuals.

87. *Barron v. Mayor & City Council of Baltimore,* 32 U.S. 243 (1833).

88. *Civil Rights Cases,* 109 U.S. 3 (1883); *United States v. Harris,* 106 U.S. 629 (1883).

89. On several occasions the Court has strained against this limit and found a number of ways around it, as by holding that certain private actions were taken in concert with state actors, *United States v. Guest,* 383 U.S. 745 (1966), or that the Thirteenth Amendment, abolishing slavery, unlike the Fourteenth Amendment, worked on individuals as well as states and that it gave Congress the power to abolish "all badges and incidents of slavery." *Jones v. Alfred H. Mayer Co.,* 392 U.S. 409 (1968).

90. *See Heart of Atlanta Motel, Inc. v. United States,* 379 U.S. 241 (1964), and the earlier discussion of that case.

91. 5 U.S. 137 (1803). There was, to be sure, another leg to the argument on behalf of Congress's power in *Morrison:* that the states, by unequal laws and unequal enforcement of the laws, had denied women the equal protection of the laws against rape and violence.

92. 521 U.S. 507 (1997).

93. 494 U.S. 872 (1992).
94. 374 U.S. 398 (1963).
95. *Kimel v. Fla. Bd. of Regents,* 528 U.S. 62 (2000).
96. *Bd. of Trustees of the Univ. of Ala. v. Garrett,* 531 U.S. 356 (2001).
97. *Boerne,* 521 U.S. at 519–20.
98. *Fla. Prepaid Postsecondary Educ. Expense Bd. v. College Sav. Bank,* 527 U.S. 627 (1999); *College Savings Bank v. Fla. Prepaid Postsecondary Ed. Expense Bd.,* 527 U.S. 666 (1999).
99. Congress set up a nationally binding system of trademarks under the commerce power. U.S. Const. art. I, §8, cl. 8.
100. *The Persian Wars,* VII.35. "Xerxes flew into a rage at this, and he commanded that the Hellespont be struck with three hundred strokes of the whip and that a pair of foot-chains be thrown into the sea. . . . He also commanded the scourgers to speak outlandish and arrogant words: 'You hateful water, our master lays his judgement on you thus, for you have unjustly punished him even though he's done you no wrong! Xerxes the king will pass over you, whether you wish it or not! It is fitting that no man offer you sacrifices, for you're a muddy and salty river!' In these ways he commanded that the sea be punished and also that the heads be severed from all those who directed the bridging of the Hellespont."
101. *See* Chapter 3.
102. In *South Dakota v. Dole,* 483 U.S. 203 (1987), the Court approved conditioning a state's receipt of highway funds on its raising its drinking age to twenty-one. The Court asked only that there be some connection between the condition and the purpose of the funding program, which it found in the connection between highway safety and discouraging teen-age drinking. A tougher standard requiring that the condition apply to how the funds were actually spent so far has found only one vote. The dispute anticipates the disagreement about how closely the Court would monitor whether legislation was "appropriate" to enforce the guarantees of the Fourteenth Amendment. In this case the Court was decisively unwilling to start down the road it later opened in *Lopez* and *Boerne. See also South Carolina v. Baker,* 485 U.S. 505 (1988).
103. *Marbury v. Madison,* 5 U.S. (1 Cranch) 137, 177 (1803).
104. "Judicial Review: A Practicing Judge's Perspective," 78 *Tex. L. Rev.* 761, 772 (2000).
105. *Dolan v. City of Tigard,* 512 U.S. 374 (1994); *Nollan v. Cal. Coastal Comm'n,* 483 U.S. 825 (1987).

3. Separation of Powers

1. *Youngstown Sheet & Tube Co. v. Sawyer,* 343 U.S. 579, 634–35 (1952) (Jackson, J., concurring).
2. *See* Joseph Story, *Commentaries on the Constitution of the United States*

§427 (5th ed. 1891) (1833) ("It has been observed, with great correctness, that although the spirit of an instrument, especially of a constitution, is to be respected not less than its letter yet the spirit is to be collected chiefly from the letter. It would be dangerous in the extreme to infer from extrinsic circumstances that a case, for which the words of an instrument expressly provide, shall be exempted from its operation.").

3. And unlike the *Declaration of the Rights of Man and of the Citizen* promulgated in 1789 by the revolutionary National Assembly of France, which stated in Article 16: "A society in which the observance of the law is not assured, nor the separation of powers defined, has no constitution at all."

4. *See* Gerhard Casper, "An Essay in Separation of Powers: Some Early Versions and Practices," 30 *Wm. & Mary L. Rev.* 211, 221 (1989). This may be because the federal Constitution at several points is more austere in its language than John Adams's text for Massachusetts, even though his was one of the models for the Constitution of 1789. In any event, the Massachusetts Constitution and its injunction were quite extreme among state constitutions at the time, many of which violated the principle of the separation of powers in a variety of more or less drastic ways. *See* Casper, *id.,* at 215–17.

5. The method of choosing justices of the Supreme Court is placed in Article II, §2 (the Appointments Clause) of the Constitution, as their appointment, with the advise and consent of the Senate, is a power of the President. *See* U.S. Const. art. II, §2, cl. 2.

6. Bruce Ackerman has written that the origin of our national institutions deprives any one of them of the claim to speak in the name of the people or of the nation as a whole. *See, e.g.,* Bruce Ackerman, *We the People: Foundations* 300–14 (1991); Bruce Ackerman and Neal Katyal, "Our Unconventional Founding," 62 *U. Chi. L. Rev.* 475, 568–73 (1995). The Preamble to the Constitution does indeed proclaim that the people are the ultimate source of its authority, but they are represented by the ensemble of institutions that together represent them. In the most formal sense the ultimate authority under our Constitution may be said to be the complexly described entities assigned the power to ratify and amend the Constitution.

7. W. B. Gwyn, "The Meaning of the Separation of Powers," 195 *Tulane Studies in Political Science* vol. IX (1965) identifies five purposes of the doctrine: "(1) to create greater governmental efficiency; (2) to assure that statutory law is made in the common interest; (3) to assure that the law is impartially administered and that all administrators are under the law; (4) to allow the people's representatives to call executive officials to account for the abuse of their power; and (5) to establish a balance of governmental powers"); *see also* Cass R. Sunstein, "Constitutionalism after the New Deal," 101 *Harvard L. Rev.* 421, 432–37 (1987).

8. *See* Montesquieu, *The Spirit of Laws,* bk. XI, ch. 4 (David W. Carrithers ed., 1977) (1748) ("Where the legislative and executive powers are united in the same person, or in the same body of magistracy, there can be no liberty . . .").

9. *See* James Madison, *The Federalist No. 47,* at 301 (Clinton Rossiter ed., 1961) ("The accumulation of all powers, legislative, executive, and judiciary, in the same hands, whether of one, a few, or many, and whether hereditary, self-appointed, or elective, may justly be pronounced the very definition of tyranny.").

10. *See* Michael Grant, *History of Rome* 67–71 (1978).

11. *See* Gordon S. Wood, *The Creation of the American Republic, 1776–1787,* at 197–255 (1998) (reviewing debates about bicameralism in the states and the Constitutional Convention). The story of Pennsylvania, *see id.* at 83–90, which so impressed the French revolutionary constitution-makers, is particularly interesting. If one looks back further in the history of political theorizing, then the looming presence of Aristotle, who is the first to speak of types of constitutions and of the mixed constitution as one such type, displays this same concern with the forms of participation by the different social orders rather than with anything resembling our present separation of powers concerns.

12. Sun Yat-sen, for example, envisioned a five-power constitution consisting of the following: legislature, judiciary, executive, civil service examinations, and censorship. Sun borrowed the first three from Western government and the last two from traditional Chinese governmental powers. "Such a government," he wrote, "will be the most complete and the finest in the world, and a state with such a government will indeed be of the people, by the people, and for the people." Sun Yat Sen, *The Three Principles of the People* 358 (Frank W. Price trans., Commercial Press 1929). *See also* Sun Yat Sen, *Memoirs of a Chinese Revolutionary* 191–206 (Sino-American Pub'g Co., 2d ed. 1953) (1918) (reproducing a speech by Sun entitled "The Fivefold Constitution"). For an argument against exporting America's separation-of-powers model to other nations, see Bruce Ackerman, "The New Separation of Powers," 113 *Harvard L. Rev.* 633 (2000).

13. Congress has traditionally also passed what is called special legislation dealing with discrete instances, most frequently private bills naturalizing named individuals and settling particular claims against the government.

14. That "the Congress shall have Power To lay and collect Taxes . . . to pay the Debts and provide for the common Defence and general Welfare of the United States" has never been taken as a global grant of a managerial role to Congress to provide for the common defense and general welfare, but rather a power to make *rules* about taxation, the revenues of which Congress may by legislation allocate for these broad purposes. This is the spending power as Hamilton conceived it. There has been controversy about the breadth of meaning of this clause, but only as to whether the appropriations themselves must be limited to the more specifically enumerated ends. This restrictive view of the spending power—which was Madison's—was definitively rejected in *United States v. Butler,* 297 U.S. 1, 65–66 (1936). Hamilton had maintained the contrary.

15. Curiously, the rigorous Massachusetts conception of separation of pow-

ers includes no such limitation, and John Adams's Constitution specifically gives the Supreme Judicial Court the task of issuing advisory opinions on "solemn occasions." Mass. Const. pt. II, ch. III, art. II. The Supreme Court, by contrast, early declined any such authority in *Hayburn's Case,* 2 U.S. 409 (1792).

16. *See* Bureau of the Census, *U.S. Dep't of Commerce, Statistical Abstract of the United States: 2000,* at 355 tbl. 556 (2000) [hereinafter *Statistical Abstract*]. This estimate is based on 1999 federal civilian employment figures, subtracting employees from the Departments of State and Defense.

17. Jonathan Turley, " 'From Pillar to Post': The Prosecution of American Presidents," 37 *Am. Crim. L. Rev.* 1049, 1081 n.171 (2000) (collecting estimates of federal civilian employment in 1800).

18. *Statistical Abstract, supra* note 16, at 7, tbl. 1.

19. *See* David A. Strauss, "The Irrelevance of Constitutional Amendments," 114 *Harvard L. Rev.* 1457, 1472 n.37 (2001) (collecting federal civilian employment numbers). The 240,000 figure is an estimate of all federal civilian employees; the number would be slightly smaller if foreign affairs employees were not counted.

20. *Id.*

21. "[O]ne of the great functions conferred upon Congress by the Federal Constitution is the regulation of interstate commerce and rates to be exacted by interstate carriers for the passenger and merchandise traffic. The rates to be fixed are myriad. If Congress were to be required to fix every rate, it would be impossible to exercise the power at all. Therefore, common sense requires that . . . Congress may provide a Commission, as it does, . . . to fix those rates. . . ." *J. W. Hampton & Sons v. United States,* 276 U.S. 394, 407–08 (1928) (Taft, C.J.)

22. *See Bowsher v. Synar,* 478 U.S. 714, 759–64, 776 (1986) (White, J., dissenting).

23. It may also be assumed—though no case has tested the point—that the offices must be created in connection with some substantive power of Congress: a postmaster general to administer the post offices, departments and their heads to oversee the regulation of interstate and foreign commerce, federal judges to sit in the "tribunals inferior to the Supreme Court" that Congress may "constitute" under Article II, §8, cl. 9. No office untethered to a substantive power has been created.

24. *Bowsher,* 478 U.S. at 721–27 (striking down, as violating the separation of powers, a portion of the Gramm-Rudman-Hollings Act that effectively gave executive power to a comptroller general, who was removable by Congress and thus should not have such power). *See also Metropolitan Washington Airports Auth. v. Citizens for the Abatement of Aircraft Noise, Inc.,* 501 U.S. 252, 265–77 (1991) (striking down, as violating the separation of powers, a congressional transfer of two major airports that gave veto power over decisions regarding the airports to a congressionally appointed board).

25. *See INS v. Chadha,* 462 U.S. 919, 946–51 (1983). *See also* U.S. Const. art. I, §7, cl. 2 ("Every Bill which shall have passed the House of Representatives and the Senate, shall, before it becomes a Law, be presented to the President of the United States . . ."); U.S. Const. art. I, §7, cl. 3 ("Every Order, Resolution, or Vote to which the Concurrence of the Senate and House of Representatives may be necessary (except on a question of Adjournment) shall be presented to the President of the United States; and before the Same shall take Effect, shall be approved by him, or being disapproved by him, shall be repassed by two thirds of the Senate and House of Representatives, according to the Rules and Limitations prescribed in the Case of a Bill.").

26. This was Justice Byron White's argument in his *Bowsher* and *Chadha* dissents. *See Bowsher,* 478 U.S. 759–76 (White, J., dissenting); *Chadha,* 462 U.S. at 967–1003 (White, J., dissenting).

27. *See* François Furet, *Revolutionary France, 1770–1880* 132 (Antonia Nevill trans., 1992).

28. *See Articles of Confederation,* art. IX, ¶5; Furet, *supra* note 27, at 134.

29. *See, e.g., Articles of Confederation,* art. IX; *see* Furet, *supra* note 27, at 132–34.

30. 524 U.S. 417 (1998).

31. John Manning has noted about the Constitution, "The entire document is exceptionally careful and detailed in the way it allocates powers and, in many cases, in the specific ways it provides for their exercise. . . . For example, Article I, Section 7 carefully specifies bicameralism and presentment as the default rule, but (as *Chadha* points out at p. 955) many clauses specifically authorize elements of Congress to act without bicameralism and presentment in carefully defined circumstances. *See* Art. I, §2, cl. 6 (initiating impeachment); Art. I, §3, cl. 5 (trial of impeachment); Art. II, §2, cl. 2 (advice and consent to appointments); Art. II, §2, cl. 2 (treaty ratification). The degree of detail in specifying Congress's powers and the manner of their exercise make it very unlikely that Congress can give itself authority under the Necessary and Proper Clause to act in a mode not contemplated by Article I."

32. I put aside inferior officers appointed by the "courts of law."

33. U.S. Const. art. II, §3.

34. 343 U.S. 579 (1952).

35. *Id.* at 641.

36. *Id.* at 646, 653.

37. U.S. Const. art. I, §8, cls. 12, 13.

38. *Youngstown,* 343 U.S. at 653–54.

39. *See* John Ferling, *John Adams: A Life* 333 (1992) (noting that Adams himself believed that his decision to keep Washington's cabinet members "resulted in the ultimate destruction of his presidency").

40. *See Myers v. United States,* 272 U.S. 52, 127–28 (1926).

41. 5 U.S. 137, 177 (1803).

42. 37 U.S. 524, 609–10 (1838).
43. The following discussion of the Bank War is drawn from my book *Order and Law. See* Charles Fried, *Order and Law* 149–50 (1991).
44. The participants in the Bank War obviously thought of it as a political crisis, and, unlike today, there was never any recourse to the courts. Nonetheless, Jackson's closest advisers discussed the issue in legal terms. Then Secretary of the Treasury Louis McLane felt that he could remove the deposits only in the face of sufficient objective evidence that they were not safe in the bank; according to him, Congress had decided that the deposits were safe (in response to a request by Jackson that the House investigate the bank), and its determination was deserving of a strong presumption. The Attorney General, Roger Taney, believed that the Secretary of the Treasury had absolute discretion over the deposits, though the opinion of Congress might be given some deference. To him, the opinion of one House of Congress was irrelevant; if Congress wanted to order the funds removed or retained, it would have to follow the rules of bicameralism and presentment and pass a law. Jackson made Taney Secretary of the Treasury and Taney did the deed. In 1835 President Jackson named Taney Chief Justice of the Supreme Court.
45. The following discussion is drawn primarily from Michael Les Benedict, *The Impeachment and Trial of Andrew Johnson* (1973), and from the excellent historical overview contained in *Myers v. United States,* 272 U.S. 52 (1926).
46. U.S. Const. art. I, §9, cl. 7.
47. *See* Stephen G. Calabresi and Christopher S. Yoo, "The Unitary Executive During the First Half-Century," 47 *Case W. Res. L. Rev.* 1451, 1516 (1997) (referring to the Tenure of Office Act of 1820 and calling it "the first substantial limitation on presidential control of federal patronage").
48. *See Humphrey's Executor v. United States,* 295 U.S. 602, 619 (1935) (quoting a letter from Roosevelt to Humphrey, the FTC official he sought to dismiss).
49. President's Commission on Administrative Management, 74th Cong., 2nd sess., pp. 39–40.
50. *Statistical Abstract, supra* note 16, at 355 tbl. 556.
51. *See* Cindy Loose, "What So Proudly They Served—Presidential Appointees Depart with a Big Sigh of Relief," *Wash. Post.,* Jan. 16, 1997, at A01.
52. President's Comm. on Admin. Mgmt., *Report of the Committee with Studies on the Administrative Management in the Government of the United States* 37 (1937). The commission was popularly known as the "Brownlow Commission."
53. 272 U.S. 52 (1926).
54. *Id.* at 117 (emphasis added).
55. 295 U.S. 602 (1935).
56. *Id.* at 628.
57. In *Wiener v. United States,* 357 U.S. 349 (1958) (Frankfurter, J.) the Court

applied the decision to removal of a member of the War Claims Commission, whose function was characterized as of an "intrinsic judicial character." *Id.* at 355. The case also developed the law beyond *Humphrey's Executor* in that the Court implied a limitation on removal from the nature of the office itself, while in the earlier case the limitation or removal was stated in the statute itself.

58. 487 U.S. 654 (1988).

59. *Id.* at 689.

60. The Court based that decision on the long-standing practice of federal courts appointing interim United States attorneys and one quite old precedent. *Id.* at 676–77 (citing *United States v. Solomon,* 216 F. Supp. 835 (S.D.N.Y. 1963)).

61. Alexander Hamilton, *The Federalist No. 70,* at 423 (Clinton Rossiter ed., 1961) ("Energy in the executive is a leading character in the definition of good government. . . . Decision, activity, secrecy, and dispatch will generally characterise the proceedings of one man, in a much more eminent degree, than the proceedings of any greater number; and in proportion as the number is increased, these qualities will be diminished.").

62. Montesquieu, *supra* note 8, at bk. IX, ch. 6.

63. A. V. Dicey, *Introduction to the Study of the Law of the Constitution* (10th ed. 1959).

64. *See, e.g., Morrison v. Olson,* 487 U.S. 654, 731 (1988) (Scalia, J., dissenting).

65. *See* Stephen Breyer, *Breaking the Vicious Circle: Toward Effective Risk Regulation* (1993).

66. Edward Coke, *Reports* 63, 65 reprinted in 77 *Eng. Rep.* 1342, 1343 (1907).

67. Montesquieu, *supra* note 8, bk. IX, ch. 6.

68. Mass. Const. pt. I, art. XXIX.

69. 2 U.S. (2 Dall.) 409 (1792).

70. Aurora (Philadelphia), March 31, 1803, a memorial presented to the Pennsylvania legislature (emphases in original), quoted in Richard E. Ellis, *The Jeffersonian Crisis: Courts and Politics in the Young Republic* 167 (1971). *See also* Wood, *supra* note 11, at 159–61; Ellis, *supra,* at 5–16.

71. *See generally* Casper, *supra* note 4 (reviewing the structure of early state constitutions and illustrating different approaches to the separation of powers). The very controversy out of which *Hayburn's Case* arose, where the political branches sought to enlist the aid of the judges in performing one of the more delicate and provocative tasks left over from the Revolutionary period, indicates that it was quite natural at the time to think of courts and judges as a general resource for the accomplishment of difficult administrative tasks.

72. *See, e.g.,* Vicki C. Jackson and Mark Tushnet, *Comparative Constitutional Law,* chs. 5 and 6 (1999).

73. James Madison, *The Federalist No. 51*, at 322 (Clinton Rossiter ed., 1961).

74. *See* Dicey, *supra* note 63, at 328–405, 388–89.

75. Even though these adjudicative functions are generally carried out by a distinct cadre of professional "administrative law judges," protected by their status as civil servants and working under often very strict guidelines, the Court has generally insisted that at the end of the day their work be reviewable by the Article III judiciary.

76. Attributed to Ibn Hanbal, 6:75 al-Bayhaqi 10:96, *quoted in* Frank E. Vogel, *Islamic Law and Legal System: Studies of Saudi Arabia* (2000).

77. *Exodus* 18:21 (KJV).

78. *Marbury v. Madison*, 5 U.S. 137, 177 (1803).

79. U.S. Const. amend. I.

80. *Marbury*, 5 U.S. at 166.

81. 2 U.S. 408, 409 n.(a) (1792).

82. *See, e.g.*, Alexander M. Bickel, *The Least Dangerous Branch* (1962); Akhil Reed Amar, "The Two-Tiered Structure of the Judiciary Act of 1789," 138 *U. Pa. L. Rev.* 1499 (1990); Akhil Reed Amar, *A Neo-Federalist View of Article III: Separating the Two Tiers of Federal Jurisdiction*, 65 *B.U. L. Rev.* 205, 258 (1985) ("The power to structure the federal judiciary is not trivial; it has real bite. It comprehends the power to create an unreviewable Article III Tax Court—or an Abortion Court.").

83. Of course such determinations invite disuniformity of result and the inelegant spectacle of state courts interfering with federal functions. It is to avoid these consequences that the Constitution provided for federal courts. The untoward results I note would simply be the result of Congress's having removed the federal courts from the scene.

84. This is a very brief summary of one of the most elegant and profound pieces of legal writing in American jurisprudence. *See* Henry M. Hart, Jr., "The Power of Congress to Limit the Jurisdiction of Federal Courts: An Exercise in Dialectic," 66 *Harvard L. Rev.* 1362 (1953).

4. Speech

1. I shall sometimes in this chapter refer simply to "the First Amendment," although the amendment addresses religion as well. The religion clauses are the subject of Chapter 5.

2. *Patterson v. Colorado*, 205 U.S. 454, 462 (1907) (Holmes, J.). Holmes cited Blackstone's *Commentaries* for this proposition, which he reluctantly abandoned in *Schenk v. United States*, 249 U.S. 47 (1919). Under this narrow conception, even seditious libel might be compatible with the First Amendment. The Sedition Act of 1798, 1 Stat. 596 (1798), for example, which barred the publication or utterance of "false, scandalous, and malicious writing [against] the Government of the United States . . . ," criminalized

what today would be characterized as core political speech. Though the Jeffersonians believed the Sedition Act violated the amendment, the Supreme Court never reviewed it. It was not until 1931 that the First Amendment was invoked successfully in the Supreme Court. *See Near v. Minnesota,* 283 U.S. 697 (1931). For a review of discussions and of litigation in courts other than the Supreme Court, *see* David M. Rabban, *Free Speech in Its Forgotten Years* (1997). The controversy regarding the original meaning of the First Amendment is surveyed and evaluated in Rabban, "The Ahistorical Historian: Leonard Levy on Freedom of Expression in Early American History," 37 *Stan. L. Rev.* 795 (1985).

3. Alexander Meiklejohn, *Free Speech and Its Relation to Self-Government* (1948).
4. John H. Ely, *Democracy and Distrust* ch. 5 (1980).
5. Meiklejohn conceded that art, literature, philosophy, and the sciences should be included in the First Amendment because they help "voters acquire the intelligence, integrity, sensitivity, and generous devotion to the general welfare that, in theory, casting a ballot is assumed to express." Alexander Meiklejohn, "First Amendment Is an Absolute," 1961 *Sup. Ct. Rev.* 245.
6. *See generally* Richard Posner, "The Right of Privacy," 12 *Ga. L. Rev.* 393 (1978); Plato, *The Republic* (Allan Bloom trans., 2d ed. 1991).
7. *Whitney v. California,* 274 U.S. 357, 375 (1927) (concurring opinion).
8. *West Virginia State Bd. of Educ. v. Barnette,* 319 U.S. 624, 633, 642 (1943).
9. *See* R. H. Coase, "The Market for Goods and the Market for Ideas," 64 *Am. Ec. Rev.* 384 (1974).
10. *See* John Stuart Mill, *On Liberty* 13 (Stephan Collini ed., 1989) ("Over himself, over his own body and mind, the individual is sovereign."). For an excellent recent discussion of this work and review of the literature, see Daniel Jacobson, "Mill on Liberty, Speech, and the Free Society," 29 *Phil. & Pub. Affairs* 276 (2000).
11. *Compare* U.S. Const. amend. I with F.R.G. Const. art. V, §1 ("Everyone has the right to freely express and disseminate his opinion in speech, writing, and pictures and to freely inform himself from generally accessible sources."); Spain Const. rt. XX, §1 ("The following rights are recognized and protected: a) to express and disseminate thoughts freely through words, writing, or any other means of reproduction. b) Literary, artistic, scientific, and technical production, and creation. c) Academic freedom. d) To communicate or receive freely truthful information through any means of dissemination. . . ."); and S. Afr. Const. ch. II, §16 (1) ("Everyone has the right to freedom of expression, which includes—(a) freedom of the press and other media; (b) freedom to receive or impart information or ideas; (c) freedom of artistic creativity; and (d) academic freedom and freedom of scientific research.").

12. *See* H. L. A. Hart, *Essays on Bentham: Studies in Jurisprudence and Political Theory* 254 (1982); Hans Kelsen, *Introduction to the Problems of Legal Theory* (Bonnie L. Paulson and Stanley L. Paulson trans., 1992).

13. *See generally* Kent Greenawalt, *Speech, Crime, and the Uses of Language* (1989).

14. Indeed, the price may be so high that it is equivalent to prohibition. Certain civil wrongs, assaults, defamation, for which victims are given the right to sue, may express a judgment that the conduct should not occur at all, but giving the victim control over enforcement suggests that his consent—purchased or otherwise—removes the wrong and so draws the sting of the prohibition to some extent.

15. In other systems—those of South Africa, Germany—where the constitution is interpreted and applied by a special court with a more frankly political form of legitimacy, the courts are readier to avow and exercise this more globally political function.

16. *See* Elena Kagan, "Private Speech, Public Purpose: The Role of Governmental Motive in First Amendment Doctrine," 63 *U. Chi. L. Rev.* 413, 462–63 (1996).

17. *Cf. Schneider v. State,* 308 U.S. 147 (1939).

18. That government must justify the burdens it imposes is not peculiar to free speech doctrine. It is an aspect of a more general rule which is indeed a distinctive feature of our constitutional law, that the subject of a governmental imposition may always demand that government justify that imposition. See Chapter 6. This is what it means to recognize a broad and ill-defined range of what are called liberty interests, imposition on which may, however, easily be justified by government's showing what is called a legitimate interest. This showing is so easily made that individuals rarely press for the justification. But where, as in the case of First Amendment rights, those interests receive heightened protection, the government's burden of justification is correspondingly greater and so attains enough weight to be constitutionally noticeable. *See Bverf GE 55,* 159 (1980); *Ferreira v. Levin,* 1996 (1) S.A. 984 (Constitutional Court of South Africa).

19. *See* G. E. M. Anscombe, *Intention* (Harv. Univ. Press 2000) (1957).

20. "A command is speech brigaded with action, and permissible commands may not be disobeyed." *Parker v. Levy,* 417 U.S. 733, 768 (1974) (Douglas, J., dissenting) (military command).

21. *Masses Publ'g Co. v. Patten,* 244 F. 535, 540 (S.D.N.Y. 1917) (L. Hand, J.).

22. This is true of the acceptance of a contract, but the contract proposal surely supposes reflection and evaluation of the offer. It is also true that a contract offer is a formal act, which combined with its acceptance produces of its own force a fact in the world. That is why in particular cases it is necessary to distinguish between contract offers that do, and those that do not, have any persuasive elements.

23. *See Bernstein v. United States Dep't of State,* 974 F. Supp. 1288 (N.D. Cal.

1997) (holding unconstitutional export controls on encryption codes), *aff'd* 176 F.3d 1132 (9th Cir. 1999), in turn *vacated and reh'g en banc granted* 192 F.3d 1308 (9th Cir. 1999); *cf. Lotus Development Corp. v. Borland International, Inc.,* 49 F.3d 807 (1st Cir. 1995) (Computer program instruction as a "method of operation" not protected "expression").

24. *United States v. Progressive, Inc.,* 467 F. Supp. 990 (W.D. Wis. 1979).
25. *Youngstown Sheet & Tube Co. v. Sawyer,* 343 U.S. 579, 653 (1952) (Jackson, J., concurring).
26. 395 U.S. 444, 447 (1969).
27. Mill, *supra* note 10, at 56.
28. *See* Oliver Wendell Holmes, Jr., *The Common Law* 64–70 (Dover Pubs. 1991) (1881); Herbert Wechsler, William Jones, and Harold Korn, "The Treatment of Inchoate Crimes in the Model Penal Code of the American Law Institute: Attempt, Solicitation, and Conspiracy," 61 *Colum. L. Rev.* 571 (1961).
29. Compare *Gitlow v. New York,* 268 U.S. 652, 667 (1925) ("That a State in the exercise of its police power may punish those who abuse this freedom by utterances inimical to the public welfare, tending to corrupt public morals, incite to crime, or disturb the public peace, is not open to question.") with *Whitney v. California,* 274 U.S. 357, 377 (1927) (Brandeis, J., concurring) ("[E]ven imminent danger cannot justify resort to prohibition of [speech], unless the evil apprehended is relatively serious.").
30. *Yates v. United States,* 354 U.S. 298, 321–22, 324–25 (1957).
31. *Masses Publ'g Co. v. Patten,* 244 F. 535, 540 (S.D.N.Y. 1917).
32. *Gitlow v. New York,* 268 U.S. 652, 673 (1925) (Holmes, J., dissenting).
33. *Whitney v. California,* 274 U.S. 357, 377 (1927) (Brandeis, J., concurring).
34. *United States v. Dennis,* 183 F.2d 201, 212 (2d Cir. 1950), *aff'd* 341 U.S. 494 (1951). This formulation echoes Hand's earlier formulation for identifying tortious creation of danger in *United States v. Carroll Towing Co.,* 159 F.2d 169, 173 (2d Cir. 1947).
35. *Dennis v. United States,* 341 U.S. 494, 570 (1951) (Jackson, J., concurring).
36. In one formulation Holmes stated the intent and imminence requirements disjunctively: "I do not doubt for a moment that by the same reasoning that would justify punishing persuasion to murder, the United States constitutionally may punish speech that produces *or* is intended to produce a clear and imminent danger that it will bring about forthwith certain substantive evils that the United States constitutionally may seek to prevent. . . . It is only the present danger of immediate evil *or* an intent to bring it about that warrants Congress in setting a limit to the expression of opinion where private rights are not concerned." *Abrams v. United States,* 250 U.S. 616, 627–28 (1919) (Holmes, J., dissenting) (emphasis added).
37. *Brandenburg v. Ohio,* 395 U.S. 444, 452, 456 (1969) (Douglas, J., concurring) (paragraphing omitted).

38. "When clear and present danger of riot, disorder, interference with traffic upon the public streets, or other immediate threat to public safety, peace, or order, appears, the power of the State to prevent or punish is obvious." *Cantwell v. Connecticut,* 310 U.S. 296, 308 (1940); *Feiner v. New York,* 340 U.S. 315 (1951).

39. *Terminiello v. City of Chicago,* 337 U.S. 1 (1949); *Gregory v. City of Chicago,* 394 U.S. 111 (1969); *Edwards v. South Carolina,* 372 U.S. 229 (1963).

40. 424 U.S. 1 (1976) *(per curiam)*.

41. 504 U.S. 191 (1992) (plurality opinion).

42. A plurality held that the prohibition survived strict scrutiny. Justice Scalia concurred on the ground that the vicinity of the polling place was not a public forum and that therefore this content-specific but viewpoint-neutral regulation was permissible.

43. It has not been applied to the procedural guarantees of the Bill of Rights such as the right to grand jury indictment, trial by jury, or the right to counsel in criminal trial. It may be that the escape for extreme circumstances implicit in the strict scrutiny standard is supplied by the more flexible due process standard, which tests restraints on liberty similar to those that result from criminal prosecution and conviction so long as the restraints on liberty are not formally designated as punishment. *See United States v. Salerno,* 481 U.S. 739 (1987); *Kansas v. Hendricks,* 521 U.S. 346 (1997).

44. For classifications on the basis of race or touching on fundamental liberties, the Court will apply strict scrutiny. *See United States v. Carolene Products Co.,* 304 U.S. 144, 152–53 n.4 (1938); *Adarand Constructors, Inc. v. Pena,* 515 U.S. 200 (1995). Classifications based on sex are subject to "heightened" or "intermediate" scrutiny. *See Craig v. Boren,* 429 U.S. 190 (1976). Other classifications are subject to the "rational basis" test. *See Williamson v. Lee Optical of Oklahoma,* 348 U.S. 483 (1955). *See* Chapter 7.

45. *Chaplinsky v. New Hampshire,* 315 U.S. 568, 572 (1942) (Murphy, J.) (involving the phrases "damned racketeer" and "damned fascist" addressed to a city marshal).

46. *Valentine v. Chrestensen,* 316 U.S. 52 (1942) (involving "purely commercial advertising").

47. *United States v. One Book Entitled Ulysses by James Joyce,* 72 F.2d 705, 707 (2d Cir. 1934).

48. Model Penal Code §251.4 (Official Draft 1980).

49. 354 U.S. 476, 481 (1957). ("Although this is the first time the issue has been squarely presented to this Court, either under the First Amendment or under the Fourteenth Amendment, expressions found in numerous opinions indicate that this Court has always assumed that obscenity is not protected by the freedoms of speech and press.").

50. *See* Robin L. West, "The Difference in Women's Hedonic Lives: A Phenomenological Critique of Feminist Legal Theory," 15 *Wis. Women's L.J.*

149 (2000). *See* Robin L. West, "Constitutional Skepticism," 72 *B.U. L. Rev.* 765, 777–78 (1992).

51. 378 U.S. 184, 199 (1964) (Warren, C.J., dissenting).
52. Alexander Bickel, 22 *The Public Interest* 25–26 (Winter, 1971) (quoted in *Paris Adult Theatre I v. Slaton,* 413 U.S. 49, 59 (1973)).
53. First Amendment doctrine has been stretched to accommodate the "environmental" argument to this extent: businesses selling sexually explicit materials may through zoning regulations either be concentrated in "adult entertainment zones" or dispersed throughout the commercial areas. In either case the justification is not that the material they purvey may be the subject of regulation but that communities may take steps to protect against the persons and activities that grow up alongside such establishments, what are called their "secondary effects." *Renton v. Playtime Theatres,* 475 U.S. 41 (1986); *Young v. American Mini-Theatres, Inc.,* 427 U.S. 50 (1976). What can be said to support this line of reasoning is that the harm does not come about because of the persuasive effect of the expression, but at one remove, because of the commercial and criminal opportunities that are presented to muggers, prostitutes, and dope peddlers in the presence of large numbers of persons who are interested in the persuasive effect of the expression. Whether the burden on such expression is nonetheless justified is discussed in the section on burdens below.
54. *See Stanley v. Georgia,* 394 U.S. 557 (1969).
55. "The expense of spirit in a waste of shame is lust in action" (William Shakespeare, *Sonnet 129*).
56. *Paris Adult Theatre I v. Slaton,* 413 U.S. 49, 109, 112–13 (1973) (Brennan, J., dissenting).
57. *Miller v. California,* 413 U.S. 15 (1973).
58. *Id.* at 23–24 (citations omitted) (emphasis in original). One of the more hilarious entailments of the *Miller* requirement that the forbidden material be "specifically defined" is that statutes and ordinances have had to become as offensive as the matter they seek to proscribe.
59. *See Jenkins v. Georgia,* 418 U.S. 153 (1974).
60. *See Pope v. Illinois,* 481 U.S. 497 (1987).
61. *See Butler v. Michigan,* 350 U.S. 352 (1957); *Reno v. American Civil Liberties Union,* 521 U.S. 844 (1997).
62. *See New York v. Ferber,* 458 U.S. 747 (1982).
63. *See Osborne v. Ohio,* 495 U.S. 103 (1990).
64. *Ashcroft v. Free Speech Coalition,* 535 U.S. 234 (2002).
65. Recall Justice Murphy's formula in *Chaplinsky, supra* note 45 and accompanying text.
66. "It is only the present danger of immediate evil or an intent to bring it about that warrants Congress in setting a limit to the expression of opinion where *private rights are not concerned.*" *Abrams v. United States,* 250 U.S. 616, 628 (1919) (Holmes, J., dissenting) (emphasis added).

67. 376 U.S. 254 (1964).
68. The Court rejected the argument that this award was not within the First Amendment at all for the reason that it was not an instance of action by the state.
69. *See supra* note 2.
70. In *Beauharnais v. Illinois*, 343 U.S. 250 (1952), the Court sustained a conviction under a state criminal libel statute of the publisher of a pamphlet accusing the African-American community in Chicago of posing a danger of rapes, robberies, and racial "mongrelization." The Court invoked the *Chaplinsky* exception and the long tradition of criminal libel laws to justify the Illinois judge's refusal to give a "clear and present danger" instruction. Although never explicitly overruled, the case cannot any longer be good law, as the speech condemned there is indistinguishable from the racist speech in *Brandenburg. See also Collin v. Smith*, 578 F.2d 1197 (7th Cir. 1978), *cert. denied*, 439 U.S. 916 (1978) (concerning a local ordinance forbidding a march by the American Nazi Party through a community with a large Jewish population).
71. Who is a public figure is a subject of some complexity and obscurity, but the nuances of that aspect of the doctrine need not detain us. *See Gertz v. Robert Welch, Inc.*, 418 U.S. 323 (1974); *Dun & Bradstreet, Inc. v. Greenmoss Builders, Inc.*, 472 U.S. 749 (1985).
72. As for the victim's pain or anger just at having nasty things said about him—perhaps only to his face—I deal with that in the next section.
73. *See* Richard Posner, *Economic Analysis of Law* 97 (3d ed. 1986).
74. *See, e.g., Miami Herald Publ'g. Co. v. Tornillo*, 418 U.S. 241 (1974) (holding unconstitutional a state law requiring newspaper to give equal space to political candidates to reply to attacks).
75. This suggestion is based on Pierre N. Leval, "No-Money, No-Fault Libel Suit: Keeping Sullivan in Its Proper Place," 101 *Harv. L. Rev.* 1287 (1988).
76. *See Rosenfeld v. New Jersey*, 408 U.S. 901 (1972) (the use of "mother-[fucking]" to describe teachers and officials at school board meeting); *Lewis v. New Orleans*, 408 U.S. 913 (1972) (an insult directed at police officers making an arrest, specifically calling them "m[otherfucking] fascist pig cops"); *Gooding v. Wilson*, 405 U.S. 518 (1972) ("White son of a bitch, I'll kill you," addressed to arresting officer).
77. *Terminiello v. City of Chicago*, 337 U.S. 1 (1949) (reversing the conviction of a speaker who addressed a hostile crowd gathered outside an auditorium in which he was speaking as "slimy snakes" and "scum").
78. John Hart Ely, *Democracy and Distrust* 114 (1980).
79. *See* Daniel Jacobson, "Freedom of Speech Acts? A Response to Langton," *Phil. & Public Affairs* 64 (1995); Richard Delgado, "Words That Wound: A Tort Action for Racial Insults, Epithets, and Name-Calling," 17 *Harv. C.R.-C.L.L. Rev.* 133, 172–79 (1982); Charles R. Lawrence III, "If He Hollers Let Him Go: Regulating Racist Speech on Campus," 1990 *Duke L.J.* 431;

Mari J. Matsuda, "Public Response to Racist Speech: Considering the Victim's Story," 87 *Mich. L. Rev.* 2320 (1989); Catharine A. MacKinnon, "Pornography, Civil Rights, and Speech," 20 *Harv. C.R.-C.L.L. Rev.* 1 (1985).

80. *See, e.g.,* Sarah Lyall, "Critic of Holocaust Denier Cleared in British Libel Suit," *N.Y. Times* (Apr. 12, 2000) at A1 (noting that denial of the Holocaust is not itself a crime in Britain, but is in Germany); Michel Marriott, "Rising Tide: Sites Born of Hate," *N.Y. Times* (Mar. 18, 1999) at G1 (noting that it is easier to censor "hate speech on the Internet in nations like Canada, Britain and Germany—nations where hate speech is illegal—than in the United States. . . ."); Michael L. Siegel, "Hate Speech, Civil Rights, and the Internet: The Jurisdictional and Human Rights Nightmare," 9 *Alb. L.J. Sci. & Tech.* 375, 396 (1999) (noting the conflicts between banning hate speech and §§18–19 of the United Nations Universal Declaration of Human Rights, which provide for freedom of opinion and expression).

81. *See, e.g., Oncale v. Sundowner Offshore Servs., Inc.,* 523 U.S. 75 (1998); *Burlington Indus., Inc. v. Ellerth,* 524 U.S. 742 (1998); *Faragher v. City of Boca Raton,* 524 U.S. 775 (1998). This is to be contrasted with so-called quid pro quo harassment where an employer implies that acceptance of sexual advances is a condition of employment or promotion. Such a term of employment is obviously discriminatory, and like any other condition must be conveyed in some kind of communication. Those communications are not protected as free speech, but are closer to performatives.

82. *See Gebser v. Lago Vista Indep. Sch. Dist.,* 524 U.S. 274 (1998).

83. *See Arguello v. Conoco, Inc.,* 207 F.3d 803 (5th Cir. 2000), *cert. denied* 531 U.S. 874 (2000).

84. *See Harris v. Forklift Sys., Inc.,* 510 U.S. 17 (1993).

85. *See* Richard H. Fallon, Jr., "Sexual Harassment, Content Neutrality, and the First Amendment Dog That Didn't Bark," 1994 *Sup. Ct. Rev.* 1.

86. Threats of rape may suffice for this purpose. Such threats were involved in *Oncale v. Sundowner Offshore Servs.,* 523 U.S. 75 (1998).

87. *See supra* note 70.

88. *See, e.g., Baty v. Williamette Indus., Inc.,* 172 F.3d 1232 (10th Cir. 1999) (affirming a finding of hostile environment when the defendant, *inter alia,* displayed "a poster of a 'half naked, clad in a bikini, woman.' ").

89. Consider the former speech code at the University of Pennsylvania, which prohibited "any behavior, verbal or physical, that stigmatizes or victimizes individuals on the basis of race, ethnic or national origin, . . . and that has the purpose or effect of interfering with an individual's academic or work performance; and/or creates an intimidating or offensive academic, living or work environment." Ethan Bronner, "Big Brother Is Listening," *N.Y. Times* (Apr. 4, 1999) at A23. *See also Silva v. Univ. of New Hampshire,* 888 F. Supp. 293 (1994) (enjoining, on the basis of the First Amendment, the university from suspending a professor for a claimed violation of the univer-

sity's sexual harassment code); *Doe v. Univ. of Michigan*, 721 F. Supp. 852 (E.D. Mich. 1989) (striking down the University of Michigan's policy); *UWM Post, Inc. v. Bd. of Regents of Univ. of Wis. Sys.*, 774 F. Supp. 1163 (E.D. Wis. 1991) (striking down the University of Wisconsin's policy as overbroad); *Dambrot v. Central Mich. Univ.*, 839 F. Supp. 477 (E.D. Mich. 1993) (striking down Central Michigan's speech code). Harvard Law School's policy (visited on March 10, 2001) is available at *http://www .law.harvard.edu/administration/hr/harassment.html*. And private institutions, which of course are not bound by the First Amendment, have regularly explained their imposition of rigid standards of political correctness by the wish to avoid liability in harassment cases. *See Burlington Indus., Inc. v. Ellerth*, 524 U.S. 742, 765 (1998) (establishing the importance of sexual harassment policies in an employer's affirmative defense to a claim of harassment).

90. *See* the section on commercial speech below.

91. *See, e.g., Patterson v. McLean Credit Union*, 491 U.S. 164 (1989).

92. *See Young v. New York City Transit Auth.*, 903 F.2d 146, 152–54 (2d Cir. 1990), *cert. denied*, 498 U.S. 984 (1990) (upholding against First Amendment challenge NYCTA prohibitions against all begging and panhandling in certain public transit facilities).

93. *See Kovacs v. Cooper*, 336 U.S. 77, 86 (1949); *Martin v. City of Struthers, Ohio*, 319 U.S. 141, 143, 148 (1943). If my tormentor is in the same dormitory, he cannot pursue me to my room.

94. *Gibbons v. Ogden*, 22 U.S. 1 (1824).

95. *See Valentine v. Chrestensen*, 316 U.S. 52 (1942) ("The ruling was casual, almost offhand."). *Cammarano v. United States*, 358 U.S. 498, 514 (1959) (Douglas, J., concurring).

96. *See* Chapter 5.

97. 198 U.S. 45 (1905).

98. *See Bolger v. Youngs Drug Prods. Corp.*, 463 U.S. 60 (1983) (invalidating statute forbidding mailing of unsolicited advertisements of contraceptive products).

99. I draw here on my brief *amicus curiae* in *City of Cincinnati v. Discovery Network, Inc.*, 507 U.S. 410 (1993), which held that a city may not limit the placing of newspaper distribution boxes on city streets to major dailies to the exclusion of publications listing real estate for rent or sale and announcing courses available at a commercial adult education program.

100. *Pittsburgh Press Co. v. Pittsburgh Comm'n on Human Relations*, 413 U.S. 376, 385 (1973).

101. *Barnes v. Glen Theatre, Inc.*, 501 U.S. 560 (1991) (plurality opinion) (finding the erotic message conveyed by nude dance performances in principle not beyond protection afforded freedom of expression).

102. *Virginia State Bd. of Pharmacy v. Virginia Citizens Consumer Council, Inc.*, 425 U.S. 748, 761, 763 (1976).

103. *44 Liquormart, Inc. v. Rhode Island,* 517 U.S. 484, 518 (1996) (Thomas, J., concurring in part and concurring in the judgment).
104. *See United States v. Carolene Products, Co.,* 304 U.S. 144 (1938); *Clover-leaf Butter Co. v. Patterson,* 315 U.S. 148 (1942).
105. *See also Rubin v. Coors Brewing Co.,* 514 U.S. 476 (1995) (striking down regulation forbidding stating alcoholic content of beer and malt liquor, where direct regulation of alcoholic content would have been valid).
106. *Central Hudson Gas & Electric Corp. v. Public Serv. Comm'n of New York,* 447 U.S. 557, 565 (1980).
107. *See, e.g., Bd. of Trustees v. Fox,* 492 U.S. 469 (1989).
108. *Posadas de Puerto Rico Assoc. v. Tourism Co. of Puerto Rico,* 478 U.S. 328 (1986).
109. *See 44 Liquormart, Inc. v. Rhode Island,* 517 U.S. 484, 501 (1996); *id.* at 518 (Thomas, J., concurring in part and concurring in the judgment). Justice Thurgood Marshall, speaking for the Court in *Linmark Assoc., Inc. v. Willingboro,* 431 U.S. 85 (1977) had come to the same conclusion: "The [town, in forbidding the posting of 'For Sale' and 'Sold' signs] acted to prevent its residents from obtaining certain information. . . . The [town] has sought to restrict the free flow of these data because it fears that otherwise homeowners will make decisions inimical to what the [town] views as the homeowners' self-interest and the corporate interest of the township. . . . If dissemination of this information can be restricted, then every locality in the country can suppress any facts that reflect poorly on the locality, so long as a plausible claim can be made that disclosure would cause the recipients of the information to act 'irrationally.' " 431 U.S. at 96.
110. There are a few state laws that purport to prohibit knowingly false statements in political campaigns. Enforcement is rare and lower courts are split on their constitutionality. *See In re Chmura,* 626 N.W.2d 876 (Mich. 2001); *State of Washington ex rel. Public Disclosure Comm'n v. 119 Vote No! Committee,* 957 P.2d 691 (Wash. 1998).
111. For an excellent analysis of commercial speech which is much less expansive than the one I offer here, *see* Robert Post, "Reconciling Theory and Doctrine in First Amendment Jurisprudence," 88 *Calif. L. Rev.* 2353, 2371–2374 (2000).
112. *See, e.g., Cornelius v. NAACP Legal Defense and Educ. Fund, Inc.,* 473 U.S. 788 (1985) (upholding the exclusion of political and advocacy groups from a fund-raising drive conducted in federal offices, but remanding for a determination "whether the exclusion of respondents was impermissibly motivated by a desire to suppress a particular view."); *Rust v. Sullivan,* 500 U.S. 173 (1991) (upholding Health and Human Services Department regulations forbidding publicly funded public health projects from encouraging, promoting, or advocating abortion).
113. *See Murdock v. Pennsylvania,* 319 U.S. 105 (1943); *Minneapolis Star & Tribune Co. v. Minnesota Commissioner of Revenue,* 460 U.S. 575 (1983).

114. *See Oklahoma Press Publ'g Co. v. Walling*, 327 U.S. 186 (1946). *See also Associated Press v. NLRB*, 301 U.S. 103 (1937) (concerning the applicability of labor laws to newspapers).
115. 501 U.S. 663 (1991).
116. *See Miami Herald Publ'g Co. v. Tornillo*, 418 U.S. 241 (1974).
117. *Bartnicki v. Vopper*, 532 U.S. 514 (2001) (law forbidding publication of illegally intercepted messages); *Ladue v. Gilleo*, 512 U.S. 43 (1994) (law forbidding almost all signs on residential property banned "too much" speech, even if content-neutral).
118. *Compare Cornelius v. NAACP Legal Defense and Educ. Fund*, 473 U.S. 788 (1985) with *Rust v. Sullivan*, 500 U.S. 173 (1991).
119. 408 U.S. 92 (1972). To the same effect is *Carey v. Brown*, 447 U.S. 455 (1980).
120. *See United States v. Eichman*, 496 U.S. 310 (1990); *Texas v. Johnson*, 491 U.S. 397 (1989).
121. In the actual flag-burning cases the government and the dissenters came up with a number of explanations. They all came down to protecting the set of messages that the flag unburnt conveys. Some would have invoked a compelling interest to protect that message. Others that the flag was unique and therefore outside First Amendment analysis. And still others that flag burning was a sort of generic instance of fighting words in the sense that disrespect to the flag gave particularly painful offense to many people.
122. The relevant portion of the Texas statute read: "Section 42.09. Desecration of a Venerated Object. (a) A person commits an offense if he intentionally or knowingly desecrates: (1) a public monument; (2) a place of worship or burial; or (3) a state or national flag. (b) For purposes of this section, 'desecrate' means deface, damage, or otherwise physically mistreat in a way that the actor knows will seriously offend one or more persons likely to observe or discover his action." (Tex. Penal Code Ann. §42.09 (1989)).
123. *United States v. O'Brien*, 391 U.S. 367, 376–77 (1968).
124. 478 U.S. 697 (1986).
125. 501 U.S. 560 (1991) (plurality opinion).
126. 468 U.S. 288 (1984).
127. 460 U.S. 575 (1983).
128. *Id.* at 581, 583, 585 (paragraphing deleted).
129. "No one supposes . . . that the First Amendment prohibits a state from preventing the distribution of leaflets in a church against the will of the church authorities." *Martin v. City of Struthers, Ohio*, 319 U.S. 141, 143 (1943).
130. *Cox v. New Hampshire*, 312 U.S. 569, 574, 576 (1941) (allowing a local authority to require parade permits "to prevent confusion by overlapping parades or processions, to secure convenient use of the streets by other travelers, and to minimize the risk of disorder.").
131. *See supra* text accompanying notes 92–93.
132. *Cf. Connick v. Myers*, 461 U.S. 138 (1983); *Bethel Sch. Dist. No. 403 v. Fraser*, 478 U.S. 675 (1986).

133. *See Wooley v. Maynard,* 430 U.S. 705 (1977) (striking down state requirement that automobiles display a slogan some found objectionable on their
license plates); *West Virginia State Bd. of Educ. v. Barnette,* 319 U.S. 624
(1943).

134. *See Marsh v. Alabama,* 326 U.S. 501 (1946) (treating a company town as a
municipality).

135. *Hague v. CIO,* 307 U.S. 496 (1939).

136. *Commonwealth v. Davis,* 162 Mass. 510, 511 (1895) (Holmes, J.), *aff'd
sub nom. Davis v. Massachusetts,* 167 U.S. 43 (1897).

137. 307 U.S. at 515. Though *Hague* is an important early articulation of this
right, the notion that streets and parks have "time out of mind, been used
for the purposes of assembly" may be overstated.

138. Harry Kalven, Jr., "The Concept of the Public Forum: Cox v. Louisiana,"
1965 *Sup. Ct. Rev.* 1, 13.

139. *See Benefit v. City of Cambridge,* 424 Mass. 918 (1997).

140. *See Commonwealth v. Pike,* 428 Mass. 393 (1998) (banishment from state
an unconstitutional condition of probation).

141. *See Gregory v. City of Chicago,* 394 U.S. 111 (1969); *Edwards v. South
Carolina,* 372 U.S. 229 (1963); *Shuttlesworth v. City of Birmingham,* 394
U.S. 147 (1969).

142. *See Kovacs v. Cooper,* 336 U.S. 77 (1949); *Saia v. New York,* 334 U.S. 558
(1948); *Ward v. Rock Against Racism,* 491 U.S. 781 (1989).

143. *Martin v. City of Struthers, Ohio,* 319 U.S. 141, 148 (1943).

144. *United States v. Grace,* 461 U.S. 171, 177 (1983).

145. *See* text accompanying notes 111–119 above; Charles Fried, "Types," 14
Const. Commentary 55 (1997); Kagan, *supra* note 16.

146. For a general discussion of this and other kinds of disciplining devices, *see*
Fried, "Types," *supra* note 145, at 56–68.

147. *Police Dep't v. Mosley,* 408 U.S. 92, 95 (1972). *See also R.A.V. v. City of St.
Paul,* 505 U.S. 377, 386 (1992) ("Fighting words are thus analogous to a
noisy sound truck. . . . As with the sound truck, however, so also with fighting words: The government may not regulate use based on hostility—or favoritism—towards the underlying message expressed.").

148. *See Schneider v. State,* 308 U.S. 147 (1939).

149. Fried, *supra* note 145 at 63–64; Kagan, *supra* note 16 at 440–43.

150. But *see* Justice Harlan's concurrence in *United States v. O'Brien,* 391 U.S.
367 (1968) (Harlan, J., concurring).

151. Narrow tailoring is also required in commercial speech, but that is a context
in which government claims an authority to regulate the speech element of
commercial speech as such.

152. This would cross the boundary that John Rawls drew between a right and
the worth of that right. *See* John Rawls, *A Theory of Justice* 204–05 (1972).

153. Ordinary citizens cannot afford mass media expression, but as consumers
they determine to a degree what mass media will offer them.

154. *Hague v. CIO,* 307 U.S. 496, 515 (1939).

155. *Int'l Soc'y for Krishna Consciousness [ISKCON] v. Lee,* 505 U.S. 672, 700 (1992), *aff'd Lee v. ISKCON,* 505 U.S. 830 (1992) (Kennedy, J., concurring in judgment).

156. *ISKCON,* 505 U.S. at 710 (Souter, J., concurring in judgment in *ISKCON v. Lee* and dissenting from *Lee v. ISKCON*).

157. *ISKCON,* 505 U.S. at 678; *cf. Brown v. Louisiana,* 383 U.S. 131 (1966) (Black, J., dissenting); *United States Postal Service v. Council of Greenburgh Civic Ass'n,* 453 U.S. 114 (1981).

158. *Perry Education Ass'n v. Perry Local Educators' Ass'n,* 460 U.S. 37, 45–46 (1983) (internal quotation marks, brackets, and citations omitted).

159. *See Southeastern Promotions, Ltd. v. Conrad,* 420 U.S. 546, 573 (1975) (Rehnquist, J., dissenting).

160. *See, e.g., Bd. of Regents of Univ. of Wis. v. Southworth,* 529 U.S. 217 (2000); *Heffron v. Int'l Soc'y for Krishna Consciousness, Inc.,* 452 U.S. 640, 655 (1981).

161. *See Cornelius v. NAACP Legal Defense and Educ. Fund,* 473 U.S. 788 (1985) (plurality opinion).

162. *Rust v. Sullivan,* 500 U.S. 173 (1991). *But see Legal Servs. Corp. v. Velazquez,* 531 U.S. 533 (2000). *Rust* allows government to dictate what doctors in federally financed programs may say. *Velazquez* holds it unconstitutional to attempt to limit the kinds of arguments federally funded legal services lawyers may make.

163. Croatia Const. art. 3 ("journalists shall have their right to freedom of reporting and access to information."); Estonia Const. art. 44 (giving citizens right to information from government); S. African Const. §32 (giving all citizens the "right of access to (a) any information held by the state . . .").

164. *See, e.g.,* Freedom of Information Act, 5 U.S.C.A. §552 (2001); Arkansas Freedom of Information Act, Ark. Code Ann. §25-19-101 (Michie 2000); Delaware Freedom of Information Act, Del. Code Ann. tit. 29, §10001 (2000); Illinois Freedom of Information Act, 5 Ill. Comp. Stat. 140/1 (West 2001).

165. The First Amendment has spread its protection widely to private individuals' publication of information the government wanted to keep secret and had a right to keep secret, but which somehow or other got out. The Pentagon Papers case, *New York Times Co. v. United States,* 403 U.S. 713 (1971), is the signal instance of this. *See also Bartnicki v. Vopper,* 532 U.S. 514 (2001) (radio commentator protected from liability for broadcasting a recording of a newsworthy conversation illicitly made by a third party).

166. 448 U.S. 555 (1980).

167. 395 U.S. 367 (1969).

168. *See supra* note 116 and accompanying text.

169. *CBS, Inc. v. FCC,* 453 U.S. 367 (1981).

170. *See, e.g.,* Cass R. Sunstein, "Free Speech Now," 59 *U. Chi. L. Rev.* 255, 276 (1992).

171. *See Jackson v. Metropolitan Edison Co.*, 419 U.S. 345 (1974) (holding a public utility not subject to constitutional obligations to accord due process to its customers); *Moose Lodge No. 107 v. Irvis*, 407 U.S. 163 (1972) (holding a liquor licensee not subject to the constitutional prohibition on race discrimination).

172. *See* the discussion of cable television and the Internet at notes 179 and 184–86.

173. *See Leathers v. Medlock*, 499 U.S. 439 (1991); *City of Los Angeles v. Preferred Communications, Inc.*, 476 U.S. 488 (1986).

174. *Turner Broad. Sys., Inc. v. FCC*, 520 U.S. 180 (1997); *Turner Broad. Sys., Inc. v. FCC*, 512 U.S. 622 (1994).

175. 518 U.S. 727 (1996).

176. *See supra* note 116 and accompanying text.

177. They might be offering satellite services (another nest of problems).

178. *See generally City of Los Angeles v. Preferred Communications, Inc.*, 476 U.S. 488 (1986).

179. *Cf. Members of City Council v. Taxpayers for Vincent*, 466 U.S. 789 (1984) (holding that a prohibition on posting signs on public property applied to political posters attached to utility poles is a reasonable time, place, and manner restriction under *O'Brien*).

180. *Denver Area Educ. Telecomm. Consortium, Inc. v. FCC*, 518 U.S. 727, 740 (1996).

181. *Nixon v. Shrink Mo. Gov't PAC*, 528 U.S. 377, 400–02 (2000) (Breyer, J., concurring). This is the approach advocated by Cass Sunstein. *See* Cass R. Sunstein, "Words, Conduct, Caste," 60 *U. Chi. L. Rev.* 795, 837 (1993); Cass R. Sunstein, "Pornography and the First Amendment," 1986 *Duke L.J.* 589, 622.

182. *Nixon*, 528 U.S. 377, 400 (2000) (Breyer, J., concurring); *Turner Broad. Sys., Inc. v. FCC*, 520 U.S. 180, 226 (1997) (Breyer, J., concurring).

183. *See* Fried, "The New First Amendment Jurisprudence: A Threat to Liberty," 59 *U. Chi. L. Rev.* 229 (1992).

184. *See* Lawrence Lessig, *Code and Other Laws of Cyberspace* (1999) and my review, Charles Fried, "Perfect Freedom or Perfect Control?," 114 *Harv. L. Rev.* 606 (2000) (book review).

185. *See, e.g.*, Alfred C. Yen, "Internet Service Provider Liability for Subscriber Copyright Infringement, Enterprise Liability, and the First Amendment," 88 *Geo. L.J.* 1833 (2000); Brian E. Daughdrill, "Personal Jurisdiction and the Internet: Waiting for the Other Shoe to Drop on First Amendment Concerns," 51 *Mercer L. Rev.* 919 (2000); Stephen Fraser, "The Conflict Between the First Amendment and Copyright Law and Its Impact on the Internet," 16 *Cardozo Arts & Ent. L.J.* 1 (1998); Robert Kline, "Freedom of Speech on the Electronic Village Green: Applying the First Amendment Lessons of Cable Television to the Internet," 6 *Cornell J.L. and Pub. Pol'y* 23 (1996).

186. *See* Lessig, *supra* note 184, at 122–41; Fried, "Perfect Freedom," *supra* note 184, at 622–30.
187. *See* Copyright Act of 1976, 17 U.S.C. §502 (authorizing courts to grant temporary and final injunctions for copyright infringement "on such terms as it may deem reasonable to prevent or restrain infringement.").
188. *See* the discussion of the *Cowles* case *supra* text accompanying note 115.
189. U.S. Const. art. I, §8, cl. 8.
190. *See, e.g., Fogerty v. Fantasy, Inc.,* 510 U.S. 517, 527 (1994); *Feist Publ'ns, Inc. v. Rural Telephone Serv. Co.,* 499 U.S. 340, 349–50 (1991).
191. For a pre-Internet case considering the interplay of the fair use doctrine and First Amendment concerns, see *Harper & Row Publishers v. Nation Enterprises,* 471 U.S. 539 (1985).
192. *See Universal City Studios, Inc. v. Remeirdes,* 82 F. Supp. 2d 211 (S.D.N.Y. 2000) (preliminary injunction), 111 F. Supp. 2d 294 (S.D.N.Y. 2000) (permanent injunction).
193. 537 U.S. 186 (2003). I was one of several counsel to the challengers in this case.
194. *See* note 189 and accompanying text.

5. Religion

1. Michael W. McConnell, "The Origins and Historical Understanding of Free Exercise of Religion," 103 *Harv. L. Rev.* 1409, 1423 (1990).
2. *Id.* at 1430.
3. *Zorach v. Clauson,* 343 U.S. 306, 313 (1952) ("We are a religious people whose institutions presuppose a Supreme Being").
4. The Seventh Amendment guarantee of a right to a civil jury in federal court, for instance, is limited to cases analogous to those that would have counted as "suits at common law" in the late eighteenth century. *See Colegrove v. Battin,* 413 U.S. 149, 152–57 (1973).
5. *McCollum v. Bd. of Educ.,* 333 U.S. 203 (1948).
6. McConnell, *supra* note 1, at 1423, 1436, 1438–1440.
7. The clearest expression has been in dissenting opinions by Justice Potter Stewart. *See Zurcher v. Stanford Daily,* 436 U.S. 547 (1978); *Branzburg v. Hayes,* 408 U.S. 665 (1972).
8. *See* Charles Fried, "Five to Four: Reflections on the Voucher Case," 116 *Harv. L. Rev.* 163, 183–184 (2002).
9. Michael W. McConnell, "Why Is Religious Liberty the 'First Freedom'?," 21 *Cardozo L. Rev.* 1243, 1248 (2000) (footnotes omitted).
10. Philip Kurland, "Of Church and State and the Supreme Court," 29 *U. Chi. L. Rev.* 1 (1961).
11. 494 U.S. 872 (1990).
12. 374 U.S. 398 (1963).
13. 494 U.S. 872 (1990).

14. *Sherbert,* 374 U.S. at 402.
15. *See* Chapter 4.
16. *Sherbert,* 374 U.S. at 404.
17. *Id.* at 403. The Court quotes from a political association case, *NAACP v. Button,* 371 U.S. 415, 438 (1963).
18. *See* Chapter 4.
19. *See Tony and Susan Alamo Found. v. Sec'y of Labor,* 471 U.S. 290 (1985) (religious organization operating gas stations and other businesses staffed by "volunteers" must comply with wages-and-hours laws).
20. 98 U.S. 145 (1878).
21. *Id.* at 164, 167.
22. 494 U.S. 872, 878–879 (1990) (citations and internal quotation marks omitted).
23. *City of Boerne v. Flores,* 521 U.S. 507 (1997). *See* Chapter 2.
24. *Id.*
25. *Goldman v. Weinberger,* 475 U.S. 503 (1986).
26. *Lyng v. Northwest Indian Cemetery Protective Ass'n,* 485 U.S. 439 (1988); *Bowen v. Roy,* 476 U.S. 693 (1986).
27. *See id.*
28. The term "religious gerrymander" appears to have been coined by the second Justice Harlan. *See Walz v. Tax Comm'n of the City of New York,* 397 U.S. 664, 696 (1970) (Harlan, J., concurring).
29. 508 U.S. 520 (1993).
30. *Frazee v. Ill. Dep't of Employment Security,* 489 U.S. 829 (1989); *Hobbie v. Unemployment Appeals Comm'n. of Fla.,* 480 U.S. 136 (1987); *Thomas v. Review Bd. of Ind. Employment Security Div.,* 450 U.S. 707 (1981).
31. *Wisconsin v. Yoder,* 406 U.S. 205 (1972).
32. *McDaniel v. Paty,* 435 U.S. 618 (1978).
33. *O'Lone v. Estate of Shabazz,* 482 U.S. 342 (1987).
34. *Goldman v. Weinberger,* 475 U.S. 503 (1986).
35. *See supra* note 26.
36. *United States v. Lee,* 455 U.S. 252 (1982) (interest in a comprehensive, uniform tax system); *Bob Jones Univ. v. United States,* 461 U.S. 574 (1983) (public policy against granting tax-exempt status to racially discriminatory educational entities).
37. 455 U.S. 252 (1982).
38. *Id.* at 255.
39. *United States v. Ballard,* 322 U.S. 78 (1944) (upholding mail fraud conviction of persons claiming healing powers as ministers of the "I Am" movement).
40. 476 U.S. 693 (1986).
41. 366 U.S. 599 (1961).
42. *Id.* at 611.
43. Justice Frankfurter's lengthy concurring opinion, in which Justice Harlan

joined, did not disagree with the Chief Justice on the grounds at issue here, but concentrated on points of its own.

44. *Braunfield*, 366 U.S. 606–07 (emphasis added).

45. *See* Michael W. McConnell, "The Problem of Singling Out Religion," 50 *DePaul L. Rev.* 1, 12–15 (2000).

46. *See, e.g., Martin v. City of Struthers*, 319 U.S. 141 (1943); *Cantwell v. Connecticut*, 310 U.S. 296 (1940).

47. *Pierce v. Soc'y of the Sisters of the Holy Names of Jesus and Mary*, 268 U.S. 510 (1925).

48. *Meyer v. Nebraska*, 262 U.S. 390 (1923).

49. Kurland, *supra* note 10, at 7–8 (noting the "essential soundness" of the Court's reasoning in *Reynolds v. United States*, 98 U.S. 145 (1878), which Kurland paraphrased as follows: "To permit individuals to be excused from compliance with the law solely on the basis of religious beliefs is to subject others to punishment for failure to subscribe to those same beliefs."); *see also id.* at 94 (noting the "problem whether an exemption from a validly promulgated police regulation framed in terms of religious belief constituted a violation of the 'establishment clause' ").

50. *See Reynolds v. United States*, 98 U.S. 145, 164 (1878) (quoting Thomas Jefferson: "Believing with you that religion is a matter which lies solely between man and his God; that he owes account to none other for his faith or his worship; that the legislative powers of the government reach actions only, and not opinions—I contemplate with sovereign reverence that act of the whole American people which declared that their legislature should 'make no law respecting an establishment of religion or prohibiting the free exercise thereof,' thus building a wall of separation between church and State.").

51. 403 U.S. 602, 612–13 (1971).

52. For examples of such exemptions, see McConnell, *supra* note 45, at 3–6.

53. The Court departed from the *Lemon* test in *Allegheny County v. American Civil Liberties Union*, 492 U.S. 573, 593 (1989), which held that "[t]he [Establishment] Clause, at the very least, prohibits government from appearing to take a position on questions of religious belief or from 'making adherence to a religion relevant in any way to a person's standing in the political community,'" but returned to it shortly thereafter.

54. *See Lynch v. Donnelly*, 465 U.S. 668, 674–78 (1984) (observing that "[o]ur history is replete with official references to the value and invocation of Divine guidance in deliberations and pronouncements of the Founding Fathers and contemporary leaders" and that this history "may help explain why the Court consistently has declined to take a rigid, absolutist view of the Establishment Clause").

55. Justice William Rehnquist, as he then was, in *Wallace v. Jaffree*, 472 U.S. 38 (1985), seemed willing to contemplate a return to the textual meaning of the Establishment Clause.

56. *See, e.g.,* Petitioner's Brief, *Mitchell v. Helms,* 530 U.S. 793 (2000) (No. 98–1648), 1999 WL 639126, at 33–38 (August 19, 1999).
57. *See Everson v. Bd. of Educ. of Ewing Township,* 330 U.S. 1, 16 (1947) (Black, J.).
58. Compare *Lynch v. Donnelly,* 465 U.S. 668 (1984) (no violation of establishment of clause) with *Allegheny County v. American Civil Liberties Union,* 492 U.S. 573 (1989) (violation).
59. 370 U.S. 421 (1962).
60. *See* Fried, *supra* note 8, at 163–172.
61. Michael W. McConnell, "Coercion: The Lost Element of Establishment," 27 *Wm. & Mary L. Rev.* 933 (1986).
62. *See* Chapter 4; *see also Wooley v. Maynard,* 430 U.S. 705 (1977).
63. *Kedroff v. Saint Nicholas Cathedral,* 344 U.S. 94 (1952).
64. 505 U.S. 577 (1992).
65. *Id.* at 592–93.
66. *Santa Fe Indep. Sch. Dist. v. Doe,* 530 U.S. 290 (2000).
67. *See, e.g., Capitol Square Review and Advisory Bd. v. Pinette,* 515 U.S. 753, 777 (1995) (O'Connor, J., concurring in part and concurring in judgment); *Wallace v. Jaffree,* 472 U.S. 38, 73, 76 (1985) (O'Connor, J., concurring in judgment).
68. *Lynch v. Donnelly,* 465 U.S. 668, 687–88 (1984).
69. *Bd. of Educ. of Westside Cmty. Schs. v. Mergens,* 496 U.S. 226, 249 (1990) (use of school facilities by after-school "Christian club" to be judged from the perspective of "an objective observer in the position of a secondary school student").
70. *Everson v. Bd. of Educ.,* 330 U.S. 1, 16 (1947) (Black, J.).
71. *Walz v. Tax Commission,* 397 U.S. 664 (1970) (challenge to New York City property tax exemption for religious buildings rejected; only Justice Douglas dissented).
72. *Mueller v. Allen,* 463 U.S. 388, 417 (1983) (Marshall, J., dissenting) (quoting *Everson,* 330 U.S. at 16). In that case, the Court held that a Minnesota statute, which allowed state taxpayers to deduct expenses incurred in providing tuition, textbooks, and transportation for their children attending elementary or secondary school did not violate the Establishment Clause by providing financial assistance to sectarian institutions. The dissenters complained that the Court did not admit that its decision in effect overruled earlier decisions such as *Meek v. Pittenger,* 421 U.S. 349, 372–73 (1975), and *Wolman v. Walter,* 433 U.S. 229, 255 (1977).
73. *Lemon v. Kurtzman,* 403 U.S. 602, 625 (1971).
74. *Roemer v. Md. Public Works Bd.,* 426 U.S. 736 (1976); *Hunt v. McNair,* 413 U.S. 734 (1973).
75. *Tilton v. Richardson,* 403 U.S. 672 (1971).
76. *Bd. of Educ. of Cent. Sch. Dist. No. 1 v. Allen,* 392 U.S. 236, 248–49 (1968).

77. *Meek,* 421 U.S. at 372–73; *Wolman,* 433 U.S. at 255.
78. *Mitchell v. Helms,* 530 U.S. 793 (2000).
79. *Comm. for Pub. Educ. and Religious Liberty v. Regan,* 444 U.S. 646, 662 (1980).
80. *Levitt v. Comm. for Pub. Educ. and Religious Liberty,* 413 U.S. 472, 482 (1973).
81. *See Mitchell* 530 U.S. at 808 ("[W]e acknowledge what both the Ninth and Fifth Circuits saw was inescapable—*Meek* and *Wolman* are anomalies in our case law. We therefore conclude that they are no longer good law.").
82. *Tilton v. Richardson,* 403 U.S. 672, 686 (1971) (plurality opinion) (Burger, C.J.) ("The skepticism of the college student is not an inconsiderable barrier to any attempt or tendency to subvert the congressional objectives and limitations."). A curious in-between place is occupied by *Bowen v. Kendrick,* 487 U.S. 589 (1988), in which the Court rejected a facial challenge to a federal grant program to organizations, specifically including religiously affiliated organizations, to teach unmarried teenagers the wisdom of avoiding early pregnancies, preferably by abstaining from sex.
83. 413 U.S. 756 (1973).
84. The grant was available to parents with less than $5,000 annual income. The full tax credit was available to parents earning less than $9,000, declining to nothing for parents earning $25,000. The decision also invalidated a provision for grants to nonpublic schools for maintenance and repairs. *Id.* at 764–66.
85. *Id.* at 783.
86. 463 U.S. 388 (1983).
87. *Id.* at 394.
88. *Id.* at 397.
89. *Id.* at 399.
90. *Id.* at 408–11 (Marshall, J., dissenting).
91. 536 U.S. 639 (2002).
92. 521 U.S. 203 (1997) (overruling *Aguilar v. Felton,* 473 U.S. 402 (1985)).
93. 474 U.S. 481 (1986).
94. 509 U.S. 1 (1993).
95. For a discussion of the role of dissent in this case and in general, see Fried, *supra* note 8.
96. *See* Chapter 7.
97. *Good News Club v. Milford Cent. High Sch.,* 533 U.S. 98 (2001); *Rosenberger v. Rector and Visitors of the Univ. of Va.,* 515 U.S. 819 (1995); *Capitol Square Review and Advisory Bd. v. Pinette,* 515 U.S. 753 (1995); *Lamb's Chapel v. Center Moriches Union Free Sch. Dist.,* 508 U.S. 384 (1993); *Widmar v. Vincent,* 454 U.S. 263 (1981).
98. These sentences are taken directly from the Introduction and Summary of Argument of the brief of the Solicitor General as *amicus curiae* in *Hobbie v.*

Unemployment Appeals Comm'n of Fla., 480 U.S. 136 (1987). I omit quotation marks because I wrote those words. The Court, including Justice Scalia, the author of *Smith,* rejected that argument and adhered to its decision in *Sherbert.*

99. Pub. L. No. 95-341, 192 Stat. 469 (codified as amended at 42 USC §1996).
100. *Corporation of Presiding Bishop v. Amos,* 483 U.S. 327 (1987).
101. *United States v. Seeger,* 380 U.S. 163, 165–66 (1965). *See also* the several opinions in *Gillette v. United States,* 401 U.S. 437 (1971) (exemption refused to draftee who objected to participation not in all but only in unjust wars, as elaborated in Roman Catholic theology); *Welsh v. United States,* 398 U.S. 333, 342–43 (1970) ("objection to war must rest on moral, ethical or religious principles" not "upon policy pragmatism or expediency") (plurality opinion); *id.* at 344, 345, 356 (statute must be read as limited to "those opposed to war in general because of theistic beliefs" not "nontheistic religious" or "secular" beliefs, a line that Congress is forbidden to draw by the Establishment Clause) (Harlan, J., concurring).
102. *Welsh,* 398 U.S. at 356.
103. Jesse H. Choper, "Defining 'Religion' in the First Amendment," *U. Ill. L. Rev.* 579 (1982).
104. Imagine the dilemma of a soldier devoted to art ordered for good strategic reasons to destroy some great architectural monument.
105. McConnell, *supra* note 1, at 1410–1416. McConnell argues that the priest-penitent privilege, like other exemptions from legal duties that conflict with religious obligations, is constitutionally required by the free exercise clause in the absence of a sufficiently compelling need. The law generally also absolves spouses from testifying against each other, but not children or parents, and certainly not friends. Journalists frequently invoke the ethics of their profession to refuse revealing their sources. Though some statutes have created privileges of various degrees of impermeability, these privileges have rarely been held to be constitutionally compelled. Is a statutory or common law priest-penitent privilege a violation of the Establishment Clause—especially when the testimony is crucial to proving the justice of a third person's claim?
106. H. L. A. Hart, *The Concept of Law* (2d ed. 1994).
107. Kent Greenawalt, "Religion as a Concept in Constitutional Law," 72 *Cal. L. Rev.* 753, 764 (1984).
108. Some religions—is Buddhism one such?—may deny that they appeal beyond the processes of reason and evidence available to all. In that case, I suppose, they lose the claim to any special treatment beyond that accorded to freedom of the mind in general. Perhaps some among them would for that reason decline even to make that claim. There are those who speak of the religion of reason, and they would surely be entitled to no more than reason claims—which is quite a lot. See Chapter 4.

109. "For the Jews require a sign, and the Greeks seek after wisdom: But we preach Christ crucified, unto the Jews a stumblingblock, and unto the Greeks foolishness; . . ." I *Corinthians* 1.22–23 (KJV).

6. Liberty and Property

1. *See* Owen M. Fiss, *The Irony of Free Speech* (1996); Cass R. Sunstein, "Lochner's Legacy," 87 *Colum. L. Rev.* 873, 883–84 (1987); Cass R. Sunstein, *Democracy and the Problem of Free Speech* (1993).
2. *See Selected Essays on Political Economy* 144 (George B. de Huszar ed., 1964).
3. Principal historical materials are collected in *Founders' Constitution,* 302–42 (Philip Kurland ed., vol. 5, 1987). *See* Alexander Hamilton, *Remarks Regulating Elections, NY Assembly, cited in Founders' Constitution, supra* at 313. ("The words 'due process' have a precise technical import, and are only applicable to the process and proceedings of the courts for justice"); *see also* E. Corwin, *Liberty Against Government,* 23–57 (1948); John Hart Ely, *Democracy and Distrust* 15 (1980).
4. *Founders' Constitution, supra* note 3, 343–67.
5. U.S. Const. art. 1, §9.
6. *Dred Scott v. Sanford,* 60 U.S. (19 How.) 393 (1856).
7. Missouri Compromise Act, Act Cong. March 6, 1820, 3 Stat. 545, §8.
8. The Supreme Court held that the federal courts did not have jurisdiction to decide Scott's case. The Court notoriously held that African-Americans were not citizens under the Constitution, but an "inferior class of beings." Accordingly, Scott could not be considered a citizen of any state, as is required for diversity jurisdiction to exist. 28 U.S.C. §1332; *Dred Scott,* 60 U.S. at 403–30. The Court nevertheless went on to discuss the due process question.
9. *Dred Scott,* 60 U.S. at 450. Taney goes on to point out that because the Constitution explicitly acknowledges slave owning as a species of property, Congress is not free to treat that property in a distinct and disfavored way. *Id.* at 451.
10. 198 U.S. 45 (1905).
11. *Id.* at 56.
12. *Whitney v. California,* 274 U.S. 357, 373 (1927) (concurring opinion).
13. Quoted in Zechariah Chafee, Jr., *Free Speech in the U.S.* 31 (1954).
14. *Pacific Mut. Life Ins. Co. v. Haslip,* 499 U.S. 1, 38 (1991) (Scalia, J., concurring).
15. *Mathews v. Eldridge,* 424 U.S. 319 (1976); *United States v. Salerno,* 481 U.S. 739 (1987).
16. The same requirements have been incorporated piecemeal through the Fourteenth Amendment to apply to the states as well as the federal government.

17. *United States v. Salerno*, 481 U.S. 739 (1987).
18. *Kansas v. Hendricks*, 521 U.S. 346 (1997); *Kansas v. Crane*, 122 S. Ct. 867 (2002).
19. *State Farm Mutual Automobile Insurance Co. v. Campbell*, 123 S. Ct. 1513 (2003); *BMW of N. Am., Inc. v. Gore*, 517 U.S. 559 (1996); *Honda Motor Co., Ltd. v. Oberg*, 512 U.S. 415 (1994).
20. *In re Murchison*, 349 U.S. 133, 136 (1955); *Tumey v. Ohio*, 273 U.S. 510 (1927).
21. *Mathews v. Eldridge*, 424 U.S. 319 (1976).
22. *M.L.B. v. S.L.J.*, 519 U.S. 102 (1996); *Foucha v. Louisiana*, 504 U.S. 71 (1992); *Argersinger v. Hamlin*, 405 U.S. 951 (1972); *Gideon v. Wainwright*, 372 U.S. 335 (1963); *Powell v. Alabama*, 287 U.S. 45 (1932).
23. *Bancoult v. Secretary of State for Foreign and Commonwealth Affairs and Another*, 2 WLR 1219 (Q.B. 2000).
24. *Ex parte Quirin*, 317 U.S. 1 (1942).
25. This phrase, quoted by Justice Souter in his concurring opinion in *Washington v. Glucksberg*, 521 U.S. 702 (1997), was most famously deployed by Justice Harlan in his dissent in *Poe v. Ullman*, 367 U.S. 497 (1961). Justice Harlan in turn quoted from *Allgeyer v. Louisiana*, 165 U.S. 578 (1897). The history of the phrase is instructive. Its first appearance in *Allgeyer* signaled the first full-blown statement of a robust doctrine of substantive due process, applied to a state law seeking to restrict the use of out-of-state insurance companies. Justice Harlan applied the phrase to a Connecticut statute forbidding the use of contraceptives, and Justice Souter used it in connection with a state law criminalizing physician-assisted suicide.
26. Benjamin Constant, *The Liberty of the Ancients Compared with That of the Moderns* (1819); Isaiah Berlin, *Two Concepts of Liberty: An Inaugural Lecture* 7 (1958). Constant juxtaposes this liberty of the moderns with what he calls the liberty of the ancients, which refers to a collective right of self-governance, as opposed to a right against the government. Berlin characterizes this negative freedom as the freedom simply to be left alone.
27. *See* Randy Barnett, *Restoring the Lost Constitution: The Presumption of Liberty* (2003).
28. *Coppage v. Kansas*, 236 U.S. 1 (1915).
29. *See* Sunstein, "Lochner's Legacy," *supra* note 1; Charles Fried, "Is Liberty Possible?" in *Liberty, Equality, and Law: Selected Tanner Lectures on Moral Philosophy* (Sterling McMurrin ed., 1987); Thomas W. Merrill, "The Landscape of Constitutional Property," 86 *Va. L. Rev.* 885 (2000).
30. Richard A. Epstein, "A Critical Reappraisal," 18 *J.L. & Econ.* 293, 315 (1975).
31. It is a further implication of this clause in the Fifth Amendment that government may not take private property for what is not a public purpose, even if it does pay just compensation. *See Hawaii Housing Auth. v. Midkiff*, 467 U.S. 229, 241 (1984) (dictum).
32. U.S. Const. art. I, §10.

33. 524 U.S. 498 (1998).
34. The Court had embraced this form of incorporation in using the Due Process Clause to incorporate against the federal government the Fourteenth Amendment's promise that no state may deny any person the equal protection of the law.
35. Rare but it happens: in *BMW of N. Am., Inc. v. Gore*, 517 U.S. 559 (1996), an Alabama court awarded $2 million in punitive damages to a doctor because the automobile manufacturer had not disclosed to him that a part of his new car had been repainted, a discrepancy that decreased its value by $4,000. Three members of the Court concluded that there was not only a failure of process, but that quite apart from any failure in the proceedings, the outcome itself was so unfair as to be constitutionally unacceptable. *See also State Farm Mutual Automobile Insurance Co. v. Campbell*, 123 S. Ct. 1513 (2003).
36. 481 U.S. 704 (1987).
37. 481 U.S. at 716–18 (internal citations omitted).
38. *Erie R.R. Co. v. Tompkins*, 304 U.S. 64 (1938).
39. *Southern Pacific Co. v. Jensen*, 244 U.S. 205, 222 (1917) (Holmes, J., dissenting).
40. *Accord Nollan v. California Coastal Comm'n*, 483 U.S. 825 (1987) (easement of passage over a person's land a traditional estate in land); *Loretto v. Teleprompter Manhattan CATV Corp.*, 458 U.S. 419 (1982) (physical occupation of buildings which occurred in connection with cable company's installation of cable wires constituted a "taking" for purposes of Fifth Amendment); *Webb's Fabulous Pharmacies, Inc. v. Beckwith*, 449 U.S. 155 (1980) (interest is the property of the owner of the principal that generated it); *Andrus v. Allard*, 444 U.S. 51 (1979) (Eagle Protection Act of Migratory Bird Treaty Act prohibiting commercial transactions in preexisting avian artifacts do not violate Takings Clause).
41. *See, e.g., Lucas v. S. Carolina Coastal Comm'n*, 505 U.S. 1003 (1992).
42. *See, e.g., Hawaii Housing Auth. v. Midkiff*, 467 U.S. 229 (1984).
43. *See also Loretto v. Teleprompter Manhattan CATV Corp.*, 458 U.S. 419 (1982).
44. *Penn. Cent. Transp. Co. v. City of New York*, 438 U.S. 104 (1978); *Euclid, Ohio v. Ambler Realty Co.*, 272 U.S. 365 (1926).
45. *United States Trust Co. v. New Jersey*, 431 U.S. 1 (1977); *United States v. Winstar Corp.*, 518 U.S. 839 (1996).
46. *Energy Reserves Group, Inc. v. Kansas Power & Light Co.*, 459 U.S. 400, 413 (1983) ("Unless the State itself is a contracting party, 'as is customary reviewing economic and social regulation, . . . courts properly defer to legislative judgment as to the necessity and reasonableness of a particular measure.' ").
47. *See, e.g., Manigault v. Springs*, 199 U.S. 473 (1905) ("parties, by entering into contracts, may not estop the legislature from enacting laws intended for the public good.").

48. *Williamson v. Lee Optical,* 348 U.S. 483 (1955).
49. James Bradley Thayer, "The Origin and Scope of the American Doctrine of Constitutional Law," 7 *Harv. L. Rev.* 129, 144 (1893).
50. *See, e.g., United States v. Lopez,* 514 U.S. 549, 603 (1995) (Commerce Clause) (Souter, J., dissenting); *Va. State Bd. of Pharmacy v. Va. Citizens Consumer Council, Inc.,* 425 U.S. 748, 784 (1976) (commercial speech) (Rehnquist, J., dissenting).
51. *But see Muller v. Oregon,* 208 U.S. 412 (1908); *Weaver v. Palmer Bros. Co.,* 270 U.S. 402 (1926).
52. 300 U.S. 379 (1937).
53. 123 S. Ct. 2472 (2003).
54. 478 U.S. 186 (1986).
55. *See also Webster v. Reproductive Health Servs.,* 492 U.S. 490 (1989).
56. *Washington v. Glucksberg,* 521 U.S. 702, 750 (1997) (Stevens, J., concurring).
57. *Id.* at 785 n.16 (Souter, J., concurring); *id.* at 737–38 (O'Connor, J., concurring).
58. 367 U.S. 497 (1961).
59. *Id.* at 539, 548 (Harlan, J., dissenting).
60. *See Allgeyer v. State of Louisiana,* 165 U.S. 578 (1897).
61. 342 U.S. 165 (1952).
62. *Id.* at 172. Today this would be an easy case. In *Mapp v. Ohio,* 367 U.S. 643 (1961), the Supreme Court held that the Fourth Amendment was incorporated into the Fourteenth Amendment, and that that incorporation included the federal remedy of the exclusionary rule. The officers' conduct would be a clear case of an unreasonable search and seizure.
63. 268 U.S. 510 (1925).
64. 262 U.S. 390 (1923).
65. Edward H. Levi, *An Introduction to Legal Reasoning* (1948); Benjamin N. Cardozo, *The Nature of the Judicial Process* (1921).
66. 381 U.S. 479 (1965).
67. 405 U.S. 438 (1972).
68. 410 U.S. 113 (1973).
69. There has also been dispute whether slaves and their descendants and artificial persons—that is, corporations—are persons in the constitutional sense. The Fourteenth Amendment explicitly resolved affirmatively the first dispute, which was implicated in the *Dred Scott* case. As to corporations, they are also considered persons for the purposes of the Due Process Clause but are not considered citizens under the Fourteenth Amendment's Privileges and Immunities Clause, which, in part, explains why the Bill of Rights has been incorporated against the states through the Due Process Clause.
70. Judgment of February 25, 1975, 39 *Bverf GLI* (1975) (translated in Jonas and Gorby, "West German Abortion Decision, a Contrast to *Roe v. Wade,*" 9 John Marshall J. Prac. & Proc. 605 (1976)).
71. 505 U.S. 833 (1992).

72. *Casey* interpreted *Roe*'s "essential holding" as recognizing a woman's right to choose abortion before viability while, at the same time, recognizing the state's legitimate interests from the outset in protecting the health of the mother and the potential life of the fetus. Decisions following *Roe* may have gone beyond this interpretation of the right to choose, *see, e.g., Akron v. Akron Center for Reproductive Health,* 462 U.S. 416 (1983), but *Casey* basically reaffirmed that which *Roe* stood for, simplifying the trimester framework to a viability standard and applying an "undue burden" standard to those state measures affecting a woman's reproductive choice.

73. These quotes are drawn respectively from *Palko v. Connecticut,* 302 U.S. 319, 326 (1937) and *Moore v. East Cleveland,* 431 U.S. 494, 549 (1977).

74. *Michael H. v. Gerald D.,* 491 U.S. 110 (1989).

75. *Moore v. East Cleveland,* 431 U.S. 497 (1977).

76. *Zablocki v. Redhail,* 434 U.S. 374 (1978) (also holding that the child support statute violated the Equal Protection Clause because members of the affected class could be deprived of their fundamental right to marry).

77. *Turner v. Safley,* 482 U.S. 78 (1987).

78. 530 U.S. 57 (2000).

79. Mary Ann Glendon, *Abortion and Divorce in Western Law* 22–25 (1987).

80. 408 U.S. 564 (1972).

81. Indeed the terms in which such due process claims are made are often quite vague. In *Michigan v. Ewing,* 474 U.S. 214 (1985), a medical student claimed he had a substantive due process right to retake a qualifying examination he had failed. He had enjoyed plenty of process, with personal appearances before a review board of his faculty. The Court (overturning a contrary decision by the Court of Appeals) ruled that he had no property right in his continued enrollment and so his dismissal from it—even if "arbitrary and capricious"—denied him of nothing to which he was entitled.

82. 397 U.S. 254 (1970).

83. *Id.* at 275–78 (Black, J., dissenting) (internal citations omitted) (internal quotation marks omitted).

84. *Lucas v. S. Carolina Coastal Comm'n,* 505 U.S. 1003, 1016 n.7 (1992) ("Regrettably, the rhetorical force of our 'deprivation of all economically feasible use' rule is greater than its precision since the rule does not make clear the 'property interest' against which the loss of value is to be measured . . . The answer to this difficult question may lie in how the owner's reasonable expectations have been shaped by the State's law of property—i.e. whether and to what degree the State's law has accorded legal recognition and protection to the particular interest in and with respect to which the takings claimant alleges a diminution in or elimination of value.").

85. *Arnett v. Kennedy,* 416 U.S. 134 (1974) (plurality opinion).

86. *Cleveland Bd. of Educ. v. Loudermill,* 470 U.S. 532, 541 (1985).

87. Henry J. Friendly, "Some Kind of Hearing," 123 *U. Pa. L. Rev.* 1267 (1975).

88. The classic statement is *Mathews v. Eldridge,* 424 U.S. 319 (1976).
89. *See Bishop v. Wood,* 426 U.S. 341 (1976).
90. *Baker v. McCollan,* 443 U.S. 137 (1979).
91. *Collins v. City of Harker Heights, Tex.,* 503 U.S. 115 (1992).
92. *County of Sacramento v. Lewis,* 523 U.S. 833 (1998).
93. *DeShaney v. Winnebago County Dep't of Social Servs.,* 489 U.S. 189 (1989).
94. *Paul v. Davis,* 424 U.S. 693 (1976).
95. *Daniels v. Williams,* 474 U.S. 327 (1986).
96. *Monroe v. Pape,* 365 U.S. 167 (1961); *Tennessee v. Garner,* 471 U.S. 1 (1985).
97. 436 U.S. 149 (1978).
98. "[N]or shall any *State* deprive any person of life, liberty, or property, without due process of law" (emphasis added).

7. Equality

1. Paul D. Carrington, "Remembering Jefferson," 2 *Wm. & Mary Bill Rts. J.* 455 (1993).
2. As Samuel Johnson asked: "How is it that the loudest yelps for liberty come from the drivers of slaves?" *See generally* Joseph J. Ellis, *American Sphinx: The Character of Thomas Jefferson* (1998); John Chester Miller, *A Wolf by the Ears: Thomas Jefferson and Slavery* (1977).
3. *Bolling v. Sharpe,* 347 U.S. 497 (1954).
4. Ronald Dworkin, *Sovereign Virtue: The Theory and Practice of Equality* (2000).
5. Peter Westen, "The Empty Idea of Equality," 95 *Harv. L. Rev.* 537 (1982). *But see, e.g.,* Kenneth L. Karst, "Why Equality Matters," 17 *Ga. L. Rev.* 245 (1983); Steven J. Burton, "Comment on Empty Ideas: Logical and Positivist Analyses of Equality and Rules," 91 *Yale L.J.* 1136 (1982); Kent Greenawalt, "How Empty Is the Idea of Equality?" 83 *Colum. L. Rev.* 1167 (1983).
6. "The Senate of the United States shall be composed of two Senators from each State, elected by the people thereof, for six years, and each Senator shall have one vote. The electors in each state shall have the qualifications requisite for electors of the most numerous branch of the State Legislature." U.S. Const. amend. XVII. It is a nice question whether there is anything in the Constitution that guarantees the right to vote for the chief executive of the state. Perhaps article IV, §4: "The United States shall guarantee to every State in this Union a Republican form of government. . . ." although the guarantees of protection against invasion and, on application of the legislature, against domestic violence that immediately follow suggest that this guarantee is against outside imposition or a coup d'état.
7. *See, e.g., Kramer v. Union Free Sch. Dist. No. 15,* 395 U.S. 621 (1969) (vot-

ing in school district elections may not be limited to district residents who either have children in the district's schools or are subject to property taxes to pay for the schools).

8. *See, e.g., FCC v. Beach Communications,* 508 U.S. 307, 313–14 (1993).

9. *See Railway Express Agency, Inc. v. New York,* 336 U.S. 106 (1949) (Jackson, J., concurring). For an excellent reformulation of Jackson's point, see Gerald Gunther, *Foreword: In Search of Evolving Doctrine on a Changing Court: A Model For a Newer Equal Protection,* 86 *Harv. L. Rev.* 1, 20–24 (1972).

10. Charles Fried, "Types," 14 *Const. Commentary* 55 (1997).

11. *Cleburne v. Cleburne Living Ctr., Inc.,* 473 U.S. 432, 452 (1985).

12. 413 U.S. 528 (1973).

13. 517 U.S. 620 (1996). The amendment read: "No protected status based on homosexual, lesbian or bisexual orientation. Neither the state of Colorado, through any of its branches or departments, nor any of its subdivisions, municipalities or school districts, shall enact, adopt, or enforce any statute, regulation, ordinance or policy whereby homosexual, lesbian, or bisexual orientation, conduct, practices or relationships shall constitute or otherwise be the basis of or entitle any person or class of persons to have or claim any minority status, quota preferences, protected status or claim of discrimination."

14. 405 U.S. 438 (1972).

15. *Allegheny Pittsburgh Coal Co. v. County Comm'n of Webster County,* 488 U.S. 336, 344–45 (1989). The decision was rather unconvincingly distinguished in *Nordlinger v. Hahn,* 505 U.S. 1 (1992), in which a similar effect was produced, but explicitly, by a California popular initiative mandating acquisition value for property valuations. In *Allegheny* the unequal valuations were reached under a legislative mandate for equal valuations.

16. *Village of Willowbrook v. Olech,* 528 U.S. 562 (2000).

17. *See* Chapter 6.

18. *Slaughter-House Cases,* 83 U.S. (16 Wall.) 36 (1872).

19. 100 U.S. 303 (1879).

20. 163 U.S. 537 (1896).

21. *Id.* at 559 (1896) (Harlan, J., dissenting) ("But in view of the Constitution, in the eye of the law, there is in this country no superior, dominant, ruling class of citizens. There is no caste here. Our Constitution is color-blind, neither knows nor tolerates classes among citizens.")

22. 347 U.S. 483 (1954).

23. *Holmes v. Atlanta,* 350 U.S. 879 (1955).

24. Charles Black, Jr., "The Lawfulness of the Segregation Decisions," 69 *Yale L.J.* 421 (1960).

25. 388 U.S. 1 (1967).

26. For a comprehensive discussion of this and other topics dealing with intimate relations between the races, see Randall Kennedy, *Interracial Intimacies: Sex, Marriage, Identity, and Adoption* (2003).

27. *See* Chapter 6.
28. Black, *supra* note 24.
29. *Korematsu v. United States,* 323 U.S. 214 (1944) (*Korematsu* seems to be the first reference to race as "suspect class").
30. *See* Black, *supra* note 24, at 424 (explaining that what made separate unequal was the practical meaning of segregation in society, and rejecting the "fiction" of separate but equal).
31. Ronald Dworkin, *Law's Empire* 388 (1986).
32. *Regents of the Univ. of Cal. v. Bakke,* 438 U.S. 265, 407 (1978) (Blackmun, J., dissenting) ("In order to get beyond racism we must first take account of race.").
33. *See* Theodore W. Allen, *The Invention of the White Race,* vol. 1, *Racial Oppression and Social Control* 21–24 (1995); Michael Omi and Howard Winant, *Racial Formation in the United States: From the 1960s to the 1990s* 55 (1994).
34. *Strauder v. West Virginia,* 100 U.S. 303, 308 (1879); *Hernandez v. Texas,* 347 U.S. 475 (1954).
35. *See* Chapter 5. *See Lynch v. Donnelly,* 465 U.S. 668 (1984) (O'Connor, J., concurring).
36. 304 U.S. 144, 152 n.4 (1938); *see also* Louis Lusky, "Minority Rights and the Public Interest," 52 *Yale L.J.* 1 (1942).
37. *Dean Milk Co. v. City of Madison,* 340 U.S. 349 (1951); *Minnesota v. Clover Leaf Creamery Co.,* 449 U.S. 456 (1981); *H.P. Hood & Sons v. Du Mond,* 336 U.S. 525 (1949); *Baldwin v. G.A.F. Seelig, Inc.,* 294 U.S. 511 (1935).
38. *See* John Hart Ely, *Democracy and Distrust* (1960).
39. J. M. Balkin, Some Realism About Pluralism: Legal Realist Approaches to the First Amendment, 1990 *Duke L.J.* 375.
40. *See* Laurence H. Tribe, "The Puzzling Persistence of Process-Based Constitutional Theories," 89 *Yale L.J.* 1063 (1980).
41. Women have been the majority of voters since 1964 because there have been more voting-age women than men in the population, even though their turnout was lower than men's until the mid-1970s. In the 1988, 1992, and 1996 presidential elections, 52 percent of voters were women. *See* Richard A. Seltzer, Jody Newman, and Melissa Vorhees Leighton, *Sex as a Political Variable: Women as Candidates and Voters in U.S. Elections* 64, 125 (1997).
42. *Reed v. Reed,* 404 U.S. 71 (1971).
43. *See, e.g., Schlesinger v. Ballard,* 419 U.S. 498 (1975); *Stanley v. Illinois,* 405 U.S. 645, 656 (1972).
44. 429 U.S. 190 (1976).
45. In his plurality opinion in *Frontiero v. Richardson,* 411 U.S. 677 (1973), Justice Brennan analogized women to "discrete and insular minorities," who, despite their numbers, are "vastly underrepresented in [the] Nations' decisionmaking" because of past discrimination. *Id.* at 686 n.17. Unable to

obtain a majority for the proposition that gender classifications warrant strict scrutiny, Justice Brennan, in *Craig v. Boren*, announced that gender would be treated under intermediate scrutiny, requiring that "classifications by gender must serve important governmental objectives and must be substantially related to achievement of those objectives." *Craig*, 429 U.S. at 197.

46. Justice Brennan maintained that, while the Oklahoma legislature's statistics, establishing that .18 percent of females and 2 percent of males were arrested for drunk driving, were "not trivial in a statistical sense," they did not justify a sex-based classification. *Id.* at 201–02. Justice Rehnquist, in his dissent, criticized Brennan's easy dismissal of these numbers, noting that other surveys indicated that nationwide arrests for drunk driving among those under 18 had increased 138 percent, and that 93 percent of all persons arrested for drunk driving were males. *Id.* at 223.

47. *Bradford v. Illinois State*, 83 U.S. (16 Wall.) (1872).

48. *See Frontiero v. Richardson*, 411 U.S. 677, 685–86 (1973).

49. Reva B. Siegel, "She the People: The Nineteenth Amendment, Sex Equality, Federalism, and the Family," 115 *Harv. L. Rev.* 947 (2002).

50. *Michael M. v. Superior Court*, 450 U.S. 464 (1981) (upholding California's statutory rape law, punishing the male, but not the female participant, on the grounds that the statute aimed to prevent illegitimate pregnancy, and was thus intended to protect, rather than punish, the female).

51. *Wengler v. Druggists Mut. Ins. Co.*, 446 U.S. 142 (1980); *Orr v. Orr*, 440 U.S. 268 (1979); *Schlesinger v. Ballard*, 419 U.S. 498 (1975).

52. This reasoning best explains the outcome in *United States v. Virginia*, 518 U.S. 515 (1996), in which the Court held the Virginia Military Institute's exclusion of women unconstitutional, explaining, "neither federal nor state government acts compatibly with the equal protection principle when a law or official policy denies to women, simply because they are women, full citizenship stature—equal opportunity to aspire, achieve, participate in and contribute to society based on their individual talents and capacities." *Id.* at 532.

53. I speak of biological gender, as does the law, not gender as a social construct, which may have a variety of forms and gradations. It is the legal construction of gender out of the biological that is, after all, the subject of this analysis.

54. *Reed v. Reed*, 404 U.S. 71, 76 (1971).

55. *See Craig v. Boren*, 429 U.S. 190, 197–98 (1976); *United States v. Virginia*, 518 U.S. 515, 531 (1996) (requiring an "exceedingly persuasive" justification for gender-based classifications).

56. "The aged in this Nation . . . unlike, say, those who have been discriminated against on the basis of race or national origin, have not experienced a 'history of purposeful unequal treatment' or been subjected to unique disabilities on the basis of stereotyped characteristics not truly indicative of their

abilities." *Mass. Bd. of Retirement v. Murgia,* 427 U.S. 307, 313 (1976). *See also Kimel v. Fla. Bd. of Regents,* 528 U.S. 62 (2000). Furthermore, the aged in this nation differ from Justice Stone's "discrete and insular minorities" in their ability to procure great, perhaps disproportionate, advantages from legislatures due to their often high voting rates and disposable income.

57. 473 U.S. 432 (1985).

58. 531 U.S. 356 (2001).

59. The case plays out a theme first struck in a race case, *Palmore v. Sidotti,* 466 U.S. 429 (1984), in which the Court had held that the prejudice a child raised by a biracial couple would almost certainly encounter did not justify denying custody to the child's white mother who had married a black man.

60. *Cleburne,* 473 U.S. at 445 ("the legislative response . . . negates any claim that the mentally retarded are politically powerless in the sense that they have no ability to attract the attention of the lawmakers.").

61. Robin West, *Progressive Constitutionalism: Reconstructing the Fourteenth Amendment* (1994). *See also* William E. Forbath, "Caste, Class and Equal Citizenship," 98 *Mich. L. Rev.* (1999); Frank I. Michelman, "The Supreme Court, 1968 Term—Foreword: On Protecting the Poor Through the Fourteenth Amendment," 83 *Harv. L. Rev.* 7 (1969).

62. David Currie, *The Constitution of the Federal Republic of Germany* (1994); Mary Ann Glendon, *Comparative Legal Traditions* (1982).

63. S. Africa Const., chap. 3, §§26–28.

64. 394 U.S. 618, 627.

65. 411 U.S. 1 (1973).

66. *Kadrmas v. Dickinson Pub. Schs.,* 487 U.S. 450, 458 (1988).

67. *Lindsey v. Normet,* 405 U.S. 56 (1972).

68. *Memorial Hospital v. Maricopa County,* 415 U.S. 250 (1974). This case held that the Arizona statute requiring a year's residence in the county as a condition of receiving nonemergency hospitalization or medical care for free created an unconstitutional classification that impinges on the right to travel by denying newcomers basic necessities of life, so this case uses *Shapiro*-like reasoning but hangs its hat on the right to travel, not a right to health care.

69. *Gideon v. Wainwright,* 372 U.S. 335 (1963). And in misdemeanor cases if the convicted defendant is to be sentenced to incarceration. *Argesinger v. Hamlin,* 407 U.S. 25 (1972). This ruling was later expanded to cases where the state sought other grave impositions: involuntary commitment of the insane in *Foucha v. Louisiana,* 504 U.S. 71 (1992), and termination of parental rights in *M.L.B. v. S.L.J.,* 519 U.S. 102 (1996).

70. *Forsyth County, Georgia v. Nationalist Movement,* 505 U.S. 123 (1992); *Murdock v. Pennsylvania,* 319 U.S. 105 (1943).

71. *See* Chapter 4.

72. *Carey v. Brown,* 447 U.S. 455 (1980).

73. 408 U.S. 92 (1972).

74. *Speiser v. Randall,* 357 U.S. 513 (1958).
75. 383 U.S. 663 (1966).
76. Archibald Cox, "The Supreme Court, 1965 Term—Foreword: Constitutional Adjudication and the Promotion of Human Rights," 80 *Harv. L. Rev.* 91 (1966).
77. "We conclude that a State violates the Equal Protection Clause of the Fourteenth Amendment whenever it makes the affluence of the voter or payment of any fee an electoral standard. Voter qualifications have no relation to wealth nor to paying or not paying this or any other tax." *Harper,* 383 U.S. at 666.
78. *See id.* at 684 (Harlan, J., dissenting) (suggesting that property qualifications, a "traditional part of our political structure," would be constitutional had they not been eliminated through wide popular debate). While no case has addressed whether property qualification are per se unconstitutional, *Quinn v. Millsap,* 491 U.S. 95 (1989), held that property qualifications in an election for members of a local government reorganization committee would be "a form of invidious discrimination." *Id.* at 107.
79. *Reynolds v. Sims,* 377 U.S. 533 (1964); *Avery v. Midland County Texas,* 390 U.S. 474 (1968); *Kirkpatrick v. Preisler,* 394 U.S. 526 (1969).
80. The most dramatic inequality is assured by the Twelfth Amendment, which in certain instances gives each state one vote in the election of the President.
81. *Reynolds,* 377 U.S. at 562.
82. *Bd. of Estimate of City of New York v. Morris,* 489 U.S. 688 (1989).
83. *See, e.g.,* Theodore Eisenberg, "Disproportionate Impact and Illicit Motive: Theories of Constitutional Adjudication," 52 *N.Y.U. L. Rev.* 36 (1977); Charles R. Lawrence III, "The Id, the Ego, and Equal Protection: Reckoning with Unconscious Racism," 39 *Stan. L. Rev.* 317 (1987); David Benjamin Oppenheimer, "Negligent Discrimination," 141 *U. Pa. L. Rev.* 899 (1993); Michael J. Perry, "The Disproportionate Impact Theory of Racial Discrimination," 125 *U. Pa. L. Rev.* 540 (1977).
84. 406 U.S. 535 (1972).
85. This distinction might explain why the Court, in *Bush v. Gore,* 531 U.S. 98 (2000), was willing to strike down the uneven and possibly prejudicial variety of counting schemes decreed by the Florida Supreme Court for the presidential election of 2000, while not purporting to address the variety of long-standing counting schemes in the states, counties, and precincts across the nation.
86. 426 U.S. 229 (1976).
87. *Cf. Gomillion v. Lightfoot,* 364 U.S. 339, 341 (1960); *Mobile v. Bolden,* 446 U.S. 55, 69–70 (1980), illustrating the problem of intent.
88. One of the rare, now infamous, instances in which a race-based classification survived strict scrutiny was *Korematsu v. United States,* 323 U.S. 214 (1944). In *Korematsu,* an order excluding all persons of Japanese ancestry from the West Coast was deemed justified by the "pressing public necessi-

ties" of World War II and by the claimed difficulty of separating loyal from disloyal Japanese-Americans.

89. *Green v. County School Board,* 391 U.S. 430 (1968).

90. *Swann v. Charlotte-Mecklenburg Bd. of Educ.,* 402 U.S. 1 (1971).

91. *Griffin v. County Sch. Bd. of Prince Edward County,* 377 U.S. 218 (1964).

92. *Swann,* 402 U.S. at 27.

93. *Regents of Univ. of Cal. v. Bakke,* 438 U.S. 265, 352 (Brennan, J., concurring in the judgment in part and dissenting in part).

94. See, *e.g., Adarand Constructors, Inc. v. Pena,* 515 U.S. 200 (1995) (5–4); *Metro Broadcasting, Inc. v. FCC,* 497 U.S. 547 (1990) (5–4); *Wygant v. Jackson Bd. of Educ.,* 476 U.S. 267 (1986) (5–4); *Fullilove v. Klutznick,* 448 U.S. 448 (1980) (plurality opinion).

95. 438 U.S. 265 (1978).

96. This was assumed by majorities in both of the 2003 University of Michigan affirmative action cases discussed below. *But see Hopwood v. Texas,* 236 F.3d 256, 274–75 (5th Cir. 2000) (holding that diversity rationale advanced in *Bakke* was not binding in challenge to state university law school's affirmative action plan).

97. *Compare* Owen M. Fiss, "Groups and the Equal Protection Clause," 5 *Phil. & Pub. Affairs* 107 (1976).

98. A signal example was Marshall's opinion for the Court in *Emporium Capwell Co. v. Western Addition Community Organization,* 420 U.S. 50 (1975). Some black employees of Emporium, complaining of discrimination, in addition to relying on the representation of their union, organized collective action of their own and sought redress from the employer. The National Labor Relations Act says that a board-certified union is the exclusive bargaining agent for all employees in a unit. In the Court of Appeals Judge Charles Wyzanski wrote a particularly plummy dissenting opinion stating: "To leave non-whites at the mercy of whites in the presentation of non-white claims which are admittedly adverse to the whites would be a mockery of democracy. Suppression, intentional or otherwise, of the presentation of non-white claims cannot be tolerated in our society even if, which is probably at least the short-term consequence, the result is that industrial peace is temporarily adversely affected. In presenting non-white issues non-whites cannot, against their will, be relegated to white spokesmen, mimicking black men. The day of the minstrel show is over."(485 F.2d 917, 940 (1973)). Justice Marshall would have none of it. Marshall powerfully restated the policy of the labor laws that employee strength lies in all union members making common cause through their unions. On Marshall, *see* generally Mark Tushnet, *Making Civil Rights Law: Thurgood Marshall and the Supreme Court, 1936–1961* (1994); Mark Tushnet, *Making Constitutional Law, Thurgood Marshall and the Supreme Court, 1961–1991* (1997); Juan Williams, *Thurgood Marshall: American Revolutionary* (1998).

99. *Bakke,* 438 U.S. at 407 (1978) (Blackmun, J., dissenting).

100. *Metro Broadcasting, Inc. v. FCC,* 497 U.S. 547 (1990).
101. *Id.*
102. The concept of a benign use of racial classification may be traced to a seminal analysis by Ronald Dworkin—Ronald Dworkin, *Taking Rights Seriously* 224 (1977)—who later also formulated the distinction between race as a forbidden end and race as a forbidden category. *See* Ronald Dworkin, *Law's Empire* 388 (1986).
103. *Adarand Constructors, Inc. v. Pena,* 515 U.S. 200, 245 (1995) (Stevens, J., dissenting).
104. 488 U.S. 469 (1989).
105. *See Local 28 of Sheet Metal Workers Int'l Ass'n. v. EEOC,* 478 U.S. 421 (1986); *Fullilove v. Klutznick,* 448 U.S. 448 (1980).
106. *Croson,* 488 U.S. at 493 ("Classifications based on race carry a danger of stigmatic harm. Unless they are strictly reserved for remedial settings they may in fact promote notions of racial inferiority and lead to a politics of racial hostility.").
107. Justice Marshall in dissent suggested that it was roughly halfway between the 50 percent black population of the city and the percentage of black subcontracting work, which was near zero.
108. 123 S. Ct. 2325.
109. 123 S. Ct. 2411.
110. 446 U.S. 55 (1980).
111. 42 U.S.C. §1973. *See* Pamela S. Karlan, "Undoing the Right Thing: Single-Member Offices and the Voting Rights Act," 77 *Va. L. Rev.* 1 (1991); Samuel Issacharoff, Pamela S. Karlan, and Richard Pildes, *The Law of Democracy* 441–545 (1998).
112. *See* Samuel Issacharoff, Pamela S. Karlan, and Richard Pildes, *The Law of Democracy* 546–670 (1998).
113. Between 1989 and 1992, the number of black congressmen increased from 25 to 38. The number of Latinos in Congress also increased from 10 to 17 during the same period.
114. The term "gerrymander" was coined in 1812 after Gilbert Stuart saw a redistricting map of Essex County, Massachusetts, signed into law by Governor Elbridge Gerry.
115. 509 U.S. 630 (1993).
116. *Id.* at 647. The case puts me in mind of *Board of Education of Kiryas Joel Village School District v. Grumet,* 512 U.S. 687 (1994), which held a statute creating a special school district for members of a religious group—the Satmar Hasidim—an unconstitutional establishment of religion. There too the Court found offensive the drawing of political lines on the constitutionally impermissible basis of religion—"a state may not delegate its civic authority to a group chosen according to religious criterion"—and once again the legislative motive had been one of accommodation not subordination.
117. *See, e.g., Davis v. Bandemer,* 478 U.S. 109 (1986). In *Davis,* Democrats

claimed an equal protection violation when a gerrymander caused Democratic voting strength to be substantially understated. The Court held that equal protection was not violated, stating unconstitutional discrimination only occurs "where the electoral system substantially disadvantages certain voters in their opportunity to influence the political process effectively" and not simply when there is a "mere lack of proportional representation."

118. *Easley v. Cromartie,* 532 U.S. 234, 248 (2001).
119. *Adarand Constructors, Inc. v. Pena,* 515 U.S. 200, 214–18 (1995).
120. *Bd. of Trustees of Univ. of Ala. v. Garrett,* 531 U.S. 356 (2001) (holding invalid Congress's attempt to abrogate sovereign immunity for state employer violations of the Americans With Disabilities Act); *Kimel v. Fla. Bd. of Regents,* 528 U.S. 62 (2000) (holding Congress exceeded its Fourteenth Amendment remedial authority in allowing employees to sue state employers for ADEA violations); *Fla. Prepaid Postsecondary Educ. Expense Bd. v. College Savings Bank,* 527 U.S. 627 (1999) (invalidating Patent Protection Remedy Clarification Act which abrogated state's sovereign immunity for claims of patent infringement); *City of Boerne v. Flores,* 521 U.S. 507 (1997) (invalidating Religious Freedom Restoration Act in which Congress attempted to overrule Supreme Court holding in *Employment Division of Oregon v. Smith*).
121. 481 U.S. 279 (1987).
122. John C. Jeffries, Jr., *Justice Lewis F. Powell, Jr.* 487 (2001).
123. *See* William G. Bowen and Derek Bok, *The Shape of the River: Long-Term Consequences of Considering Race in College and University Admissions* (1998).

Afterword

1. *See* Morton J. Horwitz, *The Warren Court and the Pursuit of Justice* (1998); Frank I. Michelman, *Brennan and Democracy* (1999); Richard A. Posner, "In Memoriam: William J. Brennan, Jr.," 111 *Harvard L. Rev.* 9, 10 (1997); Charles Fried, *Remarks at Supreme Court Ceremonies in Memory of Justice Brennan* (May 22, 1998) (transcript available in the Harvard Law School Library); *cf.* Frank I. Michelman, "The Supreme Court, 1968 Term—Foreword: On Protecting the Poor Through the Fourteenth Amendment," 83 *Harvard L. Rev.* 7 (1969).
2. 505 U.S. 833, 846 (1992) (holding that *Roe v. Wade,* 410 U.S. 113 (1973), should not be overturned).
3. This is not a development I would welcome. *See* Fried, "The New First Amendment Jurisprudence: A Threat to Liberty," 59 *U. Chicago L. Rev.* 225 (1992).
4. *See Turner Broadcasting Systems v. FCC,* 520 U.S. 180, 220 (1997) (concurring opinion); *Denver Area Telecommunications Consortium v. FCC,* 518 U.S. 727, 740 (1996) (plurality opinion).
5. *Bartnicki v. Vopper,* 532 U.S. 514, 535 (2001) (concurring opinion).

6. *Nixon v. Shrink Missouri Government PAC,* 528 U.S. 377, 399 (2000) (concurring opinion).

7. *See,* for example, Justice Breyer's comparative discussions of capital punishment in *Ring v. Arizona,* 536 U.S. 584, 618 (2002); of campaign finance in *Nixon v. Shrink Missouri Government PAC, supra;* of lengthy delays in carrying out death sentences in *Knight v. Florida,* 528 U.S. 990 (1999) (dissenting opinion); and of federalism in *Printz v. United States,* 521 U.S. 898, 976 (1997) (dissenting opinion).

Table of Cases

Index